Teacher Preparation Classroom

TEA...

MEI
PRENTI

...mo at
...eacherprep/demo

Your Class. Their Careers. Our Fut... ...prepared?

We invite you to explore our new, innovative and engaging website and all that it has to offer you, your course, and tomorrow's educators! Organized around the major courses pre-service teachers take, the Teacher Preparation site provides media, student/teacher artifacts, strategies, research articles, and other resources to equip your students with the quality tools needed to excel in their courses and prepare them for their first classroom.

This ultimate on-line education resource is available at no cost, when packaged with a Merrill text, and will provide you and your students access to:

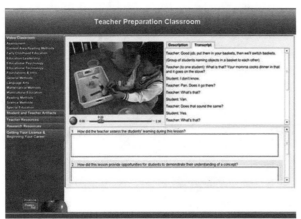

Online Video Library. More than 150 video clips—each tied to a course topic and framed by learning goals and Praxis-type questions—capture real teachers and students working in real classrooms, as well as in-depth interviews with both students and educators.

Student and Teacher Artifacts. More than 200 student and teacher classroom artifacts—each tied to a course topic and framed by learning goals and application questions—provide a wealth of materials and experiences to help make your study to become a professional teacher more concrete and hands-on.

Research Articles. Over 500 articles from ASCD's renowned journal *Educational Leadership.* The site also includes Research Navigator, a searchable database of additional educational journals.

Teaching Strategies. Over 500 strategies and lesson plans for you to use when you become a practicing professional.

Licensure and Career Tools. Resources devoted to helping you pass your licensure exam; learn standards, law, and public policies; plan a teaching portfolio; and succeed in your first year of teaching.

Access Code previously been used?

Students:
To purchase or renew an access code, go to **www.prenhall.com/teacherprep** and click on the "Register for Teacher Prep" button.

Instructors:
Email **Merrill.marketing@pearsoned.com** and provide the following information:
- Name and Affiliation
- Author/Title/Edition of Merrill text

Upon ordering *Teacher Prep* for their students, instructors will be given a lifetime *Teacher Prep* Access Code.

K-12 CLASSROOM TEACHING
A Primer for New Professionals

Third Edition

Andrea M. Guillaume
California State University, Fullerton

PEARSON

Merrill
Prentice Hall

Upper Saddle River, New Jersey
Columbus, Ohio

Library of Congress Cataloging-in-Publication Data

K-12 Classroom Teaching: A primer for new professionals/Andrea Guillaume – 3rd ed. p. cm.
  Includes bibliographical references.
  ISBN-13: 978-0-13-158024-4 (alk. paper)
  ISBN-10: 0-13-158024-8
1. First Year teachers—United States. 2. Teaching—United States.
I. Guillaume, Andrea M.
LB2844.1.N4G85 2008
371.1—dc22

2007023855

Vice President and Executive Publisher: Jeffery W. Johnston
Executive Editor: Darcy Betts Prybella
Editorial Assistant: Nancy Holstein
Development Editor: Christina Robb
Production Editor: Kris Roach
Photo Coordinator: Valerie Schultz
Production Coordination: S4 Carlisle Publishing Services
Design Coordinator: Diane C. Lorenzo
Cover Designer: Jason Moore
Cover Image: Super Stock
Production Manager: Susan Hannahs
Director of Marketing: David Gesell
Marketing Coordinator: Brian Mounts

This book was set in Korinna by S4 Carlisle Publishing Services. It was printed and bound by Bind-Rite Graphics/Robbinsville. The cover was printed by Phoenix Color Corp.

Pearson Education Ltd.
Pearson Education Singapore Pte. Ltd.
Pearson Education Canada, Ltd.
Pearson Education–Japan

Pearson Education Australia Pty. Limited
Pearson Education North Asia Ltd.
Pearson Educación de Mexico, S.A. de C.V.
Pearson Education Malaysia Pte. Ltd.

10 9 8 7 6 5 4 3 2 1
ISBN 13: 978-0-13-158024-4
ISBN 10:   0-13-158024-8

For Alexander and Zachary,
alpha and omega.

PREFACE

By learning you will teach; by teaching you will learn.

—Latin proverb

K–12 Classroom Teaching: A Primer for New Professionals is a core text for elementary and secondary preservice teachers who are taking introduction to teaching courses, field experience courses, or general methods courses. It is also a quick but thorough core text for inservice teachers who are gaining certification at the same time they are beginning to teach. Instructors of specialized methods courses or foundations of education courses will find this primer a useful supplemental text.

K–12 Classroom Teaching presents useful, practical points of view that can provide meaning and direction behind new teachers' actions related to a number of central educational issues. It uses clear, reader-friendly language to concisely explore key aspects of classroom teaching, including the context of teaching today, strategies for learning about students, educational stances, planning and assessment, instruction and instructional strategies, classroom management and discipline, and professional growth. Chapters include a balance of up-to-date discussions of educational issues, research findings, and practical advice. The selection and presentation of topics is guided by a conceptual approach that emphasizes the active nature of learning to teach.

CONCEPTUAL APPROACH

K–12 Classroom Teaching: A Primer for New Professionals is based upon the premise that teaching is goal directed, interactional, and mindful of the local setting in its efforts to encourage learners' growth. Two core convictions are that classroom teaching is complex and that today's teachers face special difficulties given current demands and events at home and abroad. It takes the conceptual approach that in the face of these challenging conditions, teachers at their best are guided by:

- a clear sense of what they hope to accomplish.
- an understanding of the context and of what research shows to be effective.
- a set of professional knowledge and skills.
- a sense of ethics concerning what is right.
- a sense of responsibility to value and enhance the learning of every student.

Building these dispositions, commitments, and understandings is hard work, so this text approaches the process of learning to teach (and of learning in general) as an active, social one. Through its content and through its approach, the text encourages readers to reflect on past experience, to question assumptions, to consider multiple sources of information, and to commit to enacting well-defined notions of good practice that address learners' diverse needs and honor the dignity of the human experience.

ORGANIZATION OF THE TEXT

Chapters are arranged topically, and content of later chapters draws from the work the reader accomplishes in earlier chapters.

- In Chapter 1, the text begins with an exploration of the distinct character of classroom teaching. Chapter 1 explores this character through six propositions of teaching that lay a foundation for the entire text through their content and their implications for each chapter's presentation of information. These propositions include:
  1. Teaching looks easy . . . from the outside.
  2. Every teacher is part of a system.
  3. Teaching is directed toward the goal of fostering change.
  4. Teaching is more than telling.
  5. There is agreement on what teachers need to know and be able to do.
  6. Teachers can be effective and yet not just alike.
- Chapter 2 stresses the importance of understanding the philosophical bases found in educational practice and of developing one's own stance toward education. Subsequent chapters ask readers to use their stance to guide their decisions related to the chapters' content.
- Chapter 3 explores the growing range of strengths and needs exhibited by students in U.S. schools and urges new teachers to use knowledge of specific students as a starting point for their instructional decisions.
- Chapter 4 addresses instructional planning both in the long range and in the short term. It guides teachers in making decisions about resources and student groupings and presents a variety of unit planning approaches and standards-based lesson planning.
- Chapter 5 introduces six pieces of general advice for instruction using the mnemonic device COME IN: Connect, Organize, Model, Enrich, Interact, and consider Nature and Needs. The chapter argues that this advice can encourage rigorous learning through rich and purposeful instruction.
- Chapter 6 shares instructional strategies and discusses the strengths and potential drawbacks of models such as direct instruction and inquiry.
- Chapter 7 explores principles of assessment and offers a variety of assessment strategies in keeping with those principles. Special attention is given to current concerns about accountability and its focus on student achievement as required by the No Child Left Behind Act.
- Chapter 8 addresses classroom management.
- Chapter 9 focuses on encouraging appropriate student behavior in ways that respect students, prevent misbehavior, and encourage self-control.
- Finally, Chapter 10 addresses issues of professional involvement and growth for new teachers.

FEATURES OF THE TEXT

Readers and reviewers of the second edition of *K–12 Classroom Teaching* commented positively on a variety of the text's characteristics, and those have been retained in the third edition. They include the text's condensed format, its readable style, its useful ideas, and its personal approach.

In keeping with the text's active approach to learning, a number of special features can also be found throughout the text.

Warm-Up Exercises. Because past experience influences present learning, chapters begin with warm-up activities that help readers access their thinking related to major points about to be explored.

Presentation of Information. Key concepts are presented in clear language. Figures are often used to present information in a succinct format.

Video Clips. Video support is incorporated into every chapter. Video clips from Merrill's Teacher Prep Web site (www.prenhall.com/teacherprep) provide opportunities for readers to see concepts in action. Every chapter includes one or more video inserts to bring chapter content to life. And, so that readers can apply their knowledge and practice of new concepts and skills, each chapter includes an end-of-chapter exercise that requires video analysis.

Teaching Tips. Plentiful practical classroom suggestions are placed in boxes throughout each of the chapters.

Words from Teachers. The voices of previous readers, now teachers, offer advice and writing samples that are presented in many chapters. Examples include a metaphor for teaching, sample stances, daily schedule structures, and poems.

Parting Words. Rather than concluding with a traditional summary, chapters conclude with some final words of advice related to the issues at hand.

Web Sites. Web sites related to the chapter's content are provided. Web sites provide connections to professional organizations and instructionally related resources and materials.

Opportunities to Practice. Application exercises conclude each chapter. They are meant to extend readers' connections with the content in a variety of ways that directly relate to the world of the classroom.

Blank Forms. Opportunities to Practice exercises, along with many figures throughout the text, provide for structured practice and application of the chapters' key ideas. Examples include blank observation guides, lesson plan forms, and assessment and management plans.

NEW TO THIS EDITION

The third edition of *K–12 Classroom Teaching: A Primer for New Professionals* responds to the dynamic conditions teachers today face. It also responds to the suggestions of previous readers and reviewers. A number of content shifts are also evident.

→ Content has been updated to reflect *current trends and research.* Examples of current topics include:
  - Differentiated instruction and Universal Design (Chapter 3)
  - Increased attention to the needs of English learners (Chapters 1, 3, 4, and 5)
  - Increased attention to the needs of students with disabilities (Chapters 1, 3, 4, 5, 6, 8, and 9)
  - Increased attention to the needs of advanced and gifted students (Chapters 3, 4, and 5)

→ *Issues related to secondary teachers* (middle school, junior high school, and high school teachers) have been incorporated more directly. Research and perspectives addressing the special conditions faced by secondary students and teachers are incorporated throughout the text. Two examples include:
  - Conflict management and school violence (Chapter 9)
  - Student use of personal technology (Chapter 9)

→ *Issues that face teachers and students across our nation* have been more directly addressed. These include:
- Federal legislation such as the No Child Left Behind Act of 2001
- Teacher induction
- Standards for teachers
- Academic content standards for students
- Accountability (a theme that runs throughout chapters)
- Educational inequities and the achievement gap (a theme that runs throughout chapters)
- Standards-based instruction and student achievement (Chapters 4 and 7)
- School-based efforts to use student data in planning (Chapters 7 and 10)

→ *Family–school connections* are addressed in several chapters, drawing tighter links among the team members who work together on behalf of students.

→ Issues related to *instructional technology* are incorporated throughout each chapter of this edition. Examples include:
- Issues of access to technology (Chapter 1)
- Assistive technology (Chapter 3)
- Technology as a means to connect students and the world (Chapters 4, 5, and 6)
- Management of student assessment results (Chapters 3 and 7)

→ Video clips are incorporated in every chapter (see page ix)

SUPPLEMENTS

An electronic instructor's manual is available on the Instructor Resource center at www.prenhall.com without cost to instructors using *K–12 Classroom Teaching: A Primer for New Professionals* as part of their courses. The comprehensive instructor's manual includes the following components:

Chapter overview and key outcomes. An at-a-glance preview of the chapter and a listing of some outcomes students should be able to demonstrate after reading the chapter

Chapter outline and graphic organizer. Two different presentations of the chapter's key points

PowerPoint presentations. Slides that present information related to the chapter content and can be used to spark classroom discussions.

Sample class activities. Activities that can be used to access readers' prior knowledge, connect the text's main points to their lives and practice, and extend their practice

Test bank items. Assessment tasks and traditional test items

The test bank items in the instructor's manual are available in TestGen software in both Macintosh and PC formats and can also be found on the Instructor Resource Center. TestGen also provides a user-friendly interface for instructors who want to create their own tests.

ACKNOWLEDGMENTS

I am grateful to my colleagues at California State University, Fullerton, and the surrounding schools for their expertise and assistance in the development of this edition.

- Thanks to Kim Case for her assistance in obtaining schedules from practicing teachers, and to Richard Kravitz and Susan Zack for those schedules. Thanks to Loretta for hers as well.
- Thanks to colleagues (who are also friends) for their expertise and assistance: Donna Bennett, Barb Finnell, Chris Blum, and Ruth Yopp.

- Special thanks to Tim Green for his expertise and generosity in reviewing the information related to technology throughout the text.

Thanks, too, to family members:

- My mom, Lu Ann Berthel, who called and asked what she could do.
- My boys at home—husband and sons—for friendship, support, and all they teach me.

Finally, thanks to my colleagues in the wider profession of education for their perspectives and for the wisdom that continues to shape the evolution of this text.

- Thanks to those who reviewed the second edition and provided valuable insights and directions for development of the third edition. They are E. Jane Irons, Texas Women's University; Gene Eakin, Oregon State University; Jan Handler, Mount Mercy College; Helen L. Harrington, University of Michigan; Martha V. Whitwell, University of Mississippi; Amy P. Dietrich, The University of Memphis; and Andrea Sabatini McLoughlin, Long Island University at C.W. Post.
- I deeply appreciate the support of Christina Robb at Merrill/Prentice Hall. This text definitely bears her mark.
- Thanks are in order, too, to Darcy Betts Prybella and the production team at Merrill/Prentice Hall and Carlisle Publishing Services.

BRIEF CONTENTS

CONTENTS

CHAPTER EIGHT
Managing the Learning Environment 213

CHAPTER NINE
Encouraging Appropriate Behavior 243

CHAPTER TEN
Growing in Your Profession 277

Note: The pronouns *she, he, her,* and *his* are used variously throughout the text to represent either teacher or student.

Note: Every effort has been made to provide accurate and current Internet information in this book. However, the Internet and information posted on it are constantly changing, so it is inevitable that some of the Internet addresses listed in this textbook will change.

Before You Begin Reading

Chapter One

Learning is an active process. Your current beliefs, motivations, and goals will shape what you learn as you interact with this text. Before you read, complete the following chart. What are your core convictions about teaching right now? What do you know to be the case? For example, do you believe that U.S. schools are better than ever? Have lost their way? Next, record your goals as an educator. Why have you selected teaching? What do you hope to accomplish? For example, is your greatest hope to help students see the power of your subject matter? To foster empathy in your students? As you read, revisit your work here. Learning is a process not only of adding to our knowledge stores, but of also modifying or discarding notions that are incomplete, less than accurate, or outmoded. Revise your work as you continue learning about your profession.

Warm-Up Exercise for the Nature of Teaching	
My Core Convictions about Teaching and Learning	**My Goals as a Teacher**

CHAPTER *One*

The Nature of Teaching

In the United States, children play school, spend many years as students in classrooms, and encounter countless media images of teachers. All these sources push us toward the conclusion that, before we ever become adults, we know all there is to know about teaching. However, a more careful look suggests that our earlier experiences with teaching may not provide information that, after all, helps us to *teach* well. What is teaching? How is it different from other things people do? How does one teach well? The following six propositions help to distinguish teaching from other activities and to combat common misconceptions about teaching:

1. Teaching looks easy . . . from the outside.
2. Every teacher is part of a system.
3. Teaching is directed toward the goal of fostering change.
4. Teaching is more than telling.
5. There is agreement on what teachers need to know and be able to do.
6. Teachers can be effective and yet not just alike.

TEACHING LOOKS EASY . . . FROM THE OUTSIDE

The prevailing perception is that teaching is simple. Unlike medicine or law, the profession of teaching does not inspire awe by conjuring up visions of a scary knowledge base or of harrowing training experiences. Because most of us have had, as children, years of classroom experience, we may assume that we know

Teaching looks easy from the outside.

Scott Cunningham/Merrill

3

Exercise 1 in Opportunities to Practice at the close of this chapter presents a number of recently offered metaphors for the many roles of teachers. Take a look, and think about your own vision related to these roles.

all that teachers know. And, on a larger scale, current national calls for accountability require schools to raise student achievement in a linear fashion each year. Some experts (e.g., Amrein & Berliner, 2002, 2003; Cochran-Smith, 2003; Rose, 2004) argue that such requirements are based on simplistic notions about the often complicated relationships among factors such as tests, teaching, and learning. Not until we step in front of a classroom for the first time—and not until we examine the myriad of factors that influence student learning—may we realize how difficult teaching can be.

Teaching is difficult partly because classrooms are complex (Doyle, 1986). First, teachers are required to serve in several roles. They need to serve as advocate (Kaplan, 2003), instructor, observer, evaluator, coach, activities director, supply master, and confidante, for instance. In their varied roles, teachers make many decisions about different kinds of issues. Some estimate that teachers make hundreds of decisions per day (Danielson, 1996). Teachers need to think about students' safety, their learning, and their other needs simultaneously, all while they also consider their own personal and professional issues.

Second, classrooms are complex because of the number and rate of events that occur there. Many things happen at once, they happen quickly, and events tend to overlap. As the number of learners increases or the learners' maturity level decreases, the challenges can increase, but in all classrooms teachers must make quick judgments without the benefit of time to reflect or weigh the consequences of their actions. Third, although particular classrooms have common elements, every learning situation is different. Individual learners' experiences and needs affect the nature of the class. Students start the year in different places academically and socially, have different interests and preferences, and go home to different circumstances. The physical, **sociocultural,** and historical setting of the class varies as well. Consequently, as teachers and their students spend time together, they build a shared history. That is why an outside observer may miss inside jokes, be confused by a class's accepted procedures, or fail to see why a single comment could irritate others.

A fourth way in which classrooms are complex is that, because people affect each other, the act of teaching is inherently uncertain. It is difficult for even an experienced teacher to predict with certainty how a class will respond to a lesson. Classrooms are also unpredictable because as teachers we may pursue goals that are unclear, our base of authority may be in question, and we are usually unsure of the outcomes of our efforts, especially long-range outcomes (Jackson, 1986). Although the desire to touch the future is a strong draw for many teachers (Eisner, 2006), we are often left uncertain about the effects of our efforts. What happens to students after they leave us? What did they learn? Did they learn *because of us* or *in spite of us?* Teaching Tip 1.1 gives a quick strategy to discover what students learn from day to day.

Finally, teaching is a complex act because it reaches into time both before and after face-to-face interaction with students. It requires preparation, and it requires reflection and revision. Because classrooms are complex, it takes *years* to master the craft of teaching (Berliner, 2004). Both careful study and reflective experience are necessary.

Have you seen the television commercial that hawks deodorant by admonishing us to "never let them see you sweat"? That commercial seems to

Good teaching is neither obvious nor simplistic.

—*National Board for Professional Teaching Standards (2002)*

EXIT CARDS

Use *exit cards* to quickly discover some things about what your students learn during your lessons. At the close of a lesson, period, or day, distribute index cards or slips of paper and ask students to respond to one or two brief prompts such as, "List one thing you learned today," "Solve for x," or "What question do you still have after today's lesson?" Students leave the cards in a container by the door as their ticket out. Study the cards quickly and start the next lesson by addressing the exit card results.

capture the first aspect of teaching: Teaching looks easy . . . from the outside. Seldom are the daily events of teaching witnessed by the public. Though public attention on teaching and on student performance is high, few people witness the day-to-day conditions under which teachers are expected to encourage learning and to manage the complexity of the classroom without a drop of perspiration. Further, classroom complexity is compounded because classrooms exist as part of a larger system.

EVERY TEACHER IS PART OF A SYSTEM

No teacher serves as an island; no teacher teaches solely for his own purposes. Instead, a teacher serves at the center of a set of nested circles of influence, as shown in Figure 1.1. Imagine an archery target. You, the teacher, are in the

FIGURE 1.1   *Circles of influence that affect classroom teachers.*

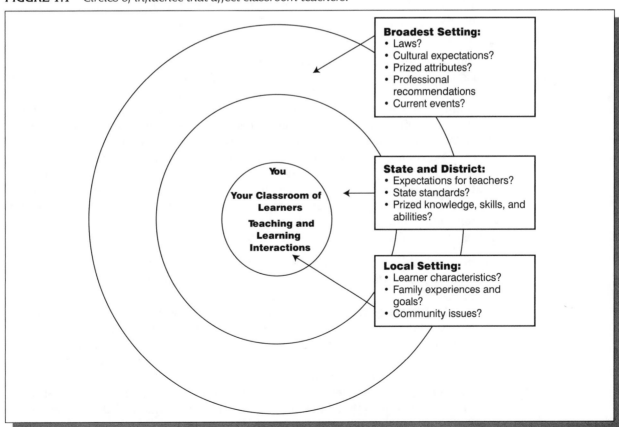

bull's-eye, and the outermost ring contains society in the broadest sense. As a teacher, you are expected to act in ways that are consistent with the rules and goals of society. These rules guide your actions as a citizen, and, more specifically, they direct you as a teacher. Laws govern many aspects of your behavior (as summarized in Figure 1.2) as well as your professional practice.

The most sweeping example of recent legislative action on classroom practice is the federal **No Child Left Behind Act of 2001.** The act was motivated by persistent disparities in student achievement—**achievement gaps**—between the performance of U.S. students overall and subgroups of the population such as minority students, students with disabilities, and students whose families face poverty. The act (often called NCLB) was designed to improve **student achievement** and increase **school accountability** for that achievement. Although you can visit the NCLB homepage at http://www.ed.gov/nclb to read the act itself, its major requirements include:

- Development by all states of student content standards
- Annual assessment of students in grades 3 through 8 to determine proficiency in mathematics and reading in line with content standards
- Measurement of all school districts for adequate yearly progress (AYP) and continuous improvement based on this AYP benchmark
- Meeting of AYP for each of nine student subgroups (based on factors such as ethnicity, physical disability, and poverty)
- Requirement for all schools to have highly qualified teachers

NCLB has changed our classrooms in a number of ways, and its effects appear at this point to be mixed and uncertain. The Center on Education Policy (2006), which conducts research on NCLB across the nation, points to a number of positive effects of NCLB to date, including the following:

- Concerted efforts to align content standards (goals), instruction, and assessment
- Better use of student assessment data to plan instruction and meet student needs
- Increased student achievement on state tests

Similarly, the U.S. Department of Education (2006) states, "No Child Left Behind is *Working,*" and cites all-time high scores in national measures of reading and mathematics and a lessening of the achievement gap.

Some analyses (e.g., Lee, 2006), however, do not support a lessening of achievement differences, and perusal of test score data and analyses found at the Nation's Report Card Web site indicates that changes in national scores are not statistically significant. The **National Assessment of Education Progress,** or NAEP, assesses student progress across the 50 states. Visit http://nces.ed.gov and go to "Nation's Report Card" to study scores for yourself. Critics of NCLB condemn its assumptions such as the use of sanctions as a motivator for improvement and identical achievement targets set regardless of students' initial performance (Rose, 2004). Some deleterious practices associated with NCLB include the following:

- the narrowing of the school curriculum to those subjects tested annually, namely reading/language arts and mathematics (Center on Education Policy, 2006).
- a lack of attention to students whose performance is perceived as less crucial for attaining targeted percentages of students deemed proficient. Such groups may include gifted students and students whose performance is so low that they are unlikely to meet proficiency requirements, even with academic interventions (Booher-Jennings, 2006).
- "gaming" practices wherein personnel focus on meeting achievement targets rather than on fostering student learning (Booher-Jennings, 2006; Rose, 2004).

FIGURE 1.2 *Teachers and the law.*

1. *Public schools must not promote worship.* Schools may teach about religion if the intent is not to worship.

   If a public school allows some groups to meet there, it must provide equal access and allow religious-based groups (such as religious clubs) to meet there as well. The groups cannot be school sponsored (Alexander & Alexander, 2005).

   Students cannot be required to salute the flag if their religious convictions or matters of conscience (in some states) prohibit it (Fischer, Schimmel, & Kelly, 1999).

2. *Academic freedom has limits.* Education is a marketplace of ideas (Alexander & Alexander, 2005). Teachers are permitted to address controversial topics and use controversial methods if they are educationally defensible, appropriate for the students, and are not disruptive. School boards have authority to set curriculum and methods.

3. *Teachers' private activities must not impair their teaching effectiveness.* Although teachers hold the same rights as other citizens, their conduct is held to a higher standard. When teachers' private lives weaken their classroom effectiveness, it is possible that they may be dismissed. Sexual relationships with students are cause for dismissal (Fischer et al., 1999).

4. *Students have rights to due process.* Teachers' and schools' rules and procedures must be fair and reasonable, and justice must be administered even handedly. Due process is important for such issues as search and seizure, suspension, and expulsion (McCarthy, Cambron-McCabe, & Thomas, 1998). Families of students with disabilities have additional due process procedures related to special education services (Fischer et al., 1999).

5. *Teachers must not use academic penalties to punish behavior.* Students' academic grades cannot be lowered as a result of disciplinary infractions. Students must be allowed to make up work that accumulates during suspensions or other disciplinary periods (McCarthy et al., 1998).

6. *Corporal punishment must not be misused.* Fewer than half the states allow corporal—or physical—punishment (Underwood & Webb, 2006). In states where it is allowed, corporal punishment must be delivered while the teacher is not in a state of anger, it must fit the crime and the student's age and condition, and it must not lead to permanent injury or run the risk of such (McCarthy et al., 1998). Disciplinary actions that serve to humiliate a child may be illegal too.

7. *Teachers must protect children's safety.* Teachers must act in place of the parents (Alexander & Alexander, 2005), providing prudent, reasonable supervision to protect children from harm. They can be held negligent if they do not do so.

   Teachers and schools can protect children's safety by establishing and enforcing rules pertaining to safety and by providing prudent, reasonable care in their supervision (Fischer et al., 1999).

8. *Teachers must not slander or libel their students.* Teachers must say and write only things about students that they know objectively to be true. Even confidential files must not contain statements that demean a student's character, background, or home life. Statements should be based on relevant observable behavior (Fischer et al., 1999). Teachers must share information only with personnel who have a right to such information.

9. *Teachers must copy instructional materials in accordance with copyright laws.* The reproduction without the author's permission of copyrighted instructional materials, including print sources, visual images, videotapes, and computer software, is restricted to conditions of fair use. Examples of fair use are a single copy of a book chapter for a teacher's own use, or a copy of a poem. Teachers may not make copies to replace collected works, nor may they make copies of consumable materials. Teachers may not make copies of computer software, and they are greatly restricted in their use of videotape in the classroom (Fischer et al., 1999; McCarthy et al., 1998). Teachers should consider materials found on the World Wide Web to be copyright protected, unless the materials state that they are public domain (Underwood & Webb, 2006).

10. *Teachers must report suspected child abuse.* All states require teachers to report suspected physical or sexual abuse, and no state requires certainty, only reasonable cause to believe that abuse is present (Fischer et al., 1999). If the state requires teachers to report suspected abuse to an agency, then a teacher's report to a principal or district does not satisfy the agency requirement; the teacher must also report to the agency (Underwood & Webb, 2006).

11. *Teachers need to know the law.* Ignorance is no excuse.

12. *Teachers should be aware of emerging legal issues.* One is educational malpractice, which can be either instructional (wherein students fail to learn) or professional (wherein school personnel misdiagnose, provide improper placements, or misadvise students) (Underwood & Webb, 2006).

Source: Adapted from McDaniel (1979). Corroborated and updated with Alexander and Alexander (2005); Fischer, Schimmel, and Kelly (1999); McCarthy, Cambron-McCabe, and Thomas (1998); and Underwood and Webb (2006).

The No Child Left Behind Act is currently under consideration for reauthorization, and educational theorists and researchers alike continue to scrutinize NCLB and its results.

By moving toward the center of the target in Figure 1.1, you travel through rings that represent increasingly local and specific settings. The settings found in these rings often have narrower and more explicitly defined purposes and expectations. For example, states develop **content standards** across the curriculum, and these standards influence state and local **textbook adoptions,** professional development activities for teachers, and learning opportunities for students.

A local source of influence on classrooms is the family. Effective teachers respond to the values and dreams of the families they serve and make use of the resources offered by families and their communities (Gonzalez, Andrade, Civil, & Moll, 2001; Moll, Amanti, Neff, & Gonzalez, 1992). In fact, research consistently links effective family involvement programs with increased student achievement (e.g., Jeynes, 2005; Sheldon & Epstein, 2005). See Teaching Tip 1.2 for some ideas for getting to know families and communities.

Others who affect new teachers include the experienced educators who direct and supervise their growth. Examples include university supervisors, **mentors,** and site administrators. These individuals can hold a powerful influence on teachers and represent the interests and values of the profession by serving the school or university as an institution.

The relationships among circles of influence (Figure 1.1) are dynamic and often riddled with tension and dilemma. Throughout history, the interactions among rings have frequently been emotionally, culturally, and politically charged. Which influences should receive priority? How do we as teachers manage demands from different sources and levels, especially when they compete?

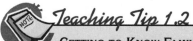

Teaching Tip 1.2

GETTING TO KNOW FAMILIES AND COMMUNITIES

Get to know your students' families and their community. Be ready to take the time and effort required to build sustained relationships. Try some of these ideas:

- Visit the school's Web site and the Web site of the city in which the school is located. What are the local issues and priorities?
- Drive or walk through the community. Visit its places of business. Talk with shoppers. If you have a good relationship with a family in the community, ask for a guided tour.
- Meet with families and talk with them about their students. Ensure that the meeting times and places accommodate families' schedules and preferences. Some of these may work:
  - Meeting at school for breakfast, coffee or tea, or a potluck
  - Meeting at sites in the community where families usually gather
  - Meeting at a park for a back-to-school barbeque or picnic
- Search out and respect families' communication preferences. Find out which family member(s) have responsibility for the student, and ask which form of communication—such as school-door conversations, cell phonecalls, or e-mails— they prefer. Be respectful about where you send messages and the number of messages you send. Also ask which language families prefer to use with school personnel. Get help from a translator as appropriate.
- Find out about families' goals for their students. Relationships are often based on shared goals, and inquiring into families' goals can build common ground.
- Use written surveys completed at home and in the home language, if appropriate, to get to know families.

What are the opportunities and constraints offered by the many sources of influence? Questions such as these require us to consider—and reconsider—carefully the role of education in our society.

Sources of influence in the various rings offer many opportunities: The United States is one of the world's wealthiest nations and has an estimated literacy rate of 99% (according to the *World Factbook*; Central Intelligence Agency, 2006). We are leaders in fields such as technology and medical innovations. These are potentially positive sources of influence. However, sources of influence also offer constraints. Although the United States is a wealthy nation, Kozol's work (1991, 2000, 2005) painfully documents the experiences of public school students who experience institutionalized racism in unsafe and woefully understocked urban schools. Although citizens of the same state and country as their peers in better-maintained schools, students in many urban and less affluent suburban schools, Kozol reports, can expect funding rates half those of nearby affluent schools. We continue to find disparate levels of wealth in American schools (Berliner, 2006). Berliner's research indicates that students who face poverty face more severe health issues, lower academic achievement, and diminished life chances. Recent reports (e.g., Fordham Foundation, 2006) suggest that current reform efforts have done little to raise achievement for the United States' neediest students.

As another example of disparity, despite the prevalence of technology in our society at large, our students view each other across a **digital divide.** Home access to computers and the Internet continues to vary by demographic and social status (DeBell & Chapman, 2006). White students are more likely to use these technologies than are African Americans or Latinos, and families with higher incomes and educational attainments are also more likely to use technology. Latino immigrants are the least likely to have computer access (Fairlie, London, Rosner, & Pastor, 2006). The same divide exists for students who have physical disabilities. Limited access to technology may serve to further constrain opportunities for participation in the economy and in society. Thus, even though the United States is a country rich with opportunities, patterns of inequity exist, and those patterns affect what happens in classrooms and in the lives of students.

Differences in achievement or educational experience based on gender, race, or **socioeconomic status** *may be exacerbated by the* **digital divide,** *or disparities in access to high-quality technology, the Internet, and effective computer-assisted instruction (Lazarus & Mora, 2000)*

Liz Moore/Merrill

Historical influences at every level can also shape what happens in individual classrooms. Current events change us. Imagine for a moment how different life is for Americans since the horrific events of September 11, 2001. More recently, teachers and students have been affected by school-based acts of violence such as the 2006 shootings of students in an Amish school in Pennsylvania and, at the university level, the appalling 2007 shootings at Virginia Tech. These events have shaped policies and procedures in schools, and they have affected the outlooks of many students and their families. We are a different people now.

It may appear, then, that the general direction of influence for the rings or sources of influence seems to be inward: Each of the concentric layers can shape what happens in classrooms so that many forces press teachers to act in certain ways and to accomplish certain ends. Fortunately, the schools and the people who work within them can act to lessen inequities in order to improve life for people in the classroom, and in the outer layers. In the case of the digital divide, for example, schools often serve as an equalizing factor by providing access to technology that may not be available in students' homes (DeBell & Chapman, 2006).

The courts, too, are used in the United States to address inequities. A notable recent example is the Williams case in California, a class-action lawsuit brought about by families who contended that their students, attending poorly funded schools, were denied equal access to the resources necessary to meet the state's challenging content standards (California Department of Education, 2006; Powers, 2004). The suit drew sharper attention to the **opportunity gap,** noting inequitable opportunities to learn based on factors such as school funding, and resulted in a settlement of nearly a billion dollars, with the effects to be felt by millions of California students in the years to come.

Finally, our students themselves offer a tremendously powerful source of influence to improve their world. For example, many students in schools across the nation responded to the tragedy of Hurricane Katrina with humanitarian efforts to ease the suffering of affected families and communities. As students examine local conditions, challenge existing practices, and participate in **social action** or **service learning** projects (e.g., Allen, 2003; Bomer & Bomer, 2001; Darling-Hammond, French, & Garcia-Lopez, 2002; Eastin, 2002; Stephens, 1995), they shape their communities. Many argue that students should be similarly encouraged to shape life within the classroom. A body of literature on **democratic classrooms** and education for democratic purposes (e.g., Allen, 1999; Bomer & Bomer, 2001; Charney, 1997; Education Commission of the States, 2000; Fuhrman & Lazerson, 2005; Kohn, 1998; Rush, 2006) seeks to harness the influence of students in molding classrooms that reflect the goals, interests, and spirit of each student as a caring member of the learning community and of society. In democratic classrooms, students learn to care for each other and participate in decision making as they take responsibility for their behavior and learning. Democratic practices are especially important in diverse classrooms because they equalize status differences that may arise given student differences. See Teaching Tip 1.3 for some ideas for encouraging democratic processes.

Thus, because teachers are part of a system, they must recognize the influence of other people in the local setting. The bull's-eye includes not only you, the teacher, but also your students. Students exert influence. Teaching is **interactional.** Although you as the teacher may be awarded more status and power, students are participants who must be considered in your instructional decisions. In fact, students are at the center of your instructional decisions; teaching is meant to encourage learning.

In sum, as a teacher you are expected not only to teach toward your own ideals and aims but also toward the goals of the nested groups—rings on the

TEACHER PREP

All students and their families have legal rights, and a number of laws protect the rights of students with special needs. Watch as a parent talks about how she and her family used the law to get their student's special educational needs met. Go to the Teacher Prep Web site Video Classroom Special Education, Module 5, Video 1. What might the general education teacher have done differently to work more effectively with the student and his family?

DEMOCRATIC CLASSROOM PRACTICES

Try some of these ideas to build democratic classrooms:

- Have students help make the rules for classroom behavior via collaborative rule making (Effrat & Schimmel, 2003).
- Hold a compliments circle. Instruct students in how to give a compliment to a peer who recently did something that was helpful or noteworthy. Teach students, also, to receive compliments. Pass an item from speaker to listener. (I recently used a foam rock, and students started their compliments with, "You rock because . . . ") Caution: Set up your circles to ensure that every person receives a compliment within one or two sessions. Do not allow compliments that focus on appearance or possessions.
- Use learning contracts or other self-selected learning plans to encourage students to direct their own study. Provide support along the way.
- Allow students to conduct self-critiques of their work and resubmit after revision.
- Use learning activities where the expertise of every class member is necessary, regardless of students' status. For instance, you may give each member of a small group just one bit of information. Each group member must rely on the others' information to accomplish the goal.

target—to which you belong. No doubt you will have opportunities to witness and manage tensions that result from the competing goals found in different rings. Part of your job will be to negotiate at least temporary solutions for the dilemmas found in competing goals. Take a few minutes to consider the goals and expectations of the circles of influence that envelop you. What influence do you hope to have in each of the rings? Try jotting your notes on Figure 1.1.

TEACHING IS DIRECTED TOWARD THE GOAL OF FOSTERING CHANGE

Why are you here? Look back at your chart from the beginning of this chapter. Many teachers select education as a profession because of the desire to help "light the candle" or watch the "lightbulb click on" as they help students learn. Others hope to help students realize the power of an education to improve life. All teachers strive for change in their learners. Teachers are expected to nudge learners toward improvement. Learners should come to know more, to know more deeply, or to have enhanced skills, abilities, or attitudes through their time with you. Although certainly teachers are affected by their learners, and effective teachers must continue to grow over time, instructor improvement is not the universal goal of teaching. The goal of teaching is change for the learner. What changes are expected? Who creates the change? Which methods are used? The answers to these questions vary by teacher and circumstance, but in every case we expect that learners will leave the setting different from when they entered it. The hope of a teacher is to make a positive difference in learners' lives.

Teaching becomes complicated by the fact that teachers usually pursue many—and sometimes conflicting—goals. For instance, although a teacher may strive to help learners become more independent, she also needs to encourage order, and she may do so by praising conformity ("I like the way that Sung is sitting so nicely!"). Learners also pursue their own agendas, including ones that may contradict the teacher's goals. My son Alex provides two examples. When his first-grade teacher stepped into the hall for a brief conversation with a colleague, Alex immediately seized the moment and leapt onto his chair. Fists and face raised to the sky, he screamed "Let's party!" A decade later, Alex is still partying. As a cross-country runner, he and his teammates stuff money into their socks for the long Wednesday run. Although their *coach's* goal is that they shave minutes off their five-mile times, *the runners'* goal is to pick up tacos and ice cream bars and enjoy life along the way. No matter how reluctant the learners, teaching is directed toward the goal of fostering change for the learners.

Do teachers in fact make a difference in the lives of learners? NCLB pushes for **highly qualified teachers** in every school. Research (e.g., Darling-Hammond, 2000; Laczko-Kerr & Berliner, 2002, 2003) indicates that enhanced teacher preparation is associated with improved student learning, and research reported by Berliner (2004) finds that expert teachers have greater student achievement gains. Further, reviews of the literature (e.g., U.S. Department of Education, 2003) present compelling evidence that individual teachers can, indeed, have a powerful effect on student learning. Overall, it appears that the single most influential in-school contributor to student learning is the teacher.

TEACHING IS MORE THAN TELLING

Part of the perception that teaching is easy stems from the mistaken notion that teaching and telling are the same thing: If a teacher *says it*, students will *know it*. Certainly a well-delivered lecture can be a powerful learning tool, but we cannot presume that knowledge travels directly from the mouth of the teacher to the mind of the learner. We know that factors such as teachers' experience and expectations affect student learning. We also know that what students learn is affected by many factors such as their physical characteristics, perspectives, preferences, and prior experiences. Knowledge is constructed as learners bring their perspectives and experiences to bear on new information. Teachers need to help students connect new information to their own lives.

Because classrooms are interactive and dynamic, "teaching as telling" does not capitalize on the learners' goals or on the power of their experiences. It also does not draw directly from current theories on how children learn. Figure 1.3 summarizes current views on how people learn.

Teaching is more than telling.

Barbara Schwartz/Merrill

FIGURE 1.3 *Influential views on how people learn.*

Behaviorist Approaches

- Hold that learning occurs continuously and can be intentional or unintentional.
- Focus on observable behaviors and shaping them through rewards and punishments, or consequences.
- Reinforcers include grades, praise, and tangible items. Punishment can take the form of time-outs, detentions, and names on the board for misbehavior.
- Theorists include Skinner (1971), and, more recently, Bandura.

Information Processing Approaches

- Focus on how information is selectively perceived, stored in memory, and retrieved.
- Liken the brain to a computer, a system with limited capacity that processes information according to logic and rules. Information is received through the senses and then is perceived by the mind. It enters short-term memory either from the process of sensation or from long-term memory. Concepts are stored through schemata (systems of linked concepts).
- Teachers should be systematic in their instruction to enhance learning. Some important activities are gaining students' attention, accessing background knowledge, focusing on organization of ideas, providing feedback, and supplying meaningful practice.
- Theorists include Gagne (1985) and Miller (Miller, 1956; Miller, Galanter, & Pribam, 1960).

Constructivist Approaches

- Focus on processes by which students *build* knowledge rather than *receive* it.
- Hold that we continually check new information against our mental rules in order to internalize and act on information.
- Purport that learning is social, and "disequilibration," or cognitively unsettling experiences, cause learners to reorganize cognition at higher levels.
- Students should confront their current thinking by actively testing and refining their ideas. Heterogeneous groups provide opportunities for students to challenge and support each other's thinking.
- Theorists and researchers include Bruner (1986), Driver (1989a, 1989b), Piaget (1952), and Vygotsky (1978).

Multiple Intelligence Theory

- Challenges the notion that intelligence is a single construct and suggests instead that people can be smart in many different ways.
- Holds that intelligences are many and currently include (1)logical or mathematical, (2)linguistic, (3)musical, (4)spatial, (5)bodily or kinesthetic, (6)interpersonal, (7)intrapersonal, and (8)naturalist intelligences.
- Urges schools and teachers to broaden the kinds of experiences offered to children.
- Practitioners find the theory powerful for questioning the assumption that a certain level of performance in one area is necessarily associated with a similar level of performance in another area.
- Developed by Howard Gardner, first in 1983, and explored more fully in recent works (including Gardner, 1999, 2006).

Brain-Based Research

- Draws from neuroscience and suggests that the brain functions holistically, processing many kinds of information (such as emotions and facts) at once.
- Holds that the search for meaning and pattern making is innate.
- School experiences should be directly guided by how the brain functions by providing numerous complex and concrete experiences that are rich in sensory stimulation and embedded within human contexts.
- Some writers (Bruer, 1997), including proponents (Jensen, 2000), caution against making large inferential leaps to classroom contexts. Research is new and limited.
- Popular proponents include Caine and Caine (1994; Caine, Caine, McClintic, & Klimek, 2005) and Jensen (2005).

FIGURE 1.4 *Teachers cannot pour knowledge into students' needs.*

One trend that emerges from these views on how people learn is that learning seems not to be a simple matter of reception. Instead, it appears to be about active engagement, about questioning, and about facing misunderstandings and building better understandings by organizing information in meaningful ways (Bransford, 2000; Gagnon & Collay, 2001; Marlowe & Page, 1998; National Research Council, 2000). Because human learning appears to be a complicated affair, teaching as purely telling can short-circuit learning by ignoring the large variety of strategies that teachers can use to help encourage growth. That is why skilled teachers have rich repertoires of **instructional strategies** from which they select as they consider their goals, their learners, and the settings in which they teach. Further, teachers can foster learning without telling by encouraging students to learn via texts, by themselves via experiences, and from each other through discussion and inquiry (Finkel, 2000). A teacher does more than deliver a monologue (see Figure 1.4).

Teaching is more than telling, too, because it involves listening (Mosher, 2001; Schultz, 2003). When people are learning, they are trying to figure things out, to make sense of new information. One effective way to help learners understand things is to listen to their points of view, their musings, and their questions. *Listening* is an important strategy that teachers can employ to slow down the presentation of new information, to give learners an opportunity to sort things out, and to help learners discover what they think. Finally, because teaching is interactional, listening gives us information about the learners' reasoning that can be used to guide our moment-by-moment and longer-range instructional decisions. Teaching Tip 1.4 gives suggestions to help you—and your students—practice active listening. The fact that teaching is more than telling is reflected in the agreement on what teachers need to know and be able to do.

ACTIVE LISTENING

Try some of these ways to encourage active listening in your classroom—for you *and* the students.

- Teach listening behaviors such as SLANT: Sit up, Lean forward, Ask questions, Nod, Track the speaker.
- Teach active listening strategies such as paraphrasing: "So what I hear you saying is . . . "
- Wait a bit after asking a question, and again before responding. Teach students to do the same.
- Call on multiple students to comment on any one question. Require students to link their comments to the previous student's comments.
- Have students toss a ball made of something soft to each other as they comment. Only the person holding the ball speaks.
- If a student's comments went unheard, don't repeat the student's comments for those who were not listening. Instead say, "I know your peers want to hear that. Wait just a second until . . . Okay, try again."

THERE IS AGREEMENT ON WHAT TEACHERS NEED TO KNOW AND BE ABLE TO DO

Despite the perception that most people who have attended school understand teaching, and although some individuals may appear to be "born teachers," there is a body of knowledge, attitudes, and skills that teachers can acquire with effort and experience. National and state panels codify the domains that teachers consider in their work. One of the most influential boards that has considered what it means to be an excellent teacher is the **National Board for Professional Teaching Standards** (NBPTS; see http://NBPTS.org). The NBPTS sets forth five propositions of effective practice, and these domains are assessed as experienced teachers pursue **National Board certification** (an optional, advanced certification that is meant to delineate excellent teachers). Domains of competence are assessed also for prospective and beginning teachers. Danielson's (1996) framework for teaching, for instance, explores domains of practice for new teachers and forms the basis for the content assessed by the Praxis examination Educational Testing Service (ETS). ETS has further explored the domains of practice by surveying practicing teachers and administrators (Tannenbaum & Rosenfeld, 1997). Many states also publish their own standards for the teaching profession. Figure 1.5 synthesizes general conclusions about excellent teaching, drawn from the National Board for Professional Teaching Standards (2002), the Praxis domains (Educational Testing Service, 2002), and various state standards for teaching.

In general, effective teachers

- understand their subject matter, human development, diversity, and learning.
- use their knowledge to plan meaningful instruction.
- create productive and humane learning environments.
- teach in ways that help students learn deeply.
- assess students' growth carefully and use results to modify their instruction.
- engage in their profession by working with families, communities, and other educators to reflect on and improve teaching and learning.

Does this sound like plenty to learn? Compare the row headings of Figure 1.5 with the chapter titles of this text and you will note that we have a whole text to begin exploration of these domains of competence together.

FIGURE 1.5 *Domains of teacher expertise.*

Subject-Matter Knowledge	• Understanding human learning and the many factors (e.g., culture and context) that affect it • Holding rich, organized understanding of the content and how it is used • Using specialized knowledge to help students build accurate and deep understandings of the content
Planning	• Assessing and using students' background knowledge and incorporating it into instruction • Setting and communicating clear learning goals • Creating and selecting learning experiences appropriate for students and goals • Creating and selecting a rich variety of resources to enrich learning
Instruction	• Committing to students and their ability to learn • Providing instruction aligned with communicated goals • Building connections with previous learning • Making content understandable for all students • Teaching for meaning, critical thinking, problem solving, and creative thinking • Monitoring student responses and adjusting instruction
Assessment	• Creating or selecting assessment strategies consistent with learning goals and student needs • Measuring learning for groups and individuals • Using multiple measures to assess growth
Classroom Management and Discipline	• Creating safe climates that promote fairness, autonomy, and respect • Setting norms for social interaction • Establishing and maintaining standards of student behavior • Using routines, procedures, and time effectively
Professional Growth	• Modeling traits of an educated person • Reflecting on goals and practice • Building professional relationships • Working with families, communities, and the profession

Large bodies of research examine schooling practices, both to capture the experiences of teachers and learners and to determine promising teaching practices. Decades of research have provided some insights into how students and teachers make sense of the schooling experience, and this research has provided some directions for practice (e.g., Marzano, Pickering, & Pollock, 2001; Reynolds, 1992; Stronge, 2002). In fact, NCLB mandates the use of research-based practices that provide insights based on careful, systematic research. Many research-based practices are shared in the chapters ahead.

The questionnaire in Figure 1.6 presents an entry-level self-assessment that you can use to consider your current knowledge and skills. Mark areas that may figure prominently in a plan for your professional growth. If you like, formulate questions to capture these areas and record goals on your chart from the beginning of the chapter. You may also wish to flip ahead to chapters that will address your questions.

> What better or greater gift can we offer the republic than to teach and to instruct our young?
>
> —*Cicero*

TEACHERS CAN BE EFFECTIVE AND YET NOT JUST ALIKE

Although there are documented domains of expert teaching, few prescriptions hold in every circumstance. Teaching is uncertain and interactional. Part of teaching well is using a combination of one's own talents, insights, skills, and professional judgments to encourage students' learning and development.

Cicero's sentiment underscores the personal and giving nature of teaching: When we teach, we offer gifts to our students—gifts that depend on our traits and

FIGURE 1.6 *Questionnaire for self-analysis of teaching.*

		Strongly Disagree			Strongly Agree
1.	I can explain how people learn.	1	2	3	4
2.	I know my subject matter.	1	2	3	4
3.	I can list some ways to find out who my students are and what they know.	1	2	3	4
4.	I can plan a lesson related to a content standard.	1	2	3	4
5.	I can demonstrate more than one instructional strategy or technique that helps makes the content clear to students.	1	2	3	4
6.	I can assess students' learning based on traditional tests and at least one other measure.	1	2	3	4
7.	I can modify my instruction based on what I discover about students' learning.	1	2	3	4
8.	I know how to help students treat each other and me respectfully during class.	1	2	3	4
9.	I can structure my time and materials so there is little wasted time.	1	2	3	4
10.	I can describe two ways to involve families beyond conferences and in-class volunteer time.	1	2	3	4

triumphs as givers. Think back to two teachers who had a powerful effect on your learning. What were their gifts? If you make lists of strengths for those two teachers (Figure 1.7), you may find areas of overlap; the teachers probably shared some common strengths and abilities. These instructors probably also made

FIGURE 1.7 *Characteristics of effective teachers I have known.*

Personal Attributes	**Professional Skills, Attributes, and Abilities**
Teacher One: _____	
Teacher Two: _____	

FIGURE 1.8 *Personal characteristics that I bring to learners.*

My Personal Attributes	My Professional Skills and Abilities

unique contributions to your learning. Your lists will probably contain both personal attributes and professional skills, attitudes, and abilities.

When asked to consider their memorable teachers, my students often find commonalities such as passion for the subject matter, high expectations, and genuine regard for the learner. However, the idiosyncratic contributions that their teachers offered are many. Some mention humor, others reserve. Some mention competitive learning activities, others mention collaborative ones. Teachers bring themselves and their abilities to their students. What do you bring to the classroom? Use Figure 1.8 to display your gifts.

A NOTE ON TECHNOLOGY AND THE NATURE OF TEACHING

The fierce and pervasive influence of technology in our society affects the nature of teaching today. First, it shapes the context in which we teach. In the United States, most people use computers (91% of those 18 and younger and 64% of adults; DeBell & Chapman, 2006). We have shifted from an industry-based society to an information-based one, and global interconnectedness requires increasing technological skills. According to one federal projection, 80% of the jobs of 2010 did not exist in 2004 (Patrick, 2004). Vigorous research and development efforts pursue increasingly sophisticated and varied technologies and their applications in fields such as industry, medicine, the military, and education.

Second, technology leaves a clear mark on our students, reared in this technology-soaked society. Fully two-thirds of U.S. preschoolers use technology (DeBell & Chapman, 2006), and many of today's K–12 students may be **digital natives** (Prensky 2001, 2005/2006) who have grown up with video games, instant messaging, Internet access, and cell phones. Such learners often have different expectations for how they learn and share information.

The technological demands of our world have dramatically influenced our expectations for what students need to learn in order to become competent citizens in the twenty-first century. The No Child Left Behind Act stipulates that all students become technology literate by eighth grade, and standards such as those proposed by the International Society for Technology Education (1998) direct us toward the technological competencies our students should master for success.

Third, this technological context shapes our schools, our classrooms and other instructional contexts. By 2002, 99% of U.S. schools had at least one computer with Internet access, and the ratio of Internet-access computers to students was 4.8 to 1 (Kleiner & Lewis, 2004). One-to-one laptop programs, where every student has a laptop computer and uses it as an integral part of instruction, gather large interest (although some experts point to the lack of evidence to support a laptop program's effects on student achievement; Cuban, 2006), and students (particularly those in high school) are increasingly drawn to online instruction, which offers flexible scheduling and connects them with learners from all over the world (Cavanaugh, October 2006).

Fourth, technology shapes the ways we can teach, unleashing innovative ways to help students learn and presenting potential pitfalls that require us to gain new skills in making informed decisions about the use of technology. It also requires us to learn new equipment and to troubleshoot the equipment and software we and our students use. Technology is, likewise, changing the ways we ourselves learn, grow, and communicate in our profession. From the virtual university classrooms visited by our Second Life avatars, to our late night e-mails and podcasts, to our social networking services such as My Space, to our electronic bulletin boards and the online professional development courses and degree or certification programs we pursue, technology is shaping what it means to teach. Many of the specific influences and implications of technology on teaching and learning will be explored in each upcoming chapter.

PARTING WORDS

Common misconceptions hold that teachers work toward a single set of unquestioned goals, usually by standing in front of a calm classroom and talking. Instead, this chapter suggests that teaching is a far more complicated act. It argues that teachers must encourage learner growth of many kinds while weighing often-competing demands and carefully considering their learners and the local context. Despite the complexity of teaching, we find some agreement in the literature about the kinds of things teachers should know and be able to do, and we know that there are many ways to practice the craft of teaching well. One place to start is by forming an educational philosophy, a personal stance toward teaching, as is encouraged in Chapter 2.

Between here and Chapter 2 you will find two end-of-chapter features. "Web Sites" provides an opportunity for you to join a larger community conversation about teaching. "Opportunities to Practice" asks you to apply what you know and to connect chapter ideas with your own thoughts and practice.

WEB SITES

http://www.ednews.org/
  Education News.org. This site includes daily news related to education, updates on education law and policy, links to college and university newspapers, and links to education organizations.

http://thegateway.org/
  The Gateway to Educational Materials (GEM). This site is a consortium-run gateway that provides access to thousands of web-based resources on government, university, not-for-profit, and commercial sites. Go to "Learning and Teaching" and "search the GEM catalog."

http://www.servicelearning.org/
  National Service Learning Clearinghouse. A project of Learn and Serve America, the Clearinghouse includes national listservs and many service learning opportunities for students kindergarten through grade 12.

www.stateline.org
  Stateline.org. A public service funded by the Pew Charitable Trusts, Stateline.org publishes news and policy information. Choose a state and choose a topic, such as "education" or "social policy."

http://www.ed.gov

The U.S. Department of Education. Provides information on legislative and policy issues such as the No Child Left Behind Act. The site has resources for students, parents, teachers, and administrators. Go to the " teachers" section for job information, lesson resources, and many links to sites related to meeting students' needs.

Try Web sites in this chart to review professional organizations and related subject-area standards.

Subject Area	Standards	Related Web sites and Organizations
Arts	National Standards for Arts Education, developed by the Consortium of National Arts Education Association	http://artsedge.kennedy-center.org/ ARTSEDGE: National Arts and Education Network
English Language Arts	Standards for the English Language Arts	http://www.ncte.org National Council of Teachers of English http://www.ira.org International Reading Association
Foreign Language	National Standards in Foreign Language Project	http://www.actfl.org American Council on the Teaching of Foreign Languages
Health	Joint Committee on National Health Education Standards	http://www.aahperd.org American Alliance for Health, Physical Education, Recreation and Dance
History and Social Science	Expectations of Excellence: Curriculum Standards for the Social Studies	http://www.ncss.org National Council for the Social Studies
Mathematics	Principles and Standards for School Mathematics	http://www.nctm.org National Council of Teachers of Mathematics
Science	National Science Education Standards	http://www.nap.edu National Academies Press National Research Council
Technology	National Educational Technology Standards for Students	http://www.iste.org International Society for Technology in Education

Note: For a concise history and summary of national standards across the curriculum, visit the Mid-continent Region Education and Learning site (http://www.mcrel.org).

OPPORTUNITIES TO PRACTICE

1. Teachers and researchers alike use metaphor as a tool to examine the nuances and varied roles of teaching. An Internet search using the linked terms "teacher as" and "metaphor" yielded the following recent analogies for what it means to teach. Place a checkmark near the ones that compel you. Use them to think about your own metaphors for teaching. You may elect to conduct your own Web search related to the metaphors that make you curious.

   Teacher as . . .

   ☐ cultural broker

   ☐ consciousness of the collective

   ☐ container of anxiety

   ☐ DJ

   ☐ executive

   ☐ shaman

   ☐ facilitator and authority

   ☐ hero

   ☐ leader

   ☐ learner

   ☐ rain dancer

   ☐ archetype of spirit

2. Use the video resource to look into three classrooms for evidence related to the nature of teaching. Visit the Merrill Teacher Prep Web site and go to Foundations and Introduction to Teaching. Go to Module 1 and view Video 1: Teaching at Different Grade Levels. In that video, we see snippets of lessons from teachers at three grade levels. Complete this chart as you think about the three classrooms:

	Kindergarten	Middle School	High School
Infer ways that contextual features such as the age of the students, the time of year, and the location of the school affected the lesson. (Teaching looks easy . . . from the outside.)			
Look at each teacher's students. How might the diversity you find in each classroom affect what happens there? What aspects of diversity are probably not apparent upon viewing? (Teachers are part of a system.)			

What do you infer that each teacher was trying to help students learn? (Teaching is directed toward the goal of fostering change.)
What evidence do you have that each teacher (a) knew the subject matter, (b) knew the students, (c) knew how to effectively manage groups of learners? (There is agreement on what teachers need to know and be able to do.)
Other than talking about the content, what behaviors did each teacher use to encourage learning? (Teaching is more than telling.)
What is one individual strength that each teacher demonstrated? (Teachers can be effective and not just alike.)

3. Connect the work you did in Figures 1.1 and 1.6. In what ways have various sources of influence affected your perceived abilities as a teacher thus far? How might they influence your growth as a teacher in the future? Discuss the questionnaire in Figure 1.6 with a relatively new teacher and with an experienced one. You may wish to compare the value they place on the content of each question.

4. Go to one of the Web sites listed at the close of Chapter 1. First, find sources that influence what happens in classrooms. Add them to your work in Figure 1.1. Second, connect what you read on the Web sites with one or more of the six propositions of teaching. Talk with an experienced colleague about recent history related to that issue.

5. Interview a nonteacher about her views on effective teaching. Consider speaking with a parent, a student, or a professional who works outside of education and has little contact with students or schools. What do good teachers do? What do students wish teachers knew? How closely do your interviewee's insights match the propositions from the chapter?

6. Good readers are active readers. Try Figure 1.9 to think about the sense you made of Chapter 1.

FIGURE 1.9   *Analysis of Chapter 1.*

One point that I found interesting or useful:
One point with which I disagree:

Before You Begin Reading

Chapter Two

In his popular treatise, Robert Fulghum (1988) asserts that everything he ever really needed to know about the world, and how to be a good person in it, he learned at school . . . in kindergarten. In kindergarten he learned, for example, to share, to play fair, and to clean up his messes. Each of these could be considered a "big lesson" that applies not only to 5-year-olds, but to 55-year-olds as well.

Take a few minutes to consider the influence you hope to have on students. If they could learn only two or three things with you, what would those things be? What are the big lessons in life that you hope to help teach?

Warm-Up Exercise for Developing a Personal Stance Toward Education

I hope to help students learn or become . . .

CHAPTER *Two*

Developing a Personal Stance Toward Education

"Now in teaching, as in several other things, it does not matter what your philosophy is or is not. It matters more whether you have a philosophy or not. And it matters very much whether you try to live up to your philosophy or not. The only principles of teaching which I thoroughly dislike are those to which people pay only lip service."

—George Polya, *Mathematical Discovery*

The operative goal of classroom teaching seems obvious: Teachers teach subject matter to students. That goal appears to go largely unquestioned, particularly in today's high-accountability climate. In the opinion of some (e.g., Keller & Bichelmeyer 2004), in fact, the mission of our schools seems to have become the improvement of test scores. However, no matter how clearly defined or matter-of-fact a classroom situation may seem, no teacher can escape the burden of personal and professional judgment. Take another look at that operative goal: Teachers teach subject matter to students. *Who* should teach our students? What *subject matter* should be taught? *How?* To *which students? Under which conditions?* Toward what *end?* According to *which standards?* With which *expectations of success?*

Important questions such as these make it imperative that teachers know what they think and take guidance from a larger vision of what should be (Duffy, 1998). I urge you to form a stance—a vision of education, or educational philosophy—that sets out what you believe to be (1) the purposes of your work, (2) the nature of humans and learning, and (3) your view of what it means to teach well. Captured in words, these notions can serve as a guide for your actions. Your efforts to plan lessons, instruct, and assess students can be richer and more cohesive when shaped by a thoughtful, carefully constructed vision of education.

Is a stance toward education irrelevant in these days of prescribed curriculum and federal and state mandates that focus on narrow definitions of student success? I argue that there has never been a day when a clearly articulated, lofty vision of your work as a professional has been more important. Here are five reasons why:

1. Teaching today can be overwhelming, especially for the novice. So many decisions need to be made. So many needs must be considered. A stance toward education provides a compass for decision making.
2. Classrooms are so busy, and pressure for teacher and student performance is so high, that it is easy to lose sight of the long-term consequences of our actions. A stance can help you remember to maintain your focus on the big picture of what we hope our schools will accomplish.
3. Mandates, such as for *what* we teach and *how* we teach it, are nothing until they are implemented by actual teachers. Your choices for how you interpret mandates and how you enact them with your particular students

each minute of the day make you powerful indeed (Elmore, 1979; Web, 2002). Your vision of education provides you with guidance on how to breathe life into directives.

4. Having your own stance and understanding of the stances of others allows you to understand their perspectives and the kinds of criteria and evidence they accept. It can allow you to understand how and why you fit (or do not fit) and the language to use in speaking about issues with someone who has a different stance.

5. This chapter argues that our actions have unintended consequences. The same is true for laws and policies. Having a clear stance allows you to assess the unintended consequences that accrue (or might accrue) as a result of our collective legislative and policy decisions. This allows us to more fully determine whether the benefits of our decisions are worth the inadvertent costs.

THREE CURRICULA

Curriculum is an example of an aspect of teaching that may appear at first glance to be straightforward and prescribed. However, "curriculum" turns out to be a multifaceted notion. Eisner (1979) argues convincingly that schools teach three kinds of curricula:

1. The explicit curriculum
2. The implicit curriculum
3. The null curriculum

The **explicit curriculum** is that content which is intentionally selected and addressed through instruction. Examples include traditional subject areas such as reading, mathematics, and physical education. For **English learners,** English acquisition becomes a high priority in the explicit curriculum. The explicit curriculum also includes skills or habits that teachers purposefully select and teach. Examples may include neatness, politeness, and cooperation. For students with disabilities, the explicit curriculum might be a functional one where students learn

What are these students learning through their interactions with their teacher?

Anthony Magnacca/Merrill

UNCOVERING SCHOOL CULTURE

Part of the implicit curriculum is what students learn via their school's culture. Secondary teachers can begin to examine school culture by analyzing school documents, rules, ceremonies, rituals, and routines. Uncover school culture by examining questions such as the following (based on Wren, 1999):

- What are the messages of the school newspaper, student handbook, and yearbook?
- What are the messages of the documents available for faculty, students, families, and community members?
- What are the regular assemblies and competitions?
- What are the school-year opening and closing activities?
- What are the school's mascot, motto, colors, and other identifying symbols?
- What are the avenues for regular recognition for outstanding achievement?
- What are the school policies, and how well known and consistently enforced are they?
- Which students participate in which school activities?
- To what extent to different segments of the student population experience the culture in the same ways? In different ways?

To hear a teacher and parent discuss genocide as part of the null curriculum in the United States, go to the Merrill Teacher Prep Website Video Classroom, Multi-cultural Education, Module 6, Video 1. They continue their discussion of the null curriculum regarding Native Americans and their contributions to U.S. history and development in Foundations and Introduction to Teaching, Module 4, Video 3. To what extent does your experience with these aspects of the null curriculum match those of the speakers? What misconceptions might U.S. students have as a result of experiencing these aspects of the null curriculum?

self-care and life skills. On the other hand, the **implicit curriculum,** or hidden curriculum, is not purposefully selected. Rather, it includes the lessons taught tacitly through actions and through unconsidered consequences. Some say that the hidden curriculum is "caught" rather than "taught." Examples of the hidden curriculum may include competition and deference to authority. John Gatto, a New York Teacher of the Year, is a supporter of education, but a critic of compulsory schooling (1992, 2001). He captures his view of the hidden curriculum of U.S. schools with the lessons all teachers teach, including these two (1992) examples:

- *The first lesson I teach is confusion.* Everything I teach is out of context. I teach the un-relating of everything. I teach disconnections.
- *The fourth lesson I teach is emotional dependency.* By stars and red checks, smiles and frowns, prizes, honors and disgraces I teach kids to surrender their will to the predestined chain of command.

Do you agree with Gatto about the lessons we teach? Clearly few teachers would select these lessons as their explicit curriculum; rather, the hidden curriculum is often a set of *unintended consequences* that results from our conscious long-range decisions and our spur-of-the-moment choices. Fortunately, positive aspects of the implicit curriculum exist as well and include outcomes such as kindness, respect, and the notion that people believe in one's abilities to succeed.

One benefit of uncovering the hidden curriculum is that, once we expose it, we can determine the extent to which we are teaching the lessons we intend, and we can address the harmful lessons students may be learning with us. Additionally, many of our students may need our assistance in understanding the tacit rules of behavior transmitted through the implicit curriculum. Part of the school-level implicit curriculum, for instance, is what students learn via their school's culture. Try Teaching Tip 2.1 to analyze school culture. As another example, this time within the classroom, students who struggle to understand social relationships (such as those with **Asperger syndrome**) can benefit from their teachers' assistance in learning and using the rules by which people interact at school and away (Myles & Simpson, 2001). Overt understanding of the implicit curriculum, then, can help students to master it, and, as necessary, change it.

The third curriculum, the **null curriculum,** refers to what we learn because of the subject matter *not* taught. An elementary example of the null curriculum is found in current concerns that valuable school subjects such as science, social studies, and the arts are shrinking or disappearing from the curriculum in the face of pressures for mathematics and reading achievement that stem from the No Child Left Behind Act (e.g., Center on Education Policy, 2006; Keller & Bichelmeyer, 2004). One of my former students, now a first-year teacher, recently sent me an e-mail that included this excerpt:

> It still surprises me just how important test scores are. We always talked about it [in class], but now I see it in action. I have a science curriculum from 1993 and no time to teach it, yet I am supposed to give a grade for it. I thought of you Andi, when I went to fill in the report cards and I had to put an "N/A" for science. (personal communication, used with permission)

A secondary social studies example of the null curriculum is the subject of *genocide* (Totten, 2001). Although acts of atrocity occur the world over, several obstacles seem to prevent the subject of genocides other than the Holocaust from entering high school classrooms. As a result secondary students may have limited understanding of important events that shape our world and tell about humans' treatment of others.

Eisner's three curricula warn that every action a teacher takes—or does not take—can teach. Even instantaneous decisions and fleeting behaviors convey our stance to our learners and to our communities. Think about the powerful things you learned in school that were probably not recorded in your teachers' daily plan books. Because every action—or *in*action—can teach, a coherent philosophy or stance toward education can be a helpful guide and a reminder for us to be intentional with our words and actions. How can you develop a stance toward education that can direct you as you teach? One way is by considering a set of enduring questions.

> As with all great teachers, his curriculum was an insignificant part of what he communicated. From him you didn't learn a subject but life. . . . Tolerance and justice, fearlessness and pride, reverence and pity are learned in a course on long division if the teacher has those qualities.
>
> —*William Alexander Percy*

CONSIDERING THE QUESTIONS OF EDUCATION

Philosophy as a field of study addresses questions about beauty, logic, ethics, morality, the nature of reality, and the character of knowledge. In education, questions such as, Should education prepare students for particular functions in society or for personal enlightenment? and, Is a classical curriculum adequate for today's students? (Noddings, 1995) are deliberated daily. Of the many sets of questions proposed by educational theorists, an especially useful one was proposed by the ancient Greeks and suggested to me by James T. Dillon (1987). These questions, which parallel the concerns of the sixteenth century's famous philosopher John Comenius (Sadler, 1966), ask the following:

> Every science and every inquiry, and similarly every activity and pursuit, is thought to aim at some good.
>
> —*Aristotle*

1. What is the good? Who is the good person living in the good society?
2. What is the purpose of education?
3. What should everyone learn? Why?
4. What is the nature of learning?
5. What is (excellent) teaching?
6. What does school do?

It may be helpful for you to study the answers to these perennial questions found in existing conceptions of education before developing your own answers to them.

CONCEPTIONS OF EDUCATION FOUND IN PRACTICE

Education holds a special place in a democracy. In fact, Jefferson saw education as the foundation of a democracy; only well-informed citizens can be expected to govern themselves and throw off oppression. Current research suggests, indeed, that the more educated people are, the more likely they are to participate in political and civic life and to be tolerant and equity minded (Kingston, Hubbard, Lapp, Schroeder, & Wilson, 2003).

What does it mean to be "educated" in the United States? As we examine conceptions of education in this country, we see a history of struggle as Americans have wrestled with how best to educate youth for participation in democratic society, respond to persistent questions, and still address the concerns of the time. A number of generalizations hold true; among them are these two: First, visions change over time. Second, there are similarities found across stances. Examining those patterns of change and constancy may provide insights into your own thinking.

Curriculum researchers have traced U.S. views toward education over time, finding that visions of education are fluid and responsive to the historical, cultural, and social contexts of the people who create them while they simultaneously address the perennial struggles of education in a democracy (e.g., Kliebard, 2002; Tyack, 2003; Tyack & Cuban, 1995). Events such as the Industrial Revolution, the War on Poverty, and the race for space, for instance, each influence the trajectory of the nation's views of education as we consider the larger purpose of the schools.

Along with change over time, we can also find similarities across stances. Prakash and Waks's (1985) analysis summarizes four broad families of conceptions of educational excellence, as shown in Figure 2.1. As you study the figure,

> The role of the teacher remains the highest calling of a free people. To the teacher, America entrusts her most precious resource, her children; and asks that they be prepared . . . to face the rigors of individual participation in a democratic society.
>
> —*Shirley Hufstedler*

FIGURE 2.1   *Prakash and Waks's description of different conceptions of education.*

	What is the good?	**What is the purpose of education?**	**What is learning?**	**What is teaching?**
Technical	Efficiency Proficiency	To produce high achievement To adjust productive means to measurable ends	Memorizing Problem solving: applying facts to routines	Provides information for rote acquisition
Rational	Disciplined thinking Initiation Imagination	To transmit values by involving students in worthwhile activities Cognitive socialization of youth	Problem solving: higher-order creative and logical abilities Building complex schema	Presents ideas and concepts in a way that allows learners to see the structure of the subject Leads discussions and projects
Personal	Self-actualization (reaching individual potential)	To create opportunities so that individuals can develop along unique paths	Learning through own mistakes and experiences Introspection Being "centered" (in touch with self)	Independent, aware individuals Provides resources and space for exploration
Social	Individual development within the context of the common good Social responsibility	To provide skills for competence in civic life To teach the ability to identify and solve problems related to societal issues To foster the dispositions needed to take action	Interacting with a group Thinking beyond "I" to "we" Focusing on the disciplines only so far as they relate to relevant problems	Provides choices for group projects and actions Facilitates problem identification and solution Provides leadership

Courtesy of the Library of Congress

notice that each one of the stances (technical, rational, personal, and social) has distinct visions of what we should accomplish and how to go about accomplishing it. The technical conception of education tends to be prevalent in K–12 public education, whereas the rational model tends to prevail in universities. With its emphasis on the individual, the personal stance is less frequently found in public schools and more often occurs in private, or independent, schools and in less traditional educational endeavors such as **unschooling.** Which way of thinking is most prevalent in your area? Can you find exceptions to the technical conception?

What do these stances look like in individual teachers' stances? Figure 2.2 gives brief phrases from two teachers' (Rae Ann and Jaime) conceptions of education. Where would you place Rae Anne and Jaime in this family of stances? See if you can place Rae Anne's and Jaime's stances in one of the rows within Figure 2.1. They view their jobs as helping young people value each other and work well in groups. They see themselves as facilitators who will match their methods to students' needs and help students take an active stance in solving important problems. These positions are consistent with the social realm. Their stances are relatively conservative within the social school of thinking, however, because both Rae Anne and Jaime plan to teach core academic areas as a focus and to infuse problem solving within the schooling context. Some proponents of the social stance suggest that we use schools to reconstruct society into a system with more equitable patterns of interaction. Had they fallen within the technical stance, Rae Anne and Jaime would have placed greater emphasis on mastery of basic skills and far less emphasis on group dynamics.

Both Rae Anne and Jaime stress the importance of people working and living in groups and of the power of education to help them do so. They also both emphasize the need for teachers to draw on students' prior experiences to connect to new information. They differ, however, in the fine points of their conceptions. For instance, Jaime emphasizes dignity for the learner and a safe learning environment, whereas Rae Anne focuses more on teachers needing flexibility

FIGURE 2.2 *Excerpts from two teachers' philosophies.*

	Rae Anne	Jaime
Who is the good person living in the good society?	Considers actions before committing them Lives harmoniously and gains knowledge from his or her surroundings in order to improve the present quality of life	Recognizes cultural differences and takes pride in diversity People work, socialize, mingle with kindness and respect Actively participates in the life of the community Passionately engages in the pursuit of knowledge
What is the purpose of education?	To create equal opportunities To provide the power to obtain one's goals and dreams To broaden one's thinking To build self-esteem and character	To draw from the lives of participants To encourage social development To provide the opportunity to discover individual passions To prepare participants for active engagement in the community To encourage lifelong learning
What should everyone learn?	That which will create citizens who can contribute new ideas and understanding to society Problem solving	Positive attitudes toward challenging subject matter Real-world applications of the subject matter That which will allow citizens to participate
What is the nature of learning?	Building on previous information through interaction Asking questions Understanding, not memorizing Varies by person: doing, observing, reading	Comparing new experiences with information from previous endeavors Trial and error Watching Examining physical representations Interacting in groups Fostered by safe environment
What is (excellent) teaching?	Reaches greatest number of students possible Is flexible and willing to change methods to enrich students' learning Creates many alternate plans Searches for new information and improvement as teacher	Holds passion for education and children Models actions and behaviors desired by the society Commits to reaching every student and meeting the needs of all Plans to incorporate different ways and rates of learning Respects the dignity of the learner Taps into background knowledge

and openness to new teaching methodologies. Although the differences between these two teachers' philosophies are relatively minor, they reflect some major philosophical differences put forward and practiced in the past.

As you examine the work of Jaime and Rae Anne, you may think about the consequences of the stances they hold. Prakash and Waks (1985) argue that there is no neutral philosophy. What are the benefits of the stance you see as most prevalent? What are the drawbacks? Who wins? Who loses?

The usefulness of examining current conceptions of education lies in the fact that conceptions expose very different answers to oft-unexamined questions. We all seem to say that we want what is best for the next generation and for the nation. Examining conceptions of education helps us to realize that "best" is a matter requiring much deliberation. Bringing about the "best" requires even more. Our stances toward education are not disembodied ideals, but rather, important matters that play out daily, with great implications for the nation's children. *Please develop a stance and use it regularly to guide and examine the work you do.*

DEVELOPING YOUR STANCE

Do you recall the saying, "The last one to see the water is the fish?" Answering the seemingly simple questions of education may put you in the position of the fish, exploring the world that has been your home and thus has many aspects that may be invisible to you. Considering the questions of education means exposing some of your tacit notions about how the world is and should be. It also entails considering the fact that your perspectives have alternatives for each of the six questions.

To address these questions, think solely about your own ideas—no need to quote famous people or to write a term paper. Instead, write no more than a page to answer each of the questions, taken in order. You may stumble a bit in interpreting the questions. Interpret them any way you like, as long as they guide you in discovering what you think and capturing convictions that are central for you. Do not be tempted to include a little of every way of thinking; for instance, some ideas from the technical conception and some from the social conception. If you were to do so, elements would probably contradict each other and would not provide guidance when you need it.

After you compose a first draft, check your answers to see that you are consistent from question to question. Revise so that answers are coherent. Take out extra words. Read your answers aloud to yourself and then to a friend to be sure that your answers truly communicate your convictions. You will know when you have finished when not a word can be cut and when each reading convinces you more fully of the soundness of your stance. Teaching Tip 2.2 offers the long, if not somewhat macacbre, view in considering whether you have gotten your stance right. Here are suggestions related to the questions to get you started on composing your stance.

What Is the Good? Who Is the Good Person Living in the Good Society?

As you consider the questions of "*What is the good? Who is the good person living in the good society?*" consider your own upbringing. If you were raised as part of the **dominant culture** in the United States, or if you interacted with

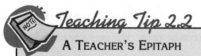

Teaching Tip 2.2

A TEACHER'S EPITAPH

An epitaph is the inscription on a person's tomb, plaque, or gravestone, commerating the life that passed. Epitaphs are typically brief and often wry. Poets often choose their own epitaphs, as do others. For example, Ludolph van Ceulen, the mathematician who dedicated his life to the task of calculating the value of pi to 35 places, had it inscribed on his headstone. Another mathematician, Paul Erdos, celebrated, "Finally I am becoming stupider no more." Looking forward, what mark would you hope to leave on the world through your profession? Compose your own epitaph, and then attempt to live up to it.

people who were part of that culture, you no doubt were exposed to American core values. Some U.S. ideals include (Banks, 2005; Pai, Adler, & Shadiow, 2006):

- Equality of opportunities
- Achievement orientation (we should all try to achieve higher goals through hard work; successful people work hard and unsuccessful people do not)
- Individualism and its emphasis on self-reliance and originality (individual success is prized above that of the family, community, and nation)
- Future time orientation (saving for tomorrow)
- Orientation toward materialism and exploitation of the natural environment

These values are not universal; other cultures, including nondominant U.S. groups, often hold alternative values. Here are two tips to get you thinking about your own values and convictions regarding the good person in the good society:

1. Look back at your work in Figure 1.1. It encouraged you to consider the system within which you teach. What expectations does your society hold for you? To what extent do those shape your view of what is possible in society?
2. List no more than 10 core values or characteristics you think a good person or society *must* possess. It is tempting to make a much longer list, but that will be less useful in guiding your actions. Try making your own list, then compare it to the thinking of others. My recent Web search for "universal values" resulted in no less than 50 proposed values. Eleven recurring values were:

• compassion	• equality	• freedom
• honesty	• respect	• service
• justice	• responsibility	• tolerance
• peace	• unity	

To what extent are *these* values *your* values? Are there some you would delete? Which must you add?

What Is the Purpose of Education?

In thinking about the *purpose of education,* consider carefully how it is that society brings its people to "the good." Look back at your list of values and convictions related to the good person and the good society. In some way, education is a vehicle to bring about those attributes. How is it that education serves as a vehicle to create "the good society"? One possible answer to this question is given in an excerpt of Martin Luther King, Jr.'s (1947) essay on the purpose of education, which he wrote as an undergraduate student:

> The function of education, therefore, is to teach one to think intensively and to think critically. . . . We must remember that intelligence is not enough. Intelligence plus character—that is the goal of true education.

Remember to think broadly about education. Remember that education and school are not the same things. Think about all of the different mechanisms that should educate and how those might work in concert (or not) to fulfill the purpose of education.

What Should Everyone Learn? Why?

Considering *what everyone should learn and why* gives you an opportunity to think about the subject matter that is important enough for each person in the society to learn. As you consider subject matter, remember that what is considered "basic" in one part of the world or at one time in history may be superfluous in another. In your response, remember to think not just about what might be considered traditional content but issues of character, skills, values, and abilities as well. Be able to explain why people should learn what you suggest, and not something else. Remember, too, that "everyone" means "*every person*"; this question addresses the common core of learnings to be mastered in the society. Here are five tips to get you thinking:

1. Look back at your list of values, characteristics, knowledge, and skills of the good person. Do you believe the good person is "born good"? Probably not entirely. Instead, he must attain (learn) at least some of those positive qualities. Look at your list of characteristics of the good person and good society and determine what knowledge, values, and skills people must learn in order to bring about the good. *That* is core subject matter.

2. Look beyond your own school experience; it is place-bound. What seems "basic" to you may not be basic at all in other settings. Learning multiple languages, dance, a musical instrument, or geometry might be considered basic in some places. Additionally, other countries tend to approach the "basics" in the classrooms differently than we do in the United States, with mathematics serving as an example (Schmidt, Wang, & McKnight, 2005). Whereas the U.S. curriculum tends to focus repeatedly over the years on topics that we see as basic (such as arithmetic), high-achieving countries tend to focus on their basics in set grade levels and then move on to other subjects.

3. Look beyond your own school experience; it is time-bound. You may believe that knowledge is unchanging and should remain constant over time. That is a defensible position, one held by many others. However, before you accept that position, consider the alternative. Perhaps as our world changes, so must the knowledge and skills we gain to find our place in it. More than two centuries ago, John Adams (1780)argued in a letter to his wife that, "I must study politics and war that my sons may have liberty to study mathematics and philosophy." And today's shifting demands (highlighted in Chapter 1) are driven by forces such as globalization and increasing technology. A world that is constantly changing may require a changing core of knowledge for its citizens.

4. Avoid suggesting that "all" subject matter is important. First, it is impossible to learn everything that is known. Second, "all" would include a body of knowledge that is for some reason odious (white supremacy doctrine?) or is now proven false (phrenology?).

5. Recall that we educate hugely diverse groups of students in the United States, and that which should be accomplished by all is a matter of ongoing and heated consideration. We wrestle with tensions such as holding high expectations for each of our learners while we simultaneously attend to vast individual differences. For instance, should your gifted students achieve the same curriculum as your students with developmental delays? As you consider such tensions, it may help to list the subjects or outcomes that are important to you and then consider whether they could in fact be grouped into categories such as things "everyone learns," "some people learn," and "a few people learn."

In sum, think broadly about subject matter; it includes life's lessons in addition to school subjects. School is but one of our educative institutions. And defining what should be core requires you to think about all learners.

What Is the Nature of Learning?

The *nature of learning* includes the nature of knowledge, the nature of the learner, and the processes by which we learn.

As you regard the nature of knowledge, ask yourself: Is it unchanging? Tentative? Is it objective, or is it constructed by people and thus inherently subjective? Is all knowledge of the same character? For instance, is religious knowledge of the same nature as scientific knowledge? The branch of philosophy that examines the nature of knowledge is deemed *epistemology.* Your epistemological convictions will influence your decisions about both what you teach and how you teach it. For example, the conviction that scientific knowledge is tentative and changes with evidence brings the obligation to teach students values such as a preference for evidence and skills such as the testing of hypotheses.

As you regard the nature of the learner, ask: Are people inherently bad? Inherently good? What are your convictions about people in general? Will they usually do the right thing, or must they have an external motivation to do so? Is intelligence singular or manifold? Again, your convictions related to human nature will permeate your classroom decisions related to factors such as how your manage your classroom and interact with your students.

As you consider the nature of learning, ask: What are the processes by which all humans learn? How is that we take in information from the environment, make sense of it, and use it as our own? Within the larger framework of how humans learn, what are the relevant differences in learning preferences? Which is more important in your view: the commonalties of human learning, or the differences? One suggestion: It will not be very useful for you to conclude that "everyone learns differently." If we can draw no common threads through human learning, your attempts to address students' needs will be random and most probably futile.

What Is (Excellent) Teaching?

You have begun to think about *excellent teaching* through your work in Chapter 1. That is, you have thought about how teaching is different from other endeavors, you have begun to examine the domains of professional expertise, and you have thought some about how excellent teachers might be different from each other. Perhaps these five sets of question will continue to fuel your thinking:

1. Is there a set of personal attributes required of excellent teachers? To what extent is an excellent teacher an example of "the good person"? What, if any, is the teacher's special obligation to serve as a role model of a good person?
2. To what extent is an excellent teacher an integral part of "the good society"? To what extent do teachers actively shape that society?
3. Is it enough for an excellent teacher to be a good person? To what extent do you agree that teachers know and can do things that represent a unique set of professional skills? What, then, are the professional knowledge, skills, and abilities that excellent teachers have?
4. How important is it that an excellent teacher is a good learner?
5. What are an excellent teacher's moral and ethical obligations?

What Does School Do?

As you consider this question, keep in mind that "school" is just one of the educative institutions in a society. Efforts such as **home schooling** and **unschooling** (Holt, 2004) indicate that schools are just one type of institution for education. Cortes (2000) explores "the social curriculum" through its branches, including the media, the family and neighborhood, and institutions such as religion and youth groups. What unique contribution does schooling provide, for better and for worse? Try these questions:

1. What *should* schools do? What should be our mission? Should we pursue student achievement in reading and mathematics as our sole aim?
2. What can be the school's role in bringing about the good society? Berliner (2006) argues that schools continue to be asked to solve huge public

problems while we as a society ignore root causes, such as poverty, that contribute to differential student achievement.

Because you are preparing for a career spent in schools, it is important that you consider—and continue to reconsider—what those schools *do* and *can do*.

In closing, when you reflect on your answers to the six questions as a set, you will have developed for yourself a stance, a conception of education, that can be a useful guide in selecting your priorities and making professional decisions.

USING YOUR STANCE

Your stance should be reflected in your year-long plans, in your lessons, and in your minute-by-minute interactions and decisions. Further, a conception of education offers *should* statements to direct you. Questions such as "What 'should' we teach?" and "How 'should' we group students?" are answered in terms of both philosophy and empirical evidence. Use what you know about findings from educational research to enrich your stance and guide your professional decisions.

Your stance can be a useful guide for short-term instructional decisions. I know a teacher who condenses her stance into a single sentence and then copies it onto an index card that she clips to her plan book. Before leaving school each evening, sometimes feeling harried and tired, she takes one last glance at that card. If she feels that she worked in some way toward the greater good listed in her stance, she goes home happy. My students find it useful, in fact, to condense their stances not into a single sentence but into a single word (see "Word Journal" in Guillaume, Yopp, & Yopp, 2007) and then to think about how that single word guides their actions minute by minute or day by day. This year, some samples include *passion, care, cooperation, strive,* and *responsibility*. Another teacher I know shares his stance with his students via a poster and in words and occasionally asks them to provide anonymous written feedback on the extent to which he is living his vision. Check Teaching Tip 2.3 for some other ideas on using your stance in these days of accountability.

Teaching Tip 2.3

USING YOUR STANCE IN THE DAYS OF ACCOUNTABILITY

Today more than ever your stance can serve as a helpful guide for remaining true to your professional ideals. Try some tips for using your stance in the days of educational accountability:

1. Regardless of the importance of test scores, helping our students learn and use social skills should remain a top priority as we educate competent and caring citizens of tomorrow (Garrett, 2006). Use your stance to help you focus on important social goals that must co-occur with academic goals. The National Association of School Psychologists (2002) places social skills into four helpful categories:
   - survival skills (e.g., ignoring distractions and following directions)
   - interpersonal skills (e.g., sharing, joining an activity)
   - problem solving skills (e.g., apologizing and accepting consequences)
   - conflict resolution skills (e.g., dealing with teasing and peer pressure)
2. Consider state content mandates as a baseline rather than as the sole targets for what you are to teach. Good schools go beyond requirements to reach for a vision that exceeds the scope of narrow measures of learning (Keller & Bichelmeyer, 2004).
3. Use your stance as the organizing principle for your professional portfolio.
4. Post your stance-at-a-glance in your classroom. Before you shut off the lights at the end of the day, ask yourself for at least one example of how you enacted that stance in concrete ways. Set one goal for tomorrow.

Use your stance to guide your long-term instructional decisions too. As you work with your colleagues in committees that address topics such as long-term planning or assessment, continue to raise gentle questions related to the big picture of what you as a team (and we as a profession) should be striving toward. As your colleagues speak, listen for their convictions about the purpose of education. Think about how they match your own, and look for common ground. Remind yourself that when you choose one course of action, you necessarily reject others. For instance, if you emphasize only basic facts, you preclude other kinds of learning opportunities. Conversely, if you include primarily small-group projects, students have fewer experiences in working on skills as individuals. Make sure your choices are in line with achieving excellence in the long view.

Finally, revise your stance. You are an adult with many years of life experience, so your stance may not change radically over time. On the other hand, it may. Thoughtful teachers engage in frequent reflection on their experience and seek to improve their thinking as their thinking changes.

TECHNOLOGY AND YOUR STANCE TOWARD EDUCATION

As an example of a current societal demand, the high-tech context within which we live and teach today may force us to mold our stances toward education with an eye toward technology. Technology shapes the explicit, implicit, and null curriculum. Via the explicit curriculum, technology influences our views of what should be—and what is—taught today. At a broad level, we have K–12 student content standards in technology (e.g., International Society for Technology Education, 1998). Arranged in grade-clustered standards, examples include the following:

- (pre-K–2) Gather information and communicate with others using telecommunications, with support from teachers, family members, or student partners.
- (3–5) Use technology tools (e.g., multimedia authoring, presentation, Web tools, digital cameras, scanners) for individual and collaborative writing, communication, and publishing activities to create knowledge products for audiences inside and outside the classroom.
- (6–8) Apply productivity/multimedia tools and peripherals to support personal productivity, group collaboration, and learning throughout the curriculum.
- (9–12) Investigate and apply expert systems, intelligent agents, and simulations in real-world situations.

In addition to broad goals, technology forces us to teach more specific, immediate newer subject matter such as "netiquette." Teaching Tip 2.4 lists some rules of netiquette, rules my grandmother no doubt never envisioned. Issues related to the implicit curriculum abound. For instance, Burniske (2000) argues that our students are barely socialized to weigh the moral and ethical obligations that technology use brings. Additionally, technology seems to teach subtle lessons such as our expectation that vast amounts of information will be available to us, that it will be available instantaneously, and that our access to technology will connect us with people in different time zones, hundreds and thousands of miles away. For many, this expectation holds true. It also subtly shapes the things we think about and the language we use (just listen to the acronym-laced, vowel-depleted "text-speech" of students—kindergarten through grade 12—you probably hear BTW, LOL, and G2G . . . *in the sam sntnc*). Technology also shapes the null curriculum by forcing certain knowledge and skills into cold storage. Are penmanship and spelling, for example,

THE RULES OF NETIQUETTE

Electronic communication requires a different set of manners than do face-to-face, phone, and paper communications. Try some of these rules in teaching your students to communicate respectfully via their e-mails and discussion board postings. (And be sure to follow them yourself as a professional.)

- *Be nice.* The immediacy and the lack of face-to-face contact of cyberspace seems to sometimes engender a lack of civility, especially when emotions are running high. Should you press "send"? If you would not say something to the intended recipient face-to-face, do not put it in e-mail.
- *Be polite.* Remember that our culture affords respect to people of higher status as a result of factors such as professional position and age. Use proper salutations (greetings) and closings in your e-mails.
- *Be patient, and be reasonable.* Remember that 24-hour access to your own account does not entitle you to immediate information from your recipient. Exercise reasonable expectations for responses. Similarly, refrain from treating recipients as online databases or help lines. Reserve your electronic requests for information to those items you cannot locate yourself via other channels and to questions whose answers will be brief.
- *Be quiet.* It is better to "lurk" in a discussion forum to gain a sense of the culture before leaping in with your own contributions. Also remain silent with other people's e-mail addresses; do not forward addresses to third parties without their permission. Remove or hide addresses in the "to" line of your e-mails.
- *Be careful.* Use standard grammar, punctuation, and capitalization (including upper- and lowercase letters). Spell check your e-mails.

slowly being frozen out of the curriculum as a result of our increasing access to technological tools? Will keyboarding also dissapear?

Technology also requires us to think twice about our answers to the major questions of education. Here are some sample issues that may arise as you *compose your own stance.*

1. *Who is the good person living in the good society?* Does the good person necessarily competently, regularly, and ethically access technological tools to meet the aims of the good society?
2. *What is the purpose of education?* Does education—via schooling and other institutions—have different responsibilities because of technology and changing definitions of a good person?
3. *What should everyone learn? Why?* Many individuals and groups interested in education are wrestling with the shifting demands necessitated by our changing world. Much of the subject matter formerly considered "core" now seems peripheral, and new subject matter seems vital. One group (Partnership for 21st Century Skills, 2004), for instance, posits that today's students need to master three core outcomes: global awareness; financial, economic, and business literacy; and civic literacy.
4. *What is the nature of learning?* Are today's K–12 students truly *digital natives*? Prensky (2001, 2005/2006) argues that prolonged and intense exposure to technology has fundamentally changed the way young students think and process information. For instance, many students today "parallel process" rather than processing information "serially" and expect multimedia instruction. Other authors (e.g., Owen, 2004) argue that students are no more changed by technology than the adults who teach them. What do you think?

5. *What is (excellent) teaching?* Technology brings us a plethora of tools that have potential to expand or, if not well implemented, detract from student learning and development. To what extent is an excellent teacher a role model of competent technology use and innovation? What are an excellent teachers' responsibilities related to continual learning, implementation, reflection, and revision of their teaching relevant to technological tools?

6. *What does school do?* Research cited in Chapter 1 (DeBell & Chapman, 2006) finds that schools can serve to provide access to otherwise scarce technological tools. To what extent is it the school's mission to do so?

PARTING WORDS

Today's demands upon teachers' attention are great. Time is short, lists of standards or outcomes to be mastered are long, and priorities sometimes conflict. Maintaining a clear sense of focus about what you consider central to your work as a teacher can help you decide at the close of a hectic day whether you have contributed to the world through your efforts as a teacher. Having a well-formulated educational stance can help you to shape your participation in the school policies, instructional practices, committees, and co-curricular duties that are part of your professional responsibilities.

With the completion of these first two chapters, you will have built a foundation for understanding the nature of teaching and your own vision of education. This foundation will come to life in each of the dimensions of your professional decision making: planning, instruction, assessment, management, and—as the following chapter shows—basing decisions on a solid understanding of your students.

WEB SITES

http://www.vusst.hr/ENCYCLOPAEDIA/main.htm
Encyclopedia of Philosophy of Education. This site includes an alphabetic listing of philosophers of education and relevant works. It also includes links to other Web sites that treat philosophy.

http://tip.psychology.org/
Explorations in Learning & Instruction: The Theory into Practice Database. This site can help you think about your stance on what it means to learn by exploring 50 theories of learning and instruction.

http://cuip.net/jds/
The John Dewey Society. The society's mission is to "keep alive John Dewey's commitment to the use of critical and reflective intelligence in the search for solutions to crucial problems in education and culture." There are links to the society's journals, including online access to articles.

http://philosophyofeducation.org/
Philosophy of Education Society. This site includes information on the Philosophy of Education Society, provides access to its publications, and includes links to other organizations and resources addressing philosophy of education topics.

http://www.bc.edu/libraries/research/guides/s-philoseduc/
Research Guide: Philosophy of Education. Boston College's guide gives databases, indexes, and catalogs for Philosophy of Education. As a start, scroll down to the Web sites. Very impressive!

http://www.teachingforchange.org
Teaching for Change: Building Social Justice Starting in the Classroom. Now in its third decade, this organization provides resources for teachers and others who wish to "transform schools into centers of justice." It contains resources and links for teaching about past and present issues such as the Bill of Rights project, the Montgomery bus boycotts, and the war in Iraq.

http://www.tolerance.org/
Tolerance.org. This Web site is a project of the Southern Poverty Law Center. If ideals such as tolerance, peace, or respect figure prominently in your stance, check this site's array of Web-based and free print materials to help you enact your principles.

Use the search words "My Philosophy of Education" to search and view thousands of philosophies of education students from around the nation . . . and beyond.

	Second-grade math lesson	Lower elementary reading group	Secondary mathematics lesson
Explicit curriculum			Hint: Include both math and social goals.
Implicit curriculum		Hint: How does the teacher want the students to behave?	Hint: How does the teacher want the students to behave?
Null curriculum	Hint: What content related to graphing would have been reasonable to teach during this lesson and yet was not?		

OPPORTUNITIES TO PRACTICE

 1. Examine video clips of lessons and analyze the explicit, implicit, and null curricula. Go to the Video Classroom on the Merrill Teacher Prep Web site and choose at least two of the three videos, noted next, to study the different curricula that schools teach. Complete the chart that follows to contrast curricula across lessons. Some hints are provided to get you started.

   • Second-grade mathematics: Go to the Foundations section and choose Module 6, Curriculum and Instruction. Watch Video 1. In it, you will see a teacher work with her second graders on graphing.

   • Lower elementary reading group: Go to the Educational Psychology section and choose Module 8, Behaviorism. Watch Video 2 (Reading Group). In it, you will see an elementary teacher lead a small reading group while other students work on English.

   • Secondary mathematics: Go to the Educational Psychology section and choose Module 8, Behaviorism. Watch Video 1 (Cooperative Learning). In it, you will see a secondary teacher using Student Teams Achievement Division (STAD, a cooperative learning strategy) to master estimation.

2. Four imaginary teachers (each with a different conception of education) are being interviewed. Label each teacher with the appropriate stance from Figure 2.1 technical, rational, personal, or social.

   a. In my classroom I try to include lots of . . .

   Abigail: "opportunities for kids to choose their own activities. They need to be able to follow their own interests."

   Ben: "resources for kids to learn about current, real-life issues. Then they need experience in addressing those issues."

   Cara: "opportunities for kids to memorize important facts. These facts will help them all their lives!"

   Diego: "chances for kids to think like experts in the field, like artists or scientists, for example."

   b. You will know children are solving problems in my class when . . .

   Abigail: "they have a clearer view of themselves and use that information to confront challenges. *That's* problem solving!"

   Ben: "they find something that is happening right now in the real world and I see them actually show the heart and courage to do something about it!"

   Cara: "children use their facts to solve more complex exercises. The lightbulbs just glow!"

   Diego: "children use their creativity and logic to solve classical problems or to create something new. You should see what they come up with!"

   c. Assessment of student learning . . .

   Abigail: "too often interferes with individual students' dignity and sense of self."

   Ben: "is done in groups, with the criteria developed by the students."

   Cara: "is valid only when it is an objective measurement of children's accuracy."

   Diego: "should include student portfolios, in which students display their own style and approach to the subject matter."

   d. As a teacher, I try hard to . . .

   Abigail: "place the learner at the center of all of my choices. If an activity does not meet my students' individual needs, we do not do it."

   Ben: "put my money where my mouth is. I show commitment to charitable causes."

Cara: "make it fun for children to learn the skills from the book."

Diego: "emphasize that the students and I embark on an exciting adventure together."

e. My metaphor for teacher is 'teacher as . . .

Abigail: 'a lens through which students can better know themselves.'"

Ben: 'a spark who can ignite the fire of action for the common good.'"

Cara: 'a factory leader who uses resources efficiently for the best product possible.'"

Diego: 'a sage who helps students learn to judge performance.' "

Were you drawn toward any one teacher's cluster of responses from the first exercise? These imaginary statements may provide specific examples to help you pin down your own stance toward education.

Key: Technical: Cara; Rational: Diego; Personal: Abigail; Social: Ben.

3. Stretch your thinking by imagining the implications of different stances on some common issues in classroom teaching. Try to imagine how these different conceptions would play out for the elements listed in Figure 2.3. Note that your own stance provides the final entries in the table. Check back to your row in Figure 2.3 as you read subsequent chapters . . . you may already know the punch lines!

4. Analyze school mission statements, beginning with your own school's statement. Go online and check your site's Web site or **School Accountability**
Report Card (SARC). Or, if you aren't assigned to a school yet, go to the Internet and locate some using the search term "school mission statements." Is it possible to place the statement in one of the families of educational thought from Chapter 2? Look for areas of agreement and disagreement with your own stance. Talk with experienced teachers about how mission statements are written and discuss issues such as group consensus, conceptual coherence, and enacting the mission statement.

5. The circumstances of classroom teaching sometimes present obstacles for enacting one's teaching stance. For instance, you may want students to be the ultimate judges of their work, but you are required to give standardized tests. Use Figure 2.4 to help structure your thinking and to consider how to address potential obstacles. Heads up: You will need this chart in Chapter 5.

6. Ask students with whom you work to help you find what is hidden: the implicit and null curriculum. Secondary students are often able to articulate their experience without much prompting, as suggested in Teaching Tip 2.1. For example, one secondary student told me recently that, through his school's **tracking** practices, he has learned that some kids are valued as smarter than others by the school: different classes for different kids, better teachers for more advanced students. Younger students may respond to more specific questions such as, "How do you know whether you have done a good job at school? What behaviors do teachers like? What have you not learned in school that you would like to learn?" Do you find patterns in students' responses? Is the news good?

FIGURE 2.3 *Daily implications of conceptions of education.*

	Common Learning Experiences	Prevalent Teaching Methods	Assessment Instruments	Homework Assignments	Expectations for Parents
Technical					
Rational					
Personal					
Social					
My own stance					

FIGURE 2.4 *Enacting my stance toward education.*

	My Convictions	Possible Obstacles	Strategies to Consider
A good society			
What education (and school) should do			
What everyone should learn			
How I should teach			

Before You Begin Reading

Chapter Three

Warm-Up Exercise for Starting with Students

Engage in a bit of personal introspection by writing an "I am from" poem. There is only one simple rule: Each line must begin with the words "I am from." As you compose your poem, think about all the factors that make you who you are. You may wish to think about features such as your unique qualities, your values, your ethnic heritage, your family experiences, your spiritual identity, significant events, and about your favorites in life. There are no rules about length, rhyme, meter, or sharing it with an audience.

I Am From

Read it aloud. Now reflect on your poem. What new insights (if any) did you gain? Excerpts from some recently composed poems are found at the end of this chapter. As you read them over, look for themes: Who are we? What matters to us? Themes such as immigration experiences, ethnic and national identity, conflict, the importance of family regardless of its structure, and a sense of growth seem to speak clearly. *Now imagine a world where schools knew where we were from and embraced us.*

CHAPTER *Three*

Starting with Students

"The secret in education lies in respecting the student."

—Ralph Waldo Emerson

This chapter is predicated on my belief that who your students are matters deeply to you. It is based on a teacher's moral commitment to honoring each of the people who cross the classroom's threshold every morning. And it is guided by the conviction that when we know and respect our students, we can teach them. To help you *start with the students*, this chapter is organized according to the following five sections:

Students as the Basis for your Decisions
Learning About Students
Mutual Accommodation for All Students
Providing Responsive Instruction for All Students
Using Technology to Support All Students

STUDENTS AS THE BASIS FOR YOUR DECISIONS

What do you say when people ask, "Why do you want to be a teacher?" What did you write in your chart as you prepared to read Chapter 1? Probably you like people and enjoy watching them learn. Perhaps you strive to contribute to society in a vital manner, through its youth. If you are like many educators, you believe that you can make a positive difference in the lives of students (Markow & Martin, 2005).

You enter the teaching profession at a time when achievement demands are high. The pressure that accompanies today's emphasis on student achievement is palpable, and you and your school will be held accountable for students' progress through some very distinct and public mechanisms. One of the most important aspects of your job will be the uniting of rigorous academic standards with your individual students' needs and interests. Students demonstrate a vast array of experiences, needs, and strengths, yet every one of them needs to learn and needs to meet high expectations. As a profession, we have an immense responsibility to provide the many avenues necessary to realize that goal. Only by knowing our students well can we hope to bring them toward uniform and rigorous expectations while simultaneously addressing them as valued individuals. Ensuring student success must therefore serve as the starting point for your all your decisions as a teacher, and ensuring student success must be the criterion by which you judge your own success.

Who Are Our Students?

Class sizes vary, but imagine that your class has 28 students. If those 28 students serve as a representative slice of our nation's student population, your class includes (NCES, 2006b):

- 25 students whose parents completed high school
- 19 students who live with both parents
- 9 who live in a different family structure
- 12 students who are racial or ethnic minorities (including 5 Hispanics, 4 African Americans, 1 Asian American, and 2 others)
- 10 students eligible for free or reduced lunch
- 5 students living in poverty
- 5 students who are English language learners (also deemed English learners, 3 of whom receive services for English language development)
- 4 students receiving special education services (with 2 having specific learning disabilities)
- 2 students classified as gifted

Although these statistics represent students across the nation, figures vary dramatically by region, state, and local area. For instance, all regions have increasing ethnic or racial diversity, but the numbers and patterns differ. In the West, "minority" student numbers exceed those of White students, with Hispanics predominating. In the South, African American student numbers exceed those of Hispanics. The Midwest has the lowest minority enrollment. Poverty rates and numbers of students living in large cities or rural areas vary widely too. Further, students who are minorities tend not to be spread evenly throughout classrooms or even schools; rather they are likely to attend urban or urban-fringe schools and tend to be segregated in certain schools and districts (Kozol, 2005; Ladson-Billings, 2006). Figure 3.1 gives some Internet sources for you to use to study student characteristics in your area. Be sure to examine characteristics for various schools within a single district and to compare surrounding districts in order to observe demographic patterns.

FIGURE 3.1 Sleuthing student statistics.

Use the Internet to examine statistics related to your students' characteristics and experiences. Try these sites:

- http://www.nces.ed.gov: National Center for Education Statistics. This site is rich with information, so try starting with "Condition of Education" or "Digest of Education Statistics" under "Annual Reports." Note that there is a Kid Zone for students as well.
- http://www.census.gov: U.S. Census Bureau. Start at "American FactFinder" and choose "people." You can view data nationwide and can narrow results by region, state, district, and community. See the Kid's Corner and the information for teachers too.
- http://www.mla.org: Modern Language Association. Includes a language map that can be explored in a variety of interesting ways. See what languages are prevalent across the country and in your area.
- State Department of Education: Type your state's name and "state department of education" into a search engine. Once at the Web site, check for data relating to students and schools. This information is often under "reports." School report cards are typically available for the entire state. Also try your state's Web site. Search for "State of ———". Statistics that are hard to find nationwide, such as those related to homelessness, are more available at the state level.
- County and District Offices of Education: Search for county and district offices of education for additional local information.

Students in the United States bring complex constellations of characteristics to the classroom.

Barbara Schwartz/Merrill

Clearly our students are a varied bunch, and your work with them will be made more complex and interesting by a few facts. First, within any federal category, students vary widely. Your English language learners might include, for instance, students from Native American communities of very long standing, students from other well-established linguistic communities in the United States (such as French-speaking communities in the Northeast and Spanish-speaking communities in the Southwest), and students whose families are more recent arrivals (LaCelle-Peterson & Rivera, 1994). Second, students display not just one type of characteristic, but overlapping characteristics and needs. That is, it will not be at all unusual for you to work with a student who meets the federal classification of "minority," is identified as gifted, and who exhibits a specific learning need. Third, students vary in terms of a myriad of factors such as their gender, their academic interests and development, their learning preferences, and their background experiences. For all these reasons, you can expect to be greeted with wonderfully complex constellations of learners.

What Difference Does Diversity Make?

Unfortunately, the potential of a richly diverse student population has not been fully realized in many U.S. schools. A convincing body of research indicates that despite many teachers' good intentions and caring natures, typical schooling practices tend to parallel larger patterns of societal injustice. Race, ethnicity, and poverty, for example, have direct effects on students' schooling experiences. Also, classroom structures reflect the interests of the dominant culture, sometimes making classrooms unfriendly places for students from cultures other than the dominant culture (Ladson-Billings, 2003; Nieto, 2004; Tyson, 2003).

If you are a child who is Black, Hispanic, or Native American, you will be *less* likely to use the Internet at school (NCES, 2006) and *more* likely to (NCES, 2006b, except where noted):

- attend a high-minority school.
- attend a high-poverty school.
- work with underqualified or inexperienced teachers.
- report feeling unsafe at your high school.
- have higher student-to-counselor ratios.
- be placed outside a general education setting if you have special needs.
- be placed in lower tracks and have fewer opportunities to learn high-status knowledge (Oakes, 2005).

Differences in educational experiences are related to other student characteristics as well. Understudied issues such as students' sexual orientation (Underwood, 2004) are increasingly recognized as affecting the schooling experience. Gender also continues to play a role in schooling. At the close of the twentieth century, for instance, research indicated that teachers (both male and female) tend to unknowingly favor boys and encourage their achievement while they encourage girls' compliant behavior (Wellesley College Center for Research on Women, 1992). A current gender concern is declining achievement levels for boys. Some studies now focus on the extent to which the schooling experience may place boys at a disadvantage (Younger & Warrington, 2006).

Researchers note that a combination of unequal schooling practices (Ladson-Billings, 2006) and larger societal disparities (Berliner, 2006) contribute to the pervasive achievement gaps we face today, and they note that vast changes at all levels will be necessary to pay off the "education debt," or significant educational inequities (Ladson-Billings, 2006), that have been accruing throughout our nation's history. You and I are not in charge of changing the whole world, of paying off the debt in its entirety, but we can almost certainly improve life and learning within our own local realm. Recognizing that students face a variety of conditions outside of their control that directly enhance or impede their success is an important step. As another, perhaps you will select your teaching position based on the student population you hope to serve. Maybe you will enact an educational stance that focuses on **social justice,** or the ideal that in a just society all individuals are treated fairly and share in the benefits of the society.

Certainly each of us can start by perceiving students in terms of the contributions they can make to our classrooms. You can view each student as an individual with personal experiences and qualities that will enrich the other students' learning and your own experience.

In fact, the very purpose of education, some argue, is to help us step outside our own worldview, appreciate the problems others face, see issues from multiple perspectives, and develop solutions that thoughtfully weigh many factors. In the classroom, students with special needs can help their peers learn compassion and creativity (Cozzul, Freeze, Lutfiyya, & Van Walleghem, 2004; Lieberman, James, & Ludwa, 2004; Whitehurst, & Howells, 2006). Students classified as gifted can bring a spark of intellectual curiosity to the room. English learners can bring to their English-only peers information about other places and customs, new perspectives on society and belief systems, and opportunities for exposure to other languages (Lachat, 2004).

Starting with students also includes getting to know students as people. In one nationwide survey, teachers and secondary students disagreed considerably on the extent to which they perceived that teachers know students and their communities well (Markow & Scheer, 2002). Although one-third to one-half of teachers strongly agreed with the following statements, *no more than one in four* students strongly agreed that teachers:

- know a lot about students' communities or neighborhoods.
- respect all students.
- are interested in what's best for all students.
- see students as individuals, not just members of some group. (pp. 59–60)

Fortunately, there are many ways to learn about your students and their families.

LEARNING ABOUT STUDENTS

Learning about students and their families involves us questioning our assumptions and gathering information that will direct us in our efforts to address student needs and foster success.

To hear a teacher recount an incident when a student taught her to question assumptions, go to Teacher Prep Web site, Foundations and Introduction to Teaching, Module 4, Video 4. Ouch! Can you recall a time when someone made unwarranted assumptions about you? How might such assumptions be damaging to our students?

Questioning Assumptions

Ronald, one of my middle school students, was struggling with medical and home-life issues, so I made a special point to make personal contact with him during class each day, to look him in the eye and converse with him about his life. At a conference a few months into the school year, his mother told me that Ronald *hated* my daily conversations. The shock and discomfort I still feel in recounting Ronald's episode reflects the extent of my surprise in discovering what a horrible job I had done in discovering my student's actual needs and preferences. My assumptions about what I thought would be right for my student were deeply rooted and unquestioned: I *assumed* that my effort to engage him personally would be a good and helpful thing. In Ronald's experience, my personal interest—or at least the way I conveyed it—was anything *but* helpful. Ronald taught me a difficult yet productive lesson about working with others: Question assumptions.

Part of our intelligence as humans stems from our ability to draw inferences from experience: We attach meaning to sensory data. Because we can draw inferences, we can learn and we can act, even when given only limited information. As a result, we sometimes have a tendency to think we understand each other fully when we hold just limited information, such as a person's ethnicity, political bent, or religious affiliation. To illustrate the limitations of this tendency, take a moment to peruse the poem you composed a bit ago and those found at this chapter's close to reaffirm that none of us is defined by a single experience or group membership. We each have commonalties that make us members of certain groups, but we also all have unique experiences that factor into who we are. Each of us is a dynamic product of the many painful and sweet experiences life has to offer.

Thus, when our inferences about others are based on limited information and assumptions about people's physical conditions, character, or home life, we run the risk of making faulty and counterproductive decisions. Instead, we need to realize that our assumptions may be incorrect and that we can sensitively collect information to enrich or replace our original faulty information. See Teaching Tip 3.1 for an exercise to help you avoid jumping to conclusions.

As an example, one prevalent faulty assumption is that parents—especially those of certain groups of students such as students of color—just do not care about their childrens' progress or teachers' efforts. Educators' work is so difficult that it is easy to see why some teachers may become discouraged by a perceived lack of parental involvement. However, the research on parent participation indicates solidly that parents in different ethnic groups *do care* about education and their students' success. One example is the work of Valencia and Block (2002), who review many studies documenting Mexican American families' participation in schools and the value they place on education. Similarly, in a recent nationwide survey, parents of all ethnic or racial groups were shown

Teaching Tip 3.1

THINK: WHAT ELSE?

Try this: When you are tempted to draw a conclusion, list for yourself several alternative explanations for what you see. Try asking students to do the same. It can help them learn to take other perspectives and draw conclusions based on evidence. *Here is one for practice:* One-third of your students had no family members attend Open House.

One conclusion: They don't value education. What else? They forgot. What else? They work nights. What else? They work days too. What else? They don't feel welcome at school. What else? Their student begged them not to go. What else?

to participate in general school meetings and parent conferences at the same levels (NCES, 2005a).

Sometimes life's rapid pace does indeed require us to make assumptions. When those occasions present themselves, it is important that we draw the most helpful conclusions possible. As my colleague Pat Keig unfailingly urges, we can *make the polite assumption.* It is far more productive to assume the best about people than to assume the worst. Making the polite assumption opens doors for further collaboration; making negative assumptions closes them. Gathering accurate information about our students also allow us to serve them well.

Gathering Information

*T*each thy tongue to say "I do not know," and thou shalt progress.

—*Maimonides*

How do we go about gathering information about our students? We first commit to admitting that our own knowledge is necessarily limited and to observing quietly and asking, in gentle and respectful ways, questions that will help us learn. "I thought I could learn about [the students'] culture by just having them in my classroom, but I now realize that when they're in the classroom, they're experiencing my culture, not theirs," remarked a teacher struggling to get to know her sixth graders (Frank, 1999, p. 20). In order to begin to understand your students, you will need to gather information about their lives both outside the classroom and within it.

Learning About Students' Lives. Getting to know our students requires us to step outside the classroom and learn about their lives (Grant & Sleeter, 1998). Kottler (1997) argues that teachers often expect to function as junior *psychologists.* Armed with theories of learning and development, we are prepared to look into the minds of students to teach what we think they should know. He suggests an additional role for us: Teaching as if we are anthropologists. As *anthropologists*, we would focus not so much on individual motivations as on people's cultural practices, on the knowledge base they share with others in their group that guides their thoughts, feelings, and actions. Kottler (p. 98) urges us as anthropologists to address a number of questions, all of which help yield data to help us challenge our assumptions:

- How are my cultural values and biases getting in the way of honoring those among my students who are different from what I am used to?
- What is it that I do not know or understand about this child's background that might help me make sense of what is happening?
- What is it about where this student comes from that leads him or her to respond to others they way he or she does?
- How might I investigate further the customs of this child's family?

Ethnographers, one branch of anthropologists, use naturalistic methods such as observations and unstructured interviews to address questions such as those just noted and thus gain insider information about our students' ways of living.

...ing Tip 3.2

...o KNOW STUDENTS USING THE LENSES OF AN ETHNOGRAPHER

...ggests a number of helpful methods for getting to know students
...of an ethnographer.

...t a neighborhood map and pinpoint every student's home. Walk (or
...m all to physically see where each student lives.

...: Go to a location where students congregate after school. As
...ly as possible, watch how they interact. If it is appropriate and they
... join in their activities with the goal of learning about their lives.

... Lead a conversation with a student or family member that follows the
...ortant to your interviewee. Ask a combination of "grand tour" (or big
... uestions and more specific questions about topics such as space,
...nts, people, activities, and objects.

...ng and note making: During observations and interviews, take two-
...notes. In the left column, record your observations. In the right, record
your ...erences, or the meanings you derive from your evidence.

5. Case study: Gather data about one particular student from a variety of sources
and in multiple settings. Analyze data from across sources to find patterns
related to the student's perspectives and preferences.

Teaching Tip 3.3

SAMPLE PROMPTS FOR STUDENT AND FAMILY QUESTIONNAIRES

Prompts for Students	**Prompts for Families**
	(Families, please answer those items with which you feel comfortable.)
• If I were in charge of the world. . .	
• What I appreciate about my family is. . .	• Some of the things that make my child special include. . .
• One thing I'm proud of is. . .	
• One unfair thing is. . .	• Past teachers who did well with my child were successful by. . .
• If I could help someone in need, I would. . .	
• I wish school. . .	• A struggle my child has experienced in the past is. . .
• It helps me learn when. . .	• This year, I hope my child learns. . .
• One thing I would like to learn at school is. . .	• The information or resources we could use at home are. . .
• In this class I hope we never. . .	
• I'd like you to know that. . .	• I'd like you to know that. . .

See Teaching Tip 3.2 for methods to get to know students using the lens of an ethnographer.

Some teachers gather information from family members by visiting students and families at home (Faltis, 2001) and at community happenings such as holiday celebrations or sporting events. For example, when my son Zachary was in first grade his teacher came to watch one of his soccer games. Recall that Teaching Tip 1.2, Getting to Know Families and Communities (p. 8), provides additional suggestions for becoming acquainted with students and families beyond the classroom door.

School-related information can be gained both from students and families early in the year or term. Students and family members alike can provide information about students' general interests via attitude inventories, surveys, and brief questionnaires. The questionnaires may ask for information such as each student's preferred learning experiences, possible ongoing school-related struggles, and strategies for working successfully with the student. Teaching Tip 3.3 gives sample prompts that might spur your thinking for developing your own questionnaires.

Teaching Tip 3.4

UNDERSTANDING A STUDENT THROUGH OBSERVATION

1. Select a student who does not immediately attract notice. This student may quietly pass the days without much demand for your attention.
2. Unobtrusively observe the student for a sustained period of time. Better yet, select varied times over the course of several days.
3. Take notes that describe the student's behavior:
   a. What does this student care about?
   b. Does this student show discomfort or fear? Of what?
   c. Does he have any skills or behaviors for avoiding notice?
   d. Does he initiate contact with peers? Which ones? How do they respond?
   e. How does he interact with the content? Is he on task? What evidence is there that he understands?
4. Analyze your observations:

   a. Would this student be learning more if he were more actively engaged?
   b. What forms of active engagement can you use that might show this student that you are teaching him as well as others?
   c. In what ways is this student exceptional?
   d. What could you do to get to know the student better?

ANDREA:	"If there was one thing you wish your teachers knew about you, what would it be?"
ALEX (14):	"That I have a life."

Think about whether you need to provide your questions in a different format, such as a translated handout or an oral interview, to make them accessible. Students can write letters too. I know a teacher who treats the first day of school as New Year's Day and asks students to write their goals, or resolutions, for the year. She uses students' hopes as she plans learning experiences throughout the year, and she and her students check their progress and set new goals periodically.

Many of the techniques just noted can be useful for getting to know students within the classroom context as well. You might map the classroom and observe students during breaks, for example. Also, Teaching Tip 3.4 gives a classroom observation procedure intended to surface facets of a single student's style and interactions. It may help you to gain information about a student whose particular strengths and struggles may otherwise go unnoticed. Keep your eyes open, too, for experienced teachers' methods of getting to know students. Some use lunch with the students, and many learn much about students by simply listening to their stories and perspectives (e.g., Thorson, 2003).

As the term or year progresses, we should continue to assess students' needs. Nieto (1996, p. 374) recommends, for instance, that we gather information about students' learning preferences by soliciting instructional feedback from students: "What do they like? What do they dislike? How would they change the classroom? The materials? What would they do to make it more interesting to them?" Students can provide this information anonymously in writing, or they may be open to responding to small-group or individual interviews. Other techniques for gathering information include some of the assessment strategies addressed in Chapter 7. Examples include:

- Attitude surveys ("Please rank these class activities in order of your preference.")

- Interviews ("Bring in an object that represents your favorite pastime and be ready to tell us about it.")
- Journal entries ("What is the best thing that happened in class this week?")
- Drawings and diagrams ("Draw a picture of your face as you study biology.")

In summary, students and their families can provide unique information about students' strengths, needs, and accomplishments over time and beyond the classroom. Engaging students and families in your efforts to get to know your learners not only provides you with distinctive perspectives on your students, it helps you build a partnership with families so that all parties are recognized as contributing members of the educational team.

Learning About Students' General Progress and Needs. Gathering information doesn't stop with student perspectives. You should also gather information about students' general academic progress. You might begin by checking on student records and past assessments. Look for information such as students' reading levels, English language levels, and special needs (Who has an **Individual Education Program** [IEP]? What special physical, emotional, social, and cognitive needs are present in your class?). If your students have IEPs or other mandated educational plans, you are legally bound (and of course ethically obligated) to take those plans into careful consideration.

The amount of information available regarding students' progress can be overwhelming. Many school districts use data management systems. Another way to manage numeric data so that it is useful in your planning is to create a spreadsheet that lists current assessment information for each student. An excerpt is shown in Figure 3.2. The benefit of a spreadsheet is that it can be easily re-sorted so that you can view students' scores in a variety of ways. For instance, you might sort by one variable (such as English language level) to form heterogeneous groups and another variable (such as reading level) to view the range of students' achievement. If you assess students' learning styles, as discussed in the next section, this information can also be entered on the spreadsheet. Imagine pasting re-sorted lists onto a clipboard to help you make student grouping and other planning decisions. Chapters 4 (Instructional Planning) and 7 (Assessment) give strategies for getting to know students' specific academic attainments.

Learning Styles and Preferences. Many teachers find gathering information on students' learning styles appealing. A learning style is the combination of factors that together indicate how a person perceives information, interacts with it, and responds to the learning environment. A familiar example is the scheme that divides learners' sensory modalities: visual, auditory, and kinesthetic.

FIGURE 3.2 *Excerpt of a spreadsheet listing student assessment information.*

	Reading Level	English Level	Plan
Brandon	4.9	EO	LD—Reading
Ceyda	7.0	4	
Christian	3.9	3	
Eli	6.4	4	
James	5.4	EO	
Jose	6.0	4	
Kaelani	6.2	EO	504—ADHD
	EO = English Only		

These divisions differentiate among students with preferences for learning by seeing, by hearing, and by doing. Sometimes the "learning by interacting with text" (or reading/writing) is included. Try one version of this scheme at http://www.vark-learn.com. The notion behind this and any scheme for learning styles is that each of us has different preferences, and if instruction matches those preferences, we learn better.

Assessments of learning styles are usually made in one of two ways: student self-report or teacher observation. Common self-report measures are questionnaires that give agree/disagree statements such as, "I like to see models and make things" and "I like helping other people" (Gregory & Kuzmich, 2004, p. 33). Students' scores are totaled for a number of clusters of statements, and a high total for a particular cluster is interpreted as suggesting a preferred learning style. If you work with students who can complete paper/pencil assessments, go online and search for "learning style questionnaire." Be cautious in your selection, however, because most inventories are meant to be informal and have not been carefully validated. It is important that you not rely heavily on results from informal assessments. Classroom observations and having multiple sources of information gathered over time can enhance the validity of the conclusions we draw. For instance, you can ask students questions about their preferences, and you can give them choices and observe their selections in action. You can allow students to work alone or with partners or in small groups and then tally students' choices as they work. You can also record how many and which students come to you to receive additional directions while others keep working.

However, be careful when attributing learning styles to students. Don't instruct in only one style. Some researchers are adamant that there is a connection between instruction that matches a student's learning style and academic success (e.g., Brand, Dunn, & Greb, 2002). However, the predominant perspective is far more guarded. Coffield, Moseley, Hall, and Ecclestone's (2004) exhaustive review of learning style research finds that the link between learning-style-based instruction and student achievement is tenuous at best and that the theoretical base and empirical support for most inventories is problematic.

Even proponents of learning styles claim that styles are not static; rather, a student's preferred learning style changes over time and with demands in the environment. Those authors who do locate trends of learning styles within student populations note that there is great variation among people designated as having any particular style and a good deal of overlap among people classified as having different styles (e.g., Brand et al., 2002). Thus, if we rely too much on learning styles we run the risk of viewing students as single, stationary groups.

Even given the limitations found in the research, learning styles can be helpful to teachers. Bennett (1995) presents three convincing arguments for considering learning styles. First, learning styles allow us to pinpoint student differences when students struggle to learn. This information can be particularly helpful to secondary school teachers who have less time to get to know their many students. Second, by placing emphasis on *how* students learn, we assume that students *can* learn. Third, learning styles encourage educational equity by reminding teachers that we may not reach our learners if we teach only in the ways we ourselves learn and that *differences* are not the same as *deficits*. Learning styles can help us to remember to question assumptions about how people learn, provide rich and varied input, and provide students with meaningful choices. Teaching Tip 3.5 provides eight tips for using learning styles thoughtfully in the classroom. Most of these tips focus on using learning styles to help students become more powerful learners by building awareness of their own profiles, gaining learning strategies, and using strategies flexibly to meet the learning demands they face.

Teaching Tip 3.5

TIPS FOR USING LEARNING STYLES THOUGHTFULLY IN THE CLASSROOM

1. Create a "lexicon of learning" by teaching terms related to learning styles in order to open discussion about learning (Coffield et al., 2004).
2. Teach students to be aware of their own preferences, strengths, and struggles. Questions such as "What's easy for you?" "What's hard?" can help.
3. Students in control of their learning are powerful learners. Teach students to assess their goals, motivations, and learning strategies (Harrison, Andrews, & Saklofske, 2003). Also teach them to judge the environment and the demands of the task at hand.
4. Teach students learning strategies.
5. Flexible learners are powerful learners. Teach flexibility by providing both instructional "matches" and "mismatches" for students' learning preferences. Working within one's style is comfortable and easy, but working in a mismatch encourages stretching and building new life skills.
6. Gather ongoing assessment information and adjust instruction to students' progress. For eight excellent educators, teaching to learning styles meant teaching with a constant eye toward assessing learners' success in the moment and adjusting instruction based on that success (Haar, Hall, Schoepp, & Smith, 2002).
7. Use students' preferences as a starting point to re-envision practice. Studies of students with attention deficit hyperactivity disorder found a distinct preference for afternoon (rather than morning) learning (Brand et al., 2002). How might that information affect scheduling decisions?
8. Be careful not to make it simple! People are complicated. Rather than using learning styles as one more way to label students, and thus limit possibilities, use learning styles as another set of variables that add to human complexity.

MUTUAL ACCOMMODATION FOR ALL STUDENTS

> Whether we speak of traditional democratic ideals of equality, equity, and opportunity or of the emergent democratic ideals of empowerment and emancipation as the conscious and purposeful outcomes of schooling, we must face the critical reality of our own cultural experience and bias. . . . Our personal blindness to the traditions of cultures other than our own binds us to convention, to the belief that there is one standard of conduct for all.
>
> —Hoover and Kindsvatter (1997, p. 67)

Students do not just vary in their approaches to learning. Remember your 28 hypothetical students from the beginning of the chapter? Five are acquiring English, 2 are gifted, 12 are classified as racial or ethnic minorities, 5 live in poverty, another 5 are eligible for free or reduced lunch, 2 have learning disabilities, and 2 more have IEPs for other reasons. As a result, as they sit in your class, some are hungry. Some wish you would speed up. Others wish you would slow down. Others leave for resource. Some translate for their families during the evening. Others teach you new words in Russian or Hmong. Some are years behind grade level. Others walk in knowing fully half of what you expected to teach them this year. What a crowd!

In the face of their differences, your students have some similar responsibilities at school. Each must come to meet the expectations of informed citizenship. They must master a core of knowledge considered essential. They must learn about your society's rules and history, learn to work effectively as members of a group, and come to participate responsibly in society (Goodlad, 1997). Their families, too, have responsibilities for fostering learning and contributing to the schooling experience. But students and their families are not the only ones with responsibilities. Teachers and schools also have a responsibility to grow and change to meet students' needs. What are your responsibilities to your varied group?

Starting with the students means that you must adjust for your learners and provide, in Nieto's (1996) words, **mutual accommodation.** When you watch a student struggle, you must ask yourself, "What can I do better to help the student learn?" You must continue to improve your knowledge of students and forge tighter connections with their community, gain professional knowledge and skills, and provide meaningful curriculum and responsive instruction. Figure 3.3 provides a summary of resources that you may consult as you seek to learn more about your students and their needs.

One of the places to begin is to learn about your students' special needs and legal rights. Federal and state legislation provides a number of protections

FIGURE 3.3 *Professional resources for responding to students' needs.*

Personnel resources	<ul><li>Experienced teachers on staff</li><li>Administrators</li><li>Specialists, including bilingual educators or coordinators, counselors, school psychologists, and special education teachers</li><li>Parents and other family members</li><li>Community members who wish to contribute to education by volunteering time or services</li><li>Educational researchers with expertise in your area of concern</li></ul>
Service resources	<ul><li>Computer laboratory facilities</li><li>Speech and language services</li><li>Psychological support through counselors or other services</li><li>Special education services for those who qualify</li><li>Medical, dental, vision, and hearing services available through outside agencies</li><li>Clothing and food services through charitable organizations</li><li>Occupational services</li></ul>
Professional resources	<ul><li>Electronic resources</li><li>Professional journals, often found in the school's professional library</li><li>University libraries</li><li>Professional organizations (for both teachers and groups with particular needs)</li><li>University courses or other workshops to provide specialized training</li><li>Professionals in related fields</li></ul>

for your students. What follows is a brief introduction to some categories of need prevalent in today's classrooms: special education, giftedness, and English language acquisition. You will also benefit from researching how federal, state, and local legislation regarding students' needs requires you to accommodate students' needs. Please see Figure 1.2 for a summary of some legal protections for students.

Special Education

A number of federal laws govern the services students with disabilities receive. The **Individuals with Disabilities Education Improvement Act** (IDEA) is perhaps the most important. Established in 1975 as Public Law 94–142, this legislation sought to ensure that all children receive appropriate educational services—regardless of their disabilities. (You can read the law online at http://www.ed.gov by typing "IDEA" into the search line.) Under IDEA, students with identified special needs have the right to a **free and appropriate education** in the **least restrictive environment.** As a result, students with disabilities have the right to an education that is tailored to their specific needs, and these students are to be educated, to the maximum extent possible, with their peers without disabilities. Indeed, half of all students with disabilities spend 80% of their day in a **general education** setting (NCES, 2005b). Only when the general education classroom does not provide an appropriate setting are other more restrictive settings, such as a special day class or special school, considered. Thus, the emphasis today is on **inclusion,** or the education of students with disabilities in the general education classroom. Our commitment to inclusiveness should be reflected in the language we use to refer to our students. Teacher Tip 3.6 gives advice for putting the person first.

IDEA also mandates the development and implementation of **individual education programs (IEPs)** for all students with special needs. IEPs are plans. These plans must specify annual goals, and staff and family members must

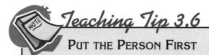

PUT THE PERSON FIRST

When speaking and thinking about students, put the person first. For example, "I am thinking of my student with ADHD," not "She's my ADHD student." Putting the exceptionality second staves off the tendency to define a person entirely in terms of a single exceptionality. (ADHD stands for attention deficit hyperactivity disorder.) Person-first terminology was established by the Individuals with Disabilities Education Act (1990).

meet regularly to discuss the student's progress. (An exercise at the end of this chapter provides an opportunity to explore IEPs in greater depth, including directing you toward sample IEPS on the Web.) In addition to IDEA, two other federal laws notably address the education of students with disabilities:

- Section 504 of the Veterans' Rehabilitation Act of 1973: This law prohibits exclusion (based solely on handicaps) of people with disabilities from participating in federally funded programs and activities. Section 504 covers any condition that interferes with learning. Conditions such as attention deficit hyperactivity disorder, asthma, depression, or diabetes might generate 504 plans, which mandate instructional modifications. These 504 plans, or accommodation plans, are similar to IEPS but are often shorter.
- Hughes Bill: This bill addresses students with behavioral problems. Before students can be referred for special education services for behavior disorders, students must receive an assessment in their natural environment and, based on the results of the assessment, a **behavior intervention plan** (BIP) that details positive behavioral supports that must be developed and implemented.

To serve your students with special needs, you will act as an important part of a team of family members, advocates they may enlist, and professionals who work to meet students' educational needs. A resource specialist, educational psychologist, speech therapist, occupational therapist, and administrator may be among those on the team. You will need to check students' records carefully to ensure that you are implementing their plans, and you will need to monitor your instruction and students' responses to ensure that you are helping them move forward.

At times you will work with students who struggle but have not been identified as having special needs. They might have persistent trouble learning, communicating, or interacting with you or the other students. If you suspect that a student has special needs that have not yet been identified, make careful observations, document those observations, collect student work samples, speak with specialists at your site, keep close contact with the family, and find out about the special education referral process at your school. Throughout this process, continue to adjust your instruction to the student's benefit.

In 2004, approximately 6.6 million students in U.S. schools received special education services (14% of all students; NCES, 2005b). Most students receiving special education services have specific learning disabilities (43% of those with special needs). Students with specific learning disabilities have adequate cognitive functioning, learn some skills well, and struggle in one or more others. The majority of students with learning disabilities face severe reading problems or problems with spoken or written language.

With the 2004 reauthorization of IDEA came a change in how learning disabilities are identified. Previously, students were identified after assessment results showed a discrepancy between a measure of their intelligence and a test of their academic performance. As a result, most learning disabilities were identified in grade 3 or later, after students had already experienced academic failure. Now, schools can use a different criterion: **response to intervention.** To be identified as having a learning disability, students must show nonresponsiveness to systematic effective instruction altered to help address their strengths and weaknesses as learners. This change in how learning difficulties are treated shifts the focus from determining eligibility for special education services to one of providing intense instruction to struggling students and making early identification as necessary so that all students can be well served before they start to fail and so that students are not misidentified as qualifying for special education merely as a result of poor instruction (Fuchs & Fuchs, 2005).

Giftedness

A student might qualify for special education services in reading, but have great mathematical talent. Gardner (2006) reminds us that there are many ways to be smart. Indeed, each of our students has gifts. However, a small segment of the population is designated as "gifted" and receives services based on that classification. In the year 2000, 2.9 million students in U.S. elementary and secondary schools were classified as gifted (6.3%; NCES 2005c). Slightly more girls were identified as gifted than boys. Definitions of giftedness vary, and states have different criteria and policies for determining eligibility. Traditionally, a single measure of intelligence was used to identify students as gifted, although there is a movement toward a more multidimensional measurement of giftedness and talent. In general, gifted or talented students show performance high above that of their age mates in intellectual, creative, artistic, or other endeavors. Gifted students are diverse, but many are problem solvers who benefit from addressing open-ended and complex problems, often related to their own interests. Many are considered to be emotionally and academically intense (Manning, 2006). Teachers who think life would be easy if their room were full of gifted students are mistaken and probably have not considered students' varied needs. In addition to their incredible gifts, advanced learners may also face a number of issues that affect classroom performance. According to Manning, classroom issues that may stem from giftedness include problematic work habits and a heightened sensitivity to others. In one study, highly gifted boys and boys with learning disabilities were alike in their classroom behavior (Shaywitz et al., 2001). Once again we are reminded that no one classification explains a person fully and that all students have needs that can stretch their teachers' skills.

Decisions about how best to serve gifted students are often heated. Examine some of the issues by reviewing the National Association for Gifted Children's (http://www.nagc.org) standards for exemplary gifted programs. Check with your school site to determine the arrangements within which students classified as gifted are served. Some districts have magnet schools for gifted students. Additionally, many schools have self-contained gifted classes. Others have **Gifted and Talented Education** (GATE) clusters within larger classes. Gifted students also frequently attend general education classes and visit resource programs or receive all of their education within their regular classroom.

Check for the referral process for identifying gifted students at your location. Although the identification process should include more than one screening device (Smutny, 2003), it often begins with a parent request or observations by the classroom teacher. When you suspect that a student may be gifted, observe the student carefully and ask questions such as, Does the student learn rapidly and possess a large store of information? Does the student exhibit originality in written or oral expression? Does the student use materials in extremely creative ways? Does the student contribute to class discussions with unique and insightful perspectives? As you observe students, be sure that you are watching all for signs of giftedness, including those exhibited by students who might be less visible than others, such as students with disabilities, students who are ethnic or racial minorities, and students who are acquiring English.

English Language Acquisition

Linguistic diversity has always been a part of our U.S. heritage, and the percentage of people who speak languages other than English is growing. Did you know that 322 languages are spoken in the United States? In terms of numbers of speakers, Spanish takes second place to English, and Chinese third (Modern Language Association, 2006). In 2004, approximately 19% of U.S. children spoke a language other than English at home (NCES, 2005d), and 11% of the student population received language services (NCES, 2006b). Although all states have English learners, the number of languages spoken and the numbers of speakers depend on location. For example, in the Los Angeles Unified School District, nearly half of all students are English learners. In the Dallas and Houston Independent School Districts, approximately a third are. In Denver County, a quarter are. In Chicago and New York, about 15% are.

Your English learners have a difficult job: They must acquire a new language (English) while they simultaneously master challenging academic content standards. It is also important that students work to maintain their primary language for a number of reasons. Among them, multilingual skills are recognized as important resources (Bilingual Education Act of 1994), and fluency in the home language boosts fluency and academic achievement in English (Krashen, 1997; Thomas & Collier, 2001). Statistics presented in Chapter 1 and earlier in this chapter indicate just how difficult the work of English learners can be, as reflected in the achievement and opportunity gaps they often face.

The civil rights case *Lau v. Nichols* (1974) expanded the rights of English learners in the United States by finding that linguistically appropriate modifications must be made so that English learners are not denied equal education opportunities. English learners are now educated in a variety of settings, such as **bilingual education programs,** pull-out programs, and mainstream English settings. Educational efforts typically focus on two goals: English language acquisition and content mastery. All content teachers need to employ a specific set of skills to ensure that English learners master grade-level content as they acquire English. Additionally, English learners often receive instruction that focuses directly on English acquisition (or English language development) regularly as well. This instruction is often provided by the regular classroom teacher although other specialists frequently assist.

Just as all of your students have a number of responsibilities to learn and to become contributing members of society, you have an awesome set of responsibilities to help them. These responsibilities require you to continue to grow and learn—to accommodate students—to ensure their success. Each time you face student experiences and needs that are outside the realm of your experience, you have the responsibility to build your knowledge and skills. Figure 3.4 suggests a variety of strategies you can employ as a professional educator to accommodate your learners' needs. Your efforts will be reflected in the responsive instruction you provide.

PROVIDING RESPONSIVE INSTRUCTION FOR ALL STUDENTS

You clearly have your work cut out for you. Meeting students' varied needs within the confines of a classroom setting is challenging, especially given the multiple demands placed on you and the pressure of a tight time schedule. Fortunately, there are a number of general approaches that will allow you to

FIGURE 3.4 *Strategies for mutual accommodation.*

Assess the students' needs and interests	1. Gather information from the students: • Interviews • Observations • Informal conversations • Interest and attitude surveys • Journal entries 2. Gather information from the family. Treat parents as experts on their children: • Beginning-of-the-year survey or conversations on students' prior experiences, hopes, and goals • Informal conferences and telephone (and other) conversations throughout the year 3. Check information gathered by the school: • Previous formal testing results • Previous successes
Provide a meaningful curriculum that incorporates aspects of the lives of the children	1. Use materials and topics of interest to the students. 2. Use problem-centered approaches. 3. Provide opportunities for student choice in what and how they study.
Make classroom adjustments for student differences	1. Watch and listen carefully to determine necessary physical and temporal modifications. 2. Trust students when they tell you about their needs. 3. Alter the physical setting to encourage success. Many physical modifications require a bit of resourceful thinking but are not expensive or difficult. 4. Include a variety of work spaces and allow for student choice.
Build your own knowledge and skills	1. Gain information about your students' life experiences. Some strategies include the following: • Read about their cultures. • Tour their community if you are not a member of it. • Listen to music that is popular with them. • Study the toy store, favorite shopping spot, or hang out. • Watch their cartoons and favorite television programs, and visit the Web sites they talk about. 2. Read the professional literature. 3. Ask expert teachers for strategies. 4. Seek out additional training opportunities.
Build connections to the home and the community	1. Invite parents and other family members to school and provide a range of activities for participation. Expect that some parents will bring younger siblings. Suggestions for participation include the following: • Guest lessons • Read alouds • One-on-one instruction • Materials preparation and clerical assistance • Room environment assistance (e.g., with pets or special centers) 2. Include other means for families to participate in school as well, such as picnics, garden projects, and field trips. 3. Send home a classroom newsletter or e-mail, in more than one language if appropriate. Include students' work and a brag section that over time mentions good news about every student. Or build a class Web site. 4. Contact each family (by phone, note, e-mail, or in person) with good news at least once during each grading period.

provide instruction that is responsive to your students and their needs. Seven are presented here:

Treat Students as Individuals
Plan for all Students with Universal Design
Differentiate Instruction
Accommodate and Modify
Shelter English Instruction
Challenge Advanced Learners
Assure Gender Equity

Treat Students as Individuals

The foundation for providing responsive instruction lies in treating students as individuals. Though this may seem obvious, many teachers proudly proclaim that their goal is to *treat everyone the same.* Such a desire is found in the colorblind perspective (Schofield, 2005), whereby educators desire to treat individuals as if their group affiliations (such as race) and prior experiences have no instructional implication. One danger in treating the students the same, according to Grant (1995), lies in the fact that it does not enhance students' learning about themselves as members of many groups. Look back at the poems at this chapter's close. The poets show their memberships in ethnic, pop-cultural, national, spiritual, and family groups. Grant (p. 10) urges: "The individual diversity and humanness that each and every student brings to school must be accepted and affirmed. Those who tend to see (or want to see) every group, and every member of that group, as the same, miss or deny the beauty of human diversity and variety."

Although all students deserve high expectations and deserve to be treated fairly and with respect, different students need different things. Teachers' emphasis on sameness often translates to their classroom practice. Research indicates that, in many general education classrooms, students are indeed treated *the same.* Students pursue the *same* objectives using the *same* activities at the *same* pace and demonstrate their knowledge using the *same* assessment. According to Cole (1995, p. 12), "Instead of being presented in a variety of modes, instruction in U.S. schools tends to be abstract, barren of application, overly sequential, and redundant."

Treating each student the same can be inherently unfair. You can meet individual needs best if you have many instructional strategies in your repertoire, build an enriched learning environment, provide for student choice, and use ongoing assessments of each student's progress. To meet the needs of your students, you need to accomplish both big things that take much time (for instance, developing a range of assignments and activities for a single outcome, learning new instructional strategies, setting long-range goals, or changing your interactional style for particular students) and smaller things that can be implemented quickly (for instance, shortening homework assignments for those who take more time or moving a student toward a helpful peer). Universal Design is one approach that can help you provide instruction that is responsive to your students as individuals.

Plan for all Students with Universal Design

Universal Design seeks to provide instruction that is built from the start—rather than modified later—to address varying needs, interests, and preferences. It arose from an interest in accessibility in architecture (see Pisha & Coyne, 2001). Rather than designing a house that must later be modified to meet the needs of occupants (perhaps by cutting curbs, widening doorways, adding grab bars, or adjusting counter heights), Universal Design suggests that the house be designed *from the ground up* to address the needs of a variety of people who might live there. Ramps, for instance, would not only help people using wheelchairs, but would also help those pushing strollers, using walkers, or carrying heavy or bulky items. So it is with Universal Design for learning: Instruction should be planned *from the ground up* to meet a variety of learning needs such as English acquisition, giftedness, emotional or behavioral difficulties, differences in motivation, and learning or physical disabilities. New technologies often play a central role in Universal Design. As you plan your units and lessons, Universal Design (Center for Applied Special Technology, 2006) recommends that you accomplish three tasks by providing *multiple means of . . .*

- *Engagement*—In order to tap into learners' interests, offer appropriate challenges and increase motivation by providing a variety of grouping strategies (individual, small group, partner) or a variety of levels of difficulty in a task.
- *Representation*—In order to help students acquire information and knowledge in a variety of ways, allow for different forms of representation—for example, by providing students with printed text, digital text, and audio recordings of a work.
- *Expression*—In order to allow students to demonstrate what they know, allow for multiple types of assessment, such as writing a report, performing a play, or creating a PowerPoint presentation.

The Universal Design Web sites listed at the chapter's close include model lessons that use the principles of Universal Design. The principles of Universal Design provide an important criterion by which you judge the quality of your instruction: How well do your lessons encourage each of your students to engage in instruction, acquire information, and represent what they know? A related approach that can assist you in providing responsive instruction is differentiated instruction.

Differentiate Instruction

Differentiated instruction helps you to account for the nearly inevitable fact that your students represent different levels of readiness, interests, and learning profiles. Differentiation begins when teachers gather information about their students' readiness (current progress), interests, and learning profiles (all explored earlier in the chapter). Next, according to Tomlinson (2001), teachers use that information to differentiate their plans in response to information about students in three ways:

- Content—*what* students learn or how we give them *access* to it.
- Process—the *activities* students pursue to *make sense of*, or process, the content.
- Product—the longer-term endeavors students create to *display* their learning.

In a differentiated classroom, the class might start out by asking questions about the topic under study, pursue different kinds of learning activities to address those questions (for instance, some may conduct interviews with experts while others read and others conduct Internet research), then come back together to share results before splitting again to refine their studies and prepare for presentations on their learning. Individual, small-group, and whole-class instruction are utilized.

Figure 3.5 draws from Tomlinson's ideas to provide a grid with questions that can guide your planning as you think about differentiating instruction. Differentiated instruction requires a sophisticated set of skills that will take some time to master. Three summary questions can set you on your way: (1) Can

FIGURE 3.5 *Sample questions to guide planning for differentiated instruction.*

	Readiness	Profile	Interest
Content	• Same or different learning objectives? • Primary language or English?	• Together or alone? • Which intelligences?	• How can choice be built into the learning goals? • What student choices in materials?
Process	• Which instructional strategies? (Read Chapter 6). • Which small-group activities? Individual assignments?	• Auditory or visual? • More structured or more open? • Together or alone?	• How to build new skills based on students' favored skills? • What choices in activities?
Product	• How to apply or extend basic ideas? • Same criteria or different? • How to support strugglers and push advanced learners?	• Variety of formats? • Which skills to teach to support product development?	• What choices in products? • What real-world interests can provide a context for product development?

and should all students learn the same content? If not, what content will you plan for each, in keeping with high expectations for all students? (2) What are the different ways students can interact with the content? And (3) What is the range of products students can use to demonstrate mastery of the content?

Accommodate and Modify

Even when you employ principles of Universal Design and differentiated instruction, there will be times when some students require additional instructional adaptations to ensure success. In those cases, **accommodations** and **modifications** allow you to proactively address individual student needs.

Accommodations make room for the abilities and needs of your students without substantially altering what they are expected to learn. Accommodations change the way students are presented with information or display their learning. For instance, your left-handers cannot see a handwriting model on the left side of the page because their hands block it as they write. To accommodate this need, you could tape two pages together so that a second model appears on the right.

Depending on student needs, you might make accommodations to the physical environment, ways you present information, materials students use, or conditions under which students display their knowledge. Examples include modified furniture, a preview of the lesson (in English or in the student's native language), textbooks with large print, a weekly homework log signed by a family member, and an oral (rather than written) test. *Accommodations,* then, change conditions without much altering expected outcomes.

On the other hand, *modifications* substantially alter what students are expected to learn. Modifications may require that students use materials at a different instructional level or that they be evaluated according to different performance criteria. For individual students, cutting a spelling list in half, allowing the use of a calculator on an assessment, and providing a word bank for use during a test are examples of modifications. Modifications are typically made for students with significant disabilities, such as severe developmental delay or traumatic brain injury.

Required accommodations and modifications are listed on students' IEPs and other educational plans. By now, though, you will have no doubt concluded that teachers have a professional responsibility to account for all learners' instructional needs, regardless of legally mandated plans. Driven by the goal of powerful learning for all, you will no doubt look for opportunities to make room for student needs whether or not students have formal plans on file.

Shelter English Instruction

Just as students' physical and cognitive needs require you to adjust your instruction, so do their linguistic needs. Responsive instruction also entails modifying lessons by lightening the cognitive, cultural, linguistic, and learning loads that can present barriers to content mastery for English learners (Meyer, 2000). The use of Universal Design and differentiated instruction addresses this goal. So does sheltered instruction. **Sheltered instruction** attempts to provide "a refuge from the linguistic demands of mainstream instruction" (Echevarria & Graves, 1998, p. 54) and is called by various names in different regions, including *content ESL* (English as a Second Language), *ESL content*, and *Specially Designed Academic Instruction in English* (SDAIE). It addresses grade-level curriculum standards but makes content accessible by embedding instruction into meaningful contexts and a supportive learning environment. Experts generally agree on methods of sheltered instruction (Center for Research on Education, Diversity & Excellence, 2002; Cummins, 1981; Echevarria, Vogt, & Short, 2004; Fillmore, 1982; Hill & Flynn, 2006; Krashen, 1981; Meyer, 2000; Swain, 1985; Thomas & Collier, 2001). They are:

1. *Supportive Environment.* In a supportive environment, the teacher respects preferences for communication styles that may differ from her own. Examples include discourse patterns and rules on interrupting, eye contact, and turn taking. In this environment, the teacher minimizes direct correction and shapes accurate English through modeling. It provides a context where people feel comfortable experimenting with language and asking questions about it. The teacher provides frequent positive reinforcement for students' legitimate successes.
2. *Focused Content.* Teachers should focus instruction on the acquisition of three kinds of English: Social English (such as that required by informal conversation) academic English (which is more sophisticated and complex and requires more time to develop), and subject-specific language that is used exclusively within particular content areas (including specialized terms such as "sextant" and "velocity"). Each lesson's content objectives should focus on just a few carefully selected main ideas. Content objectives must be rigorous and reflect grade-level expectations. A small handful of key content-related vocabulary terms should be explicitly developed during each lesson.
3. *Embedded Content.* Teachers should embed instruction within meaningful contexts where language is used for a purpose and connected to wider experiences. The acts of explaining something to a younger child or of writing a letter to a peer are examples of potentially meaningful contexts. Set a context for new information by explicitly tying it to past learning and to students' previous experiences and background knowledge, gained at home and in the community.
4. *Comprehensible Input.* Language can be made more understandable by modifying it (text and speech), guiding understanding, and scaffolding.

Teachers may provide recorded versions of class material on audiotapes or MP3 players so that students can preview material and revisit it multiple times. Teachers may also provide outlines of the text, rewrite important passages in simpler language, highlight it, provide graphic organizers, or use alternate readings (such as text materials provided in students' primary language). To make their speech more accessible, teachers may focus on **caretaker speech,** which mimics the language caretakers provide for charges by focusing on communication rather than on form. Examples of speech modifications include speech appropriate for students' proficiency level and slower but still natural speech.

5. *Increased Interaction.* English learners need plentiful opportunities to interact with peers and with their teacher to make purposeful use of the language. A variety of grouping structures, such as pairs and small groups chosen in different ways such as matching or contrasting language levels, interest, and random groupings should be used. The teacher should be included as a participant in interactions and should monitor and guide students' collaborations and use of language. For example, the vocab cards presented in Teaching Tip 3.7 can be used to encourage student conversations that include content vocabulary. The room should be arranged to facilitate conversation, and the students should talk as much—or more—than the teacher does in order to rehearse the content and practice English.

6. *Emphasis on Higher-Level Thinking.* Sheltered instruction focuses on nudging English learners to use higher-level thinking through activities such as adhering to challenging content standards; using questions that ask students to interpret and analyze ideas; providing activities that encourage students to see the whole picture related to the content in addition to its smaller parts; and requiring students to use the text and other evidence to support their opinions. Expectations must remain high (Parish et al., 2006).

Sheltered instruction is most effective with students who are beyond the earliest stages of English acquisition, although it is still better than unsupported immersion into a mainstream English language class for fostering student success. Even the best sheltered instruction reduces the achievement gap between English-only students and English learners only by half (Thomas & Collier, 2001). Although it is a relatively easy thing to suggest effective practices, it is quite another to put them into practice each day in ways that respond to specific students and their varied profiles. There are no "three easy steps," no

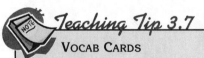

Teaching Tip 3.7

Vocab Cards

Before your lesson write three to five key terms on large cards. Give students their own smaller copies. Use these cards in a variety of ways for introducing, developing, and practicing new words. For example, begin a lesson by asking students to nominate their favorite words, or the most and least familiar words. Have them predict the word(s) that will be most important during the lesson. At their seats, ask partners to pick a card they know something about and tell their neighbor what they know. During the lesson, have students practice saying the words aloud and developing meanings in multiple ways such as drawing pictures on the backs of cards. To close the lesson, revisit students' predictions, say the words again, and use each in a sentence. Practice these words on a different day, using the cards in engaging ways. For instance, ask students to pick two cards whose words are related, or unrelated. Ask them to give examples or use them in sentences (after Guillaume & Spencer, 2006).

magic answers to provide instruction that responds to culturally and linguistically diverse students (Bartolome, 1994). Doing so is a difficult undertaking that requires strategic teaching, sustained effort, and a constant commitment to learning. It is often an uncertain enterprise in which participants give focused attention to respecting each other's cultures and perspectives, negotiate meaning, and find their way together.

Challenge Advanced Learners

Responsive instruction entails not only providing instruction that makes content accessible but also pushing students to their limits to grasp content that is as deep and as rich as their current capacities will allow. Advanced learners often require substantial modifications to the general curriculum to ensure that they, too, find new meaning each day at school. Advanced learners include those classified as gifted and those who are intensely interested in or performing at high levels for particular content areas. Many teachers find that meeting the needs of advanced learners can be more of a challenge than meeting the needs of struggling students because gifted learners often enter a grade or class knowing significant amounts of the content, move beyond grade-level content standards, and sometimes bring strong independent approaches to their learning goals and choices. They ask tough questions too. Yet our responsibility to ensure that students working at advanced levels make substantial academic progress is the same as our responsibility to the rest of our students. Gifted students' needs to learn and develop will not be met by correcting spelling tests for us, tutoring peers for most of the day, or completing additional worksheets on the same topic.

Universal Design and differentiated instruction provide useful frameworks for addressing the needs of advanced learners. Inquiry-based learning experiences (see Chapter 6) are often appropriate as well. Additional strategies you may try include acceleration, **curriculum compacting,** and modification of the depth and complexity of instruction.

In acceleration, students are moved to other settings to receive instruction at their level. A junior high school student may, for example, take mathematics at the high school or a nearby college. Or they work with materials from higher grade levels within their regular classroom.

Interactions with a variety of materials and people can help address students' learning needs.

Scott Cunningham/Merrill

In curriculum compacting, students are given a preassessment such as a written test to determine which content in an upcoming unit they have already mastered. They receive instruction with the rest of the class for nonmastered objectives and spend the rest of their instructional time pursuing projects and independent work that is more appropriate for their needs (Reis & Renzulli, 1995). Strategies that replace classroom instruction during curriculum compacting may include acceleration, community service projects, independent research, and enrichment activities. Systematic assessment of students' entry knowledge is essential for compacting to be effective.

Advanced learners can also address the same topics as their peers, but in greater depth or complexity (California Department of Education & California Association for the Gifted, 1994). Many school districts are pursuing depth and complexity to meet gifted needs in GATE programs. To alter the *depth* of the content students might:

- pursue the tools and language used by specialists in the content.
- go into greater detail.
- look for patterns related to the content, such as trends over time.
- study the underlying structure of the content.
- examine ethical considerations related to the content.
- pursue unanswered questions.

To study the content in greater *complexity,* students might examine relationships within the content, or relationships between the content and a different entity. They might also examine different points of view related to the content. Alterations of depth and complexity can be accomplished by mechanisms such as learning or interest centers (for an example, see Wilkins, Wilkins, & Oliver, 2006), differentiated assignments, student contracts, and small-group projects.

Assure Gender Equity

Gender is another student attribute that deserves teacher attention as we seek to start with our students. In subtle ways, despite efforts to be fair, schools treat male and female children differently in ways that limit members of both groups. For instance, boys are criticized and referred for special education more often than girls. Girls are often praised for behavior, but are less often encouraged to meet high academic expectations. Even the best-intentioned teachers and schools can unwittingly encourage these differences. As a result, educators continue to search for mechanisms to assist girls and boys alike in achieving potential. For example, single-sex classrooms and schools are garnering much interest today (Younger & Warrington, 2006). Horgan (1995) provides a comprehensive set of strategies for teachers who strive to create a better learning environment for all students. Teaching Tip 3.8 is an adaptation of some of Horgan's strategies.

Clearly, each of these areas of providing responsive instruction will require deep and sustained inquiry and practice. I introduce them here for two reasons. First, I hope to help you build an initial awareness and an emerging repertoire of strategies to use now, in your early days as a professional. More important, I introduce them in the hope of helping you to build a mind-set that is very different from what may exist currently for many teachers. Your students' learning needs related to gender, giftedness, exceptionality, language, or culture are not layered upon those of their "regular" needs. You build instruction from the ground up that supports the variety of needs possessed by each of your students.

To both provide a synopsis on strategies for responsive instruction and a preview of Chapter 5 (Advice on Instruction: COME IN) as it relates to starting with students, Figure 3.6 presents strategies related to six guidelines for instruction (**C**onnecting to the life the learner, **O**rganizing instruction, **M**odeling,

Teaching Tip 3.8

STRATEGIES FOR ACHIEVING GENDER EQUITY

1. Study your classroom to assess your own gender biases. Check the physical environment, activities, student feedback, and classroom management to ensure that student opportunities are not limited by gender.

2. Encourage students to take risks and set goals. This helps students to take ownership over goals and see them as achievable. Focus on progress goals (not solely performance goals) to encourage intrinsic motivation. Include intermediate and long-term goals.

3. Help students value their successes and learn from mistakes. Classroom activities should encourage legitimate success, but not 100% of the time. Students need to be challenged.

4. Keep expectations for learning high and send positive messages. Refrain from sending the message that you do not expect success from some students or that certain kinds of failure are acceptable based on gender. Avoid excessive praise for substandard performance.

5. Provide good feedback. Good feedback (a)focuses students on the relevant aspects of the problem, (b)gives information about outcomes *and* processes, (c)challenges incorrect conclusions, and(d)corrects students' flawed self-assessments.

6. Encourage appropriate attributions. Help students explain success and failure by linking performance with effort, encouraging internal explanations for success, and emphasizing specific and temporary explanations for failure. Help students focus on making choices and exercising control.

7. Challenge stereotypes. In neutral settings, ask students to think about common stereotypes. Address stereotypes found in the media. Model gender-fair language and behavior. Value both typically masculine and typically feminine perspectives and activities, and value a fuller range of what constitutes "masculine" and "feminine."

8. Use groups flexibly. Encourage children to work well within a variety of settings. Vary group compositions frequently, perhaps including single-gender groupings as one learning option. Monitor students' interactions and intervene for support.

9. Teach the null curriculum. Include readings and other activities that address the varied contributions of men and women in nonstereotypical ways.

Enriching learning, Interacting, and considering human Nature and Needs). The figure is meant to serve as a resource, not as a prescriptive list to be memorized, that can support you as you begin to think about providing instruction that meets a variety of student needs. Technology can serve as an important resource in your quest for responsive instruction as well.

USING TECHNOLOGY TO SUPPORT ALL STUDENTS

Today's technology-rich context molds your responsibilities to your students in a number of ways. So that you can lead all students forward, it is your responsibility to discover students' access to technology, their progress related to technological literacy, and the technological supports that can spur their progress. It is also your responsibility to use technology as a tool in support of rich and deep learning experiences.

We know that most U.S. students access a variety of technological resources, and their access varies by factors such as families' income level, ethnicity, and immigration status (recall research from Chapter 1). In starting with students, it is important that you discover students' access to technology. Figure 3.7 offers one quick way to discover some of the technological resources your students and their families employ. You can use this information to foster communication with families, broaden students' school access to

FIGURE 3.6 *Providing responsive instruction.*

Connect to the life of the learner	• Build a cooperative community. Encourage student interactions through a variety of heterogeneous small groups and larger groups. • Increase your own knowledge about things valued by your students. • Include students' voices and choices. • Use attitude surveys to determine students' interests and preferences. • Listen and respond to students' stories. • Include opportunities for students to investigate (indepently or in groups) issues of interest. • To the extent possible, select content that has immediate usefulness or interest. One strategy is to begin lessons or units with real-world events. • Be explicit in showing how the content is useful today and will be useful later as well (see Tomlinson et al., 2002, for practical curriculum). • Assess students' background experiences, being certain to tap into the cultural aspects of those experiences. • Expect that students have relevant experiences and bring those experiences to the surface during your instruction. • Be willing to spend time with your students out of class to develop connections. • Invite students to bring in artifacts that represent their broader realms of competence. • Provide opportunities for students to think about their thinking through journals and informal discussions. • Send home projects that students can complete with their families. Try works of children's literature for parents and children to read and respond to together and science activities with simple materials. These projects prove successful even with parents who do not read.
Organize your instruction	• Study the content carefully and analyze each of its components. • Adjust your instruction in response to student understanding. **Task analyze** concepts and skills by breaking tasks into their components and considering prerequisite knowledge. • Present information in a variety of formats to accommodate students' learning preferences. • Use predictable organizational patterns for your instruction. Draw students' attention to those patterns. • For students who need explicit structure, teach your directions for activities explicitly and check for understanding of those directions. See Teching Tip 5.3. • Use charts and previews to make the organization of the lesson and the classroom itself very clear to the learner. • Use highly organized instructional strategies for students who have difficulty with a barrage of environmental stimuli, Include direct instruction. • Keep the learning environment orderly, safe, and structured. • Teach self-management skills for students who need help in organizing their own time and behaviors.
Model	• Model your respect for human dignity. Through words and interactions, model care for each student and our expectation that learners will respect and care for each other. • Model careful listening. • Model thinking processes. For instance, help learners find the main idea in a reading passage by thinking aloud as you find the main idea. • Use repeated and simplified models for students who are in the early stages of acquiring English. Students with developmental differences may benefit from clear modeling as well. • Use student models in small groups. • Model often for students who rely less on auditory or written explanations. • Use technology to provide models that are realistic and inpeatable.

continued

FIGURE 3.6 *Continued.*

Enrich (see more ideas in Figure 5.6)	• Begin with meaningful problems. Allow students to select issues or topics that are relevant, either to individuals or to the class. • Teach for understanding, not purely rote recall. Teach a limited number of ideas well. • Use more than one form of input. Use auditory, visual, and tactile input to increase students' chances to form ideas. • Use technology frequently. • Use concrete materials to present and reinforce concepts. Examples include using mathematics manipulatives such as bean sticks and fraction bars. • Use community resources that are valued by the students, perhaps including family visitations and contributions. • Provide within-class and out-of-class opportunities for independent study. • Do not equate sticking to the basics with parched learning environments. All learners deserve rich learning opportunities. • Use Universal Design and differentiated instruction.
Interact	• Provide frequent opportunities for interaction over the content. • Foster student–student interactions and teacher–student interactions. Figure 5.5 describes active participation devices. • Monitor students' progress in the lesson carefully and provide specific feedback through verbal and nonverbal messages. • Expect different levels of interaction to be appropriate for different students. For example, new English learners should not be expected to produce lengthy English responses, especially in public. • Pair students so that they can help each other. Vary grouping arrangements so that all learners have opportunities to work with different members of the class. • Use cross-age and peer tutoring and invite volunteers to work with individuals. • Allow for student choice. • Use what you know about learning styles to provide a variety of learning experiences. • Provide opportunities for students to evaluate your teaching and their learning. • Capitalize on interactions to provide ongoing assessment information about students' progress in the cognitive, social, and physical realms.
Consider human **n**ature and developmental **n**eeds	• Observe students carefully and ask students and their families about the physical and environmental conditions that best support their learning. • Expect to see interstudent and intrastudent differences in physical, cognitive, social, and language development. • Expect that different students will have different requirements for physical space and proximity, noise, and other conditions. Arrange your classroom to include places where students can escape the crowd. • Take learners' physical and mental conditions into consideration. Will your student tire easily? Become distracted by peers? Structure your classroom and instruction to foster students' success. • Build-in opportunities for immediate success. For instance, if you have students who speak no English, provide them with opportunities to quickly master facts and skills. One example is flash cards with color words or math facts. This builds motivation and establishes a base for deeper success. • Be prepared to extend or simplify your input and provide regular changes in activities. • Provide lessons that allow for physical movement and that use music and the visual arts.

FIGURE 3.7 *Home technology survey.*

Send home a brief survey to discover the kinds of technology families use regularly. Or have older students complete it in class. One teacher was surprised to discover that all of her students' families had access to audio tape recorders and videotape players. This allowed her to send taped messages and other kinds of support home to families. Here is a brief excerpt of a sample survey.

Dear Families,

Sometimes families own or use machines that can help students and teachers do a better job. I can plan to help your students better if I know whether you use any of the following machines at home. Please place a mark by any machines you own or frequently use at home.

_____ audio tape recorder   _____ DVD player
_____ CD player   _____ Computer with Internet access
_____ Videotape player   _____ Fax machine
_____ MP3 player   _____Other:

Do you have special expertise with some form of technology that you could contribute to our class? Does anyone else at your home? If so, please write your contact information and expertise here. Thank you!

technology that may not be available at home, and provide school experiences that foster technological competence.

We know that students come to us with a variety of needs. It is your responsibility to search out the technological aids that can help each of your students to achieve to full potential. **Assistive technology** (sometimes called assistive and adaptive technology) addresses students' physical and cognitive needs. Broadly, assistive technology includes any invention that enhances the performance of people with disabilities. A wheelchair is an example. In terms of computers, assistive technology includes both hardware and software that support student performance. Assistive technology encompasses input devices—devices that allow users to feed information more easily into the computer—and output devices—devices that communicate the users' meaning in alternate forms. A few examples of assistive input devices include:

- Alternative keyboards (including those with larger or smaller keys, reconfigured keys, or keyboards made for one hand)
- Touch screens
- Sip and puff systems (activated when the user inhales or exhales)
- Electronic pointing devices (which allow the user to move the mouse on screen by use of a means other than the hands, such as eye movements)

Output devices include mechanisms such as:

- Braille embossers (which allow users with visual impairments to print from the computer)
- Screen magnifiers (to enlarge the screen display)
- Text-to-speech, or speech synthesizers (so that users with reading or visual difficulties can hear what is presented on the screen; these also provide users without oral communication a voice)

Assistive software also includes any program that enhances a person's ability to perform. Consider how spell checkers, calculators, and text magnification functions can help learners with specific needs. You own word processing program probably contains many functions designed to enhance productivity in the face of special needs. Macros, keyboard shortcuts, and customized toolbars are examples. In your word processing program, search "help" for "accessibility" features for more. Away from the desk, audio downloads of novels or other text materials can be useful to support the comprehension of students who struggle with text or would benefit from repeated readings. Cell phone videos might allow students to view a peer's performance multiple times as they learn to emulate that performance. Because you are responsible for student learning, you need to assess student needs carefully then search out and implement technologies that meet those needs.

Finally, we know from reviews of research (e.g., Metiri Group, 2006) that technology can boost learning across the content areas when thoughtfully implemented. Tools such as graphing calculators, interactive whiteboards, Web-based learning experiences, and computer-aided instruction all can support student learning. It is your responsibility to explore, become proficient in, and implement a wide range of instructional technology that can meet the specific needs and interests of your students. Many such tools are explored in the pages of this text to help you meet your goal of starting with students.

PARTING WORDS

Did I say teaching looks easy . . . from the outside? Addressing the wide range and variety of student needs is one of the most challenging aspects of classroom teaching today. Teachers who are committed to student success run the risk of growing tired as they struggle to meet so many demands. One way to avoid premature burnout is to develop an integrated approach to serving students with different needs (Faltis, 2001). If your room environment, your curriculum, your instruction and interactions, and your assessment strategies all respect the dignity of the human experience, adding new strategies and resources to your room will be less overwhelming. It also helps to remember the scope of your duties as a professional. You *must* do your best, but *all* you can do is your best. Your job is to ensure that all your students have a teacher who:

- values students as people.
- knows students as learners.
- has high expectations for student success.
- questions personal own biases and assumptions.
- provides meaningful instruction that meets student needs.
- uses every available resource to the benefit of the students.
- continues to grow and learn as a professional.

WEB SITES

http://www.chadd.org
  Children and Adults with Attention Deficit/Hyperactivity Disorder. This organization provides information and assistance related to ADHD. Especially useful is the link to its National Resource Center on ADHD, which includes information for families and teachers to help children with ADHD.

http://www.cec.sped.org
  Council for Exceptional Children. Try the "Teaching & Learning Center" in this international professional organization's site. Some resources are restricted for members only.

http://www.ldonline.org
  LDOnline is an educational program service of public television station WETA in Washington, D.C.

This site touts itself as the world's leading Web site on learning disabilities. It includes numerous helpful and easy-to-find resources for teachers and parents relating to learning disabilities and ADHD.

http://www.nabe.org
  National Association for Bilingual Education. This organization is one of a kind at the national level. It includes links to its state affiliates and research and other resources related to bilingual education.

http://www.nagc.org/
  National Associate for Gifted Children. Check contacts for gifted education in your state at "Gifted by State," and view the many informative resources at the "educators" tab.

http://www.nameorg.org
National Association for Multicultural Education. Join the listserv or check out the Resource Center.

http://www.ld.org
National Center for Learning Disabilities. This site gives factual information and policy and advocacy information concerning learning disabilities. There are early childhood, K–8, and high school sections that provide helpful information for people with learning disabilities and their teachers. For example, teens can learn tips for getting organized and building social skills.

http://www.ncela.gwu.edu/
National Clearinghouse for English Language Acquisition & Language Instructional Education Programs. This site shares information about language instruction educational programs for

English learners. You can ask an expert your questions and visit links that will be of interest to you and your students. Start with the tabs for "resources about" and "practice."

http://www.ed.gov/oela
Office of English Language Acquisition, Language Enhancement, and Academic Achievement for Limited English Proficient Students (OELA). This site contains information on federal and state initiatives for English learners. It has helpful resources and links for parents and teachers.

www.ed.gov/offices/OSERS/IDEA
Office of Special Education and Rehabilitative Services. Includes explanations of IDEA 2004. This site focuses on policy issues and is less focused on immediate classroom applications such as lesson plans.

OPPORTUNITIES TO PRACTICE

1. Watch and listen as students at different ages talk about their families and how family members help them learn and grow. Go to the video classroom at the Merrill Teacher Prep Web site and visit Child Development, Module 3, Video 3. Plan a Back-to-School night presentation that incorporates what you hear and see. These questions may help you plan your presentation:

   • For each child, which family members are likely to attend? How might you encourage the other family members to attend as well?

   • In a side conversation, what positive things might you tell the family members that their students appreciate about them? (Think, for instance, of the activities students say they enjoy with their families.)

   • The children interviewed make it clear that they feel cared for by their families and that their families help them learn and grow. What specific statement can you make to communicate your recognition that families are important members of the educational team who are clearly making vital contributions to students' growth?

   • Finally, before your presentation, you may choose to gather similar information from your other students. How might you incorporate the drawing and interview techniques to learn about your own students and their families?

2. Select an experienced teacher and conduct an interview to assess his perspectives on student diversity. If he is a secondary teacher, be sure to ascertain how he focuses on individual students despite the large numbers of students he sees each day. Sample questions include the following:

   a. What kinds of student needs are represented in your classroom?

   b. How do you take students' needs, interests, and perspectives into consideration?

   c. What kinds of challenges do you face in addressing students as individuals?

   d. What advice do you have for me as I prepare to teach all students?

3. Read the following actual scenario and give me some advice: One year I sat in the sweltering southern California summer heat and listened to the commencement speaker give projections for tremendous increases in ethnic and linguistic diversity for my state. Two credential candidates sat before me, wearing the robes that marked completion of their teacher education program. In response to the speaker's predictions, one teacher turned to the other and declared: "It's time to move to Minnesota!" [or some other state that she perceived as ethnically and linguistically homogeneous]. The other teacher groaned in agreement. I, in my own black gown and Ph.D. hood, said nothing. In sitting silently aghast, I missed an opportunity to help these new teachers respond to diversity as professionals. What should I have said or done?

4. Remember that most students with identified special needs spend at least half their day in the general education classroom. Spend some time learning about the IEP process and special education services by trying one or more of these ideas:

   a. Find the IEP form your district uses and ask to see a sample.

   b. If this is not possible, go online and use the search term "sample IEP." Try narrowing the search by also adding the name of your state, district, or county. You will see that the IEP components are very similar, despite some local differences.

   c. Shadow a special education specialist for a day.

   d. Ask if you can attend an IEP, 504, or BIPS meeting. If you are a student teacher, you are often considered part of the professional team for whom meeting attendance is appropriate, but family (and staff) permission are important.

Collect materials such as agendas and samples and take careful notes to document your discoveries. Compare your findings with those of a peer who might be working in a different setting.

5. Choose two students with different learning profiles. Ask if you can shadow them for an hour or more to experience life from the students' perspective. Observe and then compare their experiences, perhaps recording your notes on a t-chart (one column for each student) or a Venn diagram (overlapping circles where the center region represents similarities and the outer regions represent differences). Try these prompts to get you started:

- Learning opportunities (Do they read the same texts? Interact with the same technologies? Receive the same number and type of questions from their teachers? Have the same assignments?)

- Peer interactions (How do their friends compare in number? Gender? Social standing? How do their conversations compare?)

- Teacher interactions (Do they receive the same amount of attention from their teachers? Do they receive the same quality feedback? What seems to be their relationships with their teachers?)

6. Delpit (1995) finds that schools may devalue students' home language and thus decrease students' commitment to school. If your home language was not English and you attended an English-speaking school, compare your experiences to Delpit's finding. Otherwise, interview a person who spoke a language in addition to English as a young student. Analyze your school's culture in terms of the acceptance of languages other than English.

7. Use Figure 3.8 to complete a scavenger hunt for resources at your site. Tell people it is for an assignment but take careful notes for later.

FIGURE 3.8 *Scavenger hunt for educational resources.*

At your site, find someone who	
1. Can translate between English and another language	Name: Language:
2. Can give you advice on building home–school connections	Name: Ideas:
3. Has specialized training in an area related to student needs (e.g., bilingual education, differentiated instruction, special education, gifted education or technology)	Name: Training:
4. Can help you locate reading materials appropriate for a broad range of interest and ability	Name: Materials:
At your site, find materials that can	
5. Help you teach content to students who are just learning English	Materials: Location:
6. Use technology to support learning	Equipment: Location:
7. Help you arrange the classroom for students who need few distractions	Materials: Plans for use:
8. Provide challenges for students who are particularly eager learners	Materials: Plans for use:
9. Help you teach your content to students at a wide range of conceptual levels	Materials: Plans for use:
At your site, find services that	
10. Meet the needs of students whose families have financial needs	Service: Requirements for use:
11. Help students who are working on clear speech	Service: Referral process:
12. Help students with other needs	Needs: Services available:

"I Am From"
(excerpts of poems by prospective teachers)

I am from New Jersey, Florida, Germany, and Samoa.
I am from California, China, Singapore, Thailand, and
   Australia.
I am from divorces, an immigrant, and a soldier.
I am from opposing forces, wild horses, and fires that
   continue to smolder.
I am from two brutal brothers who helped me to grow.
I am from a single mother, always off to work she'd go.
I am from both good and bad, a fair mix of the two.
I am from . . . hmm I'll need to think more before I'm
   truly through.

—Joseph DeLuca

I am from life's experiences of laughter, pain, and joy.
I am from an Italian, Japanese, German, and
   Czechoslovakian heritage.
I am from the era of the bubble gum, punk, pop music,
   and fluorescent colors.
I am from a mind that yearns and seeks for knowledge.
I am from a universe where mere existence intrigues
   my soul to treasure every breath I take.

—Jennifer Junio

I am from a family that prepares meals from recipes
   brought to America in steamer trunks.
I am from a dysfunctional family that keeps the dark
   issues private.
I am from this same family; we cling to our strengths
   and display them proudly.
I am from this family. It is mine.

—Julie Clark

I am from a salvaged home where all is bright on the
   outside and has been saved on the inside.
I am from a land where no word can speak without a
   beckon, and where no answer can but agree.
I am from a rejection of the self to acceptance of the
   reflection in the mirror.
I am from many places, but headed for only one place.

—Janny Kim

I am from my faith that guides me.
I am from the mother inside me.
I am from the land of the Hispanic.
I am from a coast of diversity.
I am from the love that changed me.
I am from the education that fills me.
I am from the family who cares for me.
I am from the God who made me.

—Trista Matthews

All excerpts used with permission.

Before You Begin Reading

Chapter Four

As an adult who has experienced some success in navigating through life and its opportunities, you already know a bit about planning. Before you read Chapter 4, think about your own life and how you have planned for it thus far. Jot down some first-impression notes in response to these questions.

Warm-Up Exercise for Planning

1. When do you plan? (Hints: Think small and large. Do you plan on a daily basis? Do you plan for the distant future?)

2. What format do you use to capture your plans? (Hints: Do you use to-do lists? Do you build flow charts? Do you store plans in your memory?)

3. What do you notice about your efforts to plan? (Hints: How do plans help? How do you respond to changes?)

4. How do you know when you have accomplished your goals?

As you read Chapter 4, compare what you know about planning in the broader sense to classroom planning. Points of similarity may include, for instance, that teachers plan at different levels and use their plans to ensure that they meet goals and maintain focus on priorities.

CHAPTER *Four*

Planning

"Cheshire Puss . . . Would you tell me, please, which way I ought to go from here?"

"That depends a good deal on where you want to get to," said the Cat.

"I don't much care where—" said Alice.

"Then it doesn't matter which way you go," said the Cat.

—Lewis Carroll, *Alice's Adventures in Wonderland*

This chapter will help you devise plans to increase the likelihood that you and your students end up where you want to be. It has seven major points:

1. Planning today is shaped by our context of accountability and drive to include all students.
2. Planning starts with the students.
3. Plans are driven by what we want to accomplish, by our goals.
4. Plans should include thoughtful use of instructional resources.
5. Plans should include thoughtful decisions related to student groupings.
6. Long-term planning usually precedes short-term planning; it provides a structure for daily events.
7. Short-term planning, or lesson planning, arranges activities in logical ways for daily instruction.

PLANNING TODAY

If Alice were a teacher asking the Cheshire Cat which way to go today, the answer would have been very clear. Planning today is different than in days past. What makes planning today different from planning in other times? First, our students do. As Chapter 3 laid plain, U.S. students today are different than those in other days. For example, their ethnic makeup is different, greater proportions speak languages other than or in addition to English, they come from a variety of family structures, and many have substantial technological skills. Additionally, they represent a wide range of learning needs. You have the responsibility to provide access to important learning for all of your students, a responsibility that begins in the planning phase.

Another factor that affects the nature of planning today is the culture of accountability and reform. Long before the passage of the No Child Left Behind Act, reports such as *A Nation at Risk* (National Commission on Excellence in Education, 1983) spurred reform efforts to boost student achievement. Central to these efforts was the development and implementation of rigorous statements of expectations for student learning: content standards or **student performance standards.** Content standards tell what students are expected to know and be able to do ("The student sings alone and with others a varied repertoire of music.") and performance standards tell how they will show it ("The student sings accurately the D major scale with note names.") Several international and national organizations, with members from many kinds of institutions, have developed standards. Some of these organizations, standards, and their Web sites were presented at the close of Chapter 1 (p. 19).

As you may recall from Chapter 1, the No Child Left Behind Act requires the development and implementation of state-level content standards. States choose the extent to which they base their standards upon the recommendations of professional organizations, and the match between national and state standards varies widely. By 1998, 49 U.S. states had developed such standards (Marzano & Kendall, 1998). By 2003, all states had content standards in reading-language arts and math, and 48 had science and social studies standards as well. You can find student standards at your state department of education Web site.

How does standards-based instruction work? In standards-based instruction, the educational community first develops content standards and operationalizes them through performance standards. Next, educators develop or select tools to assess student mastery of those standards. Common assessment tools are paper/pencil tests and teacher observation. In the previous music example, where students must sing accurately in the D major scale, teacher observation of students' performance would be an appropriate assessment tool. A paper/pencil test would not. After checking students' entry-level performance related to the standard, educators plan instruction to bring about student mastery of the standard. Instruction should be in line with the expectations of the assessment. They develop or select materials that will help teachers guide students toward mastery. Textbooks were rewritten to match the standards and are a common choice of instructional material. In the singing example, music teachers will probably select materials such as recordings of songs in D major, sheet music, and perhaps musical instruments for accompaniment. Next, teachers present information and check students' progress along the way. Then students are assessed for mastery of the standard. Finally, educators analyze results and determine the next course of action: Do they move on or provide further development on the standard at hand?

You enter the profession of education at a time when we as a community have wrestled for several years to implement standards thoroughly into our practice, align all phases of instruction (planning, instruction, and assessment), face the results of standards-based assessment, and understand some of the critical implications of holding students, teachers, and schools accountable for standards. Now that educators have grappled with standards-based instruction for a time, a number of our earlier missteps in implementing standards-based instruction become clear. Some of us were, at times, overwhelmed by the sheer volume of content standards to be mastered. We may have focused too much on the surface features of the standards and assumed that each standard was of the same value as the others. And at times, some of us overrelied on our new standards-based textbooks; teaching to the standards sometimes meant *not* engaging in instructional planning and *instead* adhering closely to the sequenced and scripted directions included with our texts.

Fortunately, time and experience have allowed many educators to re-envision standards-based instruction in deeper, richer ways. Our experiences and a new body of professional literature (e.g. Hurt, 2003; O'Shea, 2005) helps us think beyond an unquestioning interpretation of the standards to use them in more powerful ways. For example:

- We have been reminded that all actions have unintended consequences (recall the implicit curriculum of Chapter 1) and that we must examine the unplanned implications of standards-based instruction that are detrimental to our students.
- We have learned that although setting high and shared expectations is a laudable goal, standards must be continually revisited to ensure that they are coherent and appropriate. For example, a recent analysis finds that the grade levels at which standards place certain mathematics concepts and skills varies widely across the nation (Center for the Study of Mathematics Curriculum, 2006).
- We have learned that we need to study standards carefully to understand their underlying, durable, and transferable learnings (Gronlund, 2004; Hurt, 2003) and to rise above the minimal performance levels set by the standards.
- We have learned that no one set of materials—such as textbooks—can ensure student mastery of standards-based content. Instead, we have learned to more adeptly use the standards as guides in choosing and using a variety of instructional resources in service of the things we want students to learn, including higher-level mastery of core ideas, essential skills, and important dispositions.

Perhaps the most important insight gained by the educational community through years of grappling with standards is that standards can, at their best, serve as powerful tools to help us focus purposefully on our students. Having unambiguous targets in mind can indeed drive us to focus clearly on what our students know, can do, and need in order to learn. Thorough understanding of expectations and accurate insights into students' progress can help us manage the tension between ensuring developmental appropriateness and high expectations for learning (Rettig, McCullough, Santos, & Watson, 2004).

Our journey as a nation of standards-based educators leads to a number of conclusions for us as instructional planners. First, teachers need to place students at the heart of our planning decisions. Second, teachers need to understand their standards at deep levels. We must systematically study the standards in order to determine underlying concepts, connections, and higher-level performances that can spring from them. Significant time investments are required. Third, every teacher, singularly and in groups, must be deeply involved in the planning (and assessment) process. Finally, teachers must be free to select the activities and materials that will help students achieve. O'Shea cautions (2005, p. 26) that "Externally prepared guides and curriculum resources can be helpful, but only teachers can make the planning decisions that will result in improved student learning."

Planning today is also different than in days past because we work within a context explicitly committed to fostering growth for all students. Caring, effective educators have always lived by that goal, but as information from Chapter 3 laid plain, our children have suffered many past failures in this regard. Caring educators continue to pursue growth for all students, and now many pieces of legislation require it. The federal laws discussed in Chapter 3 indicate that all students educated in U.S. schools have the right to an education that is appropriate for their needs, and they have the right to be educated in inclusive settings. Additionally, No Child Left Behind requires all subgroups of the student population to show adequate yearly progress in moving toward proficiency in the subject areas.

In sum, your students are no doubt diverse, and your responsibility is to plan instruction that helps every one of them succeed. Your students' learning is too important a responsibility to abdicate to others, such as textbook publishers, software developers, or the teacher next door, and careful planning can help you to help students learn and grow as much as possible during the short time they will spend in your classroom. Planning begins with careful attention to what your students know and can do.

PLANNING STARTS WITH THE STUDENTS

You have a responsibility to base your instructional decisions—what you will teach, when, and how—on a firm foundation of knowledge regarding who your students are and what they need. In fact, the major criterion for your planning decisions should be that all of your planning choices provide access to powerful learning for each of your students. In terms of planning, starting with the students entails building and incorporating knowledge of your particular students, and it includes providing access to important learning for all students.

Effective planning begins with gathering and analyzing a variety of kinds of information related to your students. When you plan instruction that draws from what students already know and can do, from their strengths and needs, and from their interests and perspectives, your lessons are far more likely to result in powerful learning for each individual. As you set goals and then plan your units and lessons, you are obligated to collect and use information pertaining to your students. Chapter 3 introduced several factors related to students as individuals and as members of groups that can be useful to you as you plan. It included gathering holistic information from families and students and information about students' general progress and needs. Examples include a review of existing records (such as IEPs and levels of English acquisition) and use of interviews and general surveys.

Planning also includes preassessment of students' content-specific needs and interests. **Formative assessment,** or assessment that guides instruction (see Chapter 7), allows you to discover what students know prior to your instruction. Some strategies to gather formative information include informal conversations, self-checks, and journal entries. Gregory and Kuzmich (2004) suggest that teachers use rapid preassessments to discover what students know. Examples are homework assignments and group problems, as in these sample tasks:

- In a primary-grade mathematics lesson before a unit on quadrilaterals, small groups of students attack a nonroutine problem, "How many squares are on a checkerboard?" Their teacher observes and takes notes on the concepts they possess, the processes they employ to solve the problem, and the gaps in their reasoning that may be present.
- In a middle grades visual arts lesson, a teacher displays a sculpture and asks students to create written lists of criteria they would use to evaluate the sculpture. He studies their lists in order to gain a sense of his students' art vocabulary.
- For a junior high science homework assignment, students analyze the errors in a hypothetical student's explanation for an observed phenomenon. The prompt reads: "Martin predicts that the water level in a container will rise as the ice it holds melts. Where does Martin's thinking go wrong?" Students discuss their analyses before submitting them.

When conducted far enough in advance, such assessments yield information that can shape instructional planning in productive ways so that you neither duplicate what students already know nor take too big a step beyond their current understandings.

TEACHER PREP

Students' own learning goals and desires should influence teachers' long-term planning. Go to the Merrill Teacher Prep Web site Video Classroom, Foundations and Introduction to Teaching, Module 4, and watch Video 2 for an example of how secondary teachers began to consider students' input. How might students' input have shaped the teachers' curricular choices in the subsequent year?

INTEREST INVENTORIES

Try writing brief surveys to assess students' interests for upcoming units of study. Here is an example from a history class.

Interest Rating: What Do You Want to Learn about U.S. Social Issues?

We will be learning about some of the issues faced by people in the United States during the late 1800s. Here are some of the social issues we will study. I want to know which issues are most interesting to you. Some of your assignments will be based on your interests. Number your choices from 1 to 5. Number 1 should be the item that is most interesting to you, and number 5 should be the item that is least interesting to you.

__treatment of minorities
__child labor
__growth of cities
__problems faced by immigrants
__Other. Tell me more:

You might have family members or know other people who could help us understand these issues. If so, tell who they are and how they might help.

In addition to students' *content knowledge* related to the topic, you should also consider their *interests*. By considering the facets of the content of most interest to the students, you will connect to their own goals and increase their motivation to learn. Your observations of the free-reading books students choose and the activities they pursue will provide some information about their interests. Additionally, you can try using simple inventories directly related to your upcoming instruction. For example, as part of their course on U.S. History Studies Since Reconstruction, Texas high school students study social changes in the United States from 1877 to 1898. To plan his unit, one teacher might distribute an interest inventory, excerpted in Teaching Tip 4.1. The teacher plans to have all students read the textbook, but students will, based on survey results, form interest groups to read other materials and complete independent assignments too. Also, the teacher plans to have students share their issue-specific knowledge later in mixed groups so that the class draws some broader generalizations about U.S. history.

In the past, equity-minded educators spoke of "access to the core curriculum," which entailed ensuring that important ideas were available to all students. Now, though, we realize that students need access not just to the *curriculum*—the facts and ideas about a subject—but to the materials and experiences that ensure their *learning*. It is not enough that teachers make materials available to their students. Instead, they must design (and then provide) instruction that builds mastery of deep, rich, and rigorous content.

Consistent with this goal, Chapter 3 introduced you to principles of Universal Design, differentiated instruction, and accommodations and modifications. Such approaches should be at the forefront of your thinking as you plan daily: To what extent do your lessons meet the wide range of learning needs? How will you push your advanced learners? How do you help struggling readers improve their skills while simultaneously helping them gain access to the content? In what ways do you encourage language development for your English learners?

As the next step in planning instruction for diverse student needs, this chapter helps you plan in ways that consider students' specific profiles to design clear and appropriate goals, to group students effectively, to use an expansive variety of resources, and to develop and organize your instruction in the long and short term. Understanding your students helps shape the next phase of planning: goal setting.

GOALS DRIVE PLANNING

As the Cheshire Cat reminds Alice, if we do not have a goal in mind, it does not much matter how we spend our time. But you and your students have places to go! You need a clear set of goals to guide you.

Kinds of Goals

What are our overall goals for our students? What kinds of knowledge or skills do we want them to possess? For instance, you might think about this by asking the question, "what are our current concerns as a nation?" Are we focused on global competitiveness? Social responsibility? Environmental responsibility? All of these simultaneously? None of these? Our concerns shape our goals for what students should know and become. Given our society's increasing reliance on technology in business, for example, many would ague that an education that does not prepare students to function and lead with technology is an inadequate education. To that end, the International Society for Technology in Education (ISTE) (1998; under revision for 2007) specifies six kinds of technological goals for students, shown in Figure 4.1.

Thus, ISTE and other standards address some of our hopes and goals for the next generation. However, although content standards in areas such as technology, mathematics, and reading spur our thinking on what students need to know, the standards do not comprise the total set of goals we want our students to master. It is your responsibility as an individual educator and our responsibility as a community to consider regularly the goals to which we will lead our young. Such consideration requires us to think beyond traditional subject matter or "book content."

Look again at your stance toward education (see Chapter 2). Your greatest hopes for your students, your goals, are probably related to their attitudes and actions. Are you interested in your students exhibiting persistence? Exercising objectivity? Taking responsibility? Employing empathy? Communicating effectively? These interests show up on many teachers' lists of goals. For instance, there is increasing interest in the goal of **emotional intelligence** (Csikszentmihalyi & Csikszentmihalyi, 2006; Elias & Arnold, 2006; Goleman, 1995, 1998). Emotional intelligence allows us to do such things as identify and manage our emotions, empathize with others, and persist in the presence of frustration. Some people predict that emotional intelligence will become highly prized in the years to come as effective teamwork becomes increasingly important.

Educated people not only *know* things, they also *feel* things and *can do* things. Theorists have, for this reason, divided the world of educational goals into three domains: the cognitive, the affective, and the psychomotor domains. Figure 4.2 presents commonly used taxonomies—or classification systems—for each of these domains. Note that in each taxonomy, the first entry is the simplest and requires the least from the learner. Higher levels

FIGURE 4.1   *ISTE's (1998) six kinds of technological goals for students.*

1. Proficient use of technological operations
2. Ethical use of technological systems that incorporates understanding of the ethical and social use of technology
3. Technological tools to enhance productivity
4. Communication via technology
5. Technological research tools
6. Problem-solving and decision-making tools

FIGURE 4.2 *Taxonomies for the domains of learning.*

Domain	Levels	
Cognitive Domain Thinking	Knowledge: Comprehension: Application: Analysis: Synthesis: Evaluation:	recall show understanding use knowledge in a new setting identify logical errors; differentiate make something new form judgments; make decisions
		(Bloom, Englehart, Hill, Furst, & Krathwohl, 1956)
Affective Domain Feeling	Receiving: Responding: Valuing: Organization: Characterization:	be aware of certain stimuli react to stimuli when asked act on a belief when not asked to do so commit to a set of values display behaviors that are all consistent with one's set of beliefs
		(Krathwohl, Bloom, & Masia, 1964)
Psychomotor Domain Doing	Imitation: Manipulation: Precision: Articulation: Naturalization:	repeat an action after observing a model perform an action without a model perform a refined action without a model or directions sequence and perform a series of acts with control, timing, and speed perform actions that are now routine and spontaneous
		(Harrow, 1969)

place increasing demands on the learner. The more complex levels require that the learner draw on the lower levels, and each level contributes to a fuller understanding, appreciation, or performance. The value of these taxonomies is that they remind us of two things: First, we teach more than just cognitive information. We need to specify goals related to different kinds of learning. Second, within each of the areas we teach, there are levels of understanding and action. Teachers need to provide opportunities for mastery across many levels. Students need to process information in increasingly deep and complex ways and to respond to their worlds via sophisticated thoughts, feelings, and actions.

The most widely discussed taxonomy in schools is Bloom's taxonomy for the cognitive domain. A variety of levels is typically represented in state standards, and teachers are expected to help students work at all levels of Bloom's taxonomy, not just at the rote recall level. Examine, for instance, a sampling of Ohio's mathematics standards for grades 11–12 (Ohio Department of Education, 2001; emphasis added):

- Develop an *understanding* of properties of and representations for addition and multiplication of vectors and matrices.
- *Apply* various measurement scales to describe phenomena and solve problems.
- *Analyze* functions by representing rates of change, zeroes, asymptotes, and local and global behavior.
- *Create* . . . tabular and graphical displays of data, using appropriate tools, including spreadsheets and graphing calculators.

Take some time to carefully study the levels of Bloom's taxonomy and work with them until they become part of your vocabulary and practice. Exercise Number 6 at the end of the chapter under Opportunities to Practice

FIGURE 4.3 *Revised levels of the cognitive taxonomy.*

Original Level and Order	Revised Level and Order
Knowledge	Remember
Comprehension	Understand
Application	Apply
Analysis	Analyze
Synthesis	Evaluate
Evaluation	Create

FIGURE 4.4 *The revised Bloom's taxonomy table.*

The Knowledge Dimension	The Cognitive Process Dimension					
	Remember	Understand	Apply	Analyze	Evaluate	Create
Factual knowledge						
Conceptual knowledge						
Procedural knowledge						
Metacognitive knowledge						

Source: Anderson et al. (2001). Reprinted with permission.

can get you started. As you work with the levels of Bloom's taxonomy, you may uncover some of the common criticisms of it. The levels are probably not linear. For example, synthesis may not always be predicated on analysis (Marlowe & Page, 1998). As a result, Anderson and colleagues (Anderson, 2005; Anderson et. al, 2001) revised the taxonomy. In the revised version of Bloom's taxonomy, two of the levels have been reordered, and their labels, originally nouns, have been replaced with verbs, as shown in Figure 4.3.

Additionally, the revised taxonomy recognizes the multidimensional nature of knowledge that can be possessed at each level: factual, conceptual, procedural, and metacognitive. Anderson et al. (2001, p. 29) define each type of knowledge as follows:

- *Factual:* The basic elements students must know to be acquainted with a discipline or solve problems within it.
- *Conceptual:* The interrelationships among the basic elements within a larger structure that enable them to function together.
- *Procedural:* How to do something, methods of inquiry, and criteria for using skills, algorithms techniques, and methods.
- *Metacognitive:* Knowledge of cognition in general as well as awareness and knowledge of one's own cognition.

The revised taxonomy is presented as a table, as shown in Figure 4.4. Both the original and revised taxonomy serve an important function: to remind teachers to provide both a solid core of basic knowledge and opportunities to act on that knowledge in more sophisticated ways. Also, teachers find that the revised Bloom's taxonomy can serve as a useful tool to help them differentiate their tasks for a broad range of student needs (Noble, 2004).

Goals, then, can fall into a number of domains, including cognitive, affective, and psychomotor. The educational outcomes teachers set also vary in terms of specificity.

FIGURE 4.5 *Goal or objective?*

Set One: Mathematics

1. Given paper and pencil, students will add two-digit numbers with 90% accuracy.
2. Students will improve their computation skills.

Set Two: Science

1. Without reference materials, students will draw a diagram of the water cycle and describe how humans can affect the cycle at two points at least.
2. Students will use scientific principles to make decisions in their own lives.

Goals Versus Objectives

Outcomes that are broad or general are typically termed *goals*. Goals drive our long-term planning. General goals encompass more specific and detailed statements. Deemed *objectives*, these specific statements guide daily instruction. Thus, objectives can be considered to be the intermediate steps students must master before their end goal is achieved. See if you can sort the statements from Figure 4.5 into goals and objectives.

Notice that the goal statements are lofty pursuits that are not yet operationalized, or put into a form that specifies students' exact actions. The specific objective statements in Figure 4.5 will help students build toward an understanding of the larger goals. Notice that though the statements in Figure 4.5 differ in terms of specificity, they are alike in a very important way: Both goals and objectives are worded in terms of what the student should be able to do. Teaching is directed toward the goal of fostering student change. As you examine national and state content standards, you will note that they also are phrased in terms of student outcomes. This keeps the focus on students and their learning. As an example, here is a 12th-grade language arts standard from the state of Wisconsin:

> Students will analyze and synthesize the concepts and details encountered in informational texts such as reports, technical manuals, historical papers, and government documents. (Wisconsin Model Academic Standards, 1998)

A few objectives related to this standard might include:

1. The learner will be able to state the criteria for locating a variety of informational sources.
2. The learner will be able to differentiate (sort into stacks) sentences from an information passage that are major concepts or supporting details.
3. The learner will compose a one-page analysis that incorporates information from more than one source.

Teachers develop and implement hundreds of objectives, and the lesson planning portion of this chapter will help you to write instructional objectives. Your objectives, though, will be shaped by your broader vision of what needs to be accomplished, by your set of goals.

Determining Goals

Professional teachers are charged with making important decisions: What should be taught? To whom? When? These decisions need to be guided by your consideration of the larger system. To develop your classroom goals for the term or year, you need to examine various sources. Recall the bull's eye of sources of influence from Chapter 1 (Figure 1.1). As you write a set of goals for student learning, consider the following suggestions, alone if necessary but in a group with other teachers if possible. For some suggestions, the perspectives of other stakeholders such as family members will enrich your thinking.

- Think again about broad contexts: What are the larger issues facing your students and families? Your state? For example, how are subgroups of students such as students of color, students with special needs, and students who are acquiring English succeeding in school? (Examining test results for your state, district, and local school can provide some insights.) What are the community priorities?
- Analyze information about your students: What do they know now? How do they learn? What would they like to learn? What are their interests and plans? What support will they need from you as they master challenging standards?
- Review your aims as a teacher: What are your hopes for students? Check your school's mission statement as well.
- Review state content standards. Spend some time studying the content expectations to which you and your students will be held. Merely glancing over them will not provide the deep understanding you need. Many teachers find it helpful to work together to examine connections across subject areas and to look for common core concepts such as "change" or "structure" (Hurt, 2003).
- Consider state standards in light of your students. Will you need to differentiate your goals based on students' progress, needs, and interests? For example, will some of your students require a set of intermediate goals to address missing knowledge? Will some need goals that take them far beyond grade-level expectations? Which students need English language development goals? What are the goals specified in IEPs and other individualized plans?
- Check grade-level articulation: What are students expected to learn in the year or years before your grade? What will their teachers in future grades expect them to know?
- Examine your materials: What goals are identified in your adopted curricular materials such as your textbooks? How do they align with your standards?

Jot down information from each of these sources. Look for areas of overlap and areas where goals seem dissimilar. Use a critical eye: Whose perspective is left out of your list of goals? Could a different set of goals be used to improve existing practice? Talk with experienced teachers and other colleagues. Prioritize the goals. Check also to see that your set includes different kinds of goals, including, for instance, social and technological goals. Figure 4.6 provides a reminder of these stages. You will keep these goals in mind as you develop your long-term plans, develop your daily schedule, and plan individual lessons. For example, if you hold goals that focus on intercultural communication, you may need to structure your schedule to include projects with investigations into other cultures. If you have several goals related to effective communication and evidence-based thinking, you may need to infuse public speaking into a number of your units. If empathy and community connections arose as essential, you may plan a service learning project that includes collaborating with a local retirement home.

PLANNING TO USE INSTRUCTIONAL RESOURCES

Once you have set goals, the world is your oyster. Look around you and determine which materials and resources are most likely to foster students' learning and development toward goals. Based on what you have discovered

FIGURE 4.6 *Goals in action.*

1. If you are working with students, gather and analyze information about them (Chapter 3).
2. Reread your stance toward education (developed through Chapter 2). Then set is aside.
3. Make a list of the three things you wish most deeply for your students. If they could walk away from their time with you with only three things, what would those things be? (Hint: Check back to your work in the Warm-Up Exercise for Chapter 2 and in Figure 2.4 for a push.)
4. Write goal statements to capture your wishes. Begin with the words, "Students will . . ."
5. Clip your goals onto your plan book and use this list of big goals to inform your planning efforts for individual subjects and students.

about your students' prior experiences, interests, abilities, and needs—and based on the high expectations you place upon students to master content—search out the resources that will push all of your students forward. A vast array of tools is available to help you and your students reach your goals.

Textbooks

Most teachers start with adopted materials such as textbooks as they make their planning decisions. In fact, many schools mandate their use. Textbooks provide a reasonable starting point because they are composed by teams of experts, are subjected to extensive reviews, are field tested, and undergo periodic revision. And, textbooks can be effective supports for student learning. One national study (Wakefield, 2006) found correlations between the frequency of textbook use and student scores on tests of knowledge of U.S. history in grades 4 and 12 (although not grade 8). Nonetheless, textbooks—like all materials—must be carefully analyzed to ensure that they are accurate and appropriate tools for your purposes.

A long history of studies and anecdotal reports explores the controversies surrounding textbooks and their shortcomings. Textbooks' match with standards may be tenuous. O'Shea (2005), for example, found that many student textbooks claiming to be standards-based provided superficial treatment of mandated content and often provided treatment at grades that did not match grade-level expectations. Through their analyses, authors (e.g., Levy, 2000; Loewen, 1996) have also found that many textbooks include content inaccuracies. Not one middle school science text at that time, for example, passed a screening for the accuracy of content by the American Association for the Advancement of Science (Jehlen, 2000). Also, despite publishers' efforts to improve texts, some continue to include ethnic and other biases such as stereotypcial portrayals of Native Americans (Hawkins, 2002). Some authors often heatedly argue that texts are boring, bland, or dumbed-down, given political and other pressures placed upon authors and publishers (Dorrell & Busch, 2000; Jones, 2000; Ravitch 2003a, 2003b).

For these reasons, it is important to study texts carefully, render your own well-supported decisions, and use textbooks judiciously. Start by examining your goals, objectives, and related standards, and then study the text for its relation to those targets. Examine the accuracy and completeness of the text, and search out possible biases. Determine the extent to which the reading level of the text matches your students' current abilities (Teaching Tip 4.2 gives an idea for matching students with text). Then think about ways to use the text in support of your goals. It will be important for you to determine the amount of judgment local policy allows you to exercise in deciding how you will use textbooks.

Teaching Tip 4.2

CHECKING THE LEVEL OF TEXT MATERIALS

You can more easily match text to students if you know the reading level of the text. Word processing programs often now report one or more different text ratings as part of the "tools" package. One measure of the text's difficulty is its Lexile rating. A Lexile measure is based on two factors: sentence length and word frequency. You can search the Lexile Web site (http://www.lexile.com) for books already rated, and you can get Lexile ratings of your own materials. Try using the analyzer on the Lexile Web site, or see if your word processing program has "Lexile" as a tool. As another use, some teachers complete Lexile ratings of students' writing to help them track changes over time. Readability depends on many factors (such as student interest and the conceptual abstractness and developmental appropriateness of the text), so readability formulas offer just one more piece of information, or a starting point, to match texts to students.

Ask your cooperating teacher, mentor, department chair, or other curriculum leader how closely you are expected to adhere to text materials. Are you required to "stick to the text"? If the answer is yes, ask a few more questions. What does it mean in your district to "stick to the text"? It can mean very different things, ranging from "use each of the activities exactly as written in the teacher's edition" to "teach to the text's objectives using your choice of activities (text and other) that will encourage learning best for your particular students." In making decisions about using texts, I encourage you to exercise your professional judgment to the fullest extent allowed by policy so that you can provide responsive instruction. For situations in which teachers are granted wide latitude, Dunn (2000) offers suggestions for strategic use of textbooks. She suggests using the textbook as

- a framework to find key ideas.
- a source of questions and possible activities.
- background reading and reference.
- the basis for cooperative learning activities.

As you consider using your texts, remember to use them as one of many resources that can help students accomplish their aims. At the least, textbooks should be supplemented with other kinds of materials.

Rich Instructional Resources

Plan your instruction to include rich resources such as primary sources, original documents, a variety of sources of print, software, maps and globes, outside speakers, family members, and visual images and recordings. Using rich resources serves many purposes. First, it helps students learn to think the way experts in the field think. Social scientists, for example, know how to interpret primary sources, conduct and analyze oral interviews, and use maps. Second, using a variety of materials ensures that students with different needs can gain access to the information. Students who struggle with reading, for instance, are placed at a disadvantage if instruction is entirely text-based (Frey, Fisher, & Moore, 2005). Also, rich source materials deepen student learning by inciting student interest and curiosity, by making the content more accessible and memorable, by helping students connect with the content, by allowing them to more effectively comprehend and practice the material, and by grounding it more fully in the real-world context within which the content will be used. Although gathering rich resources takes some thought and time, it need not

Teaching Tip 4.3

FINDING RESOURCES WHEN MONEY IS SCARCE

Resources do not need to be expensive to be useful. Imaginative teachers use strategies such as the following to obtain resources to enrich their plans.

- Talk with your parent–teacher organization. Many grant small amounts of money for instructional materials.
- Look for grants. Contact district personnel to scout out opportunities to fund promising projects.
- Get corporate support. Businesses near you will welcome the opportunity to serve the local community by donating supplies. One large retailer provided well-stocked backpacks on the first day of school each year at my sons' elementary school, for example. You can also electronically register for donations from organizations around the world. See http://www.aft.org/teachers/jft/donation.htm, for example.
- When you purchase materials, tell businesses that you are a teacher. Many businesses offer discount programs for teachers. Others provide materials at drastically reduced prices, or at cost. A florist donated an entire class set of wilted flowers for my plant dissection with fifth graders one year.
- Ask families. Send a note home (translated as necessary) asking for supplies. Do not assume that families will not contribute simply because they have low incomes. Many teachers who work with families of limited means find that families contribute generously. Throw-aways such as paper tubes, plastic grocery sacks, and cardboard may become treasures in your room.
- Visit thrift shops. I bought a class set of white men's dress shirts to use as lab coats for $2.00 a shirt.
- Use your scouts to visit garage sales. Tell family and friends what you need (Board games for your game center? Uncommon musical instruments?) and put them on the lookout. Give them a tough budget: 50 cents for a puzzle?
- Encourage your students to raise funds as a class. Some classes run recycling programs and use the proceeds to fund field trips or social action projects. Check school polices on fund raising first.
- Head to the public or university library. You can check out books, or you can stock your classroom library by attending libraries' book sales, where books are often sold for pennies.
- Borrow. Many organizations have lending libraries of materials that stretch far beyond texts. Check your local museums and state agencies. Or go national. The National Gallery of Art (http://www.nga.gov), for example, will ship loaner recordings and art samples free of charge.
- Share. Work with other teachers in your department or at your grade level to make the best of scarce resources.

necessarily require a large budget. Teaching Tip 4.3 gives some ideas for securing resources when budgets are tight.

Include technological resources in your instructional planning. Technology can be included in a number of ways. For example, to enhance the presentation of information during a lesson, the Internet offers a vast array of virtual resources. An endless collection of video clips, webcam images, multimedia files, still photographs, and the like is literally at your fingertips and waiting to enhance student learning. At the click of a mouse, you and your students can cause a tornado (http://www.nationalgeographic.com/forcesofnature/interactive), witness a caterpillar pupating (http://www.wildlifetheater.com), or experience a dramatic reading of the Declaration of Independence (http://www.independenceroadtrip.org). Each of these clips takes less than a minute to locate and can dramatically enhance your presentations.

In addition to *witnessing* computer-based technology, students need opportunities to *interact* with it (recall that the ISTE and many states and districts have developed content standards in technology). Computer-based technology found increasingly in U.S. schools includes desktop and laptop computers with Internet connections. Many teachers also augment the effectiveness of their computers by adding equipment such as cameras for videoconferencing, measurement instruments for collecting science data, and assistive technologies to increase access for students with physical disabilities. As an example, an **interactive whiteboard** is a large screen that captures a projected image. Teacher and students can "drag and drop" objects on the screen by touching the screen with their hands, rather than relying on a traditional mouse. They can also write on the screen and save their images for later reference. Although research in the area is new, anecdotal evidence (e.g., Ball, 2003; Edwards, Hartnell, & Martin, 2002) and descriptive studies indicate that teachers and students find that interactive whiteboards enhance excitement, can save time during the lesson, and can support student thinking (Metiri Group, 2006).

Research (e.g., Kulik & Kulik, 1991; Metiri Group, 2006) indicates that technology *can* support teacher effectiveness and student learning outcomes such as achievement, social development, and attitude toward the subject matter. The extent to which technology *does* facilitate teaching and learning rests largely in the care taken by the teacher to consider purposes carefully and to implement technology as a tool effectively. As you plan instruction, be sure that you keep technological goals in mind. For instance, as you plan your lessons, ask yourself how instruction might support students' technological competence by helping students

- become more proficient at using a particular piece of equipment.
- enhance productivity (through applications such as word processing, spreadsheet development, or photo editing).
- communicate more effectively.
- conduct research.
- make decisions and solve problems.

(See ISTE standards or your own local standards for specific grade-level expectations in technology.) Each chapter includes tips and examples of technology used as a teaching and learning tool, but it all starts with careful planning.

In summary, early in your planning, consider the full range of resources available to you and your students. Figure 4.7 can be used to brainstorm the kinds of resources relevant to particular lessons or units. Note that some resources may occur in more than one row, which is fine for brainstorming. Teachers also need to plan their student groups carefully.

TEACHER PREP

See an interactive whiteboard in use with middle school and elementary students. In this clip, the board is used as an assistive device to help students participate more fully in the lesson. What other student needs may be met through interactive whiteboards? Find the video at the Merrill Teacher Prep Web site Video Classroom, Special Education, Module 11, Video 2.

PLANNING FOR STUDENT GROUPINGS

In addition to planning for wise use of resources, you also have decisions to make regarding student grouping. Will you instruct students as a whole group, as individuals, or as small groups? Some common grouping practices include the following:

- *Whole class:* All students receive the same lesson from the teacher, at the same time. During work time, all students work on the same task.
- *Small group:* Students work together as subsets of the class, often in groups with three to five members. Students in different groups may receive different instruction or work on tasks specific to their group,

FIGURE 4.7 *Brainstorming instructional resources.*

Lesson Unit or Topic: Standard or Essential Question:	
Types of Resources	Brainstorming: List ideas for this type of resource (Possible sources? Actual titles?)
<u>Techno Tools</u> • What technological resources should you demonstrate? • Which tools should students use? (Think: productivity tools, research tools, communication tools) • How can technology help meet diverse needs? (e.g., assistive technology, primary language support, support for struggling readers)	
<u>Text Materials</u> • Textbook sections • Variety of types of print (newspapers, books, charts, manuals, letters, etc.) • Print in the students' environment • Print in students' home language • Student-created text	
<u>Visual Images</u> • Think about photographs, video clips, works of art, etc. • List potential Web sites or search terms	
<u>Language of the Discipline</u> • What tools do experts use? • Consider a variety of measurement tools, software applications, artistic media, data gathering strategies such as interviews, calculators, etc.	
<u>Field Experiences</u> • What expertise might family members have? Example: interviews about historical events or current experiences with the world at large • Which community members could contribute? • What sites could you use for visits to make the world your classroom? • Which contacts with faraway people may help?	

although sometimes all groups may have the same task. Groups can be heterogeneous (that is, composed of members who are different from each other on some selected variable such as reading ability or English level), or they may be homogeneous (that is, similar to each other based on a selected variable such as interest or achievement level). Groups can also be randomly formed and can be teacher or student selected.

- *Partners:* Students work in groups of two. Just like small groups, partners can be formed heterogeneously, homogeneously, or randomly. Partners can also be selected by the teacher or by students. Tutoring (same or cross grades) is a special version of partner work.
- *Individuals:* Students receive one-on-one instruction from the teacher or work on tasks that are different from those of their neighbors.

Which grouping patterns do teachers typically employ? Whole-class instruction is prevalent (McIntosh, Vaughn, Schumm, Haager, & Lee, 1993). Many teachers also use small-group instruction, including both heterogeneous groups (as in cooperative learning) and homogenous groups based on perceived ability. Heterogeneous groups are often used to maximize students' interaction with others who differ from themselves, and homogeneous groups are used to narrow the spectrum of student need within the wider range of students in the classroom. In a recent study, 63% of the primary-grade teachers surveyed used ability (homogeneous) groups for their reading instruction (Chorzempa & Graham, 2006). In another form of homogenous grouping, called **tracking**, students are assigned to classes based on their perceived ability and then stay with those classes for extended periods of time. Think, for example, about your high school experience. You may remember a variety of tracks such as a "high" or "honors" track and a "regular track."

Grouping issues are heated; answers to the question, "*Who* should learn what with *whom*?" are hotly debated. For example, it took federal legislation to ensure that students with special needs are educated, to the greatest extent possible, with their peers who do not possess special needs. Gifted students present other issues and questions. Should they be sprinkled throughout heterogeneous classes to raise expectations, provide a spark, and help their peers? Or do they have a right to be placed in homogeneous classes so that they can move quickly through a more advanced curriculum? Which grouping patterns, then, should you employ? Your stance regarding the good society and the purpose of education clearly will provide some guidance. A number of additional factors, such as your instructional purposes, come into play. Figure 4.8 provides some factors for you to consider as you plan to group students.

Existing research on student grouping should be considered as you plan your groups. We know, for example, that students have different educational experiences based on their placement in homogeneous groups or tracks. Oakes (2005) documents diminished expectations and poorer instruction for students placed in lower tracks. Chorzempa and Graham (2006), in addressing groupings *within* classes, find that primary-grade students placed in lower reading groups spend more time in noninstructional activities, interact more with workbooks and dittoes, and interact less with trade books and self-selected materials. They are also less likely to be asked critical comprehension questions. We know that groupings can affect a number of student outcomes too. For instance, students' self-assessment of academic competence can be affected by their teachers' grouping decisions (e.g., Guillaume & Kirtman, 2005).

Groupings can affect student achievement. Which is more effective in supporting student achievement: whole-class instruction or small-group instruction? In a widely cited meta-analysis (or statistical summary and analysis of research

FIGURE 4.8 *Things to think about as you make grouping decisions.*

Configuration	Possible Benefits	Possible Drawbacks	Use It When . . .
Whole class Examples: • Introducing a new concept • Read-aloud • Whole-class discussion	• Can build a store of shared experience • Can make management easier • Can allow teacher to focus preparation time on one lesson instead of several • Can maximize teacher-directed instructional time	• Can be difficult to meet full range of student needs • Can decrease student interaction • Can decrease opportunities for student choice	• Students all have necessary and equivalent background knowledge • The objective is appropriate for all students • All students can understand and benefit from the same instruction
Small groups Examples • Cooperative learning activities (see Chapter 6) • Literature circles • Group projects	• Can free up time for teacher to work with struggling students • Can provide flexibility for the teacher in modifying objectives, pace, and activities based on student needs • Can enhance opportunities for student interaction	• Can require preparation of several lessons, sets of material, or activities • Can complicate management • Can decrease student accountability • Students need to be taught to work together	• You want students to interact • Your goals include social ones • Students can enhance each other's learning • There is a range of needs or interest related to the objective
Partners Examples: • Partner reading • Peer tutoring	• Can maximize student interaction • Can enhance motivation	• Can decrease student accountability • Can decrease time on task • Students need to be taught to work together	• You want students to talk • Your goals include social ones • Students can further each other's learning
Individuals Examples: • Reteaching a missed concept • Targeting a skill important for one student	• Can pinpoint instruction for highly specific needs • Can provide valid and specific assessement information	• Can decrease overall instructional time with the teacher • Can decrease accountability for others	• Students have highly specific needs

studies; Lou et al., 1996), students at all grade levels in all subject areas and at all ability levels who were placed in small groups performed moderately better than did those who received whole-group instruction. Effects were positive for all students, but students judged lowest in ability benefited the most.

But what about *types* of small-group instruction? Which are more effective: homogeneous or heterogeneous groups? Results appear to be mixed. Lou et al.'s (1996) meta-analysis shows a slightly positive effect of homogenous groups over heterogeneous groups, but Lou's results are not consistent across students. Heterogeneous groups were best for low-ability students, and homogenous groups were best for average students. High-ability students' achievement was unaffected by the type of grouping. However, older studies (Kulik, 1993; Kulik & Kulik, 1982, 1989), in contrast, find that ability grouping often has a positive effect on student achievement for gifted students, and other studies, too, have supported homogeneous groups for students who have special needs (Vaughn, Hughes, Moody, & Elbaum, 2001).

An important conclusion about grouping arises from the research. *Grouping* does not alone cause positive effects: *Instruction* does. Positive effects of grouping on achievement are strongest when teachers are trained in using small-group instruction and when they vary their content and instruction based on their groups. In their practical text on flexible grouping, Caldwell and Ford (2002) recommend that, to maximize effectiveness, ability groups should:

- be based on assessment of specific performance related to the content to be mastered rather than on a single static measure of perceived student ability.
- be flexible rather than long-standing. That is, groups should be dissolved and re-formed as needs change.
- address a narrow range of student need (e.g., a specific skill, procedure, or interest) rather than a general perceived level.
- provide opportunities to work with a variety of peers over time.

In general, then, the research suggests that a variety of strategies can be effective and that a combination of whole-group and small-group configurations supports student learning. Gregory and Kuzmich (2004) provide a helpful suggestion to guide your planning decisions regarding student groups. They recommend that during each unit of instruction, students be given opportunities to work: in the *T*otal group, *A*lone, in *P*artners, and in *S*mall groups (TAPS). In the total group, you may model a procedure, invite a guest speaker, or present information. Alone, students may complete journal entries, summarize their learning, or self-assess. In pairs, students might conduct Internet research or peer edit. In small groups, students might brainstorm, solve a problem, or meet on shared interests.

So, as you plan your groups, think about what students know—based on assessment data of a variety of types—and what they need related both to your broad set of goals (e.g., English language acquisition? Emotional intelligence?) and to specific content objectives, and think about providing opportunities for them to work alone and together under a variety of structures and with each of their peers. Set the groups in a variety of ways, including student selection, random grouping, and teacher selection. Ensuring that students have opportunities to work regularly with different peers provides them with opportunities to gain social skills and can equalize inevitable differences in power and status. Guillaume, Yopp, and Yopp (2007) suggest a variety of random grouping strategies, including:

- Numbering off (1,2,3,1,2,3 . . .)
- Having students find a partner with the same number of siblings (or birth month, etc.)
- Distributing picture postcards, cut in half, one half per student, and then having students find the other half of theirs
- Distributing playing cards and then having students meet with peers who: Have the same number and suit (for partners), or same number (for groups of four), or same suit (for larger groups)
- Having students sign up for partners and then meeting with those partners during different times of the lesson.

When you select nonrandom groups, use a variety of criteria. If, for instance, multiple intelligences or learning styles are important for your

Many teachers bring coherence to their long-term plans by planning collaboratively.

Tom Watson/Merrill

instruction and you have assessed students' intelligences and styles, occasionally form small groups to include similar or different styles. Including a "learning style" column in your spreadsheet, as suggested on page 51, can allow you to quickly post student groups. Other criteria include student need, readiness, and English language level. Be sure to plan for both homogeneous and heterogeneous grouping structures related to these criteria. Planning effectively for student groups means knowing your students, knowing your goals, and employing a variety of grouping structures. Effective planning also includes making decisions about what to teach when, or long-range planning.

LONG-RANGE PLANNING

Although teachers plan differently, one reasonable approach is to move from the broadest level of planning down to the most specific. Long-range planning entails using your knowledge of your students, potential resources, student groupings, and set of goals to map out the year (or term) and set out a structure for weekly and daily activities. It also includes unit planning. Teaching Tip 4.4 gives some advice for long-range planning.

Year-Long Planning

With knowledge about your students and your overarching goals in mind, study your content standards for every area you teach. Then, because you teach as

Teaching Tip 4.4
ADVICE FOR LONG-RANGE PLANNING

1. Be sure that your decisions about how to use instructional time reflect your goals and priorities.
2. Remember that most lessons and units take about twice as long as expected.
3. Worry less about "covering" the material than about "uncovering" it.

part of a system, ask whether there is a **pacing guide** for your grade level or subject area. If your school has a pacing guide for you, the guide will give you direction about which standards to teach when, and it will make suggestions about the materials to use to address those standards. A pacing guide, though, is no excuse for you not to become well versed in the curricular goals your students are to attain. Only through careful study of your standards will you be able to teach in thoughtful ways that meaningfully connect ideas over time and to students' needs and interests.

If there is no pacing guide, your task is to create a curriculum map for the term or year. To do so, some teachers photocopy standards onto colored paper (one color per content area, such as "technology" and "language arts"). They cut apart the slips and group them logically. Others conduct similar activities electronically with spreadsheets or databases. Electronic copies of your standards, downloaded from your state department of education Web site, can start you on your way. As you examine standards, look for underlying concepts that might capture enduring ideas and serve as glue to hold a variety of standards together. Hurt (2003, p. xv) lists helpful questions that can guide you in studying state standards:

1. What is so important about this standard that students should know?
2. What is within, beyond, beneath, and behind standards that makes them so important?
3. How can I use this standard to teach students about something that is more durable?
4. How can I use standards to help students transfer learning to other facets of their lives and to the world around them?

Where to start if you teach multiple subjects? Many teachers find it helpful to use social studies or science as a starting point and then progress to the other subject areas. Note that this process asks you to integrate content. Integration can create powerful learning by tying standards to real-life contexts or tapping into deep understandings about life's central or enduring ideas. However, not all standards can be integrated meaningfully. Let "stand-alone" standards remain separate from your grouping and plan to address them through other structures such as opening exercises or mini-units during the year or term.

Once standards are grouped logically, they can be sequenced over the year. As you decide how much time to devote to each area of study over the year, examine a school calendar for months, scheduled breaks, and local traditions. You may choose to glue to a large chart those colored strips you have organized so carefully in the preceding step.

Although your textbook may play a central role in determining what to teach when, examine your texts only after you have studied your standards carefully. Begin reviewing the text by examining the **scope and sequence** (a chart that gives a suggested layout for the term) and other information in the **teacher's editions** to determine the units or standards that are treated in good depth in your adopted materials and those that will need additional support. This will also help you locate possible extraneous material that does not support your content standards. Use the brainstorming chart (Figure 4.7) to consider rich resources to supplement or replace the text. Think, too, about whether certain units make more sense at certain times of the year as you decide when to teach each topic. Fit your topics into the school calendar by becoming more specific in your planning: Move to unit planning.

Unit Planning

Glance through a teacher's edition and you will see that authors arrange instruction in units. A **unit** is a set of related lessons that address a single topic, theme, or skill. For example, a literature unit might address a particular book or genre. A social studies unit might address a particular group of people or a time in history. A math unit might include a single skill area such as measurement. Units range in length from just a few lessons (perhaps a week in length) to many lessons (perhaps two months). Four to six weeks tends to be a typical length for instructional units.

There are several approaches to planning units. Here are three that allow you to address your goals while maintaining flexibility in developing (or selecting) and sequencing learning activities: backwards planning, the "big idea" approach, and thematic instruction. The first format is increasingly popular as teachers plan units to meet content standards. It is called **backwards planning** or backward design (Wiggins & McTighe, 2005). This model begins with the conviction that a student's performance is key to determining what the student knows. First, the teacher identifies what students should know and be able to do at the unit's end. Second, the teacher considers what evidence the students would need to provide for the teacher to determine that they have mastered the content. After the end performance is clearly in mind, the teacher develops activities to help students prepare for the performance. To use backwards planning you might:

1. Select content standards or outcomes for mastery.
2. Unify these outcomes through a theme, an issue, or a "big idea."
3. Compose an **essential question** that students, if they answered, would demonstrate deep thinking about the content. Develop supporting unit questions as well.
4. Determine performance that you would accept as evidence that the students have mastered the content. Consider multiple measures as appropriate.
5. Select activities that lead students toward mastery.
6. Develop **rubrics,** with the students if possible, or other measures to assess each performance. (Rubrics and other assessments are addressed in Chapter 7.)
7. Review and revise until each component of the unit supports the others.

The power of the backwards planning model is that it turns the "teach my favorite activities" approach on its head and instead focuses on providing instruction that will help students meet the end goal.

A second unit planning format is recommended by experts in content areas such as social studies (Ellis, 1998; Savage & Armstrong, 2000) and science (Gega & Peters, 2002). We will call it the **"big idea" approach.**

1. Begin by determining the major ideas related to the content. Major ideas, or generalizations, are statements that connect facts and concepts. For example, "tree" is a concept, or a class of ideas with identifiable attributes. "Some trees lose their leaves" is a fact. "Trees and other organisms respond to environmental stimuli" is a generalization. It is a more inclusive statement that relates several concepts and has greater explanatory power. A sample generalization in social studies is, "All human societies change." In analyzing your content standards during year-long planning, you probably identified these generalizations. You can also find them in teacher's editions, often under the heading "Chapter Concepts." Chapters typically include three to four big ideas.

2. Once you find generalizations, write standards-based objectives and then locate activities that can help your students learn the generalizations. In selecting activities, you may draw from your texts and from other sources such as literature, current events, and **trade books** (which are any nontextbook books, including literature and teaching materials devoted to particular topical areas, typically housed in curriculum libraries or offered for sale at teacher supply stores). An earlier section of this chapter urged you to consider an abundance of resources in your planning, and Chapter 5 will reinforce the

importance of rich learning experiences that will lead to student mastery of important generalizations. Examples of enriching experiences include field trips, guest speakers, and **multimedia projects** (Green & Brown, 2002).

3. Then arrange the activities for daily instruction. Good instruction builds bridges between the students' lives and the content. You can plan lessons that begin with a "bridge" to take students from their lives into the content via an engaging question, demonstration, or other activity.

Note that, on their way to learning content generalizations, students will learn facts and concepts that should slowly coalesce to form larger under-standings. It is indeed important to teach facts and specific information. The big idea method of unit planning ensures that facts build into larger, more co-herent structures of understanding.

Another strength of this planning approach is that your focus on big ideas will ease decisions about which daily activities to cut or extend. Most teachers feel pressed for time. Using the big idea method of unit planning, you can drop activities that are less likely to help students build understanding of key con-cepts and spend more time on productive learning experiences.

A third popular approach to unit planning is **thematic instruction.** Many teachers find that integrating their content through themes allows them to address content standards efficiently and in ways that are interesting to stu-dents. Instead of being based solely on core ideas related to particular subject matters, thematic units are interdisciplinary, with learning activities emanating from the theme (Kovalik, 1993; Kovalik & Olsen; 2001; Pappas, Kiefer, & Levstik, 2006; Roberts & Kellough, 2008; Tiedt & Tiedt, 2005). Thematic units can be helpful because they present content holistically, as it might appear in life, rather than as discrete entities. Further, thematic units hold the promise of helping students with high-incidence disabilities, whose educational experience may be fragmented as a result of receiving instruction in a variety of settings, to experience content in ways that transfer across subject areas and into real-life settings (Gardner, Wissick, Schweder, & Canter, 2003). These authors sug-gest that thematic units, particularly when they are enhanced with technology, help students with disabilities to gain and practice lifelong learning skills by us-ing tools that can assist them throughout and beyond their school career. Such goals are laudable for all students.

Themes lie at the core of thematic units. Examples of themes include, for young students, *homes,* and for older students, *discoveries* or *interdependence.* Concepts from different subject areas are surfaced and linked through the use of the theme. Also, thematic units usually include choices for students, allow-ing students to select at least some of the individual and small-group learning experiences in the unit. The elements of choice and group discussion can develop a sense of ownership and community as students learn together and share their results. Pappas et al. (2006) suggest the following steps for plan-ning thematic units:

1. *Select a theme.* The theme needs to be broad enough to encompass in-formation from many subject areas but not so broad that meaningful connec-tions are lost. Keep your larger goals and students' interests in mind.

2. *Create a planning web.* Brainstorm to create a web—a semantic map—that explores the many instances in which the theme arises. Figure 4.9 gives an abbreviated version of a planning web. Notice that it does not include men-tion of traditional subject areas such as mathematics or history; it should break away from traditional compartmentalized thinking. Webbing with a colleague leads to more divergent thinking. As you web, you will note connections among ideas and can begin to categorize your ideas into groups. Jot down your ideas for resources, including books, technological materials, concrete materials, and community resources as you web.

FIGURE 4.9   *Sample planning web.*

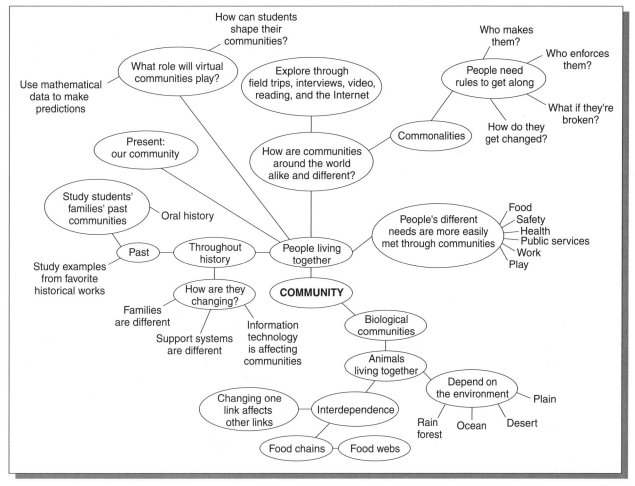

3. *Select resources.* This chapter and Chapter 5 argue that teachers should create rich learning environments. As you plan, aim to provide a wealth of resources. Include the arts, literature, other print sources, tangible materials, technology, and community resources; flip ahead to Figure 5.4 (p. 124) for other ideas.

4. *Plan activities.* Choose or create activities that address the theme, utilize rich resources, and encourage students' progress toward learning goals. Remember to include opportunities for students to choose their learning activities.

Next, teachers organize their classrooms for instruction and implement their units. It is also important to consider plans for assessment.

Experts in multicultural studies advocate thematic approaches to planning because such approaches allow teachers and students to dissolve the traditional subject-matter distinctions in favor of content organizations that revolve

How do you plan? Some teachers use index cards so they can rearrange activities as necessary. Some keep their plans in a loose-leaf notebook so that it is easy to insert other materials. Others create templates and word process their plans so that they can easily copy/paste information such as content standards into their plans. Others use Web-based programs such as Taskstream or OnCourse to author, store, and share their plans. Experiment and see which strategy works best for you.

around topics seen as immediately valuable and powerful. By restructuring the boundaries of curriculum, we may open our classrooms to more democratic and inclusive study.

In his book on ethnic studies, James Banks (2005) presents a unit planning approach that has both an interdisciplinary focus, as does thematic planning, and a focus on key generalizations, as does the big idea approach. This approach allows students to gain information through many diverse examples to build universal, cross-disciplinary generalizations related to such multicultural education topics as ethnicity, socialization, intercultural communication, and power. Banks argues that this planning approach allows learners to gain the knowledge and multiple perspectives required for participation in their increasingly diverse world. Further, Banks and others remind us that the decisions a teacher makes, including decisions about curricular planning, are not purely technical. The ways in which we arrange our content and instruction mirror our visions of what we want for our students.

Whether you use the backwards planning approach, the thematic approach to unit planning, the big idea method, a combination of these, or an entirely different approach, your plans need to utilize the information you learned about students, student groupings, resources, and instructional activities that provide access to learning for all your students. Because students typically represent a wide range in needs, interests, and learning profiles, you will need to plan for differentiated instruction, introduced in Chapter 3.

One surefire way to plan differentiated instruction is to include **learning centers.** Learning centers, often deemed "stations" or "interest groups" for secondary students, provide varied learning experiences based on assessed factors such as students' readiness and interests. You can vary students' *content, process,* or *products* in your centers or groups. For instance, based on their preferences or the teachers' assessment of their needs, during center time some students may interact with a piece of software while others work with manipulatives or study the newspaper. Students can come together and share or rotate to a new center the next day. Centers or stations also serve the useful purpose of allowing larger numbers of students to use finite sets of materials: Middle school students can all interact with expensive science materials such as microscopes or computers with temperature probes, for example, if they rotate through stations. Instead of rotating, students can be assigned to single centers or groups. For example, in the upper grades, students may work together in **literature circles** (Daniels, 2002), studying books of choice with others who made the same selection. When using centers, be sure to clearly teach students your expectations for learning and behavior and how to rotate through the groups, if movement is expected.

TEACHER PREP

Watch a second-grade mathematics teacher use centers (found at the Merrill Teacher Prep Web site Video Classroom, Educational Technology, Module 1, Video 1). How might she have assigned students to centers? How might she have taught them her expectations?

Weekly and Daily Schedules

Once you have determined a broad view of what should happen when, devise a schedule of daily and weekly events. A well-designed garden provides an analogy for a thoughtful weekly classroom schedule. According to Benzel (1997) every garden needs plants to serve as "bones," "binders," and "bursts." Bones, permanent and sturdy, provide the structure for the garden. Trees may serve as the bones, for example. Binders connect elements of the garden so that they relate smoothly to each other. Binders might be shrubs and large perennial plants. Bursts infuse the garden with color and excitement—think colorful flowers. In weekly planning for teaching, time structures provide the bones, routines and recurring events provide the binders, and engaging lessons provide the bursts.

Figure 4.10 shows two experienced teachers' classroom schedules, fourth and fifth grade at the same school, bones only. Notice that both Richard and Susie have devised structured, stable time schedules to ensure that they use

FIGURE 4.10 *Two teachers' daily schedules.*

Richard's Class (fourth grade)	Susie's Class (fifth grade)
7:50 – 8:00 Opening • Bell work • Attendance • Lunch count • Flag salute • Homework check	7:50–8:05 Opening • Opening exercises • Homework collection (with parent helpers)
8:00–9:40 Math • Warm-up • Homework correction • Math instruction	8:05–8:45 P.E. or Music • (alternating days: T, Th and W, F) 8:45–9:45 Math
9:45 – 10:07 Recess	
10:07 – 12:20 Language Arts	10:07–12:20 Language Arts
• Journal writing • Small reading groups and guided practice, follow-up activities • Grammar lessons • Writing instruction • Read-aloud • Silent reading • Vocabulary • Spelling	(We sometimes fit in a social studies or science reading or writing activity here if needed.)
12:20–1:05 Lunch	
1:05–2:00 Social Studies and Science	1:05–2:00 Social Studies or Science (alternating days)
2:00–2:10 Closing • Write in homework agendas • Cleanup	2:00–2:10 Agendas and cleanup
Special Notes: • Computer lab: T 10:20–11:05 • Music: T and Th 8:45–9:25 (don't forget instruments) • Library: Th 10:15–10:45 and as time permits • P.E.: Th 1:25–2:10 and F 8:00–8:45 (need appropriate shoes)	Special Notes for Language Arts Time (10:07–12:20): • GATE reading group with librarian on T (30 min) • GATE computers on W with parent volunteers (30 min) • Parent volunteers help with language arts T and Th • Computers on Th (45 minutes)
2:10 Dismissal	

their time well and to provide students with a sense of predictability and direction. Both teachers include similar subject areas, and they have devoted substantial instructional time to the language arts. You can see structured use of family volunteers. You also see that the school works to provide a balanced curriculum and uses specialists in technology, physical education, and the arts. Because all teachers at the site utilize the specialists, neither Richard nor Susie is free to choose the times for these subjects.

Binders are found in the routines and recurring events of these scheduled time periods. For instance, during the opening in Richard's classroom, students know they will complete "bell work" (brief review assignments that commence when the morning bell rings) and check their homework. These activities can provide a personal and academic focus for the remainder of the day's work. Another example of a binder can be seen during the closing activities, where both teachers have students write in their agendas. Bursts are the engaging activities that happen during the day during content-area instruction. Examples include hands-on investigations in science and projects during social studies.

Bones, binders, and bursts apply to teachers in departmentalized secondary schools who work within the confines of a tight bell schedule as well. They just compress their usage of bones, binders, and bursts to serve them well during a 55-minute period. Figure 4.11 shows how Loretta, a junior high teacher, structures her time over a day and a week for one period near the beginning of her year.

LESSON PLANNING

A lesson is a relatively brief instructional sequence that focuses on one or a few instructional objectives. When students master the objectives from one lesson, they are a step closer to building more complex ideas, attitudes, and actions related to the overall unit and to your guiding goals. Although lessons vary from 10 minutes to a week in length, depending on the content and on the age and sophistication of the students, lessons typically last less than an hour. The distinguishing characteristics of a lesson are that

1. It uses a set, logical structure.
2. Activities relate to each other and aim toward exploring ideas or skills related to a very limited set of objectives.

Although objectives take on different forms (e.g., Gronlund, 2004), a commonly used version is the behavioral objective (Mager, 1997). A behavioral objective is a specific statement about how students will be different at a lesson's close in terms of their knowledge, skills, attitudes, or abilities. Especially in your early days as a teacher, behavioral objectives can push you to focus on students and outcomes: What should students be able to do after your lessons?

Although many new teachers initially find that writing good objectives is time consuming and may feel artificial, repeated practice streamlines the time required and sharpens their instruction. It is worth the time. Objectives will clarify for you exactly what you want students to know, which increases the chance that students will learn it. Without objectives, plans tend to become mere scripts of what teachers do during lessons. Teaching Tip 4.5 gives advice for writing objectives.

WRITING OBJECTIVES

Look again at the following objectives, found earlier in Figure 4.5:

1. Given paper and pencil, students will add two-digit numbers with 90% accuracy.

FIGURE 4.11 *A junior high language arts teacher's schedule.*

	Monday	Tuesday	Wednesday	Thursday	Friday
Daily Schedule Period 5 8th-grade sheltered English (excerpt from plan book)	• Topic introduction • Vocabulary from literature • Language skill • Test-taking skill	• Literature connected to vocabulary • Practice language skill	• Literature connected to vocabulary • Practice language skill	• Literature connected to vocabulary • Practice language skill	• Test on vocabulary or language skill
Bones	• Six-period day, with periods 50 minutes in length. • Rotating schedule. Periods stay in order, but the first one of the day rotates through Periods 1–6. • Period 1 has five extra minutes for pledge, anthem, announcements. • No rainy day schedule. Lunch is 30 minutes long and cannot be shortened. • No assembly schedule (assemblies not held).				
Binders	• *Attendance:* Call roll. Students must answer with the phrase of the day. "I did/did not do my homework." "I like my English teacher." This is quick oral language practice. • *Opener:* Students do Daily Written Language (correct errors in passages placed on overhead transparency) and get materials ready before attendance has been taken. • *Closure:* Examples: "Tell your partner two things you learned about sonnets." "Share with someone the next step you need to take in writing your persuasive essay." • *Nightly homework:* Practice skills for Friday's test.				
Notes on Planning and Instruction (Bursts)	• *Major planning documents:* —District curriculum guide, based on California content standards —Drawn from language handbook (teacher's edition of text) —Overview schedule that lists writing activities, literature, test items to be mastered, and skills. • *Instructional methods:* Using direct instruction. Sharing pictures or photographs, reading poetry aloud, acting out vocabulary words, partner reading of literature selection, cooperative learning activities, student drawings of vocabulary words, creating flash cards with terms. • *To Do:* There is no coordination of topic or skill between the four items on the overview schedule and curriculum guide. Students might read a story about persuasion during the trimester when they are writing response to literature essays, but not during the trimester when they are writing persuasive essays. My grade-level team wants to work to coordinate these elements in the future.				

Teaching Tip 4.5

WRITING BEHAVIORAL OBJECTIVES

1. Be sure to focus on the intended *outcome* of the lesson, not on what students will do *throughout* the lesson.
2. Focus on the skill or concept involved, not the technique you will use to measure performance. (Why, for instance, have students "complete page 43"?) If you do not state the main intent, your objectives may appear trivial (Mager, 1997).
3. If the outcomes you seek are covert, add an indicator such as "circle" or "list."
4. List only the criteria and conditions that you will actually use. For conditions, think about what students may use—or not use—to demonstrate understanding, and think about real-world conditions in which they will need to use their knowledge. For criteria, if you will not check to see that all students attain 90% accuracy, do not list it in your objectives.

FIGURE 4.12   *Components of a behavioral objective.*

- **Behavior:** What, specifically, should you see the students do as a result of your instruction? (What is the studentsíobservable action on mastery?) In the first objective on page 101, students will add.In the second, they will draw and describe.
- **Conditions:** Under what conditions should students perform? (Are there limits on time? What materials may they use?) The conditions of performance are found at the beginning of each of the objectives listed. You can imagine how the conditions would change based on both the students' characteristics and the teacher's expectations for appropriate performance.
- **Criteria:** How well should students perform? (How many? How fast? With what degree of accuracy?) On page 101, The first objective gives a percentage rate for acceptable performance, and the second sets a minimal number of discussion points. You will need to think carefully about the kind and level of criteria that are appropriate for your students because your definition of success will influence the decisions you make as you plan instruction.

2. Without reference materials, students will draw a diagram of the water cycle and describe how humans can affect the cycle at two points at least.

These objectives have the three components typically specified for behavioral objectives (Popham & Baker, 1970): **behavior, conditions,** and **criteria,** described in Figure 4.12. For more examples of instructional objectives, examine your teacher's editions and other curricular materials. Check to see that each objective includes the three typically identified components of a behavioral objective.

Despite their potential to focus attention on student learning, behavioral objectives are criticized on several grounds. They are criticized, for instance, as being too driven by the teacher and as being so mechanistic that little room is left for spontaneous learning. Opinion is divided in terms of how carefully teachers should compose and adhere to objectives. Mager (1997) instructs teachers to focus on observable behaviors. Gronlund (2004) does not. Many teachers elect to include only the observable behavior, leaving the conditions and criteria implicit. I adopted this approach in a fossil lesson I taught to second graders (Figure 4.13). Until you develop skill at writing objectives and using them to guide your teaching, you probably need to write full behavioral objectives. That way, if you decide to use shorthand objectives later, your choices will be based upon a full understanding of what is implied in the objective, even if it is not stated. As you become more comfortable with planning, select the format that is most useful for you in encouraging student learning. Once you are clear on what you intend for students to learn, you are ready to make decisions about structuring your lessons.

Lesson Structure

Lessons are composed of activities that are joined meaningfully into a regular structure that addresses the objective(s). Although there are many helpful planning formats, lesson formats share similar components. Every lesson has three sections: *open, body,* and *close.*

To open a lesson, the teacher sets the stage for the lesson to come. The lesson probably begins with a "hook" that catches students' attention or a "bridge" that allows students to travel from their own worlds into the topic of the lesson. It is common for the teacher to state the objective in student-friendly language and give a purpose for the lesson. The teacher might also state behavioral standards for the lesson; such standards tell the students in clear terms how they are expected to behave during the lesson. During the body, he helps students develop concepts related to the objective. To close, the teacher and students

FIGURE 4.13 *Fossil lesson.*

Lesson Plan: How Fossils Are Made

Subjects:	Science and Reading
Grade:	Second (7-year-olds)
Students:	20 children; all English speakers, some readers
Time:	1 hour 35 minutes

Objectives

1. Students will describe the process by which fossils are made in nature.
2. Students will summarize text by sharing two important points from their reading of self-selected portions of a nonfiction text on fossils.
3. Students will explain how the mock fossils they create are the same as and different from real fossils.

Procedure

Reading Portion (35 minutes)

1. Open: On the rug: Complete a five-item opinionnaire on fossils to find out what children know. (In an opinionnaire, respondents mark their agreement with statements such as "Real fossils are made in factories.") Encourage discussion of each item to get kids talking. (8 minutes)
2. Body: Pair up the children (more accomplished readers with newer readers) and pass out multiple copies of the fossil book. Read the introduction together. Glance at the table of contents. Encourage them to read the table of contents to choose the sections that interest them. Draw upon surprises from the opinionnaire. (5 minutes)
3. Release them to partner read anywhere they like in the room. Those who wish to stay and listen to the teacher read may stay and read along. (10 minutes)
4. Back at the rug discuss something surprising that the children learned by reading. Draw from students' ideas to explain the process by which fossils are made. Use illustrations from text as support. (8 minutes)

Science Portion (1 hour)

1. On the rug: Show real fossils. Contrast them with a sample fossil made from plaster of paris.
2. Have students make their own mock fossils. Model procedure, then students work as individuals:
   a) Pass out and soften plasticine (non-hardening) clay.
   b) Release students back to their tables to select items for imprinting: shells, leaves, plastic dinosaurs (already placed at tables).
   c) When ready, have students go to back of room on hard floor to mix their own plaster of paris, pour carefully onto plasticine mold.
   d) When dry, remove fossils.
3. Close: (May need to follow lunch recess.) Reread the text, compare the process and types of real fossils with class's mock fossils.
4. Assign homework: "Tell someone at home what you know about fossils. Use yours as an example."

Assessment: Students describe the fossil-making process, referring to texts and mock fossils.

consolidate and extend what they learned. They might bridge back out from the content to their lives outside of class. Figure 4.14 offers some options that may help you as you think about structuring your lessons according to the open-body-close format.

The fossil lesson (shown in Figure 4.13) demonstrates some of these activities in its open-body-close format. Perhaps as you review the lesson, alternative ways of opening, developing, and closing the lesson come to mind. Also, I taught this lesson in a room with little technology available. Think how

FIGURE 4.14 *Activities for different lesson stages.*

	Activities for Different Stages of the Lesson Sequence: Open, Body, Close
Open	1. Capture the students' attention: Share a real object, or try using a story, a picture, a book, a video clip, or a song. 2. Present a problem. (Challenge students to solve the problem through the lesson.) 3. Provide warm-up or review exercises to engage students. 4. Elicit students' prior knowledge, experience, or opinions about the content. 5. State your objectives. 6. Preview the lesson. 7. Give your expectations for students' behavior. 8. State the purpose of what they will learn.
Body	1. Present information verbally and through graphic representations. 2. Point out critical attributes, examples, and counter-examples. 3. Model. (Described in Chapter 5.) 4. Read. 5. Discuss. 6. Use hands-on materials. 7. Work in cooperative groups to solve a problem. 8. Make charts and graphs. 9. Use your questions and those of students to explore the content. 10. Do research at the library or on the World Wide Web. 11. Use computer-assisted instruction. 12. Check on students' understanding. Adjust instruction based on their responses.
Close	1. Restate the objective. 2. Gather individual lesson pieces into a coherent whole. 3. Draw conclusions. 4. Summarize what was learned. 5. Give a brief quiz to assess understanding. 6. Ask students to state something they learned. 7. Revisit prior knowledge charts or graphs from the lessons' opening. Revise to reflect new information. 8. Show students how the learning applies to real life, or ask students to make the connections. 9. Ask what students would like to study next, or record their unanswered questions. 10. Write in journals. 11. Connect this lesson to the next by describing the problem to be solved or idea to be explored for tomorrow. 12. Hold a gallery tour (described in Figure 5.5) for students to appreciate each others' work.

technology might be used to enhance the lesson and differentiate learning experiences. What falls into each stage of the sequence indeed depends on the preferences of the teacher and students and also on the particular lesson format being employed. My fossil lesson illustrates not only an open-body-close structure but also elements common to most lesson plans.

Elements of a Lesson Plan

In addition to structuring each of your lessons to include an opening, a development phase, and a closure, you should include in your plans information that will keep you organized and that will help you communicate your intentions to yourself during teaching and to others who may wish to follow your instruction. Although you will find a great variety in lesson plans, six elements commonly included in lesson plans include the following:

1. *Housekeeping Details:* Include information about the students (such as their English language proficiency, reading levels, and behavioral needs), about the materials you will require, and other topics that may affect the lesson.
2. *Concept, Generalization, or Skill:* Remind yourself of the "big idea" you are working toward. Individual lessons should add up to bigger things. You may elect to phrase the larger learning in terms of an essential question. Include target vocabulary terms as well, keeping the number of terms fewer than five.
3. *Objectives:* State the intended outcomes of your lesson using an observable student behavior, the conditions for performance, and the criteria for success. List the relevant state standards. The typical lesson includes one to three objectives. Don't forget the cognitive affective, and psychomotor domains.
4. *Procedure:* Use the open-body-close format to structure what you will do during each step of the lesson. Primarily use general descriptions of what you will say and do. Only for important points, or when the content is difficult or new for you, will you include scripted quotations. Include enough detail so that a substitute teacher could pick up your plan and teach from it, but work on limiting the text. Think of the procedure as a to-do list that you can glance at quickly to remind yourself of what comes next.

   Include information about student groupings (remember TAPS—Total group *A*lone, *P*artners, *S*mall groups), the activities different individuals or groups may engage in, and about accommodations and modifications. Include time estimates for good time management and to help you develop realistic expectations for how much time the activities might take.
5. *Assessment:* Include a plan for how you will assess student learning in terms of the objectives and incidental learnings. Consider how you will assess your teaching as well. Note that objectives, activities, and assessments must all align.
6. *Differentiation:* Include any final notes on special considerations you need to take to attend to students' needs and interests as appropriate for this lesson.

Figure 4.15 gives a lesson plan format that can be used in many situations. The fossils lesson followed this format, as do lessons in future chapters. As you review these lessons, you may also notice that I tend to plan in fine detail. I am convinced that careful planning enhances teaching, so I encourage you to take great care in preparing good lessons for your students. The more specific and careful your individual lesson plans are, the more confident you can feel in front of the students, the more you will be able to focus on students' learning rather than on your own words and behaviors, and the more quickly you will learn from experience and be able to streamline your planning. So planning in detail is one "do" for lesson planning.

Here are some other planning "do's and don'ts." When planning lessons, Don't . . .

1. Reinvent the wheel. Begin with existing materials, and check your resources. Modify based upon your own stance, students, and standards. Lesson plans are yours for the taking. Many teachers start their short-term planning not with a blank screen but with an investigation of what other teachers have tried. Your adopted text probably has good ideas. Select from its many ideas those activities that meet the needs and interests of your particular students and that are directly related to your objectives and standards. Some schools require teachers to follow the textbook with little variation. If this is the case, study the text to analyze the quality of its activities. You can

FIGURE 4.15   Lesson plan form.

Lesson Plan		
Students: Time:		
Materials: Concepts/skills: Objectives:		
Open:	(Time:	)
Body:	(Time:	)
Close:	(Time:	)
Assessment:		
Differentiation:		

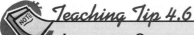

Teaching Tip 4.6

JUDGING THE QUALITY OF LESSONS FROM THE INTERNET

- Start your search with highly reliable sources such as professional organizations like the National Council of Teachers of Mathematics, the International Reading Association, and the National Council of Social Studies. Also check university- and state-based sites.
- When you find a lesson, look for its match with your content standards. Be sure to go beyond a surface-level match and aim for the bigger, transferable ideas.
- Select lessons that address more than one set of standards. For example, lessons can address social outcomes, technological outcomes, and English language development standards as they simultaneously address standards from another content area such as mathematics or health.
- Look for components of effective instruction (more to come in Chapter 5). For instance, lessons should connect with students' prior knowledge and encourage student interaction.
- Look for rigor and depth. Songs that have students memorize algorithms (such as "Please Excuse My Dear Aunt Sally" for the order of operations) may be catchy, but they do not encourage conceptual understanding.
- Remember, a worksheet printed from the Internet is not inherently better than a worksheet torn from a workbook.

tweak it just a bit, as necessary, to ensure that you provide well-structured lessons that are appropriate for your students. At the very least, ensure that you can provide a solid rationale for each instructional move you make.

The Internet is a rich source of lessons as well. Try using a search engine to search for "lesson plans" related to your topic at your selected grade level. A few likely sources are listed in the Web Sites section at the chapter's close. Teaching Tip 4.6 gives criteria for selecting high-quality lessons from the thousands that reside on the Web. Even if you are inspired by a lesson from the Web, make sure you adapt it to meet your local standards and your specific students' needs. You can develop curriculum as you gain expertise.

2. Let materials make your important decisions. Planning is not the same as finding worksheets to fill the time until lunch, or glossing over lessons so that you can finish the book by June.
3. Be intimidated if the content is new to you. Check out some books and hit the Internet to study the information you will be teaching. All teachers should expect to continue to improve their subject-matter knowledge.
4. Be lured by the promise of "fun." Student engagement is important, but not everything that is fun encourages student learning.

Do . . .

1. Focus on thorough and rigorous treatment of the content. Most teachers feel as if they are pushed along by the hands of the clock. Rather than simply mentioning topics without exploring them in depth, consider cutting out topics that do not reflect key standards or that you cannot fully explore. Devote your planning efforts to encouraging lasting and meaningful learning.
2. Plan with a partner or team. Experience and a rich supply of ideas help.
3. Anticipate students' varying responses. Develop alternate plans to address the things that may possibly go wrong.
4. Rehearse, especially if it is the first time you have taught the lesson or if you have a tough audience.

5. Prepare your materials so you are ready to go. Have your materials at your fingertips so that you feel calm and prepared as you begin your lesson.
6. Be prepared to scrap your lesson if you need to rethink it or pursue some other path that is likely to lead to significant learning. This applies even if you are being formally observed.

PARTING WORDS

One of the reasons that teaching is more difficult than the uninitiated might expect is that so much time is spent outside of instructional hours preparing effective learning experiences. There are no short cuts to good planning. Even teachers who are handed scripted materials and are asked to follow the text closely need to bring students and content together through careful planning. The more time and thought you devote to considering what your particular students need to learn and how you can help them learn it, the more likely they are to succeed.

Teaching is directed toward the goal of fostering change. This chapter was intended to help you think about structuring experiences likely to result in learning, and Chapter 5 gives advice on breathing life into your plans through your instruction.

WEB SITES

http://www.coe.uga.edu/epltt/bloom.htm
Bloom's Taxonomy: Original and Revised. This site provides an e-book that explores the original Bloom's taxonomy and the revised version. It includes links to other resources.

http://www.cast.org/research/udl/index.html
Home page for CAST, the Center for Applied Special Technology. This site includes rich resources for Universal Design for learning, including teaching modules and model lessons.

http://iris.peabody.vanderbilt.edu/
Home of the IRIS (IDEA and Research for Inclusive Settings) Center in the Peabody College of Education at Vanderbilt University. Click on "resources" and explore plentiful information on special education, including accommodations. Browse by topic or try the learning modules.

http://www.eduref.org/Virtual/Lessons/
The Teacher's Reference Desk. This site is allows you to search more than 2,000 lesson plans by grade level and subject.

http://www.free.ed.gov/
Federal resources for excellence in education. This site links you to more than 1,500 resources from a number of federal agencies.

http://www.merlot.org
Multimedia Educational Resource for Learning and Online Teaching (MERLOT). This site contains a searchable collection of peer-reviewed online learning materials. Go to "education" or "teacher education" and choose "learning materials."

http://www.teachnet.com/resource.html
This site includes lesson plans and links, power tools, and a forum for sharing your work.

Use search terms to search the Internet for additional information on selected topics, such as:

accommodations and modifications
backwards planning (sample units are found on many sites)
differentiated instruction
lesson plans (you can list grade level and topic in an advanced search)
revised Bloom's taxonomy
state standards (include your state's name)
thematic instruction

OPPORTUNITIES TO PRACTICE

1. Develop a questionnaire for families of your students to complete. Focus on information that will help you plan effective instruction. Keep the survey brief. Translate it or provide it as a recording rather than as text as necessary. Show it to a mentor before you administer it. Alternatively, develop and administer a survey to students.

2. Pick a content area and grade level of interest to you. Compare national standards for that area and level with your state's standards. How close is the match?

FIGURE 4.16 *Banks's (2005) levels of integration for multicultural content.*

Level 1: The Contributions Approach

- The mainstream perspective remains unchallenged.
- Study focuses on discrete elements that various cultures have contributed to the mainstream culture: their heroes and holidays.

Level 2: The Additive Approach

- Deeper content is introduced to the curriculum, but the structure of the curriculum remains unchanged.
- Books, readings, or lessons are added to existing materials.

Level 3: The Transformative Approach

- This approach shifts the assumption that there is one mainstream perspective and infuses the perspectives of several groups to enable students to view themes and issues from several perspectives.
- The structure of the curriculum is changed.

Level 4: The Social Action Approach

- Learning activities not only allow students to analyze issues from many perspectives but also require them to commit to personal social action related to those issues.

3. Pick a single standard. Write an essential question for it. List some objectives. List a large variety of resources that could be explored in conjunction with it.

4. The taxonomies of educational objectives (cognitive, affective, and psychomotor domains) are useful in helping teachers to broaden their scope during planning. However, the domains have been criticized in their application to classrooms. Think about a classroom instance where you learned something that you value greatly. Analyze that experience in terms of the domains of objectives:

- Which domain or domains were primarily involved?
- Which levels of understanding or performance were required?
- What, if anything, can you conclude about the classroom use of educational taxonomies?

5. Examine an existing unit that is touted as having a multicultural emphasis. Use Banks's (2005) levels of planning (from Figure 4.16) to determine the extent to which the unit can help students develop a knowledge base and view issues meaningfully from multiple perspectives. In terms of its depth of treatment, how representative is the unit you selected of other approaches that claim to be multicultural? Which level of multicultural curricular planning do you see at your site? Is that good or bad?

6. Practice Bloom's taxonomy by identifying the level of each of the following general teacher statements. Then try writing your own statement at each of the levels.

   a. Did the main character make a good choice? Why or why not?

   b. Organize the story into parts and give a good title for each part.

   c. Tell about some people in real life who have the same problems as the person in the story.

   d. Name the characters in the story.

   e. Tell the story in your own words.

   f. Make a painting or construction to represent the main characters in the story.

Key: a: Evaluate, b: Analyze, c: Apply, d: Remember, e: Understand, f: Create.

7. Write behavioral objectives for some of the following skills and concepts or choose some concepts from your upcoming lessons.

- Composing a five-sentence paragraph
- Identifying plot structure in a narrative story
- Trouble shooting a computer glitch
- Forming letters in cursive
- Explaining causes and effects of an important historical event
- Solving challenging story problems in mathematics
- Creating a device that throws marbles at least five feet
- Serving a volleyball
- Responding to a piece of music
- Analyzing the use of color in a p
- Balancing chemical equa
- Doing a cartwheel

Analyze your objectives to be c

- An observable verb (an act take to demonstrate mastery

- Conditions for performance of the observable action. Circle the conditions.
- Criteria for acceptable performance. [Bracket] the criteria.

Explain your work to a devoted friend.

8. Try sketching out a lesson plan for a videotaped lesson segment. Choose an elementary mathematics lesson (Merrill Teacher Prep Web site Video Classroom, Mathematics Methods, Module 2, Video 1) or a high school English lesson (Merrill Teacher Prep Web site Video Classroom, Educational Psychology, Module 6, Video 1). Use Figure 4.16.

- Write behavioral objectives to guide the lesson. Write one for both the cognitive and affective domains.

- What materials are required?
- Write a brief open-body-close lesson plan for the lesson. Write a "close" that is logical based on what you see in the video.
- How will you know whether students have mastered the objectives?

9. Plan a lesson using the open-body-close format. Use the form in Figure 4.15. Choose an objective for your own students or rewrite one of the plans presented in this chapter. Use this format for other plans that you teach in your own classroom as well. For extra credit, plan this lesson with a peer. Note the benefits of collaborative planning.

Before You Begin Reading

Chapter Five

Take your pick of Exercise A or B, or, if you like, do both.

Warm-Up Exercise A	**Warm-Up Exercise B**
Think back to Chapter 1, which presented six propositions for the nature of teaching. How many propositions can you remember? Write as many as you can; then refer back to Chapter 1 to complete the list and check your work.	Think back to an instance when you, with the help of a coach or mentor, learned a new physical skill. Examples include sports and crafts. Make a list of the things that your coach or mentor did that were helpful. What made the coaching successful or unsuccessful?
The Nature of Teaching	Physical skill:
1. Teaching looks	
2.	
3.	Things that helped me to learn the skill:
4.	
5.	Things that interfered with my success:
6.	
Good for you for taking the time to review and write! The six points you just reviewed provide the foundation for the advice you will find in this chapter. For instance, because teaching is goal directed, I suggest that you be organized when you teach. As you read, think about how these six propositions about teaching are reflected in the chapter's suggestions.	Now generalize. Mark the points on your list that seem to provide advice for classroom teaching. Keep them in mind as you read this chapter's advice on instruction. (Thanks to Charlotte Danielson at Educational Testing Service for this exercise.)

CHAPTER *Five*

Advice on Instruction: COME IN

"You have brains in your head.
You have feet in your shoes.
You can steer yourself
any direction you choose.
You're on your own. And you know what you know.
And YOU are the guy who'll decide where to go."

—Dr. Seuss, *Oh, the Places You'll Go!*

Dr. Seuss reminds us teachers that we are in the wonderful position of making important decisions. He also reminds us that our decisions need to be smart. We need to know what we know and use the brains in our heads as we choose how to teach. As you decide where to go in the classroom, you need to consider the stance toward education you developed through Chapter 2. Keep your stance in mind as you select strategies that are appropriate for you, for your learners, and for your setting. Always be on the lookout for opportunities to improve your stance and to add to your repertoire of teaching strategies.

This chapter is devoted to exploring six pieces of advice for instruction. Each guideline is supported by research and practice, but be warned: the presentation of each piece of advice is brief; you will probably need to reread and rehearse them in order to use them effectively. Together, these six pieces of advice invite you to . . . COME IN.

1. **C**onnect to the life of the learner.
2. **O**rganize your instruction.
3. **M**odel.
4. **E**nrich.
5. **I**nteract.
6. **C**onsider human nature and student needs.

CONNECT TO THE LIFE OF THE LEARNER

One central aspect of good teaching is forging connections. If teachers fail to help students to connect with information, then it fails to become a lasting part of them. In fact, John Dewey, considered the father of American education, held that connection—intellectual integration—was the key to learning. According to Marlowe and Page (1998), Dewey "described the mind as roaming far and wide but returning with what it found and constantly making judgments as to relationships, relevancies, and bearings upon a central theme" (p. 17).

Thus, helping students to draw connections is more than "selling" students on the relevance of our content. It is instead a necessity based on how the brain works (Caine, Caine, McClintic, & Klimek, 2005; Cole, 1995; Jensen, 2005).

Let's test this with an exercise. The next sentences will be written in English with common words; be ready to explain them in your own words:

> The cross from the midfielder was headed by the sweeper. At the far end of their pitch, the keeper caught it.[1]

What happened? Where were these people? What were they doing? And how do you know? The terms "cross," "headed," and "keeper" have many common meanings, depending on their context. Used together as they were in this sentence, they indicate that a soccer player kicked the ball, which bounced off the head of a defensive player on his team to be caught by their goalie. Phew. Only by connecting your background knowledge, gained through years of experience in the world, with the words you read could you correctly interpret the sentences. If you do not know soccer, how close did you come? What clues in the sentence connected with your knowledge?

Instruction needs to connect to—to become integrated with—students' prior experiences, to the real world and its important ideas, and to action, and it must connect classroom participants to each other. The rationale for each of these connections is made here. To help you assist students in making these varied connections, Figure 5.1 points you forward to specific tips found in later figures.

Connecting to Prior Knowledge and Experience

Learners have experiences and ways of thinking that strongly influence what they will learn and how they will learn it. Research reviewed by Marzano (2004)

FIGURE 5.1   *Tips for connecting to the life of the learner.*

Connecting to . . .	
Prior knowledge and experience	• Try Figure 5.5, Ideas for Encouraging Interaction and Active Participation. See numbers 4, 5, 6, 12, 18, 19, 20, 22, 24, 28, and 29.
The outside world and its important ideas	• Use strategies (such as analyzing newspaper articles) that place the content in a real context. • Show how information has been important to real people in different times and in different ways.
Action	• Use action projects that allow students to apply their learning. Examples include letter-writing campaigns and community improvement projects. • Have students share what they know with other audiences, such as families or other students. • Try simulation exercises and role play. • Use guest speakers.
Classroom participants	• See Ideas for Encouraging Interaction and Active Participation (Figure 5.5), numbers 2, 5, 18, 19–24, 29, and 31. • Learn students' names the first day. Encourage them to learn each others' names. • Give students a space in the room to display items that are important to them. • Share appropriate information about yourself that reveals your love of learning, your willingness to make mistakes, and your eagerness to apply the content. • Laugh—and cry—with your students. Tell your own stories and listen to theirs.

[1]Thanks to Tim Green for his help with this soccer example.

Watch an elementary teacher use a Know Want Learn (KWL) chart to help students connect their prior knowledge to their reading about the sinking of the *Titanic*. Find the video at the Merrill Teacher Prep Web site Video Classroom, Content Area Reading Methods, Module 4, Video 1. How might students' reading experience be enriched by thinking about what they already know?

shows a high positive correlation between what students know about the content when they walk in your door and what they will know when they leave. Research also indicates that the background experiences we all have sometimes run contrary to established fact and accurate explanations of the world. These alternative or growing conceptions can be difficult to change (Driver, 1981; Marzano, Pickering, & Pollock, 2001; National Research Council, 2000). Thus, your job as a teacher is to find out what students bring to the current learning situation and link it to your instruction. Surface their conceptions, challenge their misconceptions, and help them build richer, more useful ways of thinking. Strategies such as knowledge charts and clinical interviews can help you learn what students know. Chapter 7, Assessment, gives additional strategies that can be of use to you as you make it a point to include pre-assessment as a regular and important feature of your lesson and unit plans.

Connecting to the Outside World and Its Important Ideas

When asked what they liked best about school, 6% of the secondary students surveyed recently reported liking "nothing" (Markow & Martin, 2005). If those results are representative, one or two of your students per class like nothing at school. Can you identify the students? Imagine passing a significant portion of your day disconnected and unimpressed. Perhaps building explicit connections to the outside world might help students invest more in classroom life. Teaching Tip 5.1 gives an idea that may help.

In connecting to the outside world, teachers provide students with authentic settings for using and developing their academic content. Reality-based approaches also provide students with opportunities to enhance their skills at analyzing problems, gathering and summarizing important information, solving problems, and reflecting on their solutions (Cole, 1995). Approaches such as these present real-world or realistic problems that are solved by using the content under study. This helps students to perceive the relevance or importance of what they are studying and enhances motivation to learn. Examples of real-world connections include reading primary sources such as historical documents and the newspaper, beginning lessons by presenting photographs or realistic problems, and inviting guest speakers such as scientists, writers, or elected representatives into the classroom.

Authentic experiences are linked most closely to the settings in which students will use their new understanding. Important ideas are the ones worth having. For Duckworth (1996), the essence of intellectual development is the formation of connections or, in her terms, "the having of wonderful ideas."

Teaching Tip 5.1

DIGITAL STORIES

Digital stories are short (e.g., two minutes) multimedia productions that include visual images accompanied by a musical soundtrack and a narration, usually from a piece of personal writing. They tell the lives of everyday people. Digital storytelling is catching on as a way to empower youth while building both literacy and technological competence. Look at your unit plans and decide how you can include digital storytelling as one option for an upcoming assignment. Then look around you for available tools: What cameras are available? What software is available for sound editing? For now, simplify the project to use what you and your students have available. Get more information from Kajder (2006) or TechHead Stories (http://tech-head.com/dstory.htm).

Wonderful ideas

> need not necessarily look wonderful to the outside world. I see no difference in kind between wonderful ideas that many other people have already had, and wonderful ideas that nobody has yet happened upon. That is, the nature of creative intellectual acts remains the same, whether it is an infant who for the first time marks the connection between seeing things and reaching for them . . . or a musician who invents a harmonic sequence. . . . In each case, *new connections are being made among things already mastered.* The more we help children to have their wonderful ideas and to feel good about themselves for having them, the more likely it is that they will some day happen upon wonderful ideas that no one else has happened upon before. (p. 14; emphasis added)

Connecting to Action

Your long view of learners is probably related to students' future behavior patterns and decision-making abilities. What we teach children, from kindergarten on, should connect to the ways we want them to act now and as adults. They deserve immediate opportunities to act on what they learn. Social action projects can serve as a powerful mechanism to shape schools and communities into more humane and inclusive institutions (e.g., Banks, 1997; Bomer & Bomer, 2001; Nieto, 2004). Another chance for students to take action is through service learning, wherein they test and apply their content learning by serving the community (Allen, 2003; Stephens, 1995). Examples include encouraging voter registration, teaching or tutoring younger students, and planning community gardens.

Connecting Classroom Participants

When asked what they like best about school, secondary students most frequently reported "each other" (Markow & Martin, 2005). Also, students in that same survey who reported connections with their teachers also reported better attitudes toward education and school, and they have positive school experiences. Kohn (1999, p. 21) mirrors these findings when he comments on the need for human connection: "All of us yearn for a sense of relatedness or belonging, a feeling of being connected to others. . . . And all of us seek opportunities to feel effective, to learn new things that matter to us and find (or create) answers to personally meaningful questions." Indeed, students rate. "Learning new things" an impressive third place in the survey just cited (Markow & Martin, 2005).

When classroom members form a cohesive community, they can support each other in learning.

Anne Vega/Merrill

Helping students to form a cohesive group can encourage a safe environment, and it can help students learn important lessons about working as members of a group. Additionally, learning strategies that require students to work together are effective in supporting academic achievement (Bowen, 2000; Hall & Stegila, 2003; Johnson & Johnson, 1999; Maheady, Michielli-Pendl, Mallette, & Harper, 2002; Marzano et al., 2001), language development (Center for Research on Education, Diversity & Excellence, 2002; Faltis, 2001), and social and emotional growth (Goleman, 1998).

There are plenty of strategies for building a sense of community in a classroom. Most important, teachers must model respect, revealing genuine interest in students as people, and they need to encourage students to do the same for each other. If one student ridicules another, the teacher's lesson of the day must necessarily shift to address expectations for how community members are to treat each other. Several engaging techniques can foster a sense of community, as follows:

1. *Share expectations:* Hold a discussion, perhaps preceded by a journal writing session, of what class members expect from each other. What can students expect from their teacher? How do they expect to be treated by their peers?

2. *Use activities that help students get to know each other:* Choose from among many published activities that allow students to learn about each other. In an activity called "Trading Places" (Silberman, 1996), students write a favorite (e.g., book, place, song) on a sticky note, place the note on their shirts, and circulate to discuss each others' ideas. They negotiate trades of sticky notes based on self-selected criteria.

   Kagan (2000) similarly gives many games that can help build a sense of team spirit in noncompetitive and enjoyable ways. In "Smile If You Love Me," one student (Cupid) stands in the center of the circle, makes faces, and uses motions, words, and sounds to make another person smile. When people in the circle smile, they join the center of the circle as Cupids.

3. *Develop an outward symbol or sign to signify a sense of group identity:* Create a work of art, a name, a handshake, a logo, or other identification that signals your cohesion as a class. For instance, based on student Jodi's advice from her great-grandmother, my class recently decided on its motto: "Be good. And if you can't be good . . . be careful."[2]

ORGANIZE YOUR INSTRUCTION

Teaching is intentional. Professional educators do things *on purpose.* When you step into your classroom each day, you need to have goals in mind. Teachers who waste little instructional time and ensure that students are engaged affect student achievement positively (Miller & Hall, 2005). Effective instruction involves a high degree of organization. Arrange your learning activities so that they allow you and your students to reach your goals. Actively encourage them to set and reach for goals as well. This is a terrific way to start with the students, and it is effective in helping them learn (Marzano et al., 2001).

You need to be organized on more than one level: You need to organize content within and across individual lessons, and you need to organize times and tasks within the larger teaching environment.

Organizing Content

Think back to Exercise B at the beginning of this chapter, where you were invited to think about what a good coach does well. One often-cited coaching

---

[2]Used with the permission of Jodi Elmore.

TEACHER PREP

Watch a high school English teacher help students comprehend a story and its themes by composing mind maps, one form of graphic organizer. Find the video at the Merrill Teacher Prep Web site Video Classroom, Content Area Reading Methods, Module 2, Video 2. How did the maps facilitate interaction and help students think about the organization of concepts?

skill is the ability to break a complicated task (for instance, sailing, golfing, or driving a manual-transmission car) down into smaller, more easily mastered skills. As does a coach, you need to analyze the content you are teaching. It needs to be broken into chunks before it can be presented in your classroom. What size should the chunks be? What shape? In which order should you present them?

The manner in which you organize the content depends on your knowledge of the students, the amount of time you have with them, and your knowledge of the content itself. Before you teach, ensure that you have a firm grasp of the major concepts you will be teaching and that you understand the relationship among these ideas. Check your understanding by constructing a diagram or other visual representation of your knowledge. One example is a **concept map,** which relates ideas in a hierarchical structure. Figure 5.8, found in Exercise 3 at the close of this chapter, is a concept map of this entire text. Try the free trial version of popular concept mapping programs, Inspiration and Kidspiration, at http://inspiration.com.

Being able to organize your ideas into a one-page diagram helps you discover the main points and supporting details so you can structure instruction and arrange your time appropriately. Additionally, using **graphic organizers,** diagrams, and other nonlinguistic representations of the text supports student achievement (Marzano et al., 2001).

By presenting information in particular ways, your curriculum materials will also provide clues for content organization. Often textbooks follow predictable structures in presenting content. Some typical patterns for the structure of text are suggested in Figure 5.2.

As you organize your content, though, remember that textbook authors do not know your particular students when they write. Think about the organization that would best suit your purposes, even if it differs from the organization used in your curricular materials. Your learners' developmental levels provide one clue in organizing instruction. A general rule of thumb is that the less experience learners have with the content, the smaller the chunks of content need to be. For example, kindergartners, who tend to have fewer background experiences from which to draw, need consistently smaller pieces of content. Similarly, teenagers who have never heard the German language will probably not begin learning the language by reading entire essays in German. Age and other elements such as the students' capacity to learn and language proficiency affect the amount of experience students have with the content and hence the size of the chunks of information their teachers present.

FIGURE 5.2   *Some organizational patterns of content.*

Organizational Pattern	Example
Time sequence	Historical events presented chronologically
General principles to specific examples	Scientific laws and then real-world examples of them
Specific examples to general principles	Letters of the alphabet as examples of vowels or consonants
Topical	Aspects of family life within a culture: recreation, food, and work
Cause and effect	Historical events and new laws they inspired
Compare and contrast	Plants and animals
Problem and solution	An enigma and then its solution

The most common mistake novice teachers make when organizing content is to include too much information (too many chunks) in a single lesson. I also made that mistake when I taught a reading and science lesson to second graders, as I described in Chapter 4. You read my plan (Figure 4.13) for the hour-and-a-half lesson. I planned to guide the children through some reading experiences and then have them make their own fossils to build an understanding of how fossils are made. Upon reflection, I overestimated second graders' experience with text and could improve the lesson by breaking the reading portion of the lesson into even smaller chunks spread over more time. Similarly, the children's fine motor skills were not as well developed as I had anticipated, so shaping the clay molds took longer than expected.

My unreasonable expectations for students' motor development also reflects another common mistake that new teachers make: developing unrealistic expectations for their learners. Although it is critical to maintain high learning expectations for every student, it is equally important to recall that not all learners are college students. Although this point seems obvious, recall that one of the most recent and therefore potent instructional models new teachers witness is the college instructor. What works with a set of adult learners often does not work as well with less mature students.

Organizing Times and Tasks

After you arrange the content within individual lessons, place it into a framework of how activities will flow over the course of the day. When you are ready to teach, make certain that the class understands and accepts the organizational scheme you have devised. Even if you teach from great lesson plans, your learners may leave dazed unless you provide clues about the organization of content and activities—or they may leave indifferent if they perceive that they had no input into the agenda. Teaching is interactional. Students matter. Learners deserve both an overall sense of where the day is headed and clues to let them know where they are on the day's map. Teaching Tip 5.2 provides some techniques for building and sharing your organizational plan.

Teaching Tip 5.2

TECHNIQUES FOR BUILDING AND SHARING YOUR ORGANIZATIONAL PLAN

- Ask students for their expectations at the beginning of a class (e.g., "What do you hope to learn this year?").
- Write a daily agenda on the board. Try allowing learners to provide input by adding, deleting, or rearranging items.
- Provide a graphic organizer that shows how your instruction will be organized.
- Briefly tell students what will happen during the lesson.
- Preview the lesson's major points.
- If you intend to lecture, provide a note-taking form that helps student organize the information.
- During the lesson, use internal summaries and transition sentences so that students see when you are switching to a different point or activity.
- Refer back to your agenda or chart as the lessons progresses.
- Draw each lesson to closure. Try summarizing by asking students to share an important point or ask for input for the next agenda.

As you teach, events will conspire to encourage stalls and side trips. Because classrooms are crowded, busy places, it is easy for plans to be forestalled. Students, for instance, may raise interesting questions or bring up points that warrant exploration. Experienced teachers call such an instance a **teachable moment.** A teachable moment is not found explicitly listed in the daily plan book, but it presents a wonderful opportunity for learning. One difficult aspect of your job will be to decide which moments to pursue because of their rich promise and which opportunities may not be worth the time invested. That decision is not always easy, and not all students will perceive your adherence to or diversion from the plan with the same optimism. When the situation arises in my classroom, I sometimes tell students "You are raising important issues! We can certainly explore them now. We will need to modify our agenda to make room for it by deleting X. Shall we?" Use your professional judgment, and refer back to contents standards and your stance toward education and its important goals, as you decide which paths to pursue. The point is to remain intentional. Keep your goals in mind.

In terms of teachable moments and every other moment of the day, you will no doubt discover that the clearer you are in your priorities and the more organized you are, the less time gets wasted. This is especially true with giving directions. If your directions are clear and students know just what to do, they can jump in and get to work. If directions are disorganized and unclear, your students will waste time and materials, and you will waste your time and energy reteaching individuals who have made a mess or wandered off course. Teaching Tip 5.3 suggests advice for giving clear directions.

It is also easy to lose track of time. If we were to list Murphy's Laws of Classroom Teaching, at the head of the list might be "Things always take longer than expected." Keep one eye on the clock and remember your agenda to ensure that you are spending your students' time wisely.

MODEL

According to the fable, a young crab was chastised by her mother because she walked sideways, not straight ahead. Her mother, as do all crabs of her variety, also walked sideways. After trying unsuccessfully to follow her

Teaching Tip 5.3

GIVING CLEAR DIRECTIONS

Ensuring that your directions to students are crystal clear will help you and your students remain organized and productive. When giving directions, remember the following:

1. Limit your directions to no more than three steps.
2. Use more than one form of input: Say your directions aloud, post them on the board, and model them. For older students, using just two forms of input may suffice.
3. Hold up your fingers to count steps as you state your directions: "The *first* thing you will do is . . . " Be certain that, for older students, you use natural phrasing and do not overemphasize the gesture.
4. Check for understanding of the directions before you release students to work: "What is the first thing you will do?" Reteach until students demonstrate understanding.
5. No matter the age of the learner, give your directions immediately before you want students to follow them. Students may forget what to do if you give directions and then talk about something else before releasing them.

mother's admonitions to walk forward, the young crab implored her mother: "Show me!" The moral? Giving advice *through words* is easy. Demonstrating that advice *through actions* is harder . . . and is almost always more helpful for learners.

In life outside the classroom walls, we often learn by example, by being shown how to conduct ourselves. Modeling, or showing students how to carry out a skill, is a powerful instructional strategy (Cole, 1995). Think about what you want students to learn and then show them how to do it. Modeling is effective for learners of all ages, and it is appropriate in every subject area. Figure 5.3 provides four examples of modeling.

FIGURE 5.3   *Four examples of teacher modeling.*

Concepts and Skills	Modeling
Tying shoelaces	• Mr. Alvarez positions himself on the rug so his six kindergartners can see clearly. • He demonstrates each step of tying a bow, exaggerating and slowing his motions to make the steps obvious. • He asks the students to verbalize the procedure with him as he ties several times before handing each student a shoe to tie while he watches.
Cooperating with peers	• Having assigned his fourth graders to work in pairs, Mr. Pease reviews his expectations for partner work: "Partners support each other by reaching decisions together. Partners help each other when they get stuck." • He invites a student to the front of the room to play the role of his work partner. • The partners show the class how to compromise to reach decisions and how to use helpful words to get unstuck. • Mr. Pease reminds the class: "Here's what cooperation *looks like,* and here is what it *sounds like.*" • Now his students have some specific advice and behaviors to help them work together.
Writing a persuasive essay	• On a projected computer display in her seventh-grade class, Ms. Simon shows and reads aloud two examples of good persuasive essays. • She shares the criteria for effective persuasive writing and states that she will use those criteria to write her own essay. • She talks through her decisions about selecting a topic and its supporting points. • As she expresses her decisions, she writes a couple of drafts on the projected computer screen. • She and the students check to see whether the essays meet the criteria for good persuasive writing. • She e-mails her final essay to students or posts it on the class website, for students' later reference.
Solving a challenging word problem in math	• Miss Thompson reads the problem aloud to her ninth graders, varying her intonation as she reads critical components of the problem. • Using the **think aloud** strategy, She summarizes her understanding of the problem, discusses what she needs to know, and reacts to the problem to show her stance as a problem solver: "This one looks tough, but I have solved similar problems!" • She attacks the problem on the whiteboard, sharing her decisions for trying certain strategies. When her strategies do not bring immediate success, she shows students how to move forward by trying new approaches. • When she reaches a solution, she shares the joy she finds in persisting and solving a challenging problem.

Teaching Tip 5.4

TIPS FOR EFFECTIVE MODELING

1. As you plan, think about the most important elements of the skill or process you will model. List them you draw students' attention to **critical attributes** and remember that in many cases students' performances need not match yours. Their efforts may be both different from yours *and* good.
2. Verbalize your decisions; talk about what you are thinking and doing. This models **metacognition** and shows that we understand and have control over our thinking.
3. Provide plenty of good examples, including student models. Point out when the examples are different from each other and say what they have in common that makes them good. Showing different examples—**multiple embodiments**—helps students focus on the criteria for a successful performance.
4. If the behavior is complex, model sections of it and slow down your performance.
5. Model desired behaviors more than once. The less familiar students are with the skill, the more careful repetitions they need to see.
6. Model regularly, even if you are short on time.

Watch a seventh-grade science teacher model for students as they learn Bernoulli's principle. Find the video at the Merrill Teacher Prep Web site, Video Classroom, General Methods, Module 8, Video 1. Why is modeling especially important in this clip?

Modeling is important for helping students learn behaviors, such as using manners and showing consideration, as well as for helping them master content-area outcomes. When you model, try some of the suggestions in Teaching Tip 5.4.

Finally, through their modeling, teachers teach more than content-area skills, behaviors, and knowledge. Good and Brophy (1987) make the important point that through their modeling, teachers shape a healthy group climate, convey an interest in the students as people, and teach ideas about good listening and communication habits. Through teacher modeling, students learn to socialize as members of groups, to gain rational control over their own behaviors, and to respect others. Teacher modeling, then, is an important socializing force that helps teachers induce students toward the good.

Rich environments foster deeper learning.

Anthony Magnacca/Merrill

ENRICH

> Life is amazing, and a teacher had better prepare himself to be a medium for that amazement.
>
> —Edward Blishen

Because teachers are responsible for presenting a great deal of information to large groups of students in relatively brief periods of time, classrooms tend to ring with auditory input, or teacher talk. Listening is an efficient learning strategy for many students much of the time, but it does have at least six drawbacks:

1. People process information at different rates.
2. Because speech comes in a stream, listeners may not be able to separate main points and discern the supporting points.
3. It can be difficult for students to contribute to a lecture, change its pace, or connect with its content.
4. People learn differently (Gardner, 1993).
5. Students may have insufficient experience with the language of instruction or with the content to comprehend it solely by hearing it. Meaningful instruction for students acquiring English is most often embedded in realistic and rich contexts, as you will recall from Chapter 3 (Center for Research on Education, Diversity & Excellence, 2002; Echevarria, Vogt, & Short, 2004; Hill & Flynn, 2006; Krashen, 1981; Swain; 1985; Thomas & Collier, 2001).
6. Recent work in human learning suggests that varied stimulation is essential for brain development. The more varied and frequent the stimulation the brain receives, the more complex its development (Kovalik & Olsen, 2001; National Research Council, 2000).

For all of these reasons, teachers need to enrich the learning environment by providing rich input. Indeed, in a study of mathematics and science instruction, Wenglinsky (2000) found that hands-on lessons and higher-order thinking tasks resulted in higher student achievement. Think about powerful learning experiences you have had in life. Potent learning experiences tend to be full of sensations: new sights and sounds, textures and smells. We hear beautiful words and ideas that make us reconsider what we know. We try new things that just the day before seemed beyond our capabilities.

Classroom learning should mirror the most powerful kinds of learning from our outside lives. How well do our lectures, worksheets, spelling lists, and pages of math exercises live up to that challenge? As you teach, remember to fill students' lives with authentic—rich and real—opportunities to learn. Focus on meaning. Give students the chance to see and try new things, to hear the music and speech of faraway places, to experience the struggles of those fighting for independence, to touch the moist skin of the amphibians they study, to read and hear the words of people who have shaped history. Figure 5.4 gives some ideas for enriching the learning environment.

Will providing enriched experiences take more of your preparation time than would photocopying a worksheet page? Almost certainly so. You can minimize your time investment by saving your collections and by utilizing the expertise of community members and colleagues. On the other hand, do worksheets and book activities have their place in the classroom? Almost certainly so. You will need to balance the kinds of activities and input you provide, checking to see that you select a variety of activities that promote meaningful learning. Your efforts to provide rich input will pay off. Remember that you are a window to the world for your students.

Watch middle school students with and without disabilities experience enriched learning activities together by experimenting with plants, making pots, and planning to share the plants with residents at a nursing home. Find the video at the Merrill Teacher Prep Web site, Video Classroom, Special Education, Module 9, Video 3. How might the students' learning be different if the teacher had them complete worksheets instead?

FIGURE 5.4   *Ideas for enriching the learning environment.*

Look for a variety of ways to present the content and for varied representations of it.

- *Meaning:* Focus on conceptual understanding, not just rote learning. Provide authentic experiences in the content areas.
- *Many kinds of print:* Fill your room with books of different genres. Include, too, other kinds of print such as posters, recipes, student-generated work, letters, and signs (Schifini, 1994). Include text in students' primary language.
- *Picture files:* Start clipping and saving pictures to support your instruction. Pictures can be used for concept sorts or to encourage small-group discussion. Old magazines and calendars are a good place to start. Many images can be downloaded and printed as well.
- *Realia:* Find real objects to provide examples of what you read and study.
- *Works of art:* Reproductions of great works are available in teaching materials and at libraries. They can set the stage for the study of concepts from the content areas.
- *Newspapers and current periodicals:* Look in the news for examples of what you are studying. Encourage your students to do the same.
- *Technology:* Help your students access information around the world through the Internet. See the Web sites at the close of this chapter for resources that can bring the world into your room.
- *Living things:* Instead of assigning only worksheets to study insects, bring in mealworms from the pet store. Create a worm garden in an aquarium. Grow mold.
- *Music:* Many students love to sing, and nearly all love to listen. Find recordings to support your study of history and culture. Try compact discs. Make instruments in science to study sound. Dance.
- *Food:* Try foods from different places or that illustrate different scientific or mathematical applications. Make butter as an example of a physical change. When students study about George Washington, bring in George's favorite breakfast: hoe cakes and tea.
- *Real tools:* Have your students *seen* the simple tools they read about in science? Bring in wedges, screws, and pulleys. Encourage students to hunt for them also. Bring in a computer or toaster beyond repair, cut off the plug, and let the students take it apart.
- *Models:* Use physical models to provide opportunities to study hard-to-reach phenomena such as atoms, planets, rockets, or the human heart.
- *Graphic organizers:* Provide visual displays of your information (Bromley, Irwin-De Vitis, & Modlo, 1995). Try Venn diagrams to compare and contrast. Make an outline that students view before they read.
- *Guest speakers and visitors:* Bring in family members and other guests. Do you know someone who has seen war? Volunteered? Marched in a protest? Named a star? Escaped persecution? Written a book? Played professional sports? Learners' lives are enriched when they meet people with great accomplishments.
- *Field trips:* Be certain to prepare your students for the trip by building connections between their studies and what they will be experiencing in the field. List their questions before you go. Consider whether it would be appropriate for your students to record information during the trip. When you return, process the field trip by focusing on what students saw, heard, and learned. Find out if they have answered their questions. Connect questions to past and future study. Even a 10-minute walk can provide abundant learning experiences (Russell, 1990).

INTERACT

In his classic study of U.S. classrooms, Goodlad (1984) witnessed the predominance of "frontal practices," where teachers stood in front of the room, presenting information and briskly quizzing students on factual content. Thirty years later, it appears that teachers are still talking.

In one recent study, teachers talked *eight times* more than their students did (National Center for Education Statistics, 2003). Similarly, in a British study,

Teaching Tip 5.5

SHARE THE WEALTH

When you feel obliged to ask a question, try this: Ask the question. Then say, "No matter what the first answer is, I'm going to call on four more hands." Wait a few seconds, then call on four in a row. This strategy can increase student participation for both convergent and divergent questions.

teachers made 75% of the classroom discourse moves (Smith, Hardman, Wall, & Mroz, 2004). When students *do* talk, their utterances tend to be short and dependent upon the teachers' narrow requests for information. This is discouraging for all students, but the news gets worse. Students placed in low groups or tracks have poorer opportunities to interact with content (see Chorzempa & Graham's 2006 study of primary reading groups and Oakes's 2005 study of high schools). Additionally, the whole-class instruction that predominates in K–12 general education classrooms cuts opportunities for students with learning disabilities (Vaughn et al., 2001). Thus, exactly those students who need *enriched* opportunities to develop content and language mastery through interaction actually are granted *fewer*. Teaching Tip 5.5 gives one easy way to spread the participation.

Interaction is a critical component of good instruction for all students. Teaching is more than telling. Interaction allows students to build social skills, to refine their thinking, to consider alternative perspectives, to practice using language, and to provide ongoing assessment information for their teachers. Learning is personal, and students' reactions matter. As a result, teaching must be interactional; students must be active participants.

Active Participation

TEACHER PREP

Watch a middle school science teacher use *wipe boards* (or *whiteboards*) to encourage active participation for all her students. Find the video at the Merrill Teacher Prep Web site, Video Classroom, Special Education, Module 3, Video 2. Look how many more students were allowed to participate than if the teacher had called on just one student's raised hand. What is one way you might use wipe boards with your students?

Fortunately, many strategies can encourage each student to actively and overtly engage in the lesson. As you gather information about students' learning, experiences, and preferences, your interactions will vary by both participants and format. Sometimes you will interact directly with the students, and sometimes they will interact with each other. Sometimes your exchanges will be verbal, and sometimes they will be through actions, writings, or drawings. You need techniques that will allow more than one or two students to participate in both their interactions with you and with each other.

Figure 5.5 gives a list of 31 ideas for encouraging active participation. Some strategies are best for checking content mastery and others for sharing students' perspectives. Mastery strategies are listed first in each section. As you select ideas, remember that you need to use a variety of strategies, and the strategies you select should be consistent with your learners' needs and with your personal stance toward teaching.

Two themes run through these suggestions for active participation. First, active participation strategies break the traditional pattern of the teacher doing most of the talking while students either listen quietly or respond, one at a time, to the teacher's numerous questions. Second, the strategies provide tasks for students to complete so that you, the teacher, can determine whether and what students understand. These strategies promise to be more productive than asking "Does anyone have a question? Anyone *not* get it?" The bottom line: Do something that allows you to foster active participation and plentiful instruction.

FIGURE 5.5   *Active participation strategies: 31 ideas for encouraging interaction and active participation.*

Give prompts to discover what students know, think, feel, have experienced, and wonder.	

	Teacher–Student Interactions
"Tell Me"	1. *Choral response:* When questions have convergent, brief answers, all students respond at once instead of one at a time. Teacher records and discusses items with muddy responses.
	2. *Whip:* Everyone shares a brief response (word, phrase, or sentence) to a topic or question. Contributions move from one student to the next with no teacher intervention. Students are allowed to "pass."
	3. *Stand to share:* All stand when they have developed a response to a question such as, "What was an important point in the chapter?" One person shares aloud, and all with the same or similar responses sit. Sharing continues until all are sitting (Kagan, 1994).
	4. *Opinionnaire:* All respond privately to a set of statements related to the current topic, such as, "Efforts to clone humans are wrong." Responses can be formed as agree or disagree or as numbers that indicate degrees of agreement. Teacher leads a discussion to elicit students' responses.
	5. *Share a story:* Teacher elicits students' stories related to the topic. If there are many stories, students can tell their stories to smaller groups or to partners. For instance, "I have told you a story about crickets in my apartment. I would like to hear a true cricket story that you may have."
	6. *Student questions* (Dillon, 1988): Teacher provides time for students to formulate their questions about a topic. He might record them for discussion and study. For example, "We will be studying space. I have always wondered why stars twinkle. What do you wonder about space?"
"Show Me"	7. *Flash cards:* Individually or in groups students hold up color-coded or other flash cards in response to teacher's or peers' mastery questions. For example, teacher asks questions about the federal government, and students hold up red for legislative, yellow for executive, or blue for judicial. Students can also ask the questions.
	8. *Finger signals:* Students hold up numbers of fingers to respond to mastery questions (e.g., "How many sides on a triangle?"). Other gestures can also be used. For instance, "I will watch while you draw a triangle in the air."
	9. *Whiteboards:* Students record responses on individual boards, then show teacher or peers. Some examples include spelling words, cursive letter formation, French vocabulary, and brief math exercises.
	10. *Letter and number tiles:* Students have sets of ceramic, magnetic, or tag board tiles displaying letters of the alphabet or digits 0 through 9. They display their tiles in response to tasks from the teacher or peers. For instance, "Build an even number that is greater than 50." Or: "Round 5,723.86 to the tenths place. I will come around and check your tiles."
	11. *Comprehension check:* Students complete brief quizzes, written by teacher or pulled from existing materials, at the beginning or end of class. Students check their own work and analyze what they need help with before passing their papers to teacher.
	12. *Quick write:* Students respond in writing to a prompt. For example, "Before we read this chapter, please take a minute and write about a time when you felt powerless." Quick writes can spur discussion and allow all students to express feelings or experiences in writing, even if they choose not to share aloud. Quick writes are not graded.
	13. *Fuzzy points:* Near the end of a lesson, students anonymously record their fuzzy points, the concepts about which they are still unsure. Teacher collects and analyzes them for the next time.

FIGURE 5.5 *Continued.*

	Student–Student Interactions
"Tell Each Other" (Be sure to process these activities. Come together as a class and briefly share. Discuss findings.)	14. *Peer coach:* In pairs, students take turns serving as coach and coachee. Coach observes coachee solve a problem and provides praise and suggestions. Roles switch. Teacher circulates to check for accuracy and social skills (Kagan, 1994). 15. *Student-led recitation:* Students prepare written comprehension and challenge questions over course and reading material. They sit in a circle and take turns asking, answering, and evaluating each others' questions and responses (Dillon, 1988). 16. *Numbered heads together:* In small groups, students number off. Teacher (or a peer) asks a question, and group members put their heads together to discuss. Teacher calls on one number to respond for each group (Kagan, 1994). 17. *Toss the ball:* Students give a response to a factual or opinion question and toss a Koosh ball, Nerf ball, or other soft ball, to a peer, who becomes the next to answer or question. 18. *Talk to your partner:* Students turn and discuss with a nearby partner. For instance, "Tell your partner about an animal you know with protective coloration." 19. *Peer interview:* Students ask their partners questions about their experiences with a certain topic. 20. *Values line up:* Present a prompt that is likely to elicit a wide range of responses. For instance, "To help the environment, families should own only one car." Have students numerically rate their agreement with the statement and then line up in order of their numerical ratings, 1 to 10. Split the line in half and pair students with extreme scores (1 goes to 10). Instruct them to give their responses and rationales and then to paraphrase each other's points of view. Draw conclusions as a class once students are again seated. 21. *Scavenger hunt:* Prepare a scavenger hunt form that encourages discussion of students' varied backgrounds and knowledge. Allow students to circulate and record the names of peers who fit certain criteria. For instance, "Find someone who has seen a famous monument." You can also make the prompts content oriented. Students might be required to find the match for their chemical symbol, for instance.
"Show Each Other" (Process these activities, too.)	22. *Group chart:* In groups, students draw diagrams or charts to illustrate the content. Charts are displayed for class review and comparison. 23. *Group problem:* Each member of a small group is given a vital piece of information necessary to solve a problem. Only when students share their information can they solve the problem together. 24. *Snowballs:* Invite students to record their questions or perceptions on a sheet of paper. Then have them crumple the sheets into wads and, on your signal, toss them across the room. After the chaos subsides, students open the wad nearest them and respond to the question or add their own perspective in writing. Toss and respond a few times so that students can read a variety of perspectives. Process by asking for themes or questions that need to be addressed. 25. *Student quiz:* Students develop written quizzes to check their peers' mastery. They check the content before handing papers to teacher. As an option, students can complete quizzes in groups. 26. *Follow the leader:* One partner gives oral directions as the other partner tries to draw, make, or build a construction that fits the leader's description. Roles switch. Teacher leads discussion about effective communication. 27. *Sorts:* In small groups, students sort objects (such as leaves or small tools) or ideas (recorded on cards such as elements on the periodic table). In open sorts, students choose but do not reveal their criteria for sorting. Peers discern the criteria by observing groups. In closed sorts, students follow the grouping criteria given by the teacher or a peer. Older students can use multistage classifications; younger students may group by one attribute only.

FIGURE 5.5 *Continued.*

28. *Brainstorming and fact-storming:* Students in groups record as many ideas as they can generate related to a topic or solutions to a problem. Praise is given for fluency (number of ideas) and flexibility (variety of ideas). In fact-storming, students record as many relevant facts as they can. Facts can be grouped and labeled, or they can be placed on a chart for future revisions and additions.

29. *Partner journals:* Students can be paired anonymously or with friends. They respond to classroom activities and content by writing to each other. Teacher chooses whether to collect and review journals.

30. *Blackboard blitz:* During small-group work, representatives from each group simultaneously record their group's best ideas on the board. All students can view each others' ideas, and work continues while students write on the board (Kagan, 1994).

31. *Gallery tour:* Upon completion of individual or group projects, students place their projects on desks and tour the room to view other works. Students can respond to each other's works on sticky notes or on a response sheet for the author.

Sheltered Instruction

Your students who are English learners are relying on you to build in particular kinds of classroom interactions. Chapter 3 discussed the need for instruction for English learners to have an especially clear focus on the use of English through the setting of dual goals for every lesson (namely, language and content objectives) and through comprehensible input and comprehensible output (opportunities to produce spoken and written English). By sheltering your instruction, you help students work toward the triple goals of English acquisition, content mastery, and social growth. Figure 5.6 builds on those priorities by providing checkpoints for sheltering instruction.

In a sense, *every* student is an English learner. Every k–12 student should have opportunities to gain more powerful control over the English language, including the content-specific discourse considered "the language of the discipline." Students practice and refine their language through multiple opportunities to use it. Also, language provides a powerful vehicle for supporting content mastery. Meaningful opportunities to engage in elaborated, higher-level, subject-based conversations promote learning (Brophy, 1997). For these reasons, as you select strategies and plan and implement your lessons, ensure that you build in opportunities for students to use language frequently and purposefully. Review Figure 5.5 for supports for you in this goal by providing a variety of strategies to increase student interaction and talk.

Progress Monitoring

Frequent structured opportunities for interaction also provide you with feedback on students' progress and reactions. Some teachers rely on informal student feedback during their lessons: Are there dazed looks? Attentive gazes? Nods of approval? Nonverbal signals can be useful for adjusting instruction, but they are not always valid. Teachers may misinterpret students' cues—which may be culturally bound—or they may base their instructional decisions on a few unrepresentative students' responses. In addition to relying on nonverbal feedback, teachers often ask questions to check students' understanding: "Does everyone understand?" There are some drawbacks to using questions as a sole guide for encouraging interaction. One drawback is that the use of persistent questions from the teacher can serve to reinforce the power differential between teacher and students: Teacher asks, and students answer, and then await the

FIGURE 5.6 *Checkpoints for sheltering instruction.*

Supportive environment	☐ Reflects and values students' cultures and community norms ☐ Encourages language experimentation ☐ Fosters motivation (downplays explicit or negative corrections and reinforces progress)
Content focused	☐ Grade-level content standards ☐ Literacy objectives in reading, writing, listening, and speaking ☐ Develops social, academic, and specialized English ☐ Focuses on a limited number of key ideas ☐ Develops key vocabulary terms systematically
Context embedded	☐ Purposeful use of language ☐ Meaningful to students ☐ Ties to students' prior knowledge and experience ☐ Plentiful use of objects and activities that provide context (realia—or real items—props, images, recordings, and demonstrations)
Comprehensible input	☐ Modified text (simplified, alternate forms) ☐ Modified speech (caretaker speech: enunciation, slower rate, matches students' level, repetition) ☐ Use of primary language for support ☐ Guides instruction (clear directions, checks for understanding, reviews, opportunities to practice) ☐ Scaffolding (appropriate support)
Increased interaction	☐ Includes teacher–student content-driven conversations ☐ Includes student–student content-driven conversations ☐ Room is arranged for interaction ☐ Various groupings (pairs, small groups) ☐ Maximizes student talk ☐ All participants foster language use (wait time, elongated responses)
Emphasis on higher level-thinking	☐ Challenging content expectations ☐ Higher-level tasks such as evaluation and analysis ☐ Teach strategies for powerful learning

TEACHER PREP

One benefit of interaction is that students receive feedback on their performance. See paraprofessionals give plentiful feedback to their students in a special day class setting. Find the video at the Merrill Teacher Prep Web site, Video Classroom, Special Education, Module 9, Video 1. Think of one instance when you received accurate and specific feedback on your performance as a learner. How did that feedback help you learn or grow?

next question. The teacher may also draw faulty conclusions based on the sample of students who respond. Additionally, students do not need to be very old before they learn that admitting ignorance is not always perceived as a good thing to do.

Accomplished teachers listen, and they diligently search the faces and reactions of all their learners to modify their instruction. If you gather ongoing information about how students are learning and responding to the lesson, you will be better equipped to adjust your activities. Gathering and using feedback from students can help you modify your teaching and will foster learning.

Because teaching is interactional, students also deserve explicit and specific feedback. Timely and specific feedback improves learning for everyone. Give students clear and immediate information about their learning. If you use praise, precisely name students' appropriate efforts, and gently redirect efforts that are less than successful. Vary the form of your feedback to include oral, written, and nonverbal messages. Include both informal and formal messages to your students and their families.

The classroom belongs to all of you. Help students chart their own growth by sharing information about their progress and adjust your teaching based on what you learn from the students. What will you teach tomorrow? Your answer depends partly on your long-range plans, but it also depends on what happens in your classroom *today*. Teaching is more than telling.

CONSIDER HUMAN NATURE AND STUDENT NEEDS

Finally, when we start with the students, our instruction reflects students' current physical and emotional states, and it should reflect an understanding of human nature. What you know about how humans learn and behave should be reflected in your teaching. For example, we know that people are more likely to engage in activity if they are motivated to do so. Glasser (1986) states that humans have five motivations. These include the need to be safe, belong, acquire power, be free, and have fun. Your instruction will be more successful if you ensure that those needs are met.

Other examples abound. For instance, we know that people have limited ability to take in new information and that they need opportunities to process—to think about—what they hear. As a result, you will need to vary your activities within a single lesson. We know, too, that people tend to protect themselves from public displays of ignorance; they tend to avoid intellectual risks in large groups. For that reason, you will probably want to create a comfortable environment where students are free to express their questions and wonderful ideas. Using strategies such as partner discussion instead of whole-class discussion can lower students' perceptions of personal risk. Another critical human need is the need to be treated as an individual deserving dignity and respect. Each of your lessons should incorporate human nature in order to propel learning. Teaching Tip 5.6 includes a concrete example of how you can capitalize on how human memory works.

We must also recognize that at different times in their lives, humans vary predictably: They change, or develop, over time. You will need to carefully observe your students to observe their current levels of physical, emotional, and cognitive development. Watch their physical skills, the ways they interpret problems, the ways they play or talk together on the school grounds, and listen to the issues they consider important. From your readings, observations, and conversations, your understanding of your students will become richer and more reliable explanations of human development.

TEACHER PREP

Would you like more opportunities to see students from a variety of stages in order to brush up on how students change through the years? Many videos are available at the Merrill Teacher Prep Web site Video Classroom in the Child Development section. What characteristic differences do you detect in how students at various levels think, talk, and interact?

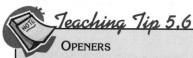
Teaching Tip 5.6

OPENERS

Because of the **primacy effect,** people tend to remember the first things they hear and see. Make your first minutes count! Start your day or your lesson with an opener that catches students' attention and draws them into the content. Here are some samples.

- "Here's a picture of my dog. In your group, estimate how many teeth a dog has." (The lesson that follows is on digestion, which starts in the mouth.)
- "Use these 12 square tiles. How many different rectangles can you and your partner build?" (The lesson that follows is on factors.)
- "Use this string to shape an outline of Peru. We'll compare in two minutes." (The lesson that follows is on South American geography.)
- "Read these headlines about the Bay of Pigs and pick the one that is false." (The lesson that follows is on President Kennedy's foreign policy.)
- "This song by the Dixie Chicks is a protest. Listen and discuss: What are they protesting? What other songs do you know that protest?" (The lesson that follows is on the First Amendment.)

In addition to being memorable, openers allow you make curricular links, practice past concepts, and address standards or topics that might not otherwise fit.

Head's up: There is a **recency effect** too. People also tend to remember the *last* thing they hear. What does this tell you about how you close your lesson and day?

Your instruction will not only need to take into account students' current levels of functioning, but it will also need to propel students' growth toward sophisticated ways of thinking, moving, and acting. To encourage development, teachers can provide varied experiences in rich physical and social environments and encourage students to confront their current understandings and ways of thinking and acting.

Additionally, your instruction must respond to the needs of your particular students. Chapter 3 encouraged you to get to know your students and use them as your instructional starting point. Your students probably display a variety of overlapping needs such as English acquisition, giftedness, and special education requirements. Responsive approaches introduced in Chapter 3 include Universal Design, differentiated instruction, and strategies for challenging gifted learners. Modifications and accommodations propel you on your journey. As you build your skills, you will continue to add to your teaching repertoire and foster student learning.

Finally, considering human needs and nature entails you looking beyond students' similarities and facing again the fact that each of your students comes to you with a unique constellation of characteristics, with an idiosyncratic set of strengths and issues. You must value all students and the contributions they will make to your life and work. When asked what you teach, perhaps your first response will be, "I teach *people.* "

Clearly your efforts to consider students' needs—both in common and unique—will require you to continue to grow and learn as a teacher. One area that will no doubt require your ongoing attention is technology and its potential to enrich your instruction for each of your students.

TECHNOLOGY AND INSTRUCTION

Used wisely, technology can dramatically enhance each component of your instruction. In a multitude of ways, technology can help you COME IN. Here are some examples.

Connect

A critical attribute of technology is that it increases *connectivity* in our lives, and so it can during your instruction. The Internet allows students to connect to the *outside world* and its events in an instant. Antarctica? The Amazon? Alabama? Argentina? Places that may be far from us physically can be virtually accessible in real time through devices such as webcams with Internet feeds. (Try http://camcentral.com, or search "webcam" and your place of interest for a glimpse of the world as it is right now.) Or read newspapers from around the world (see world newspapers in Web Sites). In online news projects such as National Neo (http://www.alphasmart.com/nationalneo/keepintouch.asp), students report local news by carrying Alpha Smart keyboards to different events, composing stories, and uploading them for others to read. Similarly, students also are increasingly creating and sharing their own podcasts to capture the world from their perspectives. When I searched for "student podcasts," I was treated to audio presentations from students in a number of countries. See the Web sites at this chapter's end for some sources that allow students to travel around the world in an instant.

Electronic technology can also facilitate connections to *action*. Because it has asynchronous and synchronous capabilities, connected computer-based technology can link students with action projects and provide a forum for virtual gathering and planning. For example, students can confer about issues together in a discussion board, or they can e-mail experts such as artists and social scientists. They might join scientific efforts by gathering local data and submitting them to larger projects. One example is the JASON project (http://jason.org).

The Internet also connects *people*. Consider your students' electronic connections: They create and visit spaces on My Space. They instant message, text message, e-mail, and use cell phones. Instructionally, we can harness students' connections via mechanisms such as discussion boards on Web sites. When they contribute to discussion boards, students share perspectives and ideas, which can equalize students' social power. For a boost in finding faraway correspondents for your class, including electronic mentors, try http://epals.com, which has registrants in nearly 200 countries.

Organize

Technology's potential to help us get and stay organized is prodigious, as we know from our personal digital assistants and home finance spreadsheets. Technology within the classroom can be used, too, to help teachers and students alike stay organized. Documents such as seating charts, computer schedules, class agendas, and plan books all are easily modified and are useful organizational tools. Chapter 8, Managing the Learning Environment, provides more information on such aids.

Technology can also serve as an indispensable tool for us in presenting information in organized ways and for teaching students to organize information. Graphic organizers such as concept maps, Venn diagrams, and retrieval charts can be created electronically, first as a demonstration, and then by students, to help students see superordinate structures and connections among data or ideas. (Search the Internet for "electronic graphic organizers".) Spreadsheets, used with students of all ages, can help them quickly find patterns that would otherwise be hidden. Common software, such as word processing and presentation programs, allows students to create outline versions of their work with a few mouse clicks. Students wishing to make decisions about priorities in content-related lists can use more specialized tools to organize and analyze information. Using Intel's Visual Ranking Tool (http://www97.intel.com/en/ThinkingTools/VisualRanking/), for instance, small groups of students rank inventions by order of importance. The tool creates statistical correlations between one group's list with the lists of other groups and the class total and allows the teacher to probe students' thinking by posing additional tasks on the screen. These applications are examples of technology's potential for helping us to organize our world in order to find connections, solve problems, and make informed decisions.

Model

Technology greatly expands our ability to supply good instructional models for our students. Students may view, for example, video clips that demonstrate how to change an oil filter, serve a tennis ball, or splint a sprained ankle. Multimedia clips of a performance are helpful because they can be magnified, played at variable speeds, and repeated endlessly as necessary. Software that models native pronunciation of a language (English or other target languages) is helpful for the same reason: The computerized model never tires of being asked to repeat a phrase. Electronic models, then, can help you differentiate your instruction by allowing students who need particular kinds of help to view models targeted to their needs.

Additionally, technology allows us to more easily capture and share appropriate *student* models, or work samples. Ask for the permission of students (and families, as appropriate) to create and keep electronic copies of their work to serve as models for future students. Sample work created by other students tends to be very well received; such models show students what is possible by someone in their peer group. And *electronic* student models are especially helpful because they are easy to store, take up little space, do not fall apart over time, and—if shared on the Web or distributed to students—can be viewed by many students repeatedly and simultaneously. If you use electronic models, take precautions to ensure that students submit their own work by structuring the assignment carefully and by providing a variety of models that are different from each other and are still of high quality.

Enrich

Given their digital nature, electronic resources can easily be used to enrich whole-class instruction or can be provided during small-group or individual work time to students who have targeted interests or needs. For example, in preparation to read one of William Shakespeare's plays, a high school English class divides into six computer-based stations to: listen to an MP3 recording of a portion of the work, examine maps of Elizabethan England, work with an interactive timeline of world events during the period, view period art, read Shakespeare's biography, or research world events that influenced the work. The teacher decides whether to assign students, based on need, to particular stations. For instance, students who may struggle in reading the play may benefit from listening to a performance of the play first. Alternatively, the teacher may allow students to follow their interests in selecting stations. Popular stations may be duplicated so that more than one computer is dedicated to them.

Interact

Technology can enhance opportunities for interaction among students and teachers. Through e-mail, chat rooms, and discussion boards, for example, we extend opportunities for content-based interactions beyond the school bell. During school, technology can foster student-to-student interaction through activities such as small-group projects that create multimedia presentations, interest centers (as in the Shakespeare example), and activities with interactive whiteboards. Technology can also encourage students to interact with the content. Web sites at this chapter's close put students in touch with some materials likely to enhance their engagement in the content. For example, virtual mathematics manipulatives are likely to encourage students to dive into challenging problems beyond what they might attempt given solely a paper and pencil. Much software, computer games, Webquests (addressed in Chapter 6), and computer-based simulations all invite students to interact with concepts and skills in potentially engaging settings. To see for yourself, explore the ancient world by downloading a free copy of Discover Babylon at http://www.discoverbabylon.org/.

Nature and Needs

Finally, technology also presents resources that, when used wisely and evaluated carefully, can help teachers capture human nature and address highly specific needs. In terms of human nature, students tend to find new technologies to be motivating. Good software addresses human needs such as the need for feedback on performance, the desire to explore and test ideas, and the benefits of multimodal presentations. Given the popularity of computer gaming and its ability to motivate many people, for instance, experts in a number of fields are currently seeking ways to harness the power of video games to teach critical thinking in the schools (Federation of American Scientists, 2006). Thus, computer-based technology at its best presents content in ways that students find motivating and that are consistent with their developmental abilities.

Computer-based technology also provides avenues to more easily address a variety of student needs (Wahl & Duffield, 2005). Teacher-created Web pages, for instance, can differentiate instruction by providing assignments that differ in terms of their levels, interests, opportunities for interaction, and products (Cunningham & Billingsley, 2003). Further, as Chapter 3 explained, assistive technology addresses physical disabilities to enhance students' access to information and their opportunities to create via the computer. Technology can also provide strategies to address specific needs such as behavioral disorders and has good potential—when teachers plan carefully—to help students with moderate to severe disabilities find success in inclusive settings (Downing & Eichinger, 2003).

PARTING WORDS

In his quote at the beginning of this chapter, Dr. Seuss celebrated the "brains in your head." If you are reading this text's chapters straight through, you are at the halfway point. Where have the "brains in your head" taken you in your journey thus far? Through Chapter 1 you considered teaching as a complex activity influenced by context and aimed at promoting learner growth. In Chapter 2, you developed a stance toward education to serve as your guide in managing the complexity of teaching and keeping your priorities clear. Chapter 3 provided a rationale and some strategies for placing your students at the center of your instructional decisions, and Chapter 4 helped you to plan instruction at different levels to address students' needs.

This chapter, Chapter 5, attempted to put "feet in your shoes" (thanks again, Dr. Seuss) by providing instructional principles that can give you a push on your journey. Its advice provides mechanisms to bring your growing professional knowledge base to life every day in the classroom. You COME IN as a teacher when you:

Connect
Organize
Model
Enrich
Interact
Consider nature and needs

You provide instruction that emphasizes the centrality of the student and the thoughtfulness required in good teaching and careful decision making. Chapter 6 provides another nudge forward by presenting a variety of instructional models that can enhance student learning in meaningful ways. Let's go.

WEB SITES

http://jc-schools.net/
Jefferson County Schools. Click on "Teachers" and look at the Quick Links. The PowerPoint collection alone is worth the trip. See the online science resources as well.

http://www.historychannel.com
The History Channel. Listen to historic speeches such as Martin Luther King's "I have a dream" speech and Amelia Earhart's discussion of the future of women in flying. I can imagine starting class each day with "This day in History."

http://www.loc.gov
Library of Congress. An incredible source for American and world history and culture.

http://www.exploratorium.edu
Museum of Science, Art, and Human Perception. An award-winning site, this one will appeal to students and includes many resources for educators. I enjoyed viewing the mouse stem cells at the "Digital Library" and the "10 cool sites."

http://www.funbrain.com
Fun Brain. Go to the Teachers Center to find games that provide good practice across the subjects, primarily for elementary content. Otherwise, play online Sudoku, the only way that wretched game should be played. Try the related Gamequarium at http://www.gamequarium.com.

http://nga.gov
  National Gallery of Art. Take a look at the online education programs, NGA Kids, and the loan programs. The gallery will send you loan materials through the U.S. mail. I have tried it; it works!

http://www.nationalgeographic.com
  National Geographic Society. The world at the click of a mouse! Go to the site index for a listing of resources. Try going to "kids" and diving in the Great Barrier Reef.

http://enlvm.usu.edu/ma/nav/index.jsp
  National Library of Virtual Manipulatives. This site gives mathematics manipulatives-based activities across the math strands and grade levels. Excellent challenge problems are provided to use in a center for early finishers or for differentiating instruction.

http://www.nytimes.com/learning
  New York Times for learning. Try out the Learning Network Web Explorer online tours. Take a look at the "Conversation starters."

http://www.si.edu
  Smithsonian Institute. Rich resources for teachers and students. Take a look at the ideas for podcasting.

http://teach-nology.com/
  Teach-nology. This site is a Web portal that offers free resources, links, and support tools to support educators in teaching with technology. Many resources are free, but access to some is limited to members.

http://www.world-newspapers.com
  World Newspapers. This site gives news from English-language newspapers around the world. See what they think in Benin and Bangladesh. Picture having your students contrast different—and international—perspectives on the same event.

  Also, to include images for your lessons, go to Google (http://www.google.com) and do an image search for your topic.

OPPORTUNITIES TO PRACTICE

1. Use the form in Figure 5.7 to analyze a lesson. You have three choices:

   - Analyze a video clip of a second-grade mathematics lesson using centers (found at the Merrill Teacher Prep Web site Video Classroom, Educational Technology, Module 1, Video 1).

   - Analyze a video clip of a seventh-grade physical science lesson (Merrill Teacher Prep Web site Video Classroom, Science Methods, Module 11, Video 1).

   - Analyze one of your own plans, perhaps one you wrote as you studied Chapter 4.

2. Take another look at the fossils lesson in Figure 4.13. Use the lesson analysis in Figure 5.7 to analyze whether, during the lesson, I followed my own advice. Record any evidence you find and then draw a conclusion for each of the six pieces of advice.

3. Implement and practice one or more aspects of COME IN through mini-lessons. Try the following examples to get you started:

   - Draw a semantic map or some other graphic organizer for a piece of text that either you or your students will read in the coming days. A concept map of this text, found in Figure 5.8, offers an example.

   - Write a daily agenda and share it with your class. Invite students' reactions and modifications.

   - Write and give a set of directions for how you want students to spend the first five minutes in your classroom each day. Use the advice for directions given in Teaching Tip 5.3. page 120.

   - Model a new behavior, either for your students or for a willing friend. Select a skill or technique that is unfamiliar to your audience and, after modeling the skill, ask for feedback on which elements of your modeling were most successful.

   - Plan to use one active participation strategy (Figure 5.5) in an upcoming lesson. If you are not currently teaching, select a strategy

FIGURE 5.7 *Lesson analysis: COME IN.*

ice	i ence
onnect	To prior knowledge: To important ideas or the real world: To action: Participants:
rganize	Content: Time and activities:
odel	Draw attention to critical attributes: Use appropriate number and pace of repetitions:
nrich	Provide rich experiences:
nteract	Strategies for active participation (verbal? written?): Sheltering Instruction: Progress Monitoring:
ature and eeds	Human nature: Developmental needs:

FIGURE 5.8 *Concept map of K–12 Classroom Teaching textbook.*

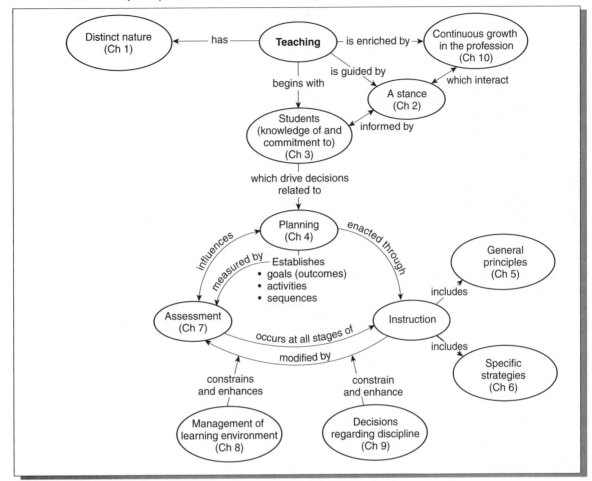

from Figure 5.5 that could have been used during a lesson you recently experienced as a student.

- Add one resource to your classroom materials. Consider adding to your picture file, or find or construct a model for a concept that is difficult to learn.

- Commit to opening an upcoming lesson with an activity that accesses students' prior knowledge. Seek to value different cultural experiences that students share. If you are not teaching now, have a conversation with a friend about an aspect of your friend's life with which you are unfamiliar. Remember to protect your friend's dignity and to appreciate what you learn.

- Watch young students play either at recess or during unstructured class time. What is the range of differences you note in their physical development? Their social development? Their reasoning? How could you improve your instruction by using this specific information? If you are not teaching, try observing people at a playground or other public place. What conclusions can you reach about physical, social, and moral functioning?

4. Write a letter or presentation for families that describes your principles of instruction. How will you teach their children? Why have you chosen those principles? Share your letter or notes with a colleague and then, if appropriate, with the families of your students.

Before You Begin Reading

Chapter Six

Your prior experience with instructional strategies will influence what you learn from this chapter. Before you read, check your familiarity with some of Chapter 6's teaching strategies by completing the following chart. Use your results to focus your efforts as you read, and check your ideas against those presented in the chapter.

Warm-Up Exercise for Instructional Strategies

Strategy	Rate your level of familiarity*	List bulleted phrases that come to mind when you think of this strategy.
1. Classroom questions	1 2 3 4	
2. Direct instruction	1 2 3 4	
3. Inquiry	1 2 3 4	
4. Cooperative learning	1 2 3 4	

*1 = I have no idea; 4 = I am a pro at using this strategy

CHAPTER *Six*

Instructional Strategies

"The difficulty in life is the choice."

—George Moore

Teaching is intended to foster change, and teaching is more than telling. Given these two propositions on teaching, how will you teach? Selecting the strategies you will employ for your lessons may be difficult. You will need to consider the needs, the research, and characteristics of your students, the demands of the content and context, and your personal stance as you choose instructional strategies. However, it can also be a great pleasure and give you a sense of power to select from a number of well-honed strategies those that you will use to respond to students' learning needs. The greater the number of instructional strategies that you master, the better able you will be to select strategies that encourage student growth. This chapter presents seven instructional strategies or approaches that can serve as the basis for your instructional repertoire. But first it addresses an essential element that must underlie your use of any instructional strategy: classroom questions.

QUESTIONS IN THE CLASSROOM

A great deal of talk can be heard in classrooms, and much of that talk is comprised of questions. Decades of research have yielded some trends about these plentiful questions. Here are six.

1. *Teachers ask many, many questions.* In fact, in one estimate teachers spend one-third to one-half of their day asking questions (Black, 2001).
2. *Students ask very few questions* (Dillon, 1988a). Dillon (1990) reviewed elementary and secondary school studies and found that each pupil asks an average of only one question per month.
3. *Teachers ask questions for a variety of purposes,* such as to check for understanding, prompt thinking, maintain lesson flow, hold student attention, and punish misbehavior.
4. *Classroom questioning exchanges are typically rapid and follow a predictable pattern* (Cazden, 1986; Dillon, 1990; Good & Brophy, 1987). In the typical sequence, known as the IRE pattern, the teacher *initiates* a question, one student *responds*, and then the teacher *evaluates* the response. A new question from the teacher usually follows.
5. *Students receive different questions based on teachers' perceptions of them.* Unwittingly, teachers sometimes use their questions to reinforce stereotypes and limit learning opportunities. For instance, students who are perceived as of low academic ability get more factually based questions and receive less time to answer them (Cotton, 2001). In research reviewed by Walsch and Sattes (2005), a sizable group of students have zero questioning interactions in class, and a small group of

"target students" (typically white males) receive a disporportionate amount of the teacher's attention in questioning.

6. *Research has not clearly linked the type or level of a question to the type or level of the response* (Cotton, 2001; Dillon, 1988b; Good & Brophy, 1987). Therefore, teachers cannot assume that asking higher-level questions will necessarily prompt higher-level responses, or the reverse.

From the research, we can conclude that teachers tend to ask many questions, and those questions are often not used to their best instructional advantage (e.g., Becker, 2000; Wimer, Ridenour, Thomas, & Place, 2001). You need to be thoughtful about your use of questions. How can you ensure that you harness the power of these potential learning tools in a way that helps you enact your stance and encourages student growth? Fortunately, research offers some promising practices. First, carefully planned questions can enhance students' opportunities to learn (e.g., Blosser, 1990; Lenski, 2001; Marzano, Pickering, & Pollock, 2001). Think about your purposes for asking questions and what you will do with the results. Make a plan to be equitable in the questions you ask and how you respond to them. Second, ensure that you listen to students' responses. Slow down the typically rapid pace of interactions and take time to appreciate students' thinking. Use wait time (Rowe, 1986). Wait three to five seconds before selecting a student to respond to a question, and wait again before responding to the student's reply. Third, ask fewer questions; encourage students to ask more.

Research supports the power of *student questions* as mechanisms that help students read with a purpose, pursue meaningful investigations, and learn in deep and connected ways (Becker, 2000; Chin & Brown, 2000; Costa, Caldeira, Gallastegui, & Otero, 2000; Middlecamp & Nickel, 2000; Orsborn, Patrick, Dixon, & Moore, 1995; Sternberg, 1994; vanZee, Iwasyk, Kurose, Simpson, & Wild, 2001). Teachers can encourage students' questions by providing time and opportunities to ask them and by using specific strategies to support students' question formation and pursuit. Teaching Tip 6.1 gives a few ideas for alternatives to asking questions. Your plans to encourage language use and to maximize the benefit of questions in your classroom will be embedded within your decisions about the strategies you will use to teach your students.

SELECTING INSTRUCTIONAL STRATEGIES

Look back to your work in the Before You Begin Reading section of this chapter. How many strategies were familiar to you? Teachers tend to teach the way they were taught. It is tempting to select strategies that feel comfortable and familiar, but part of good teaching involves taking risks and trying ideas that may, at least initially, fall beyond the realm of comfort. Several factors weigh into the choice of instructional strategy, including your stance, your students, the research, and the context.

One of the primary guides you can use in deciding how to teach your students is your stance toward education. Your hopes for students' futures, your knowledge of how people learn, and your convictions about what it means to teach well will all have direct implications for the methods you select. If you are convinced, for instance, that people learn through working together and through experience, you will necessarily choose strategies that provide for social interaction and firsthand experience. If you believe the purpose of education is the transmission of a core body of knowledge, you will select strategies that help you share information effectively. You may wish to again pull out the stance you developed through Chapter 2 and take some brief notes on what your convictions tell you about how you need to teach. (If you completed Figure 2.4, your work here is easy.)

Second, No Child Left Behind requires the use of research-based instructional methods. Slavin (2003) explains "scientifically based research" studies as those that employ experimental or quasi-experimental designs with random assignment, if possible. Put simply, studies implement an instructional product or method with one randomly selected set of students then compare their progress with those of students who received a different treatment. Researchers use statistical methods to test the likelihood that differences in the groups' scores might arise by chance. Those differences that are highly unlikely are deemed "statistically significant." The federal government has established the What Works Clearinghouse to serve as a "trusted source of scientific evidence of what works in education." You can visit it at http://www.whatworks.ed.gov. Empirical studies can, then, help you select your strategies by answering questions such as "How well has this strategy worked with other groups?" and "What happened when it was employed?"

Empirical studies, according to Slavin (2003), have not been a major criterion for educational decisions in the past, but studies can support teachers in steering clear of untested innovations and provide evidence for schools to use as they justify their programs that receive federal funding. Empirical studies can give information about how strategies have worked with other students who have characteristics and developmental levels that are similar to those of your students. For instance, there is support in the research to indicate that students with low achievement (Baker, Gersten, & Lee, 2002) and learning disabilities (Swanson, 2001; Swanson & Sachse-Lee, 2000) can benefit from **direct instruction,** a strategy presented later in the chapter.

Although the effectiveness of many strategies is documented through research that links the teaching strategy with student outcomes such as increased academic achievement (e.g., Marzano et al., 2001), in general, research does not point to any one "best" instructional strategy. For instance, in comparing the practices of teachers judged highly effective in encouraging mathematics achievement and those who were not, researchers found no discrete set of practices that was held in common by the effective teachers (Smith, Hardman, Wall, & Mroz, 2004). Research is clearer in providing information related to questions such as "Under what conditions is this strategy useful?" and "For whom?"

For this reason it is also important to gather systematic information about your own students (Grant & Sleeter, 1998; Horgan, 1995) and their responses to instructional strategies. Chapter 3 provided some strategies to learn about your students. These included, for instance, attitude surveys, informal interviews, drawings, and journal writings. Chapter 7 suggests many ways to track students' progress so that you can make informed instructional decisions.

The content and learning goals can also suggest potentially useful instructional strategies. Some of the strategies presented in this chapter focus, for example, on information mastery, and others focus on the processes by which knowledge is created, or the processes of inquiry. Though all subject matters can benefit from a discovery approach, inquiry is a special focus of science educators.

Your selection of instructional strategies, then, will be guided by your stance, your knowledge of your students, and your knowledge of each strategy's potential for accomplishing certain purposes. Each strategy places distinct demands on the teacher and learner. As you make decisions about the ways you will teach your students, consider how well a strategy will encourage the intended growth of your students.

DEDUCTIVE AND INDUCTIVE STRATEGIES

> **Deductive Strategies:** general rule → specific examples
>
> **Inductive Strategies:** specific examples → general rule

One useful distinction among strategies is the point at which the major concept, skill, or understanding is stated during the lesson. Lessons that state the concept or understanding early in the lesson are deemed *deductive*. Using **deductive strategies,** the teacher states the concept or major learning promptly and then provides practice on that concept throughout the remainder of the lesson. Deductive strategies reason from the general to the specific: They present general rules, then specific examples. **Inductive strategies** do the reverse. In an inductive, or discovery, lesson the teacher provides specific data and guides students toward discerning a general rule or rules from those data. The major concept, skill, or understanding in an inductive lesson is not explicitly stated until later in the lesson, and it is usually stated by students.

You will want to master both deductive and inductive strategies because each can address different needs and foster different kinds of student skills and attitudes. Both have been found to be effective in increasing student achievement (Marzano et al., 2001). How often you use each of the contrasting strategies will depend on your own convictions about education, your learners, and the particular setting within which you find yourself.

A SAMPLING OF INSTRUCTIONAL STRATEGIES

The remainder of this chapter presents seven instructional approaches:

> *TEACHER PREP*
>
> To watch a high school chemistry teacher lead an inductive lesson on Charles's Law, go to the Merrill Teacher Prep Web site, Video Classroom, Educational Psychology, Module 7, Video 1. Why might the teacher have elected to use inquiry rather than merely explaining the formula?

1. Direct instruction
2. Inquiry training
3. Concept attainment
4. Learning cycle
5. Concept formation
6. Unguided inquiry
7. Cooperative learning

Each is presented first through a description, then a listing of lesson stages using the open-body-close format, next an example, and finally a discussion of strengths and criticisms.

Please note that the examples are meant to be streamlined so that you can quickly and clearly focus on the critical attributes of the strategy. The teachers in the sample lessons should all have conducted a good deal of work that is not evident in the brief description of their lessons. Namely, they should have studied their content standards and determined important ideas. They should have preassessed students to determine appropriate objectives based on their grade-level standards. They should have grouped students based on a selection of relevant concerns such as student interest, English language level, learning profile, and special needs. They should have built instruction from the ground up (remember Universal Design?) to meet these various needs. Some of the lessons include technology, and all employ the advice for instruction presented in Chapter 5 (COME IN). Note that most lessons have plentiful opportunities for students to interact and develop academic language, and most of the examples include context-embedded settings for the students to work with important ideas in realistic ways, thus sheltering instruction for English learners and attempting to enhance motivation for all students. Each of the lessons includes one or two hints to how the teacher differentiated instruction to meet student needs; these hints are meant to remind you that a myriad of instructional decisions come into play during any single lesson and that instructional strategies are employed in the context of these many decisions.

Direct Instruction

The direct instruction model is one of the most widely used and helpful deductive strategies. Direct instruction, sometimes called "explicit instruction," allows teachers to impart information or skills straightforwardly to their students and to help students master strategies for learning. The direct instruction format is flexible, and because one of the teacher's primary responsibilities is to present information, it fills a vital need in most classrooms. Particularly in today's climate, when most teachers feel pressure to help students master standards in an efficient manner, direct instruction is popular.

Description of the Direct Instruction Model In a directed lesson, the teacher systematically presents information related to an objective and carefully guides students' participation to ensure mastery. The emphasis is on efficient teacher presentation and eventual student command of a convergent set of objectives. Control over information or skills initially resides with the teacher, who relinquishes control as students first practice under the teacher's supervision and then eventually demonstrate independent mastery.

Immediate and specific feedback is an important part of guided practice.

Scott Cunningham/Merrill

Stages of the Direct Instruction Model   There are a few versions of direct instruction. In the seven-step model (Hunter, 1982), the directed lesson begins with the teacher's statement of his expectations for student behavior throughout the lesson. For example, the teacher may remind his students: "I need to see you sitting up straight and staying in your seats throughout this lesson." That statement of expectations is missing from the five-step version of the direct instruction model, but its reduced number of steps may make the five-step model easier to integrate into daily planning.

In the direct instruction lesson, the teacher provides a set for learning, gives focused input, helps the students practice, ensures that they mastered the objective, and then encourages them to practice on their own. As you read through the five stages of the model, found in Figure 6.1, remember that the model provides a mere blueprint for structuring lessons. Some teachers think of the stages as options from which they can choose, so not every lesson contains all five (or seven) steps. The length of a lesson can vary so that it may take a number of sessions to complete all of the stages. Also, through a teacher's ongoing assessment of student performance, he may decide to employ some back-and-forth movement between the lesson stages. For instance, students' performance during guided practice may indicate the need for further input rather than a move forward to closure. The steps of the direct instruction model are generic, so this lesson format is used by many teachers throughout the day.

A Sample Directed Lesson   Figure 6.2 presents a brief example that presents a skill, cursive letter formation.

FIGURE 6.1   *Stages of the direct instruction model.*

Open	1. *Anticipatory set*
	  a. Focus: Briefly gain the students' attention.
	  b. Objective: State the lesson's objective in student-friendly language.
	  c. Purpose: Tell students why this objective is important.

Body	2. *Input* Provide clear information related to the objective. One or more of the following may be appropriate: • Present definitions. • Share critical attributes. • Give examples and nonexamples. • Model. • Check for understanding, usually through active participation devices. 3. *Guided practice* Allow students to practice the objective under your supervision. Circulate to provide feedback to all learners. Employ praise–prompt–leave, wherein you give specific praise related to a student's effort, provide directions about what to improve, and then leave to check another student.
Close	4. *Closure* Observe all students performing the objective without your assistance. A performance, a brief test, or an active participation device (recall Figure 5.5) can help you check mastery. 5. *Independent practice* Students practice the newly acquired objective on their own, often as homework or during individual work time. (Note: Some versions of the direct instruction model place independent practice before closure; however, that arrangement does not allow teachers to assess mastery before students practice alone.)

FIGURE 6.2 A sample direct instruction lesson.

Objective: Third-grade students will correctly form the lowercase letter *t* in cursive.	
Anticipatory set (Open)	1. Focus: "Watch me write a few words in cursive on the board and see if you can determine what they all have in common." "You are right! They all have the cursive letter *t*." 2. Objective: "By the time you leave for lunch, each of you will be able to write *t* in cursive." 3. Purpose: "*T* is important because it will help with lots of other letters we will be learning to write in cursive. Learning to write *t* will make your cursive job easier. Besides, we cannot spell *Natalie* or *Xochitl* without *t*!"
Input (Body)	4. Model: "Watch me as I form the letter *t* on the board." (Teacher describes his actions as he forms five *t*s on the board.) 5. Critical attribute: "Notice that the vertical part of *t* is closed, not like *l*. Also notice that I cross the *t* from left to right." 6. Check for understanding: Teacher draws incorrect *t*s and correct ones. He allows students to exclaim, "No! No!" or "Yes!" as he models, checking whether students are aware of the critical characteristics of the letter. "You seem ready to try your own *t*s! Let's go!"
Guided practice	7. Students use wipe boards with dry erase markers to make *t*s. The teacher selected these materials instead of pencils because he has a student with weak grip strength. Students like wipe boards better anyway. • Teacher circulates and checks each student's progress. "Raymond, you are holding your pencil just right! Remember that *t* doesn't have a loop. Close it up. I will be back to check on you soon." • Teacher has a pen with an adaptive grip ready if his student needs it.
Closure (Close)	8. "I have seen many excellent *t*s! We will do one more for the record. Please take out a piece of scratch paper. Write your name at the top and then form your best *t* for me. Make three or four *t*s if you like!" (Teacher can collect and check the slips later or circulate now and mark them as correct.)
Independent practice	9. If the students do not demonstrate mastery during closure, teacher will provide additional instruction. If the objective is mastered, teacher tells students "Aha! Remarkable *t*s! Please practice your *t*s on the whiteboard or in the salt box during center time today."

Strengths and Criticisms of Direct Instruction Research generally supports the effectiveness of direct instruction. In a meta-analysis reviewing more than 350 sources on direct instruction, Adams and Engelman (1996) found that direct instruction was highly effective in supporting student achievement. Slavin (1997) similarly found some forms of direct instruction to be effective in teaching basic skills, primarily in elementary-grade reading and mathematics. Baker, Gersten, and Lee (2002) also found explicit instruction effective for supporting mathematics acheivement for students with low achievement.

The strength of direct instruction lies in the fact that it is carefully sequenced to provide key information, to lead the students in supervised practice, and then to finally release them for independent work after they demonstrate mastery of the content. Direct instruction provides an efficient mechanism to address one central purpose of education: to pass information and skills from one generation to the next. Direct instruction shows that even when a teacher is primarily sharing information, she can do so much more than by just telling. She can carefully steer students toward control over new information or skills.

It is perhaps not surprising that direct, explicit teaching is now highly prevalent across the nation, given current interests in students' acquisition of basic literacy and mathematics skills. Also, direct instruction is comfortable for many new teachers because most directed lessons follow a predictable path, and the teacher retains control over most decisions during the lesson. Further, direct instruction exemplifies some of the principles of instruction from Chapter 5: It is highly organized, it makes use of modeling, and it is interactive.

One criticism of direct instruction offered by some (e.g., Coles, 2000) is that direct instruction's focus on the transmission of information or skills is too narrow. Because it is fully deductive, with the teacher presenting important concepts and students then practicing them, direct instruction is sometimes criticized as encouraging student passivity. The teacher retains primary control over the content, over the pace of delivery, and over selection of learning activities. Students have limited choices and control in a directed lesson. Also, direct instruction may not connect to the life of the learner or use enriched resources as readily as other instructional strategies might. It may also decrease student motivation to learn (as described by Flowers, Hancock, & Joyner, 2000).

Finally, despite its potential power, some of the research documenting the effects of direct instruction offers mixed results. This is the case in the use of directed teaching in literacy instruction today. Although some recent studies support the effectiveness of direct instruction (e.g., Din, 2000; Yu & Rachor, 2000), not every study does (e.g., MacIver & Kemper, 2002; St. John, Manset, Chung, & Worthington, 2001).

Given its strengths and weaknesses, when, if at all, will you use direct instruction? Direct instruction may be helpful when (1) it is important that all students master the same objectives to a similar degree, (2) you are interested in efficient use of time, (3) it may not be safe for students to discover concepts, and (4) students start from similar background experiences.

As a practical indicator of when it may be appropriate to use direct instruction, watch for telltale signs. When you have the urge to begin a lesson with the words "Please open to page 42" and then march your students straight through some exercises, please think *direct instruction*. Your students will almost certainly have a higher chance of success if you teach to the text's objective but structure your lesson using stages of the directed lesson. Teaching Tip 6.2 will help you use direct instruction during lessons and other times too.

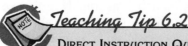

Teaching Tip 6.2

DIRECT INSTRUCTION QUICK START

Often you need to teach a skill on the spot. For example, two students need to know how to set the low hurdles before a track meet. Don't just *show* them. Use *direct instruction* to make sure they've got it. After a few tries, you will internalize the method and be able to use it naturally even without a lesson plan. Use this flow:

✔ I do it.
✔ I check that you understand.
✔ We do it.
✔ You show me.
✔ You've got it! You do it.

INDUCTIVE TEACHING

> The art of teaching is the art of assisting discovery.
>
> —*Mark Van Doren*

Inductive teaching presents a stark contrast to direct instruction. Through inductive methods, students create or discover important ideas by interacting with concrete materials or other data sources and their peers. When students analyze a poem, look for patterns in population distributions, or discover the identity of a mystery powder, they inquire.

Instead of stating the learning explicitly at the beginning of the lesson, during inductive lessons, the teacher guides students to interact with data, materials, and each other so that they discover the ideas. Additionally, whereas direct instruction focuses primarily on the *product,* or outcome, to be gained, inductive strategies also focus on the *processes* by which knowledge is formed. Reviewing state and national student content standards in science and social studies demonstrates that students literate in these subject matters not only have mastery of a body of information, they also can use the methods by which scientists and social scientists build knowledge. They can formulate questions, address their questions through appropriate methodologies, collect information, analyze it, and draw appropriate conclusions. Students learn these processes by using them, and inductive instruction provides an appropriate vehicle. Teaching Tip 6.3 provides an example of an inductive strategy, photo analysis, that can be used quickly and helps students to inquire into what they see.

Inductive methods can be convergent or divergent in nature. In convergent, or guided, approaches students are expected to discover or infer a single concept or generalization. In divergent, or unguided, approaches the number of concepts or generalizations to be formed is greater.

Although many inductive approaches exist, unfortunately, most of us have had limited experience with inductive instruction as students. This chapter presents a variety of inductive strategies. The first three are convergent, and the last two are more divergent.

Inquiry Training

Suchman's (1962) inquiry training assists students in asking questions that help them move from the observation of facts to the development of theories.

Students analyze data and draw conclusions through inductive instruction.

Barbara Schwartz/Merrill

INQUIRY QUICK START

Use inquiry in your openers to start your day or lesson and hook those curious minds. One inquiry quick start is photo analysis (Guillaume, Yopp, & Yopp, 2007). Try it:

1. Find an intriguing photo that represents a current event or your content. Use one from home, the newspaper, your textbook, or the Internet. Try searching "photo of the day" or "photo in the news."
2. Display the image for the students. You can put it on a transparency or project it on the screen.
3. Ask students to make careful observations of it: "What do you notice? What is in this quadrant?"
4. Ask students to make inferences about the photo: "When was it taken? Who are the people? What's the story?"
5. Tie it to your lesson. Come back to it at the end of the lesson and allow students to revise their inferences.

An unusual artifact can spark students' curiosity and provide a discrepant event to begin a lesson.

Parvin/Texas Memorial Museum/Pearson Education-Corporate Digital Archive

To watch a first-grade teacher use a discrepant event in science, go to the Merrill Teacher Prep Web site, Video Classroom, Science Methods, Module 10, Video 1. How might the students' engagement in the lesson change as a result of this discrepant event?

This strategy's power resides both in the way that it capitalizes on students' natural curiosity—the need to know—and in the fact that it puts students in the questioner's seat. Usually students in classrooms are expected to *answer* the questions, not to *ask* them. Asking a question can propel learning.

Description of the Inquiry Training Model   In an inquiry training lesson, the teacher presents a phenomenon, called a discrepant event, that piques curiosity. In a *discrepant event,* there is a mismatch between what students expect to happen, based on prior experience, and what actually does happen. For instance, a teacher may drop two full, unopened cans of soda into an aquarium. Students look puzzled when one floats and the other sinks (the floater is a diet drink, lacking sugar, which adds to the other can's density). For a discrepant event, I once filled a half-liter clear water bottle with water and baby oil. Although both liquids were clear, when students dropped food color into the bottle, the dye fell through the oil and dispersed in the water that rested in the bottom half of the bottle. A sample discrepant event in language arts might be a poem with no capitalization or punctuation. In social studies, it might be an unusual cultural artifact.

After presenting the discrepant event or stimulus, the teacher invites students to ask yes–no questions to develop explanations for what they observe. Through their questions, students develop and test causal connections to explain the discrepant event.

Suchman developed his model for science instruction, but as long as a teacher can locate relevant discrepant events or stimuli, inquiry training can be used across subject areas. It is useful for students of many ages, though younger children and English learners need extra support in formulating yes–no questions.

Stages of the Inquiry Training Model Figure 6.3 lists the stages of Suchman's inquiry training, moving through the presentation of the discrepant event through two stages of questioning: verification and hypothesis-testing questioning. As you read over the stages of inquiry training, please bear in mind that inquiry training is more than a guessing game. If a student states the correct explanation early on, resist the temptation to scold the student for "giving away" the answer. Treat the student's proposed explanation as yet another tentative explanation that needs to be verified through empirical testing. The social atmosphere is important; encourage students to listen to each other.

A Sample Inquiry Training Lesson Figure 6.4 relates an inquiry training lesson I have used with enthusiastic students of a variety of ages.

Concept Attainment

Recall that inductive teaching methods foster students' ability to discern patterns, impose structure, and discover important ideas by working with concrete data. The ability to categorize information is central to these processes of discovery. Categorization, or grouping items into classes, serves a number of important functions: It reduces the complexity of our environments, it helps us identify individual objects, it makes learning more efficient, it helps us make decisions without the need for testing every object's properties, and it allows us to relate and order classes of events (Bruner, Goodnow, & Austin, 1960). Further, Bruner et al. note that our understanding of the world is not purely objective. Our systems for processing new information are shaped by the ways of thinking in which we are immersed: "The categories in terms of which man sorts out and responds to the world around him reflect deeply the culture into

FIGURE 6.3 *Stages of the inquiry training model.*

Open	1. Present a discrepant event or puzzling situation.
	2. Describe the procedure: Students are to form explanations for what they see by asking questions that you can answer with yes or no.
Body	3. Allow for questions that *verify* what events and conditions students observe. Forestall causal questions until the next stage.
	4. Allow for questions that allow children to *identify relevant variables* and *test their hypotheses*.
Close	5. Guide students to state the explanations they have formulated.
	6. Prompt students to analyze their inquiry strategy.

FIGURE 6.4 *A sample inquiry training lesson.*

Objectives:	Fifth-grade students will state the necessary components of an electric circuit. Students will demonstrate the ability to test cause–effect relationships by asking relevant yes–no questions (Guillaume, Yopp, & Yopp, 1996).

Open	Preview for English learners
	• Before the lesson, teacher calls her English learners to the side of the room and allows them to handle two toy chicks that chirp only when a circuit is completed by simultaneously touching both terminals on their feet to an electrical conductor, such as skin or metal.
	• She shows them a written sign, "What makes the chick chirp?" and reads it aloud as she points and uses facial expressions to support her message.
	• The three students who share a language talk among themselves excitedly in Spanish. Her one Chinese student works with her, asking for terms and trying things out.
	1. To open the lesson: Teacher presents the toy chick to the class.
	   • The terminals are two metal rings embedded in the toy's feet.
	   • Students chatter and express curiosity about the toy.
	2. Teacher states the task: "Your job is to ask me questions that I can answer with yes or no so that you can determine what makes the chick chirp."

Body	3. Students ask questions to verify what they see and interpret as the problem.
	   • Sample questions include "Is there a battery in the chick?" and "Are you flipping a switch to make it chirp?"
	   • She allows students to discuss their questions in partner pairs, providing specific support to her English learners who will benefit from talking with each other before speaking to the class, and for her students who need more time to process ideas.
	   • When students ask questions that test causal relationships ("Are you completing an electric circuit?"), teacher asks them to save those questions for a few minutes.
	   • When children ask questions that cannot be answered with yes or no, teacher asks them to rephrase, enlisting help from peers as necessary.
	   • For newer English learners, the teacher takes their utterances and rephrases them, into yes/no questions. She points to the written version of question as well.
	   • A family volunteer in the class records the students' questions on the board for all to see.
	4. Teacher asks for questions that move into the phase of identifying relevant variables and exploring hypotheses about cause–effect relationships.
	   • For instance, "Does it have anything to do with the heat in your hand?"
	   • When students hypothesize about the materials necessary to complete the circuit, teacher responds with actions: She places the chick on metal, then wood, and finally glass so that students can see the answers to their questions.

Close	5. Teacher directs students to talk in groups about their explanations. She requires each group member (including English learners) to make a contribution, even briefly. She entertains new questions that arise from group discussions.
	6. In their groups, students write an explanation for the chirping chick on sentence strips.
	   • They post and examine the explanations: An electrical circuit requires a power source, a conductor, and in this case a load (the chirping mechanism).
	7. The class analyzes its inquiry strategy and then applies its knowledge by exploring electrical circuits with batteries, foil, and lightbulbs.
	   • She pushes her advanced learners (including GATE students and ones who excelled earlier in this lesson) to build parallel circuits after demonstrating series circuits.

which he is born. . . . His personal history comes to reflect the traditions and thought-ways of his culture, for the events that make it up are filtered through the categorical systems he has learned" (p. 10). The concept attainment model (Bruner et al., 1960) makes categorization schemes explicit and guides students to consider information conceptually toward the aim of categorizing information meaningfully.

Description of the Concept Attainment Model   One object at a time, students observe a set of objects or examples, each deemed by their teacher as belonging—or not belonging—to a particular set. As the teacher presents more examples, students make hypotheses about the rule for grouping. They test their hypotheses on additional objects, and, finally, the rule (or concept) for grouping is induced.

Stages of the Concept Attainment Model   Figure 6.5 delineates the stages of the concept attainment model. Notice that the teacher presents one item at a time. It may be necessary to change the order of presentation or to gather new items to challenge the students' emerging hypotheses. Occasionally students discover a rule that is accurate given the data they observe but is not the rule you meant to illustrate. Be certain to provide many different-looking or different-sounding examples of your concept so that students can focus on the critical attributes of the rule. If students induce a rule other than the one you planned, you may need to provide additional examples that contradict their rules. Figure 6.6 shows some angles a teacher just presented to his geometry students. Column A has angles he calls "flops." Column B has "flumps." Is the angle in the student's hand a flop or a flump? What is the rule?

A Sample Concept Attainment Lesson   Figure 6.7 presents a sample lesson using the concept attainment format.

FIGURE 6.5   *Stages of the concept attainment model.*

Before the lesson, select a concept or rule and collect a wide variety of examples and nonexamples of your concept.

Open	1. To build interest, briefly display some of the items. (Items can vary. Examples include words, objects, pictures, and places on a map.) 2. Introduce the students' task: to discover your rule for grouping.
Body	3. One at a time, present the items that serve as examples or counterexamples of your grouping. State whether each item belongs or does not belong to your group, perhaps by calling each a *yes* or a *no*. 4. Continue presenting examples and counterexamples, providing opportunities for students to share their hypothesized rules and discuss them with their peers. Guide students' discussion to be certain that their proposed rules conform with all the data you have presented. Provide examples that challenge students' erroneous rules.
Close	5. When most students have induced the rule, furnish a final chance for consensus. Allow the rule to be stated aloud for the class. 6. Invite students to explore further examples or to group the data according to a criterion they select. 7. Process the activity by making observations about the process and content as appropriate.

FIGURE 6.6   *Where should this angle be placed? Is it a flop or a flump?*

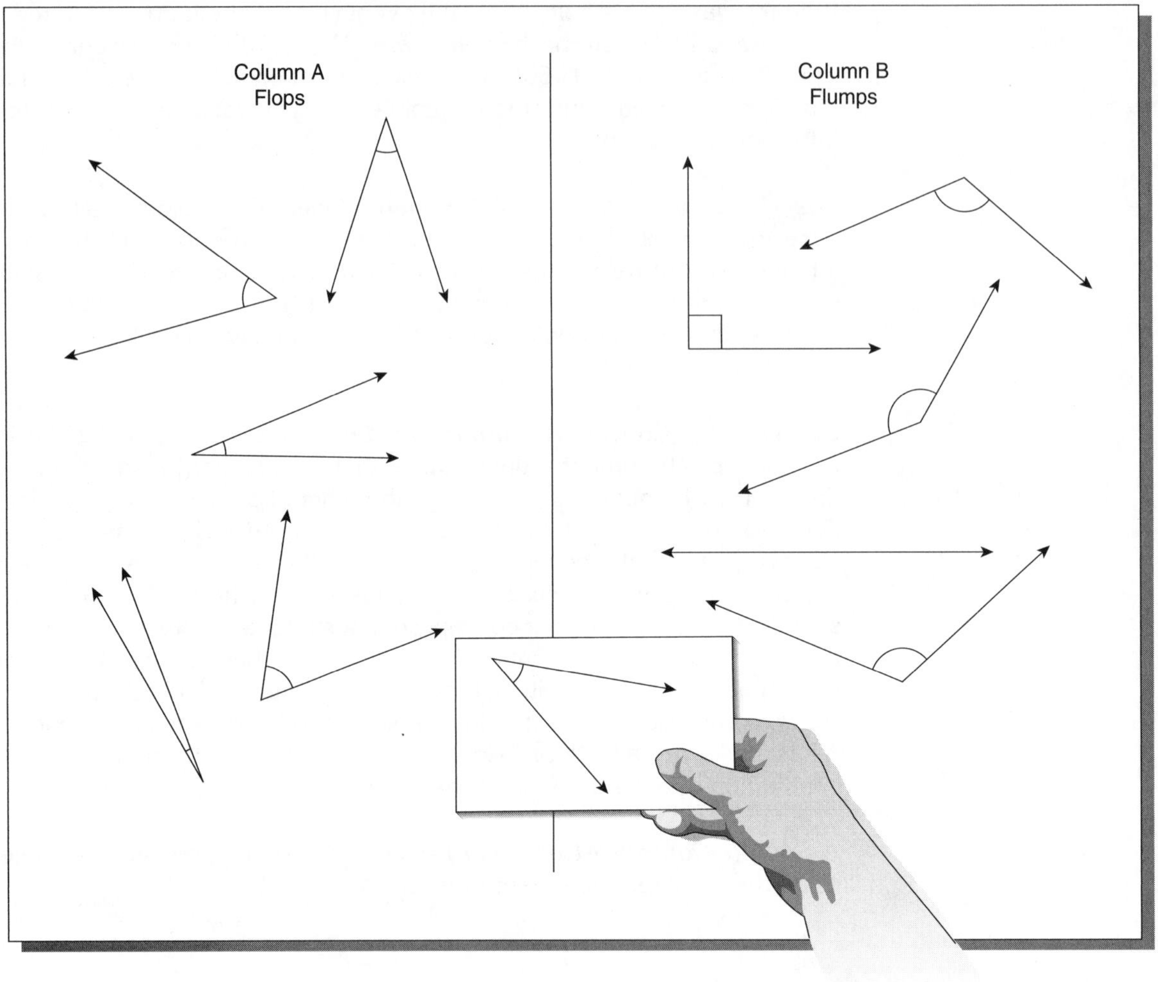

Learning Cycle

The learning cycle approach is inductive in that it moves from firsthand experiences to well-formulated understanding of the content and real-world application. It is based on constructivist learning theory that defines learning as both the process and the result of questioning and interpreting, the application of thought processes and information to build and improve our understandings, and the integration of current experiences with past experiences (Marlowe & Page, 1998). The learning cycle model differs from other inductive approaches in that the first and last stages of the lesson must be based in real-world or realistic experiences. The learning cycle approach can level the playing field by ensuring that all students have firsthand experiences to build background knowledge and deepen content knowledge. This is especially important for English learners and for students whose background experiences may be limited (Guillaume, Yopp, & Yopp, 1996). It also can foster the development of content vocabulary (Spencer & Guillaume, 2006).

Description of the Learning Cycle Model   A learning cycle begins with a real-world problem or event that piques students' interests and fuels one or more questions for exploration. A personal story, discrepant event, current event, toy, poem, or thoughtful question from a student or the teacher can all serve to engage

FIGURE 6.7 *A sample concept attainment lesson.*

Objectives:	Kindergarten students will distinguish between examples and nonexamples of a triangle. Students will group items based on relevant attributes.
	Preparation: The concept attainment strategy is new to the teacher, so he conducts Internet research to read up on it. He finds a particularly helpful set of materials at the Georgia Department of Education Web site (http://www.glc.k12.ga.us/pandp/critthink/ conceptattainment.htm).
Open	1. "Come sit with me here on the rug and have a look at some of the things I brought today." • Teacher draws two students near him. His student with a visual impairment sits on his left. His student who is physically very active sits on his right. • Teacher takes turn allowing first the student on his right and then the one on his left to pull items from a bag. • All students are allowed to handle and comment on a few of the items.
	2. "Some of these items are members of my club, and some are not. Your job today is to discover the name of my club. Then we will know which items can join and which cannot." 3. "I will place the members of my club in this hoop of yarn. Items that are not members will go outside the hoop. Ready?" He guides the hand of his student with the visual impairment over the yarn hoops. He speaks soothingly to refocus the student on his right who is beginning to bounce.
Body	4. Teacher shows one item at a time, placing it in the hoop if it is a triangle and outside if it is not. He provides plenty of examples and nonexamples that vary not only in the number of sides and angles but also in color, size, and texture. 5. After presenting five or six items, teacher encourages the children to guess where he will place subsequent items and guides them to explicitly state their hypotheses: "Whisper to your neighbor what you think is the name of my club." Teacher helps students test their hypotheses by examining the present examples and by adding others.
Close	6. When most students have demonstrated knowledge of the "triangle club" rule, teacher invites students to state it aloud: "Okay, club experts, what is the name of my club? Everyone, say it aloud on three. One . . . two . . . three!" "Triangles" students shout. 7. "Who can look around the room to find a member of my club? Who can find a nonmember?" As most students look around, teacher provides three more samples for the students at his side and for two others who especially like to work with the teacher. 8. Students share examples and nonexamples they have found. 9. "Let me see if I understand the rules about triangles, then. Does size matter? Does color? Texture?" (All: "No!") "What matters about a triangle is that it has exactly three sides and exactly three angles." 10. "After recess, I will place these objects in a center so that you can think of your own club using the objects." Teacher includes different types of triangles such as right, isosceles, and equilateral triangles, knowing that some students will be ready to informally examine the size of their angles. 11. Extension: Students are so excited by the "game" of sorting objects into clubs that the teacher creates a few drag-and-drop concept attainment Web pages for other concepts the students are studying. • They try the activities during center time in class, and they log on at night and play the games with their families too. • Some parents report playing the "club game" while they are waiting at the doctor's office or for the bus.

FIGURE 6.8 *Stages of the learning cycle.*

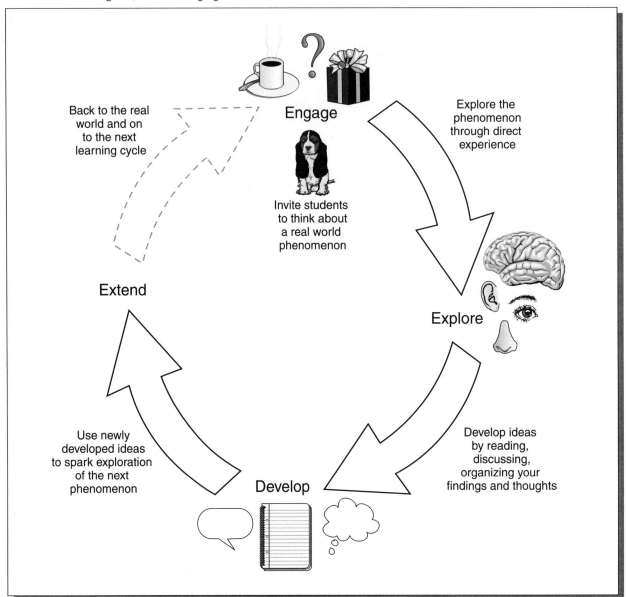

Open	1. Engage: Provide a brief real-world phenomenon, an object, or an issue that engages students' interest in the topic and fuels one or more questions for investigation.
	• Listen carefully to determine students' prior knowledge related to the topic and to expose their questions.
	• Do not provide explanations of phenomena yet.
Body	2. Explore: Provide materials so that students engage in firsthand experience with the issue under study.
	• Students begin to address their questions from the prior phase.
	• They begin to generate new concepts and questions. Observe students carefully to determine emerging concepts and vocabulary.
	3. Develop: Systematically develop the concepts that arise during the exploration phase.
	• Supply vocabulary terms appropriate given students' experiences.
	• Provide direct presentations of the information and reading experiences as necessary so that students refine their understanding.

continued

FIGURE 6.8 *Continued.*

Close	4. Apply: Present a new problem or situation that can be addressed given students' newly formed understandings.
	• Connect to the real world.
	• Use the real-world connection as the starting point for the next learning cycle.

the students. Next, students interact with data sources and concrete materials to explore the problem or question(s). Exploration builds background knowledge, from which more abstract understandings arise. After students have firsthand experiences the teacher begins to formally help students to systematize their knowledge, label concepts, and generate explanations. Finally, students apply their newly formulated knowledge to a similar real-world problem or event.

Stages of the Learning Cycle Model Different versions of the learning cycle approach to planning and instruction vary only slightly in the number of stages they propose, typically between three and five. Figure 6.8 depicts the phases of the learning cycle using one popular version of the model. This version of the learning cycle embeds assessment in each phase of the lesson. Another useful version of the learning cycle model is the 5E approach: engage, explore, explain, extend, and evaluate.

A Sample Learning Cycle Lesson The lesson in Figure 6.9 is a visual arts lesson for high school students that follows the learning cycle model. Notice that a single lesson can last more than one day and that it can make use of many kinds of resources. In following the learning cycle model, the lesson begins with a real-world phenomenon to engage the students (discussion of a painting), explores ideas related to that phenomenon (examination of the use of color in many other works), develops concepts surfaced through the exploration phase (color concepts), and ends with a connection back to the real world (creation of students' own works that make use of what they learned through the lesson, principles of color use).

Concept Formation

Hilda Taba's (1967) strategy allows learners to build new ideas by categorizing specific pieces of data and forging new connections among those data.

Description of the Concept Formation Mode Often deemed "list–group–label," concept formation should increase students' ability to process information. Students begin by developing extensive lists of data related to a topic or question. Next, they group the data based on criteria they select, and they develop labels for their groups. The labels of the groups convey a concept or generalization. Oftentimes students are asked to re-sort data in different ways. Lessons often conclude with students using the information in a new way, such as by composing an explanatory paragraph.

Concept formation can be used to induce one particular concept or can be used in a divergent manner so that a number of accurate concepts or generalizations result. It has a wide range of applications. One is to consolidate concepts at the end of a lesson, as in Teaching Tip 6.4.

Stages of the Concept Formation Model Figure 6.10 lists the stages employed in the concept formation lesson.

FIGURE 6.9   A sample learning cycle lesson.

Objectives:	Tenth-grade students will analyze works of art to determine principles of color use. Students will create their own work of art that uses color to convey a message.
Engage (Open)	1. With zydeco, Cajun, or jazz music playing in the background, the teacher shares a brightly rendered watercolor painting from New Orleans. 2. "Years ago I took my favorite vacation and bought this painting. Looking at this painting, where do you think I went?" • She supports the students' guesses by asking for their evidence. "What about the picture makes you say, 'Europe'?" • They discuss, among other student-generated topics, the architecture portrayed in the painting. 3. Once the students conclude that the painting depicts a courtyard in New Orleans, teacher asks students to examine how the artist used color to capture the sense of energy, cultural fusion, and joy that many people associate with the city. 4. To set the stage for exploration, teacher states that artists throughout time and all over the world use color to convey or enhance the message or mood of their works.
Explore (Body)	5. Teacher sets the task: "I reserved the laptops for tomorrow. Your job will be to go on a virtual tour of museums around the world and download examples of visual art that use color in a variety of ways. You will share your examples with the class." 6. The next day, the students boot up the laptops and connect to the Internet for their tour. It launches with a visit to the National Gallery of Art (http://www.nga.gov). • The teacher supplies URLs of other museum sites, and in pairs, students find examples of art that vary in their use of color to convey mood and message. • When permitted, students print out copies of the art and create a class gallery of the varied works. Or they leave the image displayed on their screens. • Teacher and students add reproductions such as posters of famous works and their own works to the gallery as well. • A few students have created and shown their own works at festivals. These are added to the gallery.
Develop (Body)	7. The following day, teacher commends the students on their diligent searching: "We have created quite the collection of works in our class gallery. Very impressive! Your next task is to study all the works to determine themes in how color is used." 8. Students tour the class gallery, grouping works that create similar moods or convey similar messages. They test the hypotheses they formed in viewing works they found with their partner on the virtual tour by studying the larger set of works found by their classmates. 9. The day ends with the students writing and submitting journal entries on their tentative conclusions about the use of color. • One student writes, for example, "When artists use a subdued palette, it expresses a calmer message. Mixing black with the colors adds an air of sadness to the work." • Two students, including one with a developmental delay, dictate their entries into the computer near the door that has speech recognition capacities. They print out their work and take it home to practice reading it. 10. That night, the teacher studies the students' entries and reproduces some of their most telling findings on overhead transparencies. If she trusted her projection system, she would display the findings using presentation software instead. 11. The next day, the teacher lectures on the use of color, drawing from the concepts and tentative generalizations about color students recorded in their journals. • She introduces terms such as "hue," "value," and "saturation" to formalize what the students stated informally in their entries. • For homework, students read from their text a chapter on the use of color. • Two or three who experience reading difficulties read a compact disc version, in which the teacher has highlighted key ideas and terms.

continued

FIGURE 6.9   *Continued.*

Apply (Close)	12. Students select a life event that evoked strong emotions from them.
	• They create a work using a medium of their choice and use color to convey their intended emotions.
	• Students plan a gallery showing, including background music related to their works. Families (and other supporters) attend the lively showing.
	• Students begin to notice, now, differences in artists' use of *line* in addition to color. Teacher begins to think about line as the next element for study.

Teaching Tip 6.4

CONCEPT FORMATION QUICK START

Use a mini-concept-formation activity to close your lesson or as a review. Here's how.

1. Choose some content terms, perhaps between 5 and 10. Remember your vocab cards from Teaching Tip 3.7? Use those. Or have the students pick the words. Be quick.
2. Put the words on cards or large sticky notes and display them. Use magnets to hold them to the board if you wrote cards. Or display them on the interactive whiteboard.
3. Have students group them. Which words go together? Regroup them in a different way.
4. Ask students to name the groups, then use the group labels in a sentence.
5. Alternatives: Students can sort cards with small groups at their seats. Or you can hand each student a card and have them move around the room to form groups.

FIGURE 6.10   *Stages of the concept formation model.*

Open	1. Challenge the students with a question about the topic that will encourage them to generate an extensive list.
Body	2. *List:* In full view, record students' contributions in the form of a list. Some teachers use sentence strips or large cards.
	3. *Group:* Invite the students to place similar objects together. Questions such as "What goes together?" can elicit grouping.
	4. *Label:* Ask students to label their new groups: "What can we call this group?"
Close	5. Call students' attention to new concepts that arise from their groupings.
	6. Categorize new pieces of information according to the students' system and invite them to regroup and label the information.
	7. You may require students to use the information in some way, such as through a writing or retelling assignment.

A Sample Concept Formation Lesson   Figure 6.11 gives a concept formation lesson I used with second graders. In this lesson, students generated many words related to the topic *water*. They sorted the words into groups that shared certain characteristics. I was surprised that students initially grouped the words according to **linguistic** clues rather than by **semantic** clues. With prompting, students regrouped words in a few different ways to discover that water can be both helpful and harmful to humans. Finally, they wrote books about how we interact with water.

Unguided Inquiry

Through unguided inquiry, students address a problem or issue through first-hand experience with plentiful materials and information sources. The teacher serves as a facilitator instead of as a presenter. Many possible answers or solutions may be generated. Glasgow (1997) touts the contemporary relevance of unguided inquiry, which he calls problem-based learning:

> In most professions, knowledge is dynamic and requires current understanding for optimal success with contemporary problem solving. Information, concepts, and skills learned by the students are put into memory associated with

FIGURE 6.11   *A sample concept formation lesson.*

Objectives:	Second-grade students will form two accurate statements about the interrelationship of humans and water. Students will group data in rule-governed ways.

Open	1. "Class, come sit with me and listen to my rain stick." Students join teacher and listen intently as she turns the column once, then twice.
	  • They chat briefly about their experiences with similar instruments.
	  • One student visited family in Chile, birth place of the rain stick.
	  • "I brought my rain stick in today because we are beginning to study weather."
	2. "Let's begin today by writing down as many water words as we know. I will write the words here on index cards."

Body	3. *List:* The class creates an extensive list of water words. Examples include *evaporation, puddle,* and *mudslide.* When the students' listing slows down, the teacher prods their thinking: How about frozen water? 4. *Group:* Teacher calls the class of 20 to the carpet, and in their circle they lay out all the index cards that list their words. "That's quite a list, my friends! Now let's think about putting some of the cards together in groups. Who sees some cards that go together?" Teacher jokes with students, suggesting that they sit on their hands, because each is so eager to group the cards. She makes a note to herself that making individual or partner cards may work even better than class cards for grouping. Students group words into those that include *-ation* within them and those that do not. Teacher praises the ingenuity of their grouping and then asks students to regroup them another way. Students continue grouping until each card is with others. Teacher encourages students to collapse groups and to consider cross-groupings. 5. *Label:* Students dictate the names of the groups they have generated, and the teacher writes group names on new cards, which she places near the three groups: *Ways water helps us, Ways water can be dangerous,* and *Other water words.*
Close	6. Teacher leads students to draw conclusions about the groups they have generated. Students conclude that humans interact with water in many ways, both helpful and harmful. 7. Teacher provides materials and instructions for students to make water pop-up books that contain two accurate sentences of ways that humans interact with water. Later, students read their books aloud to their sixth-grade buddies.
Extension:	Becasue the students were so eager to sort the cards, teacher knows students need more opportunities to work with the words. She transfers the words to a computer file and each day for the next week students begin the day by coming up to the interactive whiteboard and dragging and dropping terms into new groups.

the problem. This improves recall and retention when the students face another problem . . . Problems actively integrate information into a cognitive framework or system that can be applied to new problems. (p. 42)

Problem-based learning involves small groups of students locating and using rich resources (often with technological ones playing a prominent role) to solve a real or realistic problem. For example, first graders may need to determine the best pet for their class (Lambros, 2002). Secondary students may need to address a moral dilemma problem, such as suggesting a course of action for a doctor who was just called by a parent confessing that the parent broke into the pharmacist's shop for drugs a child needed to survive (Slavin-Baden & Major, 2004). Thus, problem-based learning and other forms of unguided inquiry can be implemented at all grade levels, in both general and special education settings, and across the curriculum (Audet & Jordan, 2005).

Description of the Unguided Inquiry Model   Unguided inquiry can be used in any subject matter through which students can personally experience a problem and then work firsthand with data to address (and perhaps solve) that problem. In social studies, for example, students may frame the problem of homelessness in the local community either by experiencing homelessness themselves or by observing others who are homeless. They work to define the problem by formulating a question, to investigate the issue through reading and interviewing, and then to generate possible solutions. Their efforts may lead them to fund-raising or other social action opportunities. In mathematics, students may design survey studies that allow them to collect, analyze, and present data and then act on their findings.

Although unguided inquiry leads students to gain understanding of disciplinary content, the teacher may not be able to determine in advance which understandings will be developed. Rather than presenting information directly, the teacher provides for a rich environment and gently guides students' efforts to discover relevant information and address the problem productively.

Stages of the Unguided Inquiry Model   Figure 6.12 gives stages of the unguided inquiry model.

A Sample Unguided Inquiry Lesson   Figure 6.13 recounts an unguided inquiry lesson, inspired by Project WILD's (2001) lesson, "No Water Off a Duck's Back." Students of all ages participate merrily in the lesson, creating and cleaning up the **simulation** of oil spills.

To watch an elementary teacher spark an unguided inquiry session on earthworm behavior, go to the Merrill Teacher Prep Web site, Video Classroom, Educational Technology, Module 1, Video 2. What skills might the students learn through pursuing their own questions?

FIGURE 6.12   *Stages of the unguided inquiry model.*

Open	1. Present or capitalize on a problem that has multiple solutions and that captures the interests of students.
Body	2. Guide students in clearly stating the problem, perhaps by formulating a question.
	3. Lead a discussion of methods that may allow students to address the problem. Set the guidelines for study. Provide access to a variety of appropriate resources, including concrete materials and information sources.
	4. Monitor students as they employ their methods, helping students to revise and refine their methods as appropriate.
	5. Encourage students to take action based on findings, when appropriate.
Close	6. Direct students to draw conclusions regarding (a) the problem and (b) the processes of investigation.

FIGURE 6.13 *A sample unguided inquiry lesson.*

Objectives:	Seventh-grade students will describe useful techniques for cleaning oil spills and state at least one possible drawback of each technique.
	Through a closing discussion or product of their choice, students will demonstrate the ability to clearly define a problem, to employ an appropriate method, and to analyze their results.
Open	1. Teacher projects an Internet image from a news magazine of an oil-soaked bird and leads students to conclude that an oil spill at sea was responsible for the bird's condition.
	2. Using Inspiration (http://www.inspiration.com), the class together begins to create a semantic map on oil spills. Students move into small heterogeneous groups and continue adding to a small-group version of the map.
	3. Teacher focuses students' attention on the portion of the map that lists a few cleanup methods: "Let's think about this part of the map. You already know some ways that specialists attempt to clean up spills at sea."
	4. Teacher shows a clear container with water and vegetable oil meant to simulate an oil spill. "Here I have my own spill."
Body	5. Teacher directs pairs of students to phrase the problem for investigation as a question. Students share their questions aloud and revise based on peers' ideas.
	6. Students spend one period reviewing books, encyclopedias, newspapers, and Internet materials to study cleanup methods. The teacher quietly assigns each student to a particular source given information on students' reading level, but she allows them to read their choice of additional materials as well. Materials include sources in Russian and Korean to provide primary language support for her English learners.
	7. The next day, students bring in some cleanup materials and place them with those gathered by the teacher. Materials include coffee filters, detergents, soaps, sponges, eyedroppers, and paper towels.
	8. In pairs, students devise and record a plan for cleaning up the vegetable oil spill. Partner groups exchange plans and ask each other a few questions to troubleshoot before spill cleanup begins.
	9. Before distributing materials, the teacher quietly pulls two students with marked behavior difficulties to her. She makes each of them manager for particular materials and reinforces the rules for handling other materials appropriately.
	10. With plans in hand, each pair creates its own oil spill using one tablespoon of vegetable oil in a pan of water. Students implement their plan to clean up the slick. Teacher monitors, prompting students to work carefully and to record their efforts in specific detail. She attempts to enrich their thinking through strategies such as visits to other student groups for observation.
Close	11. As testing concludes, teacher guides students in constructing a class chart of cleanup methods and their potential usefulness. The class also discusses drawbacks of its methods and reflects on how its future tests may be improved by the strategies students attempted in this inquiry.
	12. Students choose a format to share what they learned and to evaluate their success as problem solvers. Teacher encourages intensely curious students to conduct future investigations on cleanup methods for oil spills on land.

Strengths and Criticisms of Inductive Strategies

Each of us probably has a story that illustrates the old saying "Experience is the best teacher." Experience allows us to form rules that can be useful in guiding our behavior and solving related problems in the future. Most of us report that when we generate the rules by distilling experience rather than simply by reciting the rules we have heard stated for us, learning is more potent and tends to be longer lasting. Inductive strategies capitalize on the tremendous power of discovery learning.

Additionally, one widely professed purpose of education is to foster students' ability to think independently, to find order and patterns in the huge amount of information that confronts us daily. Inductive approaches are useful for that purpose because they provide students with opportunities to frame problems, to select appropriate methodologies, and to analyze their reasoning. To expand students' ability to face problems and complicated issues, inductive strategies focus on the processes of questioning, gathering information, and learning, in addition to content mastery.

Finally, inductive strategies make use of many principles from Chapter 5: They connect easily with the lives of the learners by using student interest and frequently allowing for some student choice in the methods of study and the pacing of the lesson. Inductive approaches address human nature and needs by sparking and sustaining curiosity and by encouraging students to be puzzlers and problem solvers. Further, inductive strategies often make use of a wide range of information sources and real-world materials, which results in an enriched learning environment. When students engage in unguided inquiry into problems they themselves experience, they have the important opportunity to question existing conditions and to work on improving one piece of the world.

Inductive strategies can be criticized for a number of reasons. First, because student input can so dramatically shape the direction of the lesson—not only its pacing but in many cases its content as well—it can be difficult for the teacher to predict a lesson's content outcomes. Releasing partial control to students can be unsettling to teachers because they must approach content and time decisions with greater flexibility, especially in divergent lessons. Whereas the outcomes in a directed lesson are clear at the outset, divergent inductive lessons such as unguided inquiry result in multiple generalizations. Some teachers feel that this divergence places heavy demands on their own stores of knowledge.

The divergent, somewhat unpredictable nature of certain inductive methods also worries some teachers because of the pressure they feel to systematically treat a large body of content information in short periods of time. Focusing study on relevant, real-life problems may not allow for orderly treatment of some of the more mundane topics teachers are expected to address.

Finally, inductive lessons require resources and time. Whereas it takes very little time for a teacher to directly *state* a generalization, *inducing* a generalization requires repeated and varied experiences. Although they can produce lasting and memorable learning, inductive strategies can be less time efficient than direct instruction.

When will you use inductive methods? Check your stance toward education to gain a sense of what you want students to be able to do as adults. If you include outcomes such as the ability to analyze information sources, to think critically and creatively, or to solve complex problems, you need to master and employ inductive strategies. Because of their potential to address both content and thought-process goals, I hope you will use inductive strategies frequently. As a general rule, when you plan your lessons, ask yourself: "Could the students effectively discover these points for themselves if I arranged conditions appropriately?" If your answer is yes, use an inductive strategy. My own stance toward education reminds me not to tell students that which they could discover on their own. The last strategy addressed in this chapter, cooperative learning, can include both inductive and deductive approaches.

Cooperative Learning

Popularized in the 1970s and 1980s, cooperative learning was formulated as an attempt to move classroom practices away from the highly individualistic and often competitive emphases of the typical American classroom. Cooperative learning includes a family of methods and structures designed to capitalize on every classroom's diversity and to enrich students' cognitive learning and social behaviors (Jacob, 1999; Johnson & Johnson, 1999). Related terms include *peer-mediated instruction* and *collaborative learning*. Often these terms

Through cooperative learning, students work together to meet goals and build social skills.

Scott Cunningham/Merrill

At the Merrill Teacher Prep Web site's Video Classroom, you can see many varieties of cooperative learning—with students with wide-ranging needs, across the curriculum, and up and down the grade levels. Try these:
- Think-pair-share (Go to Special Education, Module 4, Video 1.)
- Peer tutoring (Go to Special Education, Module 6, Video 1.)
- Cooperative learning combined with whole-group instruction (Go to General Methods, Module 9, Video 1.)
- Student-Teams Achievement Division (Go to Educational Psychology, Module 8, Video 1.)

As you watch, ask yourself how student interaction might be influencing students' social skills and cognitive outcomes.

are used interchangeably, although precise distinctions do exist. For instance, some say that cooperative learning requires a shared product of learning; collaborative learning does not.

Research on peer-mediated instruction (including cooperative learning) is extensive, with studies spanning a century, many countries, grade levels, subject areas, and populations (including general and special education) represented. Results are positive (Hall & Stegila, 2003). Cooperative learning is effective for encouraging content learning, social interaction, and students' attitudes toward learning and the subject matter. Recent examples of its effectiveness include a meta-analysis of the research by Marzano et al. (2001) and studies by Maheady, Michielli-Pendl, Mallette, and Harper (2002) and Baker, Gersten, and Lee (2002). Even very young children can use cooperative learning in its simple forms.

Description of the Cooperative Learning Model   In cooperative learning lessons, students are expected to help each other learn as they work together in small groups. Groups can be temporary or year-long. Frequently, cooperative groups include four members, but other configurations also exist. Cooperative learning is more than simply assigning students to work together and then issuing group grades. According to proponents (Kagan, 1994; Slavin, 1995) cooperative learning needs to accomplish three basic principles:

1. *Positive interdependence.* Conditions must be arranged so that students are dependent on each other for success. This interdependence can be facilitated by providing group awards or by structuring tasks so that individual students cannot complete them alone.
2. *Individual accountability.* Each student must remain accountable for exhibiting mastery of the content.
3. *Simultaneous interaction.* Lessons should keep a maximum number of students overtly active at once. This is in contrast to traditional lessons in which only one student in the entire class speaks at a time.

A fourth principle is *equal participation* (Kagan 1994). Students need to make balanced contributions to the group's work. Kagan argues that to accomplish these principles, teachers must:

- Structure teams so that they are heterogeneous. Ability, language, gender, and ethnicity may be criteria teachers use to sort students into teams where members differ.
- Use team-building and class-building activities to create the will to cooperate.
- Use management techniques specifically suited for group work. Examples include a quiet signal to regain students' attention and the use of assigned roles within teams.
- Explicitly teach social skills such as listening and conflict resolution techniques.

In sum, cooperative learning lessons structure resources and activities so that students remain responsible for their own learning and become responsible for assisting their teammates in learning.

Stages of the Cooperative Learning Model Although for many teachers cooperative learning has come to mean simply allowing students to help each other, there are scores of formal cooperative learning structures that breathe life into the principles of cooperative learning. The stages listed in Figure 6.14 do not represent a single lesson. Instead, they suggest a sequence of events that take place over an extended period of time as a teacher works to establish a cooperative learning classroom. Individual cooperative learning lessons that make

FIGURE 6.14 *Stages of the cooperative learning model.*

Form teams and set the stage	1. Select the dimensions along which students will be heterogeneously grouped.
	2. Use assessment results and demographic information to place students into groups of four that include members who differ according to the selected dimensions. For example, each group may have two high achievers, two lower achievers, and be balanced in terms of girls and boys and English and Spanish speakers. Random teams, interest teams, or skill teams may also be used.
	3. Teach a defined and explicit set of social behaviors. Examples include active listening and responding in positive ways to peers' contributions.
Implement cooperative management system	4. Select and teach a quiet signal. Examples include a raised hand, a flick of the lights, a noise maker, and patterned hand claps.
	5. Teach students to distribute and collect materials within their teams.
Build teams	6. Encourage students to rely on each other by using team-building activities. Examples include team interviews and developing team names or hats.
Teach social skills	7. Directly teach students to interact in positive ways.
	• Post a list of the behaviors you expect to see and model those behaviors for the students.
	• Consider assigning roles such as encourager and task master to help students learn skills.
	8. Monitor social skills. Reinforce appropriate social behaviors. Allow students to evaluate their own use of social skills regularly.
Use cooperative learning strategies throughout instruction	9. Select from a variety of structures to embed cooperative learning within your regular instruction
Analyze and revise	10. Monitor students' growth in social skills and encourage them to self-monitor through self-assessments.
	• Reorganize teams as appropriate.
	• Set new goals for yourself and your students based on their current work.

use of a variety of structures can be embedded within this sequence. There are plentiful structures and resources on the Web. For example, try the links at CAST's site: http://www.cast.org/publications/ncac/ ncac_peermii.html In the meantime, here are four to get you started.

1. *Jigsaw II* (Slavin, 1995): Students in heterogeneous teams read the same chapter of material, with each member focusing on particular "expert" topics in the chapter. Students meet in groups with other experts to discuss the material and decide how to present it to group members. Back in their home teams, members teach each other their expert topics, ensuring that each member has mastered all topics. Students are assessed on the material, and the teacher records both individual scores and team scores that are based on the improvement gains of each individual student.(Content mastery)

2. *Inside–outside circle* (Kagan, 1994): Two concentric circles form, and students face each other. Partnered with the outside circle person directly across from him or her, each inside circle student shares and then listens as the outside circle person shares. The outside circle rotates so new partners can converse. (Information sharing)

3. *Student-Teams Achievement Divisions* (STAD; Slavin, 1995): Based on the lesson objective, the teacher presents new information in a manner that closely relates to quizzes students will take later. Then team members practice the information together, using worksheets or other materials. Team members' responsibility is to ensure that all members have mastered the content. Next, every student takes a quiz on the material. Individuals receive scores based on their improvement over time. Team scores are determined by combining individual improvement scores. Recognition is given to teams based on their team scores.(Content mastery)

4. *Team statements* (Kagan, 1994): Each person writes an individual statement about a topic. Students share their statements and then develop a team statement that synthesizes each of the individual statements. (Thinking skills)

A Sample Cooperative Learning Lesson Figure 6.15 shares a sample lesson for second graders that uses three of Kagan's cooperative learning structures.

Strengths and Criticisms of the Cooperative Learning Model Cooperative learning offers refreshing changes to traditional classroom practice. First, it

FIGURE 6.15   *A sample cooperative learning lesson.*

Objectives:	Second-grade students will synthesize information from their aquarium field trip as evidenced by their descriptions of the murals they create.
	Students will exhibit two social skills: listening to each other and asking the teacher a question only when no group member can answer it.
Open	1. The class gets ready to learn.
	• Class is seated on the floor in a misshapen circle.
	• A fully included student using a wheelchair is sitting next to several friends who like to help out.
	• The teacher directs students to choose a partner by making eye contact with a person nearby and linking up.
	• She watches to ensure that all students are matched in a respectful way, and then she has them number off (1 and 2).

continued

FIGURE 6.15 *Continued.*

	2. Teacher states, "Here are some plastic animals like the animals we saw on our aquarium field trip. I have plenty. Partner 2, come here, choose one, talk to your partner about what you remember about the animal on the trip, and then return it to the center so that Partner 1 can choose another animal." 3. Teacher watches the partner group with her fully included student to ensure that the student's partner doesn't do too much for him. She monitors others as well. 4. Teacher compliments the students: "Do you know what I noticed as you were talking? When your partner spoke, you really listened. I could tell because you were looking at your partner, nodding and sometimes smiling. You didn't interrupt either. Careful listening is the social skill we'll practice today and tomorrow. What does it *look like* to listen carefully? What does it *sound like?*" A brief discussion ensues and the teacher charts their responses. 5. "I can tell from your conversations that you learned many things from our field trip. Today you will have a chance to share what you learned by creating a team mural. Tomorrow we will describe our murals to each other."

Body	6. Each partner group joins up with another to form teams of four and they renumber, 1–4.
	
	7. At their team tables, students fact-storm on their trip.
	  • Using a strategy called roundtable, one student writes a memory from the aquarium trip on a large sheet of paper, then passes the paper to the next member. The partner of the fully included student takes his dictation.
	  • Students continue writing for about 10 minutes, until the paper is full.
	  • "Now that you have so many animals and plants recorded, see if your team can group them in some logical way. Write on the chart."
	
	8. "Use your groupings to create a mural. Look toward the back of our room and you will see many materials you may use."
	  • Students: "Dude! Glitter!"
	  • Teacher continues: "Here's the rule for making your mural. I have made a sign that describes your job. See? Member 1, you are in control of the scissors. Only you may cut. Member 2, you are the magazine monitor. Any pictures selected from the magazine are your responsibility. You see that you may need 1 to cut for you, right? Member 3, your job is Fancy Material Captain. Glitter and crepe paper belong only to you. Member 4, markers are your job."
	  • She checks for understanding on directions. Satisfied, teacher states, "Use your charts and get to work."
	
	9. Children work until lunch on their murals.
	  • Teacher monitors to be certain that members are making their unique contributions based on their roles.
	  • When individuals ask her questions, she asks, "Have you asked each person in your group that question yet?"
	  • She applies some time pressures to keep groups productive, and she reinforces the listening skills students demonstrate.

Close	10. The next day: To share their murals and allow the teacher to assess the first objective, students use the "one stay, three stray" structure.
	  • All Number 1's stand by their group mural and describe it to three visitors.
	  • Next, Number 2's stay and describe while the others stray to see the murals of other groups.
	  • Teacher takes anecdotal notes on students' presentations.
	  • Back in their home groups, groups write one statement about what they saw and heard about other groups' murals.
	  • Statements are posted near the murals.
	
	11. Students talk briefly in their groups to evaluate their social skills.
	  • They focus on the chosen skill, careful listening.
	  • They discuss the questions "What did we do well as a group today?" and "What will we work on for next time?"

breaks the typical discourse pattern where teachers do most of the talking. It can enliven a classroom because it allows a far greater number of people to talk—to develop oral communication skills—at once. Second, cooperative learning changes the typical expectation that students need to succeed only as individuals and instead builds as norms social interaction and interdependence. Third, whereas student differences are sometimes seen as problematic, cooperative learning suggests that the more diverse the group, the richer the potential outcomes. Fourth, cooperative learning meets many of the principles addressed in Chapter 5. It is highly interactive, it capitalizes on human nature by allowing students to be actively involved throughout the lesson, and it allows students to form connections to the subject matter and with other students.

Still, cooperative learning brings some difficulties. Cooperative learning lessons can take more time than traditional presentations because students are simultaneously learning social skills. Cooperative classrooms require diligence from the teacher in terms of classroom management. It takes skill to harness students' energy and ensure that students are working productively. It can also be a challenge to guide students in solving their social difficulties when a teacher's temptation is to quickly solve the problem and move on. Finally, it is the teacher's responsibility to structure lessons that require every student to contribute to the group's work. One of the greatest challenges of cooperative learning is to bar the possibility that students can freeload.

When will you use cooperative learning? Informal techniques such as partner sharing are easily integrated into traditional instruction. Try the three cooperative techniques given in Teaching Tip 6.5. Individual lessons that employ cooperative structures are also possible. Structuring your entire classroom around the principles of cooperative learning will probably require you to receive additional training or to study some of the excellent resources that describe cooperative learning methods. As you consider cooperative learning, remember the power of your role as instructional leader. You must arrange events so that you can manage students' behavior, monitor their social skills, and ensure that they truly are helping each other succeed. Think through your activities, anticipate trouble spots, and plan some alternative responses to keep your cooperative lessons productive. Also consider whether and how technology might enhance your selection of instructional strategies.

Teaching Tip 6.5

COOPERATIVE LEARNING QUICK STARTS

Use quick collaborative activities to increase interaction, language, and learning. Here are three to get you going.

1. *Peer teach:* Pause a few times during a lesson. Have one partner re-teach the content to the other. They switch roles next time.
2. *Traveling partners:* Before the lesson begins, have students sign up for traveling partners. Each records the other's name. Or you designate the partners. They should not sit near each other. When it is time during the lesson, signal students to travel to their partners. Partners might work a problem, discuss an issue, or check over their notes. Signal when it's time to head back to their seats.
3. *Four-two-one:* At the end of a lesson, have students individually write down what they think are the four most important words from the lesson. In partners or small groups, have students share their words and then devise a list of just two important words. Everyone must agree. Finally, in partners or small groups, they pick the one word that captures the lesson best (Rogers, Ludington, & Graham, 1999).

INSTRUCTIONAL STRATEGIES AND TECHNOLOGY

Driscoll (2002) argues that human learning is contextual, active, social, and reflective. Technology can neatly address the nature of human learning, she further argues, by providing realistic contexts and engaging and interactive activities with plentiful opportunities to reflect. Although no instructional strategy *requires* use of advanced technologies, some include prevalent use of technology in meeting human learning needs. Problem-based learning is one example. Technology is useful in problem-based learning because it can provide a multitude of resources quickly. Simulations are a second example. Technology is highly useful in simulations because it allows the user to virtually manipulate time, resources, and other variables without having to experience real consequences. This is what makes computer-based simulations a prevalent training option for professions such as flight, health care, law enforcement, and the military.

Simulations are becoming more prevalent in classrooms too. Animal dissection is an example. For ethical, cost, and other reasons, some teachers and students are selecting virtual dissections over traditional animal dissections as a learning tool. Visit http://froguts.com and try out the frog and squid demos as examples of virtual dissections. Evaluations of computer-based dissections indicate that students who engage in virtual dissections can learn at rates that are at least comparable to those who engage in traditional dissections (e.g., Maloney, 2002; Predavec, 2001). Virtual dissections are not without their flaws (Allchin, 2005), however, and factors such as time spent in dissection also affect student learning.

Technology can serve as a useful tool for any instructional strategy you choose by allowing you to present information effectively, by fostering students' research, by facilitating interaction and communication (Hamm & Adams, 2002; Schultz-Zander, Buchter, & Dalmer, 2002), and expanding the array of products students create. Here are some examples.

In terms of your presentation of information, during a direct instruction lesson, you might present a video clip of the model you wish students to emulate. Or you might use graphing calculators to display and practice a concept. During a cooperative learning lesson, you might provide text at different levels (recall Teaching Tip 4.2 for leveling text) or text that is read aloud by the computer for students with different needs. You might present a political map of the United States, with state names added gradually, during a concept attainment lesson on the origin of state names. You might post words or images on an interactive whiteboard and allow students to drag and drop them into yes/no groups for concept attainment, or into related categories for concept formation.

In terms of student research, you might make the Internet available during the explore phase of a learning cycle or during the information gathering phase of unguided inquiry. To foster student interaction, you might encourage students to post and respond to each other's findings for inquiry sessions. To enhance students' products, you might allow students to create multimedia presentations (Steelman, 2005) or their own Web pages as culminating activities for cooperative learning projects. They may create and share audio recordings or word processed documents of their conclusions for concept formation sessions. As each of these examples indicates, technology provides a set of tools that can help us make effective use of the instructional strategies we choose while we simultaneously assist students in gaining technological proficiency.

PARTING WORDS

Classroom teaching is so demanding that it is easy to retreat to instructional methods that do not require us to consider best practice, to enact our stances toward education, to stretch as professionals, or to stray from the ways we were taught as children. However, teaching is more than telling. Skilled teachers can use a number of instructional strategies to suit their purposes and encourage different kinds of growth for their learners. Make learning and using a number of instructional strategies a priority, perhaps selecting one or two based on your work from the Before You Begin Reading exercise in this chapter. When you try any new strategy, think very carefully about what you will say at each point, what you will expect from the students, and what you will do if things do not go as planned. Expect that you will need repeated opportunities to practice new strategies; in fact, research on staff development suggests that a strategy may not feel natural until you try it about a dozen times. A dozen times! Further, be vigilant in thinking about how using a variety of instructional strategies can help you differentiate your instruction so that it pushes all of your students to their learning potential. The harder you work to build your instructional repertoire, the better able you will be to help your students grow and develop.

WEB SITES

Use the names of strategies given in this chapter to conduct your Internet search for teaching techniques. Examples include the following:

http://www.imsa.edu/team/cpbl/cpbl.html
  Center for Problem-Based Learning by Illinois Mathematics and Science Academy. Start with the tutorial, then move to Sample Problems.

http://www.thirteen.org/edonline/concept2class/
  Concept to Classroom. This site offers free online workshops in topics such as cooperative learning, inquiry-based learning, and Webquests. Solid information is supplemented with video.

http://www.inquiry.uiuc.edu/
  The Inquiry Page. Includes a helpful inquiry cycle and examples of inquiry in practice. Browse the inquiry units, but be sure to evaluate the submissions using your knowledge of the critical attributes of inquiry.

http://olc.spsd.sk.ca/DE/PD/instr/index.html
  Instructional Strategies Online. This site groups dozens of methods within a handful of strategies. A valuable resource, it provides background, step-by-step directions, and plentiful resources to help

you master a variety of techniques. One example from this chapter is concept attainment.

The instructional strategies presented in this chapter are just a subset of the myriad strategies you can try. Others, such as virtual field trips and simulations, are also readily available. To get started, try these sites:

http://www.awesomelibrary.org/
  Awesome Library. Look around, or search for the word "simulation" within the site and locate many activities that allow students to experience content through memorable, role-play-type activities.

http://www.uen.org/utahlink/tours/
  Virtual Field Trips by Utah Education Network. This site provides great links and prepares students for their virtual travels.

http://webquest.org/
  WebQuest News. This site presents WebQuests by their founder, Bernie Dodge at San Diego State University. Membership in the QuestGarden community has a fee, but teachers can search WebQuests by grade level and content area for free.

OPPORTUNITIES TO PRACTICE

1. The direct instruction strategy plays an important role in a skilled teacher's repertoire. A common misconception, though, is that direct instruction is the same as lecture. Restructure one of these video lesson clips to meet the five stages of the direct instruction model:

   • Elementary writing lesson on voice (found at the Merrill Teacher Prep Web site Video Classroom, Reading Methods, Module 6, Video 2).

   • High school history lesson on the Vietnam War (found at the Merrill Teacher Prep Web site Video Classroom, General Methods, Module 5, Video 1).

   This is for practice in writing a direct instruction plan (recall Figure 6.1 and use the form in Figure 6.16). Use the lesson events as a basis, but take

some license to exaggerate the five stages. This means you may need to add content or delete it to highlight the use of direct instruction.

2. Recover yourself teaching or ask for permission to observe another teacher. Tally the number of questions the teacher asks and how many the students ask. Analyze your data of question–answer patterns according to some of the topics given early (pp. 139–140) in this chapter. What is your evaluation of the questioning you observed?

3. Observe another teacher lead a lesson. Afterward, discuss with the teacher the choices he made about instructional strategies. Ask him how many of the strategies from Chapter 6 he knows and which he prefers. If an observation is not possible, try

analyzing the teacher's editions from a published curriculum series. How many of the strategies are suggested? What is your evaluation of the use of instructional strategies? What changes might you suggest?

4. Make a prioritized list for yourself of the strategies you will work to master. Busy? I suggest you choose, for a start, direct instruction and one other strategy. Study the stages of the models as if you are studying for an exam. Commit them to memory and then bring them to life through intense effort to model them each a couple times. Work with a colleague and discuss your experience.

5. Write two contrasting lessons using strategies from Chapter 6. Use an objective from your classroom or the following one: "Students will retell three major events from a story [name one] in the correct sequence." Blank lesson plan forms are included in Figure 6.16.

6. Figure 6.16 includes lesson plan formats for each of the instructional strategies in Chapter 6. Use them as you plan lessons that incorporate different strategies. Remember to include cognitive, affective, and psychomotor objectives as appropriate. Also, include assessment to match each of your objectives.

FIGURE 6.16 *Lesson plan formats.*

Direct Instruction Lesson

Objective(s):   Materials:

Expectations for behavior:

Open	1. Anticipatory set: • Focus: • Objective: • Purpose:
Body	2. Input: • Provide input: • Check for understanding: 3. Guided practice:
Close	4. Closure: 5. Independent practice:

Continued

FIGURE 6.16 *Continued.*

Inquiry Training Lesson

Objective(s):   Materials:

Open	1. Discrepant event: 2. State students' task:
Body	3. Elicit questions that verify conditions and events of the discrepant event: • Sample acceptable questions: • Sample prompts to encourage appropriate questions: 4. Elicit questions that test hypotheses: • Sample acceptable questions: • Sample prompts to encourage appropriate questions:
Close	5. Guide students to formally state their explanations:

Continued

FIGURE 6.16   Continued.

Concept Attainment Lesson

Concept or rule to be discovered:

Objective(s):

Materials (list examples and counterexamples of your concept):

Open	1. Briefly display objects: 2. State students' task:
Body	3. Present examples and counterexamples of the concept or rule (list the order in which examples will be presented): 4. Allow students to test their hypothesized rules by (a) citing their own examples and nonexamples and/or (b) talking with peers. Prompts:
Close	5. Allow the rule to be stated for the class: 6. Allow for observations of the content and process of the lesson: 7. Invite further exploration (e.g., allow students to create their own groups):

FIGURE 6.16 Continued.

Learning Cycle Lesson

Concept or rule to be discovered:

Objective(s):

Materials:

Open	1. Engage (use a real world phenomenon hook the students; elicit questions; determine background knowledge):
Body	2. Explore (work with concrete materials; determine emerging concepts and terms): 3. Develop (formally develop concepts and terms from the explore phase; use readings, direct presentations, and other methods to ensure mastery of the objective):
Close	4. Apply (provide a novel problem to which new knowledge can be applied or make some other real-world connection):

Continued

FIGURE 6.16 *Continued.*

Concept Formation Lesson

If specified, concepts or generalizations to be discovered:

Objective(s):

Materials:

Open	1. Introduce the topic and ask a question that will generate a list of terms:
Body	2. List (prompt students to generate an extensive list related to the topic): 3. Group (prompt students to group items from the list): 4. Label (prompt students to name the groups): 5. Optional: Regroup (prompt students to find other ways items can be grouped):
Close	6. Call students' attention to the concepts or generalizations that arise from their groupings. Prompt: 7. Extend learning through an additional assignment, such as a drawing, writing, or speaking opportunity:

FIGURE 6.16 *Continued.*

Unguided Inquiry Lesson	
If specified, concepts or generalizations to be discovered:	
Objective(s) (consider both content and research skill or process objectives):	
Materials (list concrete materials and information sources):	
Open	1. Present stimulus material that suggests a problem or issue for study:
	2. Guide students to state the problem in clear terms. Prompts:
	3. Decide on appropriate methods to address the problem. Prompts:
	4. Set the guidelines for study. Prompts:
Body	5. Monitor students as they employ their methods. Prompts to encourage careful study:
Close	6. Encourage students to draw conclusions regarding (a) the problem and (b) the processes of investigation. Prompts:

FIGURE 6.16   *Continued.*

Cooperative Learning Lesson

Content objective(s):

Social skill objective(s):

Materials:

Prelesson questions	a. How are teams formed? b. What quiet signal will you use? c. What team-building and class-building efforts have you taken or will you take?
Open	1. Focus students' attention and allude to the lesson's content and activities: 2. State expectations for cooperative work and teach social skills:
Body	3. Use a cooperative learning structure to present information or encourage discovery learning. Samples from Chapters 5 and 6 include the following: blackboard blitz inside–outside circle round table brainstorming jigsaw roving review four corners numbered heads together stand to share gallery walk one stay, three stray values lineups group problems peer interviews 4. Monitor students' use of social skills. Sample prompts:
Close	5. Summarize the learning. Prompts or cooperative strategy: 6. Process students' use of social skills:

Before You Begin Reading

Chapter 7

Warm-Up Exercise for Assessment

Think back to your years as a student. How did your teachers know whether and what you learned? What kinds of feedback did you receive? Take three minutes to jot down as many different assessment strategies as you can recall experiencing.

Now mark each of these statements with *agree* or *disagree:*

1. Teachers knew me as a multifaceted person with varied strengths and skills.
2. Teachers were interested in my own assessments of my work.
3. Teachers encouraged me to set my own learning goals.
4. The feedback I received from tests and other assessments helped me learn.
5. Teachers changed what they did in the classroom based on student assessment data.

Finally, evaluate your answers for statements 1 through 5. Were your experiences with assessment as a student positive? Would it have been better if teachers had assessed your learning differently?

Here is a chance for you to use effective practices from both the past and present to make a difference for today's students. Use your conclusions to help make sense of the following chapter and to build your own system for assessing student progress.

CHAPTER *Seven*

Assessment

*"O*pen your mouth and say, 'Ahhh'."

—Anonymous Physician

Just as physicians evaluate patients' well-being with physical signs and tests using well-established protocols, educators assess their clients' progress, plan appropriate interventions, and report on the health of our schools to the public. Careful assessment of student progress is both challenging and essential. Assessment is critical because it allows us to provide for students' needs. It is through assessment that we can form appropriate groups, plan responsive instruction, and differentiate our teaching to meet students' needs. Through assessment we can garner resources for our students. Assessment reveals persistent inequities that might otherwise go unnoticed. It allows us to show the public the progress we make. Assessment supports us in our serious responsibility to help all students learn rigorous content.

This chapter presents six guiding principles for assessing student learning. It then provides examples of different assessment strategies, each useful for different purposes. If you have limited experience with student assessment and would benefit by seeing descriptions of some assessment strategies, glance at the section "Assessment Strategies" starting on page 195 before reading these general guidelines.

GENERAL GUIDELINES FOR STUDENT ASSESSMENT

Effective teachers gather information of different kinds over time to ensure that their pupils are learning and that they themselves are providing appropriate instruction. An assessment instrument is not inherently good or bad. Rather, its worth depends on whether it is effective for particular purposes in specific settings. The following six guidelines can help you to select and develop instruments that are useful elements of your own system for student assessment. Assessment needs to be:

1. Tied to your stance on education
2. Driven by learning goals
3. Systematic
4. Tied to instruction
5. Inclusive of the learner
6. Integrated into a manageable system

Assessment Needs to Be Tied to Your Stance on Education

As a nation, we test what we value, for better or worse. As a professional, your views about the good society, about the purposes of education, and about teaching and learning should be reflected in the ways you assess student progress. For example, if it is important to you that students master a large body of factual knowledge, then it is essential that you use assessment strategies that carefully tap into students' mastery of facts. Likewise, if one of your goals is for students to become independent thinkers, then you need to provide opportunities for them to evaluate their own work and to show that they are growing in their capacity for autonomous thought. Check the tests and other assessment tools you use. Make sure they send a message that is consistent with the way you are convinced life should be.

Assessment Needs to Be Driven by Learning Goals

Today's accountability climate means that we continuously gauge progress of individual students, groups of students, schools, districts, states, and even nations. Student achievement results are published and scrutinized, and rewards and sanctions are based on students' growth or lack of growth as measured by standardized test scores. Schools that consistently fail to improve, for example, could be subject to takeover. You can read about this and other sanctions and accountability provisions at the NCLB page of the government's Web site (http://www.ed.gov/nclb). Students, too, are increasingly held accountable for learning, with many states requiring students to pass examinations in order to complete a certain grade level or to graduate from high school.

Central to the accountability effort is that student performance is assessed in line with our instructional goals, supplied through our content standards. We select our goals based on priorities for student learning. The planning and instruction chapters of this book (Chapters 4, 5, and 6) argue that we should teach to our goals. Then we test (or measure) what we have taught. As the accountability movement emphasizes, goals, instruction, and assessment all need to be aligned.

Most of us have at least one college horror story about course goals and class activities that had no apparent relation to the class's final examination. Those horror stories disappear when assessments are based clearly upon explicit goals. In standards-based instruction and assessment, we select or write goals that address important points and teach what is important. Then we test (or more broadly, assess) what we have taught. Remember, too, that if a concept, generalization, skill, attitude, or ability was important enough to be included in a list of instructional goals, it is important enough to be included in the list of items to assess as well. Using goals to drive assessment requires that we address different levels, time spans, and domains.

Assessment Occurs on Different Levels   Recall the bull's-eye from Chapter 1 that placed you and your students at the center of a system. Because your classroom is embedded in concentric societal layers, you and your students will participate in different levels of assessment. Figure 7.1 lists many current test-related terms.

One of our national goals is general literacy. As a result, No Child Left Behind requires all students in grades 3 through 8 to take annual statewide achievement tests in reading and mathematics. These examinations must match state content standards, the learning goals. Additionally, a sample of fourth, eighth, and twelfth graders across the United States must take the National Assessment of Educational Progress (NAEP) examination to allow for achievement comparisons across states. Visit http://nces.ed.gov/nationsreportcard/ to view a wealth of information such as your state's profile (including expenditures per pupil,

FIGURE 7.1   *Assessment and accountability terms.*

Adequate yearly progress (AYP)	A federal requirement that schools make progress in approaching the 2014 goal of 100% of students performing at "proficient" level. AYP is calculated as a percentage above the school's baseline measure. Ninety-five percent of students in all subgroups and the total school must make AYP for the school to make AYP.
Alternative (or authentic) assessment	A measure that assesses student learning in realistic contexts to show application of knowledge and skills.
Assessment versus evaluation	*Assessment* is the process of gathering information; *evaluation* is the act of judging that information, of assigning a value to it. Many use the terms synonymously.
Benchmark	In terms of NCLB, benchmarks present intermediate goals on the way to 100% proficiency.
Criterion-referenced measures	Results are evaluated based upon a comparison with an external standard. All students (or schools) are awarded the highest level if they demonstrate that level of achievement. Example: 90% = A.
High-stakes evaluation	Assessment results that have real consequences for the participants or other stakeholders. Examples include eligibility for special services, high school graduation, and the withholding of funding.
Low-performing schools	Schools that continue to have achievement scores below expectations. Sometimes other measures such as low graduation rates also are considered. These schools are required to develop plans to improve, and resources are available to help.
Low-stakes evaluation	Assessment results that are useful primarily in local and informal ways. An example is a classroom attitude survey that measures students' opinions about reading.
Multiple measures	Use of more than one instrument to determine progress. Multiple measures are an effort to decrease errors in measurement and capture students' progress more holistically. No Child Left Behind requires that AYP be based on at least one measure in addition to standardized tests.
National Assessment of Education Progress	A mandated measure of academic achievement with a nationwide sample.
Norm-referenced measures	Results are evaluated based upon a comparison with the scores of others; grading on a curve. Only a certain percentage can, by definition, achieve the highest score. Schools can be compared with other schools using norm-referenced procedures to examine achievement.
Performance levels	Determinations for criteria at different levels of achievement. Examples include "pass," "fail," "proficient," and "advanced."

percent of students with individual education programs, and percentage participation in English proficiency programs), released test items (click on "sample questions"), and achievement in several subject areas over time.

Standardized tests such as the NAEP typically provide a variety of kinds of information. They include **norm-referenced** information, which means that your students' achievement will be compared with the achievement of students in a norming group. Your school's overall achievement will also be compared with that of other schools. How well your students (or your school) score depends on the relation of their scores to those of the norming group. Additionally, standardized tests provide **criterion-referenced** information, which deems certain outcomes as "mastered" or compares performance to various levels of mastery. In fact, NCLB requires that all U.S. students reach "proficient" by the year 2014.

The public maintains an eager interest in standardized test scores because standardized tests give general information about students' progress at the school, district, state, and national levels. The public interprets standardized test scores as an important measure of the health of America's schools. Heated debates arise about the validity of standardized tests as a measure of important outcomes. Proponents argue that well-educated students should be able to communicate their knowledge via mechanisms such as carefully constructed, broad-based measures. Some vocal critics (e.g., Kohn, 1999, 2001) condemn standardized tests as incapable of measuring important outcomes, of limiting our vision of what is important, and of being biased against students of color. Some seriously doubt the ability of standardized tests to measure the types of learning and intelligence that relate to success in the real world. Sternberg (1997a, 1997b), for instance, argues that successful intelligence—the ability to adapt to one's environment to accomplish goals—is not measured by standardized tests. Sternberg also asserts that standardized tests emphasize conformity in thought instead of valuing diverse approaches to learning. Others argue that high-stakes testing has unintended consequences that restrict students' educational experience (Laitsch, 2006).

Because of the great interest—and increasingly the tangible rewards and punishments—attached to standardized tests, such measures are considered high-stakes evaluations. However, their very nature as *standardized* assessments means that they provide less information about life inside your specific classroom in order to focus on content of interest across classrooms. For instance, content measured on national examinations may not be a good match with the content selected for your locale. Also, your students' scores may remain relatively stable, but their standing can change radically based on changes of the norming group's scores. **Local assessments,** on the other hand, provide information more directly related to your instruction. Examples include your district-selected benchmark tests and assessments you use daily in the classroom. Classroom assessments serve the primary purpose of immediately fostering student learning and improving instruction.

Local instructional goals are more specific and dictate the use of classroom-based assessments. Many classroom assessments are *criterion referenced* instead of norm referenced. Through criterion-referenced tests, students' achievement is measured by comparing their scores to predetermined criteria instead of to other students' scores. For example, you may set the criterion of 85% accuracy as demonstrating satisfactory mastery of particular mathematics concepts. Local assessments are often considered lower-stakes measures (though perhaps not by students).

Both levels of assessment—large-scale and local—can contribute unique information to our understanding of students' progress. The trick is to be smart in considering the kind of information that each level of assessment can provide. Keep in mind the purpose of particular assessments as you interpret your students' progress and speak with students, families, and professionals about that progress. The kinds of assessments we select also depend on the time frames of our goals.

Different Time Spans Require Different Assessments   You have both long- and short-term goals for your students, so you need measures to assess student progress in both the long and short ranges. At the most immediate level, you will conduct assessments related to your daily lesson objectives. Assessment for each lesson needs to determine students' progress toward the lesson's objectives. With the crush of classroom events, it is tempting to restrict assessments to those that measure quick, discrete skills and ideas. But don't. Beyond single, discrete objectives, you will assess mastery of a certain standard or generalization that consists of work with several objectives. Then, for documenting students' long-range growth, you will need to gather information that allows you to track students' progress over time.

Assessment Needs to Be More Than Cognitive Based on your stance toward education and on grade-level recommendations, you probably have goals for your students in the cognitive, psychomotor, and affective (the thinking, doing, and feeling) domains. School assessments in the past have focused heavily on the cognitive domain, and as a result, teachers may have glimpsed only a segment of students' progress. A multiple-choice test, for instance, tells very little about students' attitudes toward the subject matter.

Recent development of content standards may help address this shortcoming. The National Science Education Standards (National Research Council, 1996), for instance, require students to master the *abilities* necessary to do scientific inquiry, which include, for example, *employing equipment and tools* to gather data. Those abilities include psychomotor skills. The National Science Education Standards also emphasize *appreciation* for science as a way of knowing the world and the *dispositions* and *attitudes* associated with science.

Even if your state standards do not yet address domains outside of the cognitive realm, you as a teacher have the responsibility to assess student progress in *each area* you have deemed as important given your view of what it means to be educated, local planning efforts, and your knowledge of the discipline. Match your goals across domains with at least one way to check students' growth related to those goals. Stiggins (2001) suggests that teachers use assessments to measure a variety of targets, including:

- Knowledge and understanding
- Reasoning
- Performance skills
- Proficiency in creating products
- Dispositions

You will need to think hard about ways to tap student growth for some of your goals, especially when multiple domains are addressed or when goals seem elusive. Strategies described later in the chapter, such as journal entries, observations, and attitude surveys, can help. Different kinds of goals and objectives often require different assessment strategies. Devise a plan that includes a number of ways to determine whether and what students are learning related to your varied goals.

In fact, Reineke (1998) and Walvoord and Anderson (1998) argue that even when teachers have no plans for assessing affect, assessment tends to involve a good deal of emotion for students. Walvoord and Anderson (1998, p. 13) intone

> Because grades [the results of assessments] are highly symbolic, because they reveal and complicate the bases of power in the classroom, because they so powerfully shape interrelationships among students and teacher, and because they often carry high stakes for learners, they will evoke strong emotions.

Teachers should therefore seize the opportunity to teach when students respond to evaluations with emotion: "Such moments of emotional intensity may be the most powerful teaching moments of the semester," Walvoord and Anderson suggest (1998, p. 14).

Assessment Needs to Address Incidental Learnings, Too Despite the fact that planning, instruction, and assessment must be logically linked (goals → teach → test), many things influence student learning; teaching is one. Learning can be highly individualistic. Students learn things related to our goals, but not only those things. Additionally, based on their idiosyncratic characteristics, students do not learn the same things, even given the same instruction. Therefore, you need to include in your assessment plan a means to determine, in addition to your goals for student learning, *what else* students have learned. A journal prompt such as, "What surprises did you encounter during our unit on

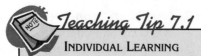

INDIVIDUAL LEARNING

Before you collect a major assignment or close a long-range unit of study, say to your students, "People learn different things. You may have learned something about yourself, about your peers, or something about the content that you did not expect." Invite students to share the things they have learned via discussion or a quick write.

Ancient Rome? What did you learn from your peers? What questions do you still have?" may tap into these serendipitous outcomes. See Teaching Tip 7.1 for an idea for assessing individual students' varied learning.

Assessment Needs to Be Systematic

No matter your stance toward education, you need to gather information about your students' learning in ways that are accurate, fair, and systematic. Because teachers busily engage in many activities at once, their conclusions about students are sometimes based on recollections of informal and fleeting observations. Unfortunately, human perception tends to be selective, and teacher memory is faulty. Reineke (1998, p. 7) reminds us that assessment involves *people:* "Assessments, formal or informal, considered or casual, intentional or not, powerfully affect people, particularly students. . . . Students' assessment experiences remain with them for a lifetime and substantially affect their capacity for future learning." Therefore, you need to develop a plan that will allow you to gather information about student learning in ways that are logical and equitable. Make a plan for collecting information in a fair manner—a valid and reliable manner—that gives students ample opportunity to display the breadth and depth of their growth and understanding.

Validity and Reliability   Being systematic will increase the chances that the measures (tests and other assessments) you use are **valid** and **reliable.** A *valid* instrument measures what it was intended to measure. Does it tap into students' understanding of the intended content? Whether an instrument measures what it should is based partly on its reliability. A *reliable* measure gives consistent results under different conditions and with different raters. It is free of error. A measure may be valid in one setting and completely inappropriate in another. When you work on being systematic with your assessments, you will guard instruments' reliability and validity.

Although the criteria of validity and reliability seem obvious, they are regularly trampled in classroom practice. One example is the sixth-grade class in which a group of English learners took their social studies instruction in Spanish (as was consistent with the school's policies for bilingual education). When it was time for the Spanish-speaking students to share what they had learned, however, they were given the same written exam—in English—as other members of the class. Their teacher probably received inaccurate information about the students' knowledge of social studies, and the experience may have eroded students' dignity, which was probably not in keeping with the teacher's stance toward education.

Another example of invalid assessment also concerns the use of language. In many classes, students who read at lower levels of proficiency are given written tests in subjects such as science and social studies with no modifications. For low-proficiency readers, written tests can be more tests of reading ability than they are of content knowledge. If teachers' intent is to gain a valid picture of students' content knowledge, teachers may need to consider altering the testing format to sidestep reading issues. For instance, it may be appropriate for struggling readers to hear written tests read aloud.

One of the best ways you can ensure that you are developing a thorough and valid understanding of students' progress is by using **multiple measures**, or many pieces of evidence collected using varied formats. This approach will help you to provide a number of chances and avenues for students to show what they know, to account for student differences, and to ensure that you are sampling different kinds of information about students' knowledge, attitudes, and development. Additionally, you may need to differentiate your assessments, just as you do your instruction, to be sure that you are systematically measuring all students' learning (see Figure 7.2).

FIGURE 7.2 *Multiple measures can be used to differentiate and help ensure valid results.*

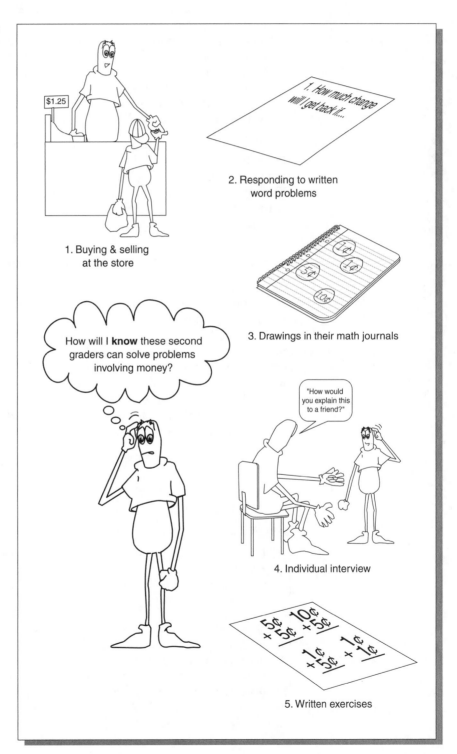

Differentiated Assessment   Our assessments can better capture our students' progress if assessments are varied and matched to students' capabilities. Chapter 3 introduced approaches to provide responsive instruction; those approaches also provide guidance for us as assessors. For instance, you may need to include additional visual supports or examples, read directions aloud, or provide extra work time. Here are other examples:

- Students with special needs may require accommodations to classroom assessment procedures; they may require larger print or highlighted key terms, for instance. They may also require modifications to the tasks such as fewer problems or the use of a calculator.
- English learners may need to express their learning in the primary language, may require the use of a dictionary, or may respond to closed-ended prompts rather than constructed-response ones.
- Struggling readers may listen to the computer read the test to them as they wear headphones.
- Gifted students may be expected to respond to an assessment prompt with greater complexity or in greater depth.

We should consider, then, adjustable classroom assessments that allow students to reveal what they know (Gregory & Kuzmich, 2004). Teaching Tip 7.2 provides one example of adjustable assessments: tiered assessments (Tomlinson, 2001; Wormeli, 2006). By being responsive, sensitive, thorough, and careful—by being fair—you can determine whether and what every one of your students is learning.

Assessment Needs to Be Tied to Instruction

The goals → teach → test cycle is indeed a cycle. As Gronlund (2004) notes, assessment actually begins in the planning phase, as you develop your objectives. Content standards provide outcomes, or targets, that typically contain a number of components captured through objectives. You study your objectives and standards in order to specify your assessments. Once your objectives and goals are in place, you provide instruction to meet them and to bring students success at assessment. Assessment results should both drive instruction and guide the selection of future learning goals. Tying assessment to instruction means that you assess *before, during,* and *after instruction* to enhance student learning and spend your planning and instructional efforts wisely.

Teaching Tip 7.2

TIERED ASSESSMENTS

1. Determine what full proficiency of the content standard would look like. What evidence would you accept as mastery?
2. Use that level as the minimum acceptable level; all students must demonstrate mastery at that level.
3. Adjust the complexity or challenge of the assessment for students who are working at higher levels of readiness. For example, students at lower levels of readiness might demonstrate proficiency by graphing linear equations where variables are whole numbers and they are given the graph. Students at higher levels might graph variables that are fractions or absolute values, and they might generate the graph themselves.
4. Learning menus and learning contracts, where students choose their assessments on occasion, are also adjustable assessments (Wormeli, 2006).

Assessing Prior to Instruction   On the day before her lesson on the Eighth Amendment, a social studies teacher hands each small group an envelope of 10 statements she selected from the supplemental workbook and cut into strips, five with true statements about the Eighth Amendment, and five with false. Strip number 3 reads, for instance, "The Eighth Amendment prohibits the federal government from punishing citizens for their crimes." The students work in their groups to sort the statements into two stacks: true or false. Statement 3 goes in the false stack. The teacher circulates and notes that most students already know about the protection against cruel and unusual punishment, but few know about the protection the Eighth Amendment provides against excessive fines. She focuses tomorrow's lesson more clearly on that provision.

This teacher's engaging 10-minute activity (a true/false sort from Guillaume, Yopp, & Yopp, 2007) is an example of formative assessment. Other ideas for rapid preassessments are homework, group problems, and brainstormed lists. Chapter 4 shared these ideas as it introduced formative assessment, or assessment that allows you to adjust your teaching to respond to student needs. Research indicates that formative assessment has a positive effect on student learning (Fuchs, Fuchs, Hamlett, Phillips, & Bentz, 1994; Herman, Osmundson, Ayala, Schneider, & Timms, 2006).

By assessing students' prior knowledge, teachers' lessons have a greater chance of connecting to what students know. Results on preinstructional assessments may tell you, for instance, that students do not have the background knowledge necessary for success in the unit you were planning or that they have already mastered the standards you intended to teach. In either case, had you not preassessed students, you would have wasted valuable instructional time and effort. Preassessments are also important in helping you to determine special interests and needs students may have so that you can differentiate your instruction to provide all students with powerful learning.

Assessing During Instruction   Everyday assessment is powerful for a variety of reasons—it links teaching and learning, and it drives teachers to learn more about not only their students, but about the craft of teaching (Atkin, Coffey, Moorthy, Sato, & Thibeault, 2005). Use a variety of strategies to find out what students are learning as you teach. Active participation strategies where each student responds during your lesson allow you to make mid-lesson adjustments.

 TEACHER TALK

Three practicing teachers reflect on the power of prior-knowledge interviews, where they talked with individual students to discover what the students knew about specific science content:

1. "My [middle school] student felt privileged to share her knowledge with me one-on-one. I don't often take the time to sit with one student and listen carefully to her view of the world."
2. "I taught my same students last year, so I know what they were exposed to in science. I couldn't believe that my prior knowledge interview student didn't have the concepts I thought I taught so well last year. He could repeat definitions that we memorized, but he hadn't glued those definitions to real ideas or explanations of the world. It was a humbling experience."
3. "I interviewed a small group of kindergartners to discover what they knew about sinking and floating. I know people learn things at home, but I was amazed at all the connections these five-year-olds made with their outside lives. They talked about going fishing, about throwing pennies into a fountain, and about playing with bathtub toys. I learned vividly that even my very young students are working hard to make sense of things."

As an example, in a graduate research course, I was teaching the concept of hypothesis testing. My students became suspiciously enamored of the papers on their desks when I asked a question to check comprehension. There, apparently, *was* no comprehension. They just sat and stared at their papers. I modified my assessment strategy: "Okay, turn to your partner. Tell him one thing you know about hypothesis testing and one thing that makes absolutely no sense. You have two minutes, then be ready to report." The use of partner talk as an active participation strategy allowed each person to safely express his fragile, newly forming knowledge, and students' questions allowed me to attack the concept in another way. Another quick and engaging way to assess students' understanding is with wipe boards, as described in Teaching Tip 7.3. Wipe boards are useful because they are less dependent on the use of language to provide assessment information, which allows a greater range of students immediate access to teacher feedback. Students can flash colored cards or complete drawings instead.

Watch a ninth-grade geography teacher assess her students' understanding after a series of lessons on the relationship between geography and economy. Find the video at the Merrill Teacher Prep Web site, Video Classroom, General Methods, Module 10, Video 1. How well have students mastered the content? How might students' responses provide information to guide the teacher's future instruction?

Assessing After Instruction   Ensure that your post-lesson assessments will allow you to determine the level at which students mastered your objective. Some checks on objectives will be brief and informal, and some will be much more complex and formal. One "quick check" strategy is to collect and analyze short student work samples. For example, to close a lesson, you may have had your chemistry students write brief responses to the prompt, "What is the difference between endothermic and exothermic reactions?" You collect their responses and sort them into two stacks: Those who stated a correct difference, and those who did not. You count how many are in each stack and determine whether to **reteach** or move on. If you need more detailed information, you could sort the incorrect examples into stacks based on students' apparent misconceptions. For example, one group may have understood something about energy entering and leaving reactions, whereas one group did not even mention energy. Based on your assessment information, you can differentiate your instruction to address students' ideas.

One of the benefits of No Child Left Behind is that it has brought teachers and other stakeholders together to scrutinize students' post-instructional assessments and products in order to make data-driven decisions (Center on Education Policy, 2006). The days when individual teachers graded stacks of papers, passed them back, and moved on seem to be numbered. Instead, professional learning communities (Annenberg Institute for School Reform, 2004; see also Chapter 10),

Teaching Tip 7.3

WIPE BOARDS

For an inexpensive class set of wipe boards, place card stock into a plastic page protector and hand it, a dry erase marker, and a tissue to each student. I have found, to date, 84 uses for these boards. Here are a few:

- Every student can now "do the problem on the board" and hold up work for you to quickly assess.
- Everyone can spell the words at a spelling bee now; this way the students who need the most opportunities to spell get to keep spelling long after they'd typically be "out."
- Place colored card stock *and* white paper in the page protector. Students can flash the colored side for "true" and the white side for "false."
- Slip the hundreds chart, worksheet, map, or periodic chart into the page protector. Students can follow your directions, practice naming countries or tracing routes, circle nonmetals . . . in short, students can stay actively involved while leaving a record of learning that you can quickly check before they erase.

grade-level teams, departmental teams, and other groups of stakeholders frequently gather to examine together evidence of student learning and make plans based on their findings. Research indicates that when teachers, students, and families discuss data related to student success, achievement is positively affected (Baker, Gersten, & Lee, 2002).

Figure 7.3 presents some strategies for assessing students before, during, and after instruction. Do some look familiar? They are active participation strategies drawn from a figure in Chapter 5; when assessment is ongoing, the line between it and instruction blurs nicely. Figure 7.3 also includes a few new strategies and descriptions. Additionally, the second part of this chapter describes a variety of assessment options that may be used during each phase of instruction (before, during, and after). As you consider selecting assessment strategies, it is important not to assess unless you have a plan for what to do with the results.

FIGURE 7.3 *Using active participation to assess student learning throughout all phases of instruction.*

Preinstruction Assessments	4. Share a story 12. Quick writes 20. Values lineup 28. Brainstorming and fact-storming • Drawings: Students draw a picture of the content and use drawings to describe their knowledge. • Four corners: Students respond to prompts that have four possible answers and then go stand in a corner of the room that matches their response. They discuss with corner mates or others. • Peer interviews: Students interview each other on prior experiences with the topic. • Prior knowledge interviews: Teacher observes students completing a task and asks a few gentle questions.
During-Instruction Assessments	1. Choral response 2. Whip 7. Flash cards 8. Finger signals 9. Wipe boards 10. Letter and number tiles 14. Peer coach 15. Student-led recitation 16. Numbered heads together 17. Toss the ball 18. Talk to your partner 27. Sorts 29. Partner journals
Post-Instruction Assessments	11. Comprehension check 13. Fuzzy points 22. Charts and diagrams (individual, group, or whole class) 25. Student quiz 30. Blackboard blitz 31. Gallery tour • Graphic organizers: Alone or with assistance, students create visual displays of content information to illustrate their understanding of key concepts and relationships.

Although traditional tests can evoke anxiety, they have a place in an assessment system because their judicious use can provide important information. Most assessment opportunities, though, should feel low risk (low stakes) to students, undertaken with the trust that the teacher is interested in improving instruction and facilitating learning. In today's high accountability context, alternative (or authentic) assessment measures are seen by many as important complements to standardized assessments in that alternative assessments can provide context-embedded, multifaceted portrayals of what students know and can do. According to Herman, Aschbocher, and Winters (1992), alternative assessments

- ask students to perform, create, produce, or do something.
- tap higher-level thinking and problem-solving skills.
- use tasks that represent meaningful instructional activities.
- invoke real-world applications.
- are scored by people using human judgment rather than by machines.
- require new instructional and assessment roles for teachers.

Alternative assessments are currently recommended across the curriculum, for students from pre-school (Grisham-Brown, Hallam, & Brookshire, 2006) through secondary school (Prouty, 2006), and for a range of student needs, including those of English learners (Media-Jerez, Clark, & Medina, 2007) and of students with special needs (Layton & Lock, 2007; Vacca, 2007).

Several alternative assessments are described in the second part of this chapter. They include products, portfolios, performance-based assessments, and interviews.

Assessment Needs to Be Inclusive of the Learner

Check back to your work from the exercise preceding this chapter and think about, as a student, the role you played in the assessment of your own learning. How often did you have choices about the content to be assessed, about the form of assessment, or about selecting the testing conditions? Many adults state that, as learners, their role in assessment was that of passive participants. Their primary role seems to have been to study in preparation for tests and then to keep their eyes on their own paper. Assessment was done *to* them, not *with* them. Further, it appears that existing assessment procedures were accepted as normal and correct. No one questioned the red ink or percentages scrawled near the top of each test. Here's hoping, though, that your own opportunities to self-assess were numerous.

The ultimate goal in assessment is self-assessment (Costa & Kallick, 2000). Costa and Kallick argue that only when they are effective self-evaluators will students be autonomous individuals who can analyze their own progress, motivate their own learning and action, and renew themselves as people. Throughout their schooling years, we should help students to set their own goals, continually monitor their own progress, and reflect accurately upon the quality of their work. Although schooling experiences often place the authority for judging students' progress squarely on the teacher and the school as an institution, we should be working to wean students away from their dependence upon authority to provide the ultimate evaluation of their work. Small actions can contribute to this goal in large ways. For instance, we should respond carefully to the first-grader's question, "Teacher, is this right?" and the twelfth-grader's query, "Is this what you want?" Do we grade our papers in pencil or pen? What color? Figure 7.4 provides numerous examples of how you can include your students' voices and choices in your assessment by helping students set goals, make assessment choices, self-reflect, and evaluate instruction. Bear in mind that these options must be considered in conjunction with other principles of assessment. For instance, you need to remain systematic in assessing learning even as you allow for student choice.

FIGURE 7.4 *Involving students in assessment.*

Goal Setting	• Students discuss previous years and create a chart at the beginning of the year of topics they would like to study.
	• Students provide input into the course content, choosing units and lessons based on assessment results and their interests.
	• Students examine their records (portfolios, work samples, and report cards) to set class and personal goals.
	• Students keep individual records of their progress. They discuss progress and revise goals with their teacher.
	• Students end an examination by answering the question, "What would you like to learn next?"
	• Students write a note to their teacher explaining what she should focus on as she assesses a piece of writing or a performance.
	• The teacher invites students to write long-term goals and seal them in envelopes. The teacher may mail these letters back to students when they reach a certain age.
Student Choice	• Students select some forms of assessment. Teachers who implement multiple intelligence theory often allow students to choose from among seven or eight assessment formats.
	• Students work in groups to list what they consider the key content to be assessed.
	• Students develop some questions or prompts for the assessment.
	• Students select writing prompts or test items from a larger bank.
	• Students respond to prompts that allow for a broad range of appropriate responses (for example, "Devise a method of sharing equally").
	• Students have some say over the assessment conditions (for instance, students are allowed to move to the library if they need isolated conditions or are allowed to have a prompt read aloud to them).
Self-Reflection and Self-Evaluation	• In small groups or in their journals, students discuss their thinking or analyze a problem.
	• Before submitting work, students analyze their growth, in writing or in a conference.
	• Before submitting work, students turn the paper over and write to their teacher: "What would you like me to know as I read this paper?"
	• Students study good and poor examples of the product to be created and assessed. They develop rubrics for use in scoring their products.
	• Students use rubrics or a checklist from the teacher to assess their own work before submitting it.
	• Students grade their own papers and hold onto the grade. They compare their analysis with the teacher's analysis and discuss.
	• Students reflect on their progress over time by comparing work samples from different time periods.
Evaluation of Teaching and Assessment	• Students rate problems and exercises for appropriate level of difficulty (too easy, just right, or too difficult) and for appropriateness of content.
	• In their journals or on anonymous slips of paper, students tell the teacher what worked well in facilitating their learning and what may have worked even better during particular lessons or units.
	• Students periodically rate the teacher's instruction, giving specific praise and criticism. Using a specific format can help structure feedback into a format most useful for the teacher, but open-ended questions are important as well.
	• The teacher regularly provides students with choices for future activities based on the class's assessment of current activities.
	• The teacher shares his instructional goals with students and revises the goals based on ongoing assessment.

Students need to be active participants in their own assessment.

Modern Curriculum Press/Pearson Learning

For an example of peer assessment, watch elementary students discus their peers' writing via a technique dubbed Author's Chair. Go to the Merrill Teacher Prep Web site, Video Classroom, Educational Psychology, Module 9, Video 1. What steps would the teacher need to have taken to help students learn to accurately assess their peers' work?

Every act of teaching—including assessment—conveys our professional convictions. If we wish to protect students' dignity, to encourage them to build responsibility for their own learning, and to foster their growth as self-assessors, then assessment must involve students' voices and choices. My son Alex taught me this lesson during his kindergarten year. In the left-hand portion of Figure 7.5 is a self-portrait Alex drew near the beginning of the year. "Good detail," said his mother. "Lots of realistic subtleties! Smart kid!" In the right-hand portion is the self-portrait Alex completed near that year's close. "Yikes!" said his mother. "Less detail. No pupils, no digits, no feet, no hair! No growth in fine motor abilities!" I struggled with my interpretation of those portraits until a wise teacher suggested that I ask *Alex* to analyze the portraits. Alex easily explained to me the significance of the second portrait. There was less detail, yes, but, he held up both arms, made fists, and flexed his biceps, "Mom, look how *strong* I am!" Alex's most treasured change of his kindergarten year was that he had become physically more capable, much stronger: Superman strong! Had I not asked Alex to attach meaning to his work, to self-evaluate, I would have been left with an unnecessarily limited conclusion about his progress. This self-portrait experience humbled me as an instructor and assessor. It taught me not to overestimate my ability to judge learning based on the information I gather. It taught me that to understand student learning in holistic terms, I need to ask the students. So that you can involve students in the process of assessment, provide opportunities for students to set goals, to have choices in assessment, to self-evaluate, and to evaluate your instruction.

In our efforts to enhance students' skills as evaluators, we can help them to evaluate products from their peers as well. Through peer assessment, students learn to assess the quality of a product or performance without reliance on the teacher. Peer assessment can be informal, such as when students edit each other's work or review homework problems together. It can also be more formal, as when students rate the social skills of group members at the close of a cooperative learning experience.

FIGURE 7.5 *Alexander's self-portraits.*

Alex's Early Kindergarten Self-Portrait	Alex's Late Kindergarten Self-Portrait

Assessment must include not only students and their peers but families as well. Professional guidelines for teachers (such as the National Board for Professional Teaching Standards, 2002) make it clear that teachers and schools need to take the lead in including families in the process of schooling, including the assessment phase. Families' role is far greater than simply ensuring that students get to bed on time and eat a hearty breakfast before the big tests. Your communication with family members about assessment should be goal-driven, multifaceted, and inclusive of their perspectives. Teaching Tip 7.4 gives a few ideas for including families as members of the assessment community. Another example is **student-led conferences** (Bailey & Guskey, 2001; Benson & Barnett, 2005), where students facilitate a discussion of their progress among family members, teachers, and themselves. This approach to conferencing seems especially popular at the middle school level, but all students can succeed with these conferences. Search "student-led conferences" on the Web for a host of resources, including guidebooks, regarding student-led conferences.

No doubt teachers in your local setting have particular ways to engage families in the ongoing conversation about student progress. Talk with an experienced teacher to determine how he shares assessment information with students and their families.

Assessment Needs to Be Integrated into a Manageable System

You have a tough job to do in your assessor role. You will assess progress every day, at many levels, and across many domains, all while remaining true to your stance on education and staying fair and respectful to your students. Stiggins

Teaching Tip 7.4

COMMUNICATING ABOUT ASSESSMENT WITH FAMILIES

- Solicit family input on learning goals.
- Frequently provide newsletters about student learning. Build a Web page for your class with samples of their learning products. Maintain e-mail contact regarding assessment information.
- Try a dialogue journal where you, a family member, and the student communicate about student progress.
- Include family members in regular assignments. One idea: Weekly, have students describe to a family member three things they learned. The family member records those things (in English, the home language, or in another format) and signs a form.
- Invite family members, baby-sitters, or friends into your class to listen to oral reading, translate, or work with students who need extra support during a test.

(2001) suggests that lack of time is a significant barrier to effective assessment. He notes four issues: (1) the scope of the school curriculum continues to expand so that teachers are responsible for assessing a broadening variety of student achievements, (2) the expectations for instruction continue to expand, (3) current assessments tend to be labor intensive, and (4) teachers are often also expected to store large amounts of assessment information.

You can manage the weighty assessment role by developing an overall system of assessment that allows you to gather the information you need to be accountable and to encourage student progress. By *system* I mean a collection of assessment instruments that allows you to focus on student learning and enact the five principles of assessment in a way that is reasonable for your circumstances. Here are 10 pointers.

In preparing portfolio entries, teacher and student discuss the significance of particular student works.

Anthony Magnacca/Merrill

1. Determine which assessment strategies you are required to use. Be certain you are prepared to use them well. Considerable staff development efforts are now typically in place to help teachers with these assessments.
2. Talk with experienced teachers about assessment. Ask to see how they maintain student records and have them describe their assessment system. Ask about the time investments required. Determine whether those teachers' systems allow them to obtain important information about their students.
3. Select a variety of instruments that will allow you to gather information about all students, in every domain, over time, and across levels. Use the information in Figure 7.6 to assess the potential of each instrument.
4. Review the guidelines for assessment from this chapter and think about specific assessment tools that will allow you to enact those guidelines. Is your system fair? Inclusive of the learner?
5. Streamline your list so that you use the minimum number of assessment strategies possible to obtain the variety and amount of information you and your students require. Drop an item from your list if you can gather the same information using another item you have already listed. Add items when you notice that certain goals or domains are missing.
6. Sit down with your school calendar or plan book and think about when and how often you should use each type of instrument.
7. Be realistic in estimating the time and effort required to implement your system.
8. Be certain that the system yields information that matches the time and energy investments it requires.
9. Monitor the effectiveness of your system. Is it accurately and humanely assessing the progress of each of your students? What modifications are you making to gain accurate information about your students with diverse cultural and linguistic backgrounds?
10. If you cannot manage your assessment system, change it.

The section that follows provides specific examples of assessment strategies that may play a role in your system.

ASSESSMENT STRATEGIES

You will select and employ a range of assessment strategies. Some will be mandated by your school, district, state, and federal government, and others you will select or develop yourself. Of these many assessments, some fall within the realm of traditional assessments, and some are more often considered alternative or authentic assessments. Traditional assessments include standardized tests and publisher- and teacher-developed paper/pencil tests. Alternative assessments include portfolios and performance-based measures. Although each can play a useful role in your assessment system, there are notable points of contrast.

The two types of assessments vary in their form, purpose, benefits, and potential drawbacks. Whereas a traditional assessment is designed to measure a narrow slice of student progress, an alternative assessment often attempts to capture a complex range of outcomes achievement over longer periods of time. Traditional tests are not designed specifically to match the conditions under which the assessed information will be used (context free or context reduced), but alternative assessments are context-embedded. Test-taking skills may thus factor into results of traditional assessments. Alternative assessments aim to share the power of assessment and subsequent planning between teacher and

FIGURE 7.6 *Assessing assessments.*

	Goal-Directed	Systematic	Tied to Instruction	Inclusive of the Learner
Traditional Tests	Most often cognitive. Select items that match objectives and what was taught. Careful to dig deeper than facts for generalizations. Write special questions for incidental learnings.	Easy to collect for every student. Objective items are most reliable.	Usually used post-instruction. Reteach based on results. Brief, self-graded quizzes can be used during instruction.	Typically not, but is possible with teacher effort.
Attitude Surveys	Great for affective domain.	Validity may be affected by students' desire to please.	Good for pre-instruction to influence planning.	Special strength. However, if you won't use results, don't ask.
Products	Can tap all three domains. Can tap integrated, complex understandings. Can span longer time periods.	If students are allowed choice, can be difficult to assess uniformly across products. Reliability is affected if work was conducted outside of class.	Find an audience to appreciate products. Think specifically about what to do with results.	Can be a strength if students are allowed choice. Encourage self-evaluation of work.
Portfolios	Can tap all three domains. Good for measuring progress toward larger goals return. Good for long-term growth.	Argued as being highly valid because entries are samples from many time periods and different conditions. Train raters for best reliability. May overestimate competence if work is completed collaboratively.	Can profoundly influence instruction. Time intensive.	Excellent potential—when author has ownership. Good for goal-setting.
Journals	A collection of entries over time can give indications of long-term development. Excellent for assessing incidental learning and affective domain.	Can be difficult to assess using a standard protocol unless prompts are very structured. Journals depend upon teachers' ability to interpret students' written words and symbols. Discussion can protect validity.	Can be used at all instructional stages. Must have an audience. Time-consuming if teacher is sole audience.	Open prompts include a great deal of student choice. Students need to be able to express themselves in writing. Students need to value the prompts for journals to be useful.

FIGURE 7.6   *Continued.*

Performance-Based Assessments	Use regularly throughout the year to collect evidence of long-term growth. Excellent for psychomotor (and other) domains.	Each student must be given the same opportunity to perform. Validity can be affected if the performance situation is uncomfortable for the student. Scoring procedures need to be clearly specified.	Many teachers obtain baseline information through performances, and then assess again after instruction.	Allow students to self-assess their performance and to evaluate your instruction to suggest the next step.
Teacher Observations	Excellent for affective and psychomotor domains.	Structured observation guides and class lists can help focus teachers' attention on certain items for all students.	Individual lessons can include a period during which teacher observes to check for student progress.	Variable, depends upon structure of the observation.
Interviews	Used primarily for cognitive and psychomotor items, but affect can naturally arise.	Allows for great depth for individual students. Tied to verbal skills.	Depth of information obtained can be very useful for instruction planning. Requires careful planning to interview all students.	Respectful questioning can allow children to share what they know, can do, and find important.
Drawings and Diagrams	Drawing uses psychomotor skills. Cognitive and affective domains can both be addressed.	Allow students to describe the meaning behind their works to ensure that you fully understand what the students are trying to convey.	Highly appropriate at all phases of the instructional cycle.	Presents tasks (drawing) that are atypical for school for many students; many students enjoy the novelty and the nonlinear, nonlinguistic opportunity. Some students do not feel comfortable drawing.

student, whereas with traditional assessments, power tends to reside more with the assessor. Traditional tests often have the benefits of efficiency and more objectivity in scoring. In contrast, alternative assessments often have the benefit of richness because information is collected over time and in a range of contexts.

Despite their potential benefits, both kinds of measures also have their criticisms. Some traditional tests, for example, are criticized for focusing on student deficits rather than on what students can do. Some are seen as providing little information related to realistic settings or the application of knowledge. Finally, they are also criticized as containing biases against students in nondominant groups (see, for example, Murphy, 1994). Likewise, alternative assessments are criticized as failing to provide sufficient evidence of validity and reliability (Bateson, 1994; Ryan, 2006). They can also lack meaningful standards, and biases against minority students also exist for alternative assessments (Howell, Bigelow, Moore, & Eroy, 1993).

This section of the chapter describes nine classroom assessment techniques. Figure 7.6 analyzes the potential usefulness of the instruments in terms of general guidelines for assessment.

Traditional Tests

Traditional paper-pencil measures can be furnished through adopted textbook series or written by teachers (most typically alone, but students can contribute items). Some common types of questions on traditional tests include objective items such as true–false, multiple-choice, fill-in-the-blank, and matching items. Analogies and case study items are less common. Objective items tend to be time-consuming to write but quick to grade and are subject to little interpretation from the grader. Open-ended questions include short-answer items, essay questions, and less traditional variations such as graphic organizers and pictorial representations of students' knowledge. Teachers' time investment with open-ended items tends to be not in the writing phase but in the assessment phase. Open-ended items require more judgment from the grader than do objective items. If you write your own tests, consider the following:

- Include a mix of forced-choice and constructed-response items so you have a richer picture of student knowledge.
- Make the response format efficient for students so that it is less tiring and so that there is no question about what they wrote. (For example, have them circle T or F rather than writing the word.)
- Make the prompts clear and specific so that students understand the parameters.
- Keep your tests short. Any test is just a snapshot.
- Include common errors among the choices. This can increase the validity of your measure. (Wormeli, 2006)

Double check your scoring to ensure that you remained consistent over time across students. Check reliability by asking a fellow teacher to score a few responses.

After you correct students' work, be sure to analyze the content they have mastered and identify the gaps in their knowledge. Use that information to reteach. Teaching Tip 7.5 gives one idea for reteaching after a multiple-choice test.

 *Teaching Tip 7.5*

TEST AND THEN RETEACH

- Analyze the results of a paper/pencil test and look for the four to seven major error patterns or gaps in students' thinking.
- Form flexible groups that are composed of students with similar gaps.
- Spend a bit of time working with each group, providing instruction tailored directly for the need they displayed on the test.

For instance, on day 1, your students take the district's multiple-choice benchmark test in mathematics. The test is computer scored and returned to you on day 3. On day 4, you spend 20 minutes in small-group time, discussing only item 1 of the test. Your groups are a, b, c, d, or e, depending on their selected answer to item 1. On the next day, you meet again for item 2, and so on for the four problems students missed most.

Attitude Surveys

Usually developed by teachers, attitude surveys are paper-pencil scales that assess students' preferences and feelings toward a topic or skill. Some prompts are closed-ended. For instance, students can rank order lists of subjects in terms of their preferences or agree/disagree with a set of items. For young students, a survey item can be read aloud while the students circle one of a continuum of faces, very happy to very sad. Open-ended items allow for a broad range of student responses. An example is "What I would like you to know about me as an artist is_____." Many teachers use attitude surveys near the beginning of the year to become acquainted with their students.

Products

Students submit items (written or constructed) to demonstrate their understanding or skill. Examples include student-composed newspapers, brochures, dioramas, posters, works of art, multimedia presentations, and scientific or practical inventions. Products can be assessed through the use of rubrics, or scoring guides that specify the criteria against which an item will be assessed.

Rubrics can be used for scoring many kinds of student works. Portfolio entries, performances, and products can all be assessed through rubrics. A **holistic rubric** (one that addresses the overall characteristics of the entry) is found in Figure 7.7 In contrast to the holistic rubric, an **analytical trait rubric** assesses individual traits, or components, of the performance separately (Arter & McTighe, 2001). An analytical trait rubric contains two major kinds of information: the scale and the dimensions. The scale—usually posted along the top of the rubric—represents the range of performance levels, such as 1, 2, and 3, or "standard not met," "standard met," and "standard exceeded." The dimensions are the individual categories upon which the work will be assessed. They are usually placed along the side. One example is: content, organization, and convention. Another example is: creativity, accuracy, and presentation. Visit the discovery school Web site noted at the close of the chapter to view many examples of analytical rubrics. You may find one to borrow. You will also find sites that allow you to create your own rubrics.

Stevens and Levi (2005) give an approach for developing rubrics that is similar to the concept formation strategy you studied in Chapter 6. Start by *reflecting* on the assignment: What is its purpose? What standard does it capture?

FIGURE 7.7 *A sample holistic rubric for scoring portfolio entries.*

Score 3	Score 2	Score 1
Entry briefly describes the item that follows but devotes more attention to careful analysis.	Entry describes the item that follows and reflects on it in brief ways.	Entry is solely a simple description of the item that follows. Description may be quite long.
Entry reflects on the author's thinking in meaningful ways.	Entry includes superficial or limited information about the author's thinking.	Entry does not include information about the author's thinking.
Entry addresses content-area concepts accurately and in ways that enrich the reader's understanding of the item that follows the analysis.	Entry addresses content-area concepts in limited, accurate ways.	Entry does not reveal content-area knowledge or content information is inaccurate.

What evidence could students provide to demonstrate their learning? Then move to *listing*. List all of the expectations for the assignment, and then list again, giving the highest level of expectations. Then *group* the expectations based on their similarities. *Label* those groups with an overarching term. These labeled groups become the rubric's dimensions. Finally, *apply* your work by fitting it into the rubric grid. You can use this process alone, with other teachers, or with your students. With students, after explaining the assignment, you could distribute sticky notes and have each student write 3–5 things that an excellent product would possess. Then students could post their notes on the board, group them by shifting them around, and, finally, label them. Students are far more likely to understand a rubric deeply if they have helped create it. At the very least, the criteria for grading should be made clear to students at the onset of the assignment. Teaching Tip 7.6 gives an idea for encouraging students to understand the characteristics of quality work.

Portfolios

In developing portfolios, students collect and analyze work samples over time and from a variety of contexts (Hebert, 2001; Stefanakis, 2002). Some items are typically chosen by the teacher, and some are student selected. Students write reflections about the entries in order to discuss their learning. Portfolios can consist of paper or other concrete objects stored in a binder, folder, or large sleeve; they can also be electronic. Students K –12 can collect and assess their work and display it in an electronic portfolio using specialized software or more commonly available presentation or word processing software. Two benefits of the electronic portfolio are its portability and multimedia format. Conduct a Web using the terms search "student portfolios" and "electronic portfolios" for plentiful examples.

Schipper and Rossi (1997) recommend five stages for incorporating portfolio assessment:

1. *Lay the groundwork.* Examine your own values and help students "name" their learning by writing explicit criteria for what constitutes high-quality performance.
2. *Collect baseline data.* Because portfolios assess long-term growth, collect samples to indicate students' initial knowledge and skills.
3. *Select and collect.* Choose artifacts for inclusion in the portfolio.
4. *Write self-assessments.* Have students analyze their work.
5. *Conference.* Meet with students to share and assess their portfolios.
6. *Celebrate.* Reflect on the students' successes.

Rubrics are sometimes used for the formal assessment of student portfolios. A teacher might use the rubric in Figure 7.7 to assess students' literature portfolio entries. He would study an entry (which might be, for example, a student writing sample) and the writer's reflection sheet on that entry to attach a score of 1, 2, or 3 to the entry. As an alternative, the teacher might award scores

Teaching Tip 7.6

No Guessing Allowed: Post Sample Works.

The more time students spend guessing what you want, the less time they spend learning. Also, guessing makes people feel dependent rather than powerful. Obtain samples of student work at each of your specified performance levels (e.g., "Not Yet," "Getting There," and "Got It!" or maybe "Developing," "Competent," and "Exemplary") Post these works on the wall—or online—with a copy of the rubric.

> ### Teaching Tip 7.7
>
> #### GETTING STARTED WITH PORTFOLIOS
>
> 1. Try it out. Start small! Tweak it for next time.
> 2. Set a low number of required artifacts. Require just a few the first time you try portfolios. If you can, space entries out somewhat over the term and include more than one kind.
> 3. Make the reflections that accompany each artifact brief. Try these prompts:
>   - What is this item?
>   - What does it show about your learning?
>   - Why is that learning important to you?
>   - How does it help you set your next goal?
> 4. Have the authors share. It's best if you can have a conference with each author, but they can share in groups too.
> 5. Make the grading of the portfolio relatively low stakes. Perhaps you will make it worth no more than one test grade.
> 6. After they submit their portfolios, have the students anonymously evaluate the assignment and give advice for next time.

to whole sections of the portfolio or to the portfolio as a complete document. Use Teaching Tip 7.7 to get you and your students started with portfolios.

Journals

Used primarily for informal assessment, journals can be completed by children as young as kindergartners. Students can respond to prompts from the teacher in pictures, symbols, or written words. They may also write with no prompt from the teacher. One of the primary benefits of journals is that they have a broad range of applications. Students can use them to describe their thinking, to document their experiences, to ask questions, to converse with a peer or the teacher, and to analyze their growth. Sample journal prompts include "What is mathematics?" and "How do you use mathematics in your daily life?" (Newmann, 1994).

Performance-Based Assessments

Students demonstrate competence by performance. Discrete skills such as cutting, counting, shooting a basket, or focusing a microscope can be assessed through student performances, as can more complex behaviors such as reading and social problem solving. Rubrics and other formal scales can be used to assess student performances. For instance, many teachers assess students' oral reading by marking and categorizing students' errors (or miscues) as they read. Then teachers analyze students' error patterns (e.g., Ashlock, 2005) to devise instructional plans to address student difficulties.

Teacher Observations

In addition to formal, performance-based assessments, teachers also observe their students working and interacting under more typical conditions. Examples include students' use of science process skills, their play behavior, and their ability to work as part of a team. To be systematic in their observations, teachers keep anecdotal records that describe their students' behaviors. Some teachers take notes on individual students, date the observations, and then collect them in file folders. This system allows teachers to analyze individual students' performances over time. A fourth-grade teacher interested in his students'

TEACHER PREP

To hear a teacher discuss the place of performance-based assessments within an assessment system, visit the Merrill Teacher Prep Website, Video Classroom, General Methods, Module 10, Video 2. To what extent do you envision using performance-based assessments in your own classroom?

progress in physical education, for example, might develop an observation record based on his state standards and then use it to observe students outdoors. Here are a few questions from an observation scale based on California standards (California Department of Education, 2005). Does the student:

1. Include others in physical activities?
2. Jump a self-turned rope?
3. Catch a fly ball?

Interviews

In clinical interviews, teachers work with one student, or just a few students, at a time. Students typically complete a task that allows the teacher to probe their reasoning. For instance, in an interview to assess a student's prior concepts in science, a teacher might sit with the student and display a house plant. The teacher may ask her pupil to describe the plant and to hypothesize about the functions of the plant's parts. In a reading interview, a teacher might ask her student to point out and discuss features of the text that help convey the text's message. In a history interview, a teacher might ask a student to examine a primary source and talk a bit about its context and significance.

Drawings and Diagrams

Drawings and diagrams allow you to tap into students' knowledge through visual means. Students can draw their understandings of specific terms, emotions, experiences, and objects throughout history. One example is provided in Figure 7.8. The left side shows Zachary's portrayal of a squid when he was

FIGURE 7.8   *Compare the two drawings and view Zachary's knowledge as emergent: What does he know about squid structure? How has it changed over time? What does he need to understand next?*

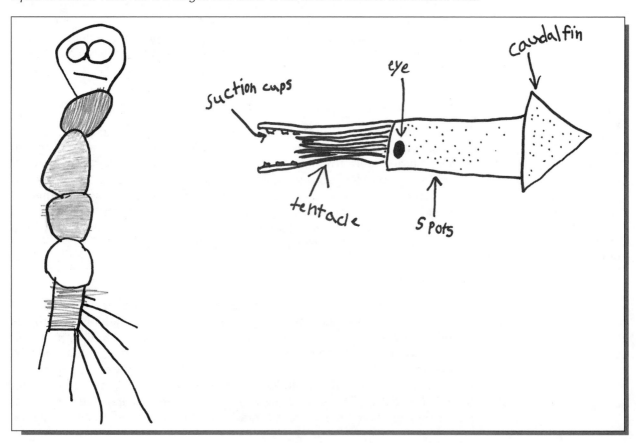

4 years old. The right column was completed 5 years later, shortly after his class studied the squid's external structures. Both pictures demonstrate that he had some understanding of the external structure of a squid, and we see significant growth over time. The right-hand drawing and his verbal explanation demonstrate that he knows quite a bit about squid, and that he has some ideas still developing, even in his later drawing. For instance, the chromatophores (spots) are actually grouped, not randomly spread over the squid's body as depicted. Worried that the suction cups might look like teeth, Zach labeled them.

Drawings used over time are often highly effective at demonstrating change in students' thinking and abilities. Drawings can be assessed by rubrics.

In addition to drawings, students can also complete a variety of **graphic organizers,** or visual displays of information where terms are grouped and represented graphically, to demonstrate what they know. One widely used organizer is the **concept map** (Novak, 1990, 1991, 1998). Research on concept mapping indicates that it support students' achievement and attitudinal development (Horton, 1993) and helps them organize and represent their knowledge (Edwards & Fraser, 1983; Novak & Gowin, 1984). As the sample concept map in Figure 7.9 shows, a major concept or term is given at the top of the map. Beneath it, subconcepts are presented hierarchically. Each concept is related to one above it with a line or an arrow and a verb phrase that specifies the nature of the relationship between the two concepts. Often concepts are connected to more than one other concept. Before being used as assessment tools, concept maps would need to be modeled and developed during instruction. In general, the more concepts listed on a map, and the more accurately and richly connected they are, the better developed the author's thinking about that topic.

Assessments typically result in student work, work that needs to be graded. What follows is some advice that can guide you in evaluating students' progress and translating it into forms that are useful to students, families, and school personnel.

FIGURE 7.9 *A concept map shows the hierarchical organization of ideas related to a particular topic, in this case novels.*

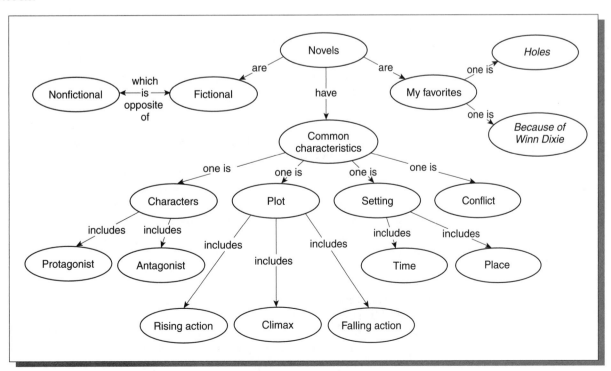

SOME ADVICE ON GRADING

Although it would seem straightforward ("Open your mouth and say 'ahh.'), the process of grading is actually riddled with a myriad of decisions and intractable dilemmas. You will need to reason your way through each issue with a good deal of thought. The grades you record need to follow the same guidelines as your assessments. In general, you need to assign and then grade the things that matter; you need to capture a rich portrait of what students know and can do; you need to be fair and systematic; and you need to be efficient. Here is some advice for grading.

1. Find a copy of the grade report used for your level before you begin teaching and entering grades. Check the alignment of the report card with your content standards. Determine whether each item is assessed every term. Use that information to guide your long-term planning. Use the report form to structure your grading, but also collect other information that is important to you and may not show up on the grade report.

2. Inform students of criteria for grades in advance. Students who receive challenging assignments and have clear grading criteria perform better than those who don't (Matsumura & Pascal, 2003). In every case possible, allow student input into grading criteria, perhaps using strategies such as backwards planning (Chapter 4).

3. Think about the role of daily homework in students' overall grades. If a student aces every test but refuses to do homework, should the final grade be an F? If so, you will be awarding a grade for something other than content mastery, which was demonstrated through exam performance. Is that other criterion reasonable and clearly specified?

4. Similarly, check grading policies for students with significant academic disabilities. How will you denote that a student may be performing consistent with capability, but still be earning a failing grade? Many teachers worry about the demoralizing effects on students who consistently earn failing grades despite their best efforts, yet these teachers appreciate the importance of consistent standards. Talk with experienced general and special education colleagues for insights.

5. Be careful of how much weight you place on assignments that are completed outside of class. Unless you specify that family members should be involved in completing a major project, you probably need to be guarded in the importance you award it. For instance, some middle school teachers are tempted to weight a science fair project heavily despite the fact that it is completed almost entirely at home. Under these conditions, the teachers cannot be sure whose work they are grading. Additionally, not all homes have the resources to support students in projects such as these. Be sure to provide in-class instructional support for any major project and have checkpoints along the way.

6. Be careful of how you award extra credit; use it to reward appropriate performance. As a counterexample, I have witnessed teachers award extra credit points when their students donate the novels they purchased to the class library. In a sense, students buy a portion of their grade if they can afford the price of a novel. Similarly, some teachers award extra credit points at the end of a term if students did not use their allotment of bathroom passes. In both of these cases, nonacademic performance (financial donations and bladder control) are rewarded with academic grades. Additionally, if you award extra credit, ensure that its weight as a portion of the grade reflects your priorities.

7. Don't write a grade on every piece of paper. Some assignments are just for practice. In fact, many teachers judge homework assignments as complete

or not and reteach to address errors. Or they collect and grade a sample of homework. Also, feedback needs to be timely for it to be useful to the learner. Don't collect stacks of papers if you cannot return them for weeks.

8. When you grade papers, be specific in your feedback. "Great job" feels good, but it doesn't give advice on how to repeat the performance for next time. If you write praise, make sure it is based on the quality of the performance and not on your opinion as an authority. "Your use of color creates a sense of excitement" is more relevant and helpful than "I love your use of color."

9. Instead of entering percentages in your grade book (paper or electronic), translate grades into smaller numbers. Some teachers use a 1- to 12-point system, others use a 1- to 5-point system. If you keep a paper grade book, consider adding the points as you record them so that your work is done at the end of the term. Using smaller numbers not only makes figuring totals easier, it avoids penalizing students for low scores the way entering tiny percentages can. (Mathematically, it is difficult to overcome even a single 23%.)

10. After you figure grades, check again that marks accurately reflect your global assessment of each student's growth. Be prepared to defend every grade you report to families. Be open to the possibility that you may have misgraded. Be ready to say what students will need to do differently for different marks.

11. Be careful in the words you write in the comment section of a grade report. Remember that those words will be the ones that follow students for years after they leave you. Include only relevant comments. Be constructive. Point out every student's growth.

Many schools now implement computerized grading and communication systems. In this way and in many others, technology will no doubt figure into your responsibilities as an assessor.

STUDENT ASSESSMENT AND TECHNOLOGY

Technology presents us with a new set of demands and offers us a wide range of tools to assist us in our efforts to understand students' progress. Because technology itself is a subject matter (recall the discussion of technology literacy goals in Chapter 4), we are required to assess students' mastery of it. Are our students meeting the NCLB goal of demonstrating technological proficiency by eighth grade? We must assess the extent to which students proficiently and ethically use technology to communicate, produce, conduct research, solve problems, and make decisions. Classroom observations and analysis of student products will be useful in assessing technological literacy.

Another emerging issue is the use of computer-based assessments for wide-scale evaluation of student progress. Envision your students taking year-end tests by clicking a mouse rather than bubbling in circles. Potential benefits of computer-based assessment include adaptivity (the tests can accommodate student needs such as visual impairments, and the tests can ask fewer questions because they judge students' responses on the spot and adjust to them) and the specificity of the results such tests can provide, but there are potential drawbacks as well (Rabinowitz & Brandt, 2001). Results are mixed as to whether students perform better on computer-based tests (see for example Hargreaves, Shorrocks-Taylor, Swinnerton, Tait, & Threlfall, 2004). Concerns include issues such as fairness and the extent to which the ease of computer-based standardized assessments might, for instance, push us to assess students even more frequently. Thus, technology is linked to assessment at all levels of education, both within the classroom and beyond.

To hear a high school geography teacher discuss technology and assessment, visit the Merrill Teacher Prep Website Video Classroom. Go to Educational Technology, Module 10, Video 1. How can the use of technology for assessments serve dual purposes?

Technology and Classroom Assessment

Within the classroom, technology provides us with a great range of options in discovering what our students know, and it provides us with a set of tools to assist us in assessment. Technology can assist us in progress-monitoring assessment. Some teachers, for instance, capitalize on **audience response systems** to provide instant information on student learning (e.g., Cavanaugh, 2006). Using these systems, students reply to a teacher's prompt using electronic devices (such as special calculators) that send responses to their teacher. Teachers analyze students' responses, determining, for example, the percentage of students who accurately answered or who chose a particular incorrect response. Some systems allow results to be printed later, and some allow the teacher to identify each student's response. This technology allows teachers to modify instruction on the spot, reteaching troublesome concepts right away rather than discovering students' misunderstandings later.

Technology also affects our summative assessments in the classroom. This chapter argued that conditions of assessment should match those of instruction. Therefore, if use of technology, such as calculators or a word processing spell checker, is prominent during your lessons, it should also factor into your assessments.

Perhaps in its most widespread assessment usage, computer-based technology can help you manage assessment results. Electronic grade books and spreadsheets make data analysis much easier. Such programs allow you to keep running percentages, weight grades, and analyze performance by assignment. You can analyze student performance in different ways to direct future instruction. For instance, Figure 7.10 shows a portion spreadsheet where I recorded subscores of students' performance on an assignment using an analytic rubric. By examining the spreadsheet, I can analyze scores by student to determine which students need further instruction or enrichment. I can also sort by subscores to determine those portions of the assignment on which students excelled and those portions that require additional instructional support. Data from Figure 7.10 suggest that, in a small group, I need to provide additional instruction for Carl and Cathy. I also need to provide instruction for the entire class on the reflection component of the assignment, given its low subscore. Despite their usefulness and their appearance of objectivity, however, electronic grade books must be carefully used so that they remain fair to students

FIGURE 7.10 *Spreadsheet on student performance.*

Last name	First name	Design	Results	Plan	Reflection	STUDENT AVG.
Black	Cathy	2	3	2	2	**2.25**
Bene	Margo	3	3	3	3	**3.00**
Caltright	David	4	4	4	3	**3.75**
Clemens	Dianne	4	3	3	3	**3.25**
Chavez	Jenna	4	3	3	2	**3.00**
D'arten	Jean	4	4	4	3	**3.75**
Fernandez	Carl	2	3	2	2	**2.25**
Gilbert	Kara	3	4	3	3	**3.25**
SUBSCORE AVG.		**3.25**	**3.38**	**3.00**	**2.63**	

and represent students' progress accurately. Guskey (2002) notes that strategies such as awarding zeroes for missing homework and treating all scores as equal and then averaging can penalize students and present inaccurate pictures of what they know. No electronic tool, therefore, relieves the teacher of the burden of careful judgment.

Some electronic assessment programs, deemed student information systems, are used by entire schools and districts. They allow teachers to post students' achievement data to the Web immediately so that students and their families can access, via password-protected accounts, assessment results and communicate with teachers at the click of a mouse. Powerschool (http://www. powerschool.com) is one example. This facilitates communication for families with Internet access by freeing them from the restrictions of teachers' limited conference time during the day. Families without Internet access at home should be guided to free public access sites such as public libraries. With knowledge that his parent has access to his grades, a student might just rethink his answer to his parent's question, "Do you have any homework today?"

Technology and Assessment beyond the Classroom

Beyond the classroom, technology provides us with means to track and analyze students' progress over time, with multiple measures, and across subject areas. This capacity allows us to see patterns more clearly and to improve our instruction. Driven by accountability concerns, there is increasing interest in computer-based data systems that track test scores and can be used to plan instructional interventions. Teachers in about two-thirds of the United States have access to tracking systems, although use of them is uneven (*Education Week*, 2006). One example is Edusoft (http://www.riverpub.com/products/edusoft), which attempts to help school districts collect and analyze student performance data from classroom tests and district benchmarks. As such management systems become more prevalent, we must be careful as educators to use them as tools that help us understand our students' progress from an important—but particular and limited—perspective and to use the knowledge we gain from such assessments as one facet of our highly detailed portrait of what our students know and can do.

PARTING WORDS

Assessment of student progress is a messy business. Something as simple as writing a letter grade on a student paper requires us to ask ourselves difficult questions such as, "What does this letter represent? Is it growth over time, or does it show that this is one of the best papers in the stack? Does it deserve this letter when the writing is so flawed, despite that it shows understanding of the content?" Teaching is a complex moral endeavor, and the weight of an evaluator's role should be great.

You probably will not relish *every* element of the assessor's role. Guiding students to establish performance standards, commenting on their work, interpreting results, and assigning grades takes large amounts of teacher time and can feel contrary to the role teachers *do* relish—that of coach and mentor. However, there is also incredible power that comes through assessment. When you conduct valid assessments, you peer through a window into a student's thinking and gain entrée to avenues that can allow you to help that student learn and grow, regardless of her starting point.

WEB SITES

http://act.org
ACT. The ACT is a widely accepted college admissions test. Read about the test your students may take. Check resources for educators and parents (including a student blog).

http://www.cse.ucla.edu/
CRESST: National Center for Research on Evaluation, Standards, and Student Testing. Contains resources that are both scholarly (see the Reports and Policy Briefs) and practical (see the pages for Teachers and Parents).

http://school.discovery.com/schrockguide/assess.html
Discovery School's Kathy Schrock's Guide for Educators: Teacher Helpers Assessment and Rubric Information. This guide contains many Web-based resources for classroom assessment and grading, including alternative assessments and report card comments.

http://www.ets.org/
Educational Testing Service. Go to "Tests" to read about many of the tests you and your students may take.

http://www.fairtest.org/
FairTest. Web site of the National Center for Fair and Open Testing, which promotes "fair, open, valid and educationally beneficial evaluations" and "works to end the misuses and flaws of testing practices." Check the "What's New" page for the Center's work directed toward NCLB, and see the K–12 testing page.

http://www.inspiration.com
Inspiration is a commercial software product that allows you and your students to develop concept maps and other graphic organizers. You can download a free trial version of the software at this site.

http://www.lasw.org/
Looking at Student Work. Gives strategies for teachers to work together and with families to examine student work for a number of purposes. The site includes protocols and strategies for analyzing student work.

http://nces.ed.gov/nationsreportcard/
The Nation's Report Card: The National Assessment of Education Progress program. Read the findings by state or subject matter. Click on "Sample Questions" to try released items in a variety of subject areas and grade levels.

http://www.nclb.gov/
The No Child Left Behind Web site. The "Toolkit for Teachers" has frequently asked questions and resources related to the law.

http://rubistar.4teachers.org/index.php
Rubistar. Create your own rubrics at this site. Continue to explore rubrics at http://www.rubrics4teachers.com.

Also try searching with search terms for specific issues and strategies in assessment. Examples include:

Authentic assessment
Classroom assessment (sites give assessment techniques)
Grade book programs (many sites have free downloads)
Performance assessment
Portfolio assessment
Standardized testing
Statewide achievement testing

OPPORTUNITIES TO PRACTICE

1. Watch as two teachers lead their students to assess their progress as writers via the portfolio process. Go to the Merrill Teacher Prep Website Video Classroom and pick one of these clips:

   • Educational Psychology, Module 13, Video 1
   • Classroom Management, Module 6, Video 1

   To what extent do you agree that your selected clip might meet the six principles of assessment?

Assessment Principle	Not at all (or cannot tell)	Somewhat	Very well
1. Tied to your stance on education			
2. Driven by learning goals			
3. Systematic			
4. Tied to instruction			
5. Inclusive of the learner			
6. Integrated into a manageable system			

2. Pull out your stance on education from Chapter 2 and the two or three overarching goals you developed in Chapter 3 as a result of your stance. Reread your stance and goals with an eye toward assessment.

   a. As you develop your assessment system, think about what kinds of information you will need to gather as a result of your view of what is important. How can you gather that information in ways that remain true to your convictions?

   b. In evaluating your assessment system, consider the following: How does this system reflect your view of the good society? Of the purpose of education? Of teaching? Of learning? If you find little concrete evidence to link your stance toward education with your system for assessing student learning, you probably need to spend a bit more time revising the system—or the stance—to more accurately reflect your professional views.

3. Use the Assessment Analysis in Figure 7.10 to evaluate the potential of one of the instruments in use in a classroom, and try it with any newly discovered assessment strategy.

FIGURE 7.11 *Assessment analysis.*

Instrument:		
Intended purpose:		

Criterion	**Evidence**	**Usefulness for Intended Purpose**
1. Instrument is consistent with my stance on education.		Low Medium High

2. Instrument will allow me to collect information related to my instructional goals.
  a. Level
  b. Time span
  c. Domain(s)
  d. Instrument can provide information on incidental learnings.
		a. Low Medium High
		b. Low Medium High
		c. Low Medium High
		d. Low Medium High

3. Instrument will allow me to collect information systematically.
  a. For every student
  b. Validly
  c. Reliably
		a. Low Medium High
		b. Low Medium High
		c. Low Medium High

4. Instrument can be explicitly tied to instruction.
  a. Before instruction
  b. During instruction
  c. After instruction
		a Low Medium High
		b. Low Medium High
		c. Low Medium High

5. Instrument can include the learner.
  a. Goal setting
  b. Student choice
  c. Self-evaluation
  d. Evaluate instruction
		a. Low Medium High
		b. Low Medium High
		c. Low Medium High
		d. Low Medium High

Overall evaluation of the instrument:

FIGURE 7.12   *Alex's drawing.*

4. If you are currently teaching, try one of the assessment strategies from earlier in this chapter. Reflect on the experience. If it provided useful information, what would you need to do to arrange your classroom to include this strategy in your assessment system?

5. Survey your students on their opinions about assessment. Use the survey to determine how they prefer to demonstrate their learning. Ask about how teachers help them learn to assess their own work. Share your results.

6. You saw Alex's kindergarten self-portraits in Figure 7.5. Now look at Figure 7.12 for the final version, completed at the end of his K–12 years. Make a list of all the ways his portraits have changed from kindergarten to grade 12. Have they retained any commonalties? (By the way, when I showed Alex the kindergarten portraits, he said, "Now I don't feel so bad about how this one looks." He appreciated his growth over time!) Where would you guide him next as an artist?

Before You Begin Reading

Chapter 8

Warm-Up Exercise for Managing the Learning Environment

Think of a store or other business that you hold in high regard: a place of business where you actually do not mind spending your time. Got it? Jot down some brief notes in response to each of the prompts.

1. Describe the physical space. What aspects of it appeal to you? Do any which make your life more difficult? Which?

2. Describe how time is used within this store or business. What aspects please you? Which irritate you?

3. Describe typical interactions in this business. What do you expect? What happens when interactions are not up to your expectations?

4. You wrote the responses from the perspective of a customer. How (if at all) would your responses have changed if you wrote from the boss's perspective? From an employee's? Analyze whether your responses can teach you anything about the way you would like to manage your classroom.

CHAPTER *Eight*

Managing the Learning Environment

"Never before have we had so little time in which to do so much."

—Franklin Delano Roosevelt

You have so much to accomplish with your students! As you guide students' progress, you must manage them as groups within a tight space, with limited materials, and with never enough time. Just as businesspeople organize time, space, and materials for safety and productivity, so will you organize in your role as classroom manager. Dexterous classroom managers organize and maintain the business end of the classroom so that noninstructional issues interfere as little as possible with learning. Effective classroom managers use a variety of instructional strategies, teach procedures and routines, maximize learning time, and engage their students fully in instruction. And that greater student engagement translates into student achievement (see the research reviewed by Bohn, Roehrig, & Pressley, 2004; including the classic research of Emmer, Evertson, & Anderson, 1980 and Evertson & Emmer, 1982).

Additionally, effective managers move beyond "productivity" and toward creating a mini "good society." Enacting your stance begins with you creating a classroom environment that clearly reflects your answer to the questions, "What do I want to accomplish? Who should these students become?" Your work as a manager reaches beyond ensuring productivity to include building a sense of community with a shared code of ethics. The environment you create should model and foster the kinds of interactions and habits you hope students will practice throughout their lives. Your job as a teacher-manager is to teach students the social curriculum, or in Charney's provocative phrase, "habits of goodness":

> When we establish a social curriculum, when we struggle to integrate ethical practice into our daily fare, we too are trying to set down habits that we want children to carry from their desks to the pencil sharpener, out into the halls, the playground, and even into the world. And we dare to envision that world far more filled with civility and honesty, with community and nonviolence than it is now . . . We teach habits of goodness most often in the way we organize the social and academic lives of our students and in the way that we bring the children into the regular activities and ceremony of the day. (1997, p. xiv)

This chapter encourages you to develop a classroom management plan that, through its ceremonies and rituals, shapes a sense of community that encourages learning in an environment that is both productive and humane. Research

REMEMBER THE LAW

Provide for physical safety.

Provide for adequate supervision.

Refresher from Figure 1.2.

indicates that classroom management systems must be coherent, consistent, positive, and proactive (Miller & Hall, 2005). In order to help you build such a system, the chapter addresses four components of classroom management:

- Creating community: Managing classroom ambience
- Managing physical space
- Managing resources: The stuff of teaching
- Managing time

CREATING COMMUNITY: MANAGING CLASSROOM AMBIENCE

Your central task as a teacher-manager is to start with the students and meld a group of individuals without common ground or goals into a classroom community. Kohn (1996, p. 101) defines the classroom community as

> a place in which students feel cared about and are encouraged to care about each other. They experience a sense of being valued and respected; the children matter to one another and to the teacher. They have come to think in the plural: they feel connected to each other; they are part of an "us."

Kohn's central ideas of connectedness, value, and respect are echoed in the words of numerous educators who stress democratic community (Allen, 1999; 2003; Bomer & Bomer, 2001; Education Commission of the States, 2000; Effrat & Schimmel, 2003). For Gootman (2001), a true classroom community is comprised of individuals who can communicate in caring ways. To foster students' ability to converse with care, teachers must help them do three things: (1) recognize and label feelings—theirs and others; (2) communicate feelings without hurting others; and (3) listen to each other, showing interest and hearing the speaker's complete message. The teacher must serve as a model community member by listening carefully and fully to students.

Clearly, the community you and your students build sets the stage for your interactions with students and pervades each of your choices about classroom management rituals and routines. Classroom community begins to develop through the tone, or ambience, you create from the first day of school. *Ambience* refers to the mood or atmosphere of your classroom environment. Some classrooms are subdued and businesslike, some are homey, and others are full of noise and excitement. Classroom ambience can vary widely and still encourage student success. Although what works best for each of us varies, you probably want to establish an ambience that

- *encourages students to take risks* by providing for emotional safety and a sense of belonging.
- *provides for intellectual stimulation* by including appealing displays, plenty of resources, and interesting objects.
- *fosters social interaction* by providing space and opportunities for students to work together.
- *conveys a sense that school is a pleasant experience.*
- *communicates your stance toward education* without you saying a word.

Metaphors and other analogies can provide a starting point for helping us think about ambience. You may recall, for instance, Jason's analogy of "teachers as pilots" from Chapter 1. Refer back to your stance on education as a guide for the kind of atmosphere you would like to establish. Skim your stance and compose a single-sentence simile: "I want my classroom to feel like a _____." Sample responses that may fill in the blank include the following:

- *Board room* (where powerful people meet to accomplish important things)
- *Garden* (where beautiful, dissimilar plants are given everything they need to flourish and bloom)
- *United Nations* (where people from around the world work toward international cooperation)
- *Home* (where people who care about each other live together in comfortable surroundings)
- *Hospital* (a clean, safe environment where people leave healthier than when they entered)
- *Sports camp* (where individuals hone their skills in preparation for the big game)

Analogies provide very different directions for the kinds of physical arrangements, displays, furnishings, routines, and activities that teachers select in managing their classrooms. Imagine, for example, how differently a home and a hospital classroom would appear at first glance:

Home	**Hospital**
- Overall atmosphere is cozy and warm	- Overall atmosphere is neat and calm
- Displays are personalized and cluttered	- Wall displays have coordinated backgrounds
- Desks are arranged in groups for interaction	- Desks are arranged in rows for efficiency
- Each group has materials at the center	- Materials are placed out of sight
- Several ongoing projects are out in view	- All surfaces are clean and shiny
- Lots of personal touches: fabric curtains, lamps, colorful rug, radio, potted plants, and rocking chair	- Colors are limited but carefully used

Select a physical arrangement, time schedule, routines, and instructional activities that build community and convey your convictions about what education should accomplish. Be forewarned, though, that you cannot establish a pleasant ambience for the year simply by coordinating your bulletin boards and buying potted plants before the school year begins. In fact, doing so may actually detract from a participatory community. Instead, you may build community by allowing students' voices and choices in the classroom environment. Bomer and Bomer (2001, p. 105) suggest that the teacher may greet students with "Welcome! We're going to spend the next week building and organizing the classroom. How do you think it should look?" It is ultimately the *people*—the way they treat each other and the way they care for their space—who define the ambience. Additionally, you can help students feel like they belong by making careful choices about the games you play; see Teaching Tip 8.1.

Allow your students to contribute to the atmosphere and teach students to help each other and to care for the room. For example, you might ask students as homework to create a map of the perfect classroom, given the furniture and resources available to you (Thorson, 2003). Students could present maps and then decide on a single map or a combination of maps to try out in your room.

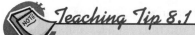

Teaching Tip 8.1

THINK TWICE ABOUT WINNERS AND LOSERS

Competitive games and assignments tend to be popular motivators for some students. However, you might undo the sense of community you try so hard to maintain by using a game where one person or group wins. One winner means the rest of us are losers. Try some alternatives: "Let's see if we can beat our best class time (or scores)." "To win this game, each team needs five examples." "Each presentation will receive an award. Be listening to see what each one does best."

You can also take an anonymous survey to determine how many of your students find friendly competition to be motivating. In my experience about one-half the students in a class enjoy competition. Then work their preferences into the classroom in ways that help them feel welcome and yet do not detract from the sense of community.

Individual class activities can span the grade levels to build community. In Common Threads (Obenchain & Abernathy, 2003), students draw and write responses to the prompt, "For fun I . . . " into wedges on a paper circle. Then chaos ensues as students find others who have wedges that align with their own. The entire interlocked set of circles is posted on a wall as a reminder that each person has interests in common with others. Teaching Tip 8.2 gives a few additional examples of strategies that can encourage a sense of community.

To review, you will actively work to build a sense of community in your classroom by:

- forging a sense of "we" from a myriad of individuals "I's."
- modeling genuine listening, respect, and regard.
- explicitly teaching students to communicate in caring ways and then reteaching whenever necessary.
- creating a certain ambience or tone through decisions related to physical arrangement, time schedules, routines, and instructional activities.
- allowing students to contribute to the creation and maintenance of the classroom environment.

Turn to Figures 8.7 and 8.8 now to begin planning for your own management system, including ambience. Community develops, in part, through your decisions about managing the classroom's physical space.

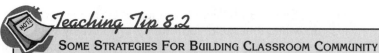

Teaching Tip 8.2

SOME STRATEGIES FOR BUILDING CLASSROOM COMMUNITY

1. Help members get to know each other through strategies such as oral history interviews, artifact interviews, and ice breakers such as "Find someone who . . . " mixers.
2. Brainstorm a list of community characteristics that members appreciate.
3. Hold regular community circles, or **classroom meetings,** where students recognize each other's efforts. Meetings are productive for all and have been shown effective for increasing the social inclusion of students with special needs (Frederickson, Warren, & Turner, 2005).
4. Invite students to plan and create a whole-class bulletin board, maybe to accompany the current unit or season.
5. Make a class scrapbook, time line, or Web site to capture its unfolding history.
6. Pay attention to students' moods and modify your plans based on their moods. For instance, you might take Period Three out under the trees just for today.
7. Eat together.

MANAGING THE PHYSICAL SPACE

Your choices in arranging the physical space allow you to use it to enact your convictions about how people learn and about good teaching. As you begin to map out your room, think about your goals and design the room to match. For instance, if social interaction and language development are key for you, you probably won't place the desks in rows. Visualize the classroom as "learning space" (Faltis, 2001). Breaking away from the traditional "teacher up front, students facing forward" pattern may allow you to identify many areas in the classroom where teaching and learning can occur. Think about the different kinds of space you and your students will need. At the elementary level, these spaces typically include an area for desks or tables for seatwork, at least one area from which you can teach the whole class, small-group work spaces, and an area for messy tasks. Secondary classrooms typically make fewer provisions for student movement or a variety of activities in part because classrooms tend to serve more specialized purposes, such as cooking rooms, weight rooms, and science laboratories. Teachers at all levels should remember to use student seats flexibly. Because a variety of grouping patterns can be effective for supporting student engagement (Bohn, Roehrig, & Pressley, 2004; Vaughn, Hughes, Moody, & Elbaum, 2001), you will no doubt want to be able to rearrange student seats so that they can work total group, alone, in partners, and in small groups (that's TAPS from Chapter 4).

Also consider using your wall space, windows, and ceiling (if allowed) to their fullest advantage. Enrich the environment with special-interest areas such as a puzzle center (you too, high school teachers), a class library, or a music center. Keep your physical setting flexible and ensure that activities and traffic can flow easily.

As you arrange for the different areas in your classroom, be certain that you can **monitor** students at all times and that they are free from the threat of physical danger. For instance, do not allow them to stand on a chair stacked on a desk so that they can reach a top shelf. In addition to safety, your choices for arranging the physical space can be used to enhance the spirit of cooperation. Glance around the room and see what the arrangement says about the balance

Rich resources are more fully utilized when they are organized efficiently.

Anthony Magnacca/Merrill

To see the physical arrangements of some elementary and secondary classrooms, visit the Merrill Teacher Prep Web site Video Classroom:

- First-grade classroom with learning centers: Go to Reading Methods, Module 7, Video 1.
- Second-grade classroom: Go to Classroom Management, Module 1, Video 1.
- Middle school classrooms: Go to Child Development, Module 12, Video 2.
- High school classrooms, including science lab: Go to Child Development, Module 11, Video 3.

What aspects of these physical environments might you incorporate into your own room arrangement?

of power, about student choice, about meaningful study, and about a sense of the group. Finally, when considering each option for the layout of space and resources, ask yourself two questions:

- Is it productive?
- Is it efficient?

Is It Productive?

Productivity requires that:

1. *The space allows for a balanced variety of activities.* You address students' physical, social, and emotional needs when you provide for shifts in movement. For young students especially, plan to balance seat time with floor time, whole-group instruction with individual or small-group work, and quiet activities with more boisterous ones. School tends to be a highly public place. Design an area that allows for privacy within safety constraints and crowded conditions.

2. *People can see and hear each other.* Charney (2002) contends that for students to feel safe they must feel seen. She arranges her classroom with few visual barriers so that when positioned at her work space, she can see the entire class. You need to be able to see students, and they need to be able to see you—and each other. Research indicates that face-to-face seating arrangements facilitate student interaction, and that students ask more questions in such arrangements (Marx, Fuhrer, & Hartig, 1999). You'll recall from Chapter 6 that student-generated questions facilitate learning.

When it's time for students to look at you for whole-class instruction, some may need to turn their desks toward you. Teach them to quickly rearrange their seats so that they can participate in the lesson. So that students can hear other members of their group during cooperative lessons, you can teach them to use "six-inch voices," which are voices that can only be heard from a distance of six inches.

3. *The students are able to focus their attention on the task at hand.* Is your directed lesson competing with a colorful bulletin board or the aquarium behind you? Are some students looking into the light because they face windows? Is the noisy science center positioned far enough away from your math group to allow students to focus on their work? Will the students working on the computers distract the others?

Is It Efficient?

Efficiency in the physical layout allows you and the students to complete tasks without delays. Efficiency requires that

1. *You can get to each of the students quickly.* Physical proximity is important for encouraging appropriate behavior, providing assistance, and ensuring safety. Jones (2000) emphasizes that the greater the physical distance between students and teacher, the less likely students are to remain **on task**. Arrange your room so that you can quickly get to each of the students by positioning furniture to create wide walkways. Jones suggests that tables and desks be arranged so that the traffic pattern forms a loop, or circuit. Figure 8.1 gives a sample floor plan with the loop marked.

2. *The students can get to each other.* Student access to peers is helpful in efficient distribution of materials and in small-group and partner work.

3. *You and the students can get to the materials.* Much time can be wasted as students wait for paper or other supplies. Position materials for easy access. For instance, store materials as close as possible to the area where they will be used. Then train students how and when to distribute and use the materials. Some teachers assign two or three students to be paper

FIGURE 8.1   *Sample floor plan with teacher's loop marked.*

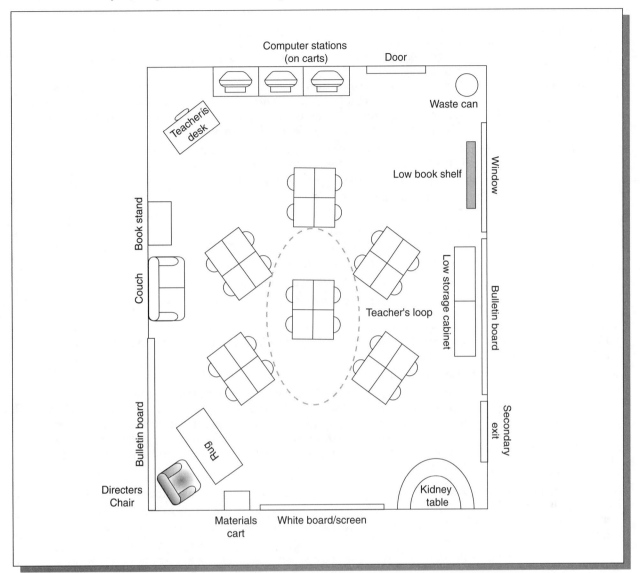

passers, so that the teacher gives a word and three assistants snap to work. In cooperative learning classrooms, each group typically has a supply sergeant who is responsible for gathering and collecting materials. If students fill the supply role in your classroom—and you have trained them well—let them know that if they cannot perform, they lose the job. Doing so prevents students from dawdling and allows them to take pride in a job that must be done well.

   4. *You and the students can get other places easily.* Arrange furniture and work areas to avoid traffic jams. Think about areas that tend to draw crowds (the pet center, the pencil sharpener, and the drinking fountain, for instance) and provide wide margins for each. Position student seats so that these high-draw areas do not interfere with their work. Be certain that all students can reach the exits quickly in times of emergency. Figure 8.2 reviews sections of the classroom's physical space and provides guidelines to consider for each area.

   While the ideas are rolling, you may want to turn ahead to Figure 8.9 and design the physical layout of your classroom.

FIGURE 8.2 *Checkpoints for a classroom's physical space.*

Work Areas	Checkpoints
Desks or tables for seatwork	• Match seating arrangements with your stance and the instruction you hope to provide. • Rows can be effective—especially for new teachers—if the instruction is good and desks are used flexibly. Rows may be useful, at least for the first days of school, until students have learned your expectations about talking and work times. But don't let rows interfere with the development of a sense of community. • In row configurations, short and shallow (many columns with few desks) is typically better than narrow and deep (few columns with many desks). • Row clusters, in which two or three desks are pushed together and yet still point forward, save space and encourage interaction. Two large, nested horseshoes serve a similar purpose and create a sense of group belonging. • Small clusters of desks (usually four) that face each other promote social interaction. Slant the groups for better views of the front board. • Try a single large circle for classroom meetings. • If possible, avoid using all the floor space for desks. • Be certain that students fit their desks. Make a switch or call the janitor if they do not.
Whole-class instruction station	• Position your media equipment so that all students can see when seated at their desks. • Use a small table or cart to keep instructional supplies available. • At the elementary level, save enough floor space so that you can pull the entire class "up to the rug" or "over to the rocking chair" to work with all students in a more intimate setting. Reading aloud and class discussions are often more effective when students are seated in close proximity. A change of pace can be good for behavior and materials management, too. Consider alternatives if students object to sitting on the floor.
Areas for small-group instruction	• If space allows, use a round or horseshoe table for small-group instruction. • If space is tight, consider using space outside the classroom door or borrow from another area such as your library. Make the area off-limits if you are instructing there. • Position yourself so that you can see all students. Keep your back to the wall.
Special-interest areas	• Include learning centers such as a class library, an author's corner, a science center, a technology area, a pet area, or an art area. Even a small counter space works. Try a claw-footed bathtub filled with pillows for reading or a tropical rain forest for independent work. • Students and their families sometimes like to contribute materials for these areas, but you will need to teach students to handle materials carefully. • Include a private area for quiet reading. This space or another may be used for students who need to be temporarily removed from the group. • Special-interest areas can be permanent or can evolve with the interests and needs of your class.
Work spaces for messy tasks	• Place the painting or art center near the sink for easy cleanup. Teach your students to place newspaper under their work and to properly care for materials. • Space outside the classroom door can be used if you can monitor all students. • Position materials for active lessons away from your whole-group instruction station so that you can monitor from afar as individuals go up to gather materials. • Place the materials distribution center away from students' work desks, to the extent possible. • Obtain a large sheet of heavy plastic or an easy-clean rug if you need to protect carpet.

FIGURE 8.2   *Continued.*

Work Areas	Checkpoints
Wall space	• Use bulletin boards for instruction. Plan for displays to be interactive. Try knowledge charts, word walls, and materials related to current topics. • Display work from all students and change the displays frequently. • Long-standing bulletin boards may include the monthly calendar, job chart, current events, and student work. • Use wall space other than bulletin boards to display classroom rules, expectations for assignments, and other items that do not change. • Make a space for your daily agenda. • Ask whether you are allowed to tape things to the walls and whether you have access to a machine that cuts out letters and other items for bulletin board displays. • It is more important for displays to be neat and to involve the students than it is for the displays to be masterpieces.
Ceiling space	• If allowed, take advantage of the ceiling for posting bold messages, student work that can be viewed from a distance, or artwork. • If allowed, consider suspending student work from above. Paper clips and string can do the trick.
Teacher's work area	• Find a secure place for your valuables. A purse, wallet, or laptop on a desk is an invitation for trouble. • Consider placing you desk it at the back of the room. Your desk is not usually the best place for giving instruction, and placing too much attention on your own work space can give a distorted message about who is important in the class.
Storage areas	• Arrange for space to hold students' lunches, jackets, and backpacks. • Store paper and other materials in cupboards. • Keep thin stacks out for easy access. Think about balancing students' responsibility to obtain necessary supplies and the fact that you would rather not run out of construction paper in October. • Place materials that present safety threats such as glue guns and craft knives well out of students' reach.

MANAGING RESOURCES: THE STUFF OF TEACHING

Managing a classroom means managing all the *stuff,* to use a technical term, that inevitably goes along with teaching. One prominent management issue is managing the paper flow. Many new teachers struggle to stay afloat of the paperwork. New teachers, who felt otherwise well prepared, often comment that they are likely to drown under the paperwork generated in the school and classroom. One of their most important management lessons during their early days in the classroom is typically devising *systems* for managing the paper flow. They develop, for example, homework folders that go home and get reviewed periodically by families, they work with family volunteers (when available) to organize upcoming materials and check in papers that come from home, they devise planners in which students record their assignments, and they identify spaces where students submit their work. Implementing systems for managing resources allows teachers to streamline their efforts and spend more time on instruction than on checking homework.

Morris (2000) provides an example of a system that can be useful for many such necessary management tasks: student numbers. He assigns each student a number, and this number is used for several purposes. For instance, students collect and mark homework as completed using their numbers rather than names. Their papers can be quickly collected and placed in numerical order for easy entry into the paper or electronic grade book. Materials, even individual crayons or pencils, can be marked with students' numbers for quick identification. Students can "sound off" by number at a fire drill to ensure that all are present. Numbers can be recorded on cards or craft sticks so that students are equitably called on to participate during discussions.

Another resource management question is how to integrate the classroom's single classroom computer meaningfully into instruction. Three-quarters of all American classrooms have between one and five computers in them. Teachers often struggle to use these single or few computers to their full instructional advantage.

The single computer can be used both as a teacher tool and as a student tool. The teacher uses it as a tool for preparing instructional materials, communicating with families, and keeping track of student progress. If the computer can be connected to a projection system so that all can see the screen, it becomes the teacher's whole-class instructional tool. He can use it to display a slide show of the digital photos of the students at work. He can use the computer to model the writing process or to do shared writing, to draw concept maps, to present short video or audio clips that enrich the lesson, or to show still photos. Examples, for instance, include using an Internet-connected computer to show a webcam, real-time image of Seoul as students read about Korea in their social studies texts or to send images of your students to their e-pals. A video clip can show a squid using jet propulsion to move, time-lapse images can capture a storm, and pictures of rare chemical elements can present difficult-to-obtain elements visually to students. In each of these cases, the computer provides students with access to information that can enhance their understanding and allow the teacher to save the products electronically. If no projection system is available, students can view images before instruction in small groups.

A single computer can also be used as a student learning tool. Individual students can provide input to larger products such as brainstorming lists. They can work in small groups to create stories, drawings, or maps. Individual students can use the computer to reinforce their lessons, for instance through drill programs that practice previously presented objectives, or by hearing content presented in their home language. Computers can be used as assessment tools, and they can be used by individuals or small groups during center time. A fifth-grade class that is learning states and capitals, for instance, may have the option of playing a "capital match" game on the computer during independent work time.

To ensure that all students work on the computer, their teacher creates a schedule and posts it so that small groups or partners can check and monitor their own visit. The teacher also may hang a check sheet near the computer so students check off their names as they complete their computer activities.

In addition to managing computer resources, experienced teachers sometimes use their resource management systems so effortlessly that it can be hard to appreciate them. Watch your mentors carefully and jot down some notes about how the teacher manages the scarce resources and plentiful paper we find in most classrooms.

MANAGING TIME

Alarming studies (e.g., Jones, 1987) indicate that teachers lose up to half of their instructional time through inefficient management. Imagine wasting *half* of the precious time you have with your students. Use your classroom time as gold; wasting a single minute costs everyone in the class, and those costs can never be recouped.

Maximizing Academic Learning Time

Using your time as gold means that you need to *maximize* the time your students spend engaged in learning and *minimize* the time they spend in other ways in your classroom. The total amount of classroom time can be divided into three nested subsets: allocated time, engaged time, and academic learning time. These aspects of time are presented in Figure 8.3, which makes it clear that your job as a time manager is more sophisticated than just ensuring that students are busy at *something*. You want the bull's-eye in Figure 8.3—academic learning time—to expand so that it crowds the other two circles. Your job as a time manager is to ensure that students are experiencing success in work related to lesson objectives. Students are not using their time well if they are staring at the right page in the text but have no idea what it means. Chapters 5, 6, and 7 present principles and strategies for providing instruction and assessment to encourage student success. Poor instruction is, at the very least, a waste of time. You can

FIGURE 8.3 *The target for classroom instructional time.*

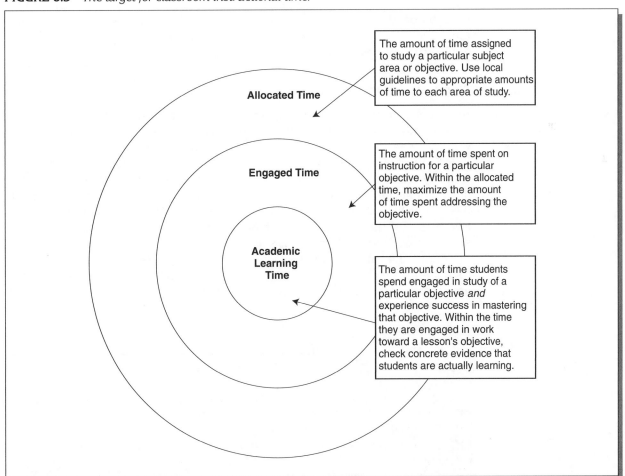

Teaching Tip 8.3

KEEPING TRACK OF TIME

It's easy for teachers and students to lose track of time during small-group or independent work time. Help students learn to gauge time by calling their attention to time requirements. Displaying a timer seems to be far more potent then telling them to watch the clock, and it removes you from the burden of timekeeper, where your announcement "time's up!" is likely to be met with a chorus of "No!" You can buy a timer to place on the overhead projector for this purpose. Or, if you have a projection system for your computer, try this free timer and stopwatch: *http://www.timeme.com/*. Students can also use it on individual computers during work times.

also maximize academic learning time by helping students learn to manage their work time. Teaching Tip 8.3 gives one suggestion for doing so.

In addition to ensuring student success during lessons, you need to minimize the amount of time you and your students spend on business items. One guaranteed way to minimize wasted time is by using **routines** for recurring events. Routines save time and offer two added benefits (Gootman, 2001): They provide confidence and security, especially for students who are accustomed to strict family structure, are lacking in structure at home, or have physiological needs for clear and calm behavioral support. Routines also provide daily practice in appropriate behavior. You will need routines for family and other classroom volunteers. Plan, for example, to have a set of materials that need preparation in case a volunteer drops in. Keep an instructional activity (such as flashcards) ready for volunteers too. Additionally, you will need both noninstructional and instructional routines.

Noninstructional Routines

An initial investment in teaching your students to run the business of your classroom will save vast amounts of time over the course of the year. Students will not need to discover your procedures, and you will not need to answer 2,043 questions about where homework belongs or whether it is okay to sharpen a pencil. Procedures and routines are especially important during the first days of class. Research indicates that effective teachers share commonalties in how they spend their early days (Bohn et al., 2004; Emmer et al., 1980; Evertson, & Emmer, 1982). Teaching Tip 8.4 gives advice based on this research to get you off to the right start.

Figure 8.4 lists some of the recurring "business" events that occur in classrooms for which you may wish to establish and teach set procedures. Clearly, your classroom would feel more like a penitentiary than a joyful learning

Teaching Tip 8.4

OFF TO THE RIGHT START

During the early days of the term, be sure to:

✔ Set high expectations for what all students can learn.
✔ Offer engaging learning activities.
✔ Establish your routines and procedures.
✔ Praise specific student success and behavior.
✔ Encourage student self-regulation.

FIGURE 8.4 *Recurring events that might benefit from a routine.*

- What to do when class begins
- What to do when class ends
- How to enter and exit the classroom
- Taking attendance
- Opening exercises
- Getting lunch count
- The rules for having water at desks or getting a drink of water
- When to use the restroom
- How to behave in each area of the classroom
- When and how loud to talk
- When to sharpen a pencil
- Where and when to get paper and other supplies
- How to head a paper
- What to do if a computer stops working
- Where and when to submit completed work
- How to gather work for absent students
- How to complete homework when returning from an absence
- What to do if the teacher steps out of the classroom
- What to do when a visitor comes
- Who will and how to help a substitute teacher
- Who will and how to run errands for the teacher
- What to do in case of emergency

environment if you were to teach and enforce rigid procedures for all of these events during the early days of school. Instead, you can teach some of the most immediate routines (what students should do when they enter the classroom in the morning, how you will take roll, what is expected in each area of the classroom) early on, checking that each routine is humane, productive, and efficient. Over time students can master each of the routines that will help them run the classroom, even in your absence. The beauty of good routines is that they set the expectation that students are responsible and capable of running the show, they help students feel secure in the predictability of their environment, they reinforce your expectation that student learning is your highest priority, and they save you from countless mundane decisions.

When you teach a routine, do it purposefully with a carefully chosen instructional strategy. I have seen some teachers gracefully coax their students into routines solely through subtle modeling. More often, direct instruction (recall Figure 6.1) is employed to efficiently ensure that each student understands and can use the routine. The younger the student, the more direct instruction may be necessary. Through direct instruction, you

- Present critical information on the routine.
- Check for student understanding.
- Practice the routine with the students.
- Observe students as they practice the routine independently.

Reteaching repairs misunderstanding at any point (Wong, 1998).

For example, Ms. Garcia wants to teach her third graders to get to work immediately when they enter the classroom each morning. She clarifies her own expectations and writes them on a chart. Then she teaches her students: "There are three things to be done each morning when you step into the classroom." Pointing to her chart and using appropriate hand gestures to support her message, Ms. Garcia states: "First, put your things away. Second, move your photo to the 'buying' or 'bringing' lunch string. Third, take out your journal and begin writing." After checking for understanding, Ms. Garcia provides guided practice: "Let's pretend it is morning now. Pick up your backpack and meet me in line. My bet is that all of you will be able to do each of our three morning tasks without a single reminder!" Students giggle as they indulge Ms. Garcia in her charade. She laughs along and provides plenty of praise for students as they get started on their own. If students fail to carry out one or more of the steps, she stops them, reteaches the step(s) they missed, and they try again. She leaves her chart posted for two weeks, until students have internalized the routine.

You will select noninstructional routines based on your own preferences and the ages of your students. Let's explore alternatives for one of the most common noninstructional routines: taking attendance.

Some teachers choose to call out students' names for daily roll so they have the opportunity to greet students as individuals: "Good morning, Tran. Good morning, Chelsea." Calling students' names in this way establishes daily positive contact with all students. However, calling each student's name aloud daily only to listen for a rote response ("Here!") is a waste of instructional time, especially for secondary teachers who have limited time with each set of students and must take attendance five or more times per day. If name-calling during roll is not used as an instructional or interactional tool, consider an alternative that takes far less time:

- As students work in their journals or complete some other task right after the bell, you can glance over the classroom to silently check and record absences. Some secondary teachers mark their seating charts to take roll.
- If students are in groups, one member can report absences for each group.
- Students enter the room and move personal markers—such as clothespins, cards, or magnets with their names on them—to a new area to indicate that they are present. One first-grade teacher I know photographs her students during the first week, cuts out the figures, and glues magnets to the back. Students move their photos each morning. She simply glances at the few remaining names or photos to determine absences. These photos can also be used for graphing experiences in mathematics. See Figure 8.5 for an example of how this strategy can be used to instructional advantage.

As you build your classroom management plan, select noninstructional routines that are appropriate for your students, that are easily managed, and that allow you to maximize the time your students have for learning.

Instructional Management and Routines

In his influential research, Kounin (1983) studied how teachers organize and manage their lessons and found that three aspects of lesson movement correlated well with management success:

- *Smoothness.* Does the lesson flow from start to finish, adhering to a set focus? Is it free from abrupt changes in what students are asked to do?
- *Momentum.* Does the lesson move along without lags created by the teacher overexplaining (the yack factor) or overdwelling (the nag factor)?
- *Group focus.* Is the teacher able to concentrate on the entire group of students as a unit?

FIGURE 8.5 *Take roll and teach . . . at the same time.*

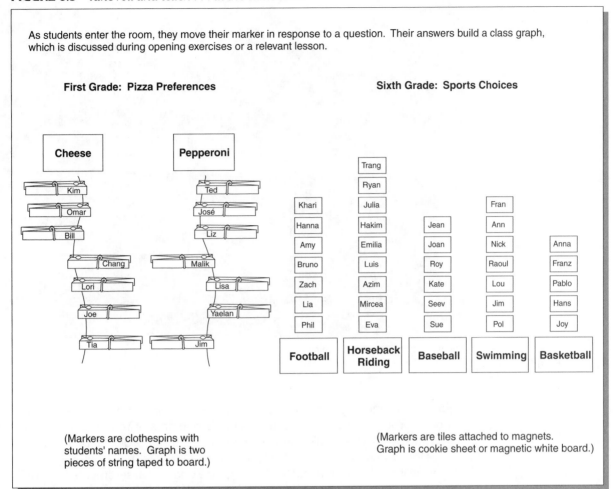

As students enter the room, they move their marker in response to a question. Their answers build a class graph, which is discussed during opening exercises or a relevant lesson.

First Grade: Pizza Preferences

Cheese | **Pepperoni**

Kim | Ted
Omar | José
Bill | Liz
Chang | Malik
Lori | Lisa
Joe | Yaelan
Tia | Jim

(Markers are clothespins with students' names. Graph is two pieces of string taped to board.)

Sixth Grade: Sports Choices

Football	Horseback Riding	Baseball	Swimming	Basketball
	Trang			
	Ryan		Fran	
Khari	Julia	Jean	Ann	
Hanna	Hakim	Joan	Nick	Anna
Amy	Emilia	Roy	Raoul	Franz
Bruno	Luis	Kate	Lou	Pablo
Zach	Azim	Seev	Jim	Hans
Lia	Mircea	Sue	Pol	Joy
Phil	Eva			

(Markers are tiles attached to magnets. Graph is cookie sheet or magnetic white board.)

In the same way that routines can help with noninstructional issues, routines can also help smooth instructional movement wrinkles. Typical creases that can be ironed out through careful attention to instruction include the following:

- Pacing
- Transitions
- Providing assistance
- Making every minute count

Pacing. **Pacing** refers to the speed at which instruction is delivered. Pacing often presents difficulties for new teachers because it demands an understanding of student development, and in-depth knowledge of students grows primarily through experience. A well-paced lesson devotes just enough time to developing concepts and ideas. Lessons must progress slowly enough to ensure student understanding but quickly enough to

1. Maintain student interest and attention.
2. Minimize opportunities for misbehavior.
3. Make efficient use of a time within a crowded classroom schedule.

To gauge the pace of your lessons, start by watching for cues from the students. You may select a couple focus students with disparate needs—for example, a student with an identified learning disability and one who learns

An effectively managed classroom results in greater academic learning time.

Karen Mancinelli/Pearson Learning Photo Studio

quickly. Do they appear anxious? You may be moving too quickly. Are they snoozy? You may need to pep things up. Is one antsy? You may need to switch activities. overwhelmed? You may need to let them process information for a bit before moving on. Do not rely solely on students' body language, though, because it can be limited and misleading. Use ongoing assessments (Figure 7.13) that provide information about student learning to adjust your pacing. Active participation devices such as unison response and finger signals, for example, give quick information about student understanding during a lesson and can help you know whether your pacing is appropriate.

As you observe a variety of experienced teachers, you will note that they pace their lessons differently, depending on both their students and their own preferences. I prefer an air of productive hurrying. I like students to glance at the clock, surprised that our time is up, when I close the lesson and say good-bye. To ensure that lessons do not drag, tell students how much time they have for each task and stick fairly closely to your stated limits. You may wish to use a timer to help you and the students keep track. Especially during group work, students of all ages seem to take as much time as they are given to complete their work. You may bend your rule a bit if they groan at your one-minute warning ("Okay, but in two minutes you will be ready to report. Hurry!"), but if you double your initial time allotment, you will teach students that they need not focus and work productively or that you can be swayed easily to relax your requirements. Send the message that time is golden. In doing so, be certain to use each spare moment to instructional advantage. Have a plan if your lesson runs short, as in Teaching Tip 8.5.

Transitions. **Transitions** are the periods between one activity and the next. Teachers at all levels need to switch activities efficiently *within* lessons. Teachers with multiple subjects also must manage transitions *between* lessons. Murphy must have a law to account for the fact that students—no matter the age—can remain attentive during an entire lesson and then hang from

WHAT TO DO WHEN—YIKES!— THE LESSON RUNS SHORT

As new teachers learn to gauge pacing, lessons occasionally take less time than expected. For *every* lesson you plan, have a brief, stand-alone activity ready in case the lesson runs short. Practice pages and extension activities are examples. Be certain that the extra activity is meaningful.

If you really get stuck, try some of the sponges in Figure 8.6 on page 231 or the independent activities listed in the upcoming subsection "Making Every Minute Count."

---

the ceiling in the two minutes between one activity and the next. To encourage smooth transitions:

1. Anticipate transitions as trouble spots. Have your own materials ready. Be watchful and businesslike.
2. Plan for transitions as a mini-lesson: What exactly do you need students to do in switching activities? Tell them. Monitor their behavior and redirect as necessary ("Stop. You forgot the part about silence. Let's try again.").
3. Practice completing transitions in limited time. Challenge students to prepare for the next lesson in less than 60 seconds. Invite them to beat their previous times. Make it a wager if you are the betting type.
4. Use a change in space to ease transitions: "Finish up your comprehension questions and meet me on the rug by the time I count down from 20."
5. Make transitions serve double duty. For example, some teachers have primary-grade students sing as they move from one activity to the next. This keeps the students instructionally focused and limits the transition period to the length of the song. A secondary teacher may play one song on a CD to signal the start and finish of the transition. Other options include reciting math facts and picking up trash as students move from one activity to the next.

Providing Assistance. Students often lose learning time during independent work periods because they sit and wait for the teacher's help. Make a plan so that you can provide assistance to all students who ask—before their hands fall asleep in the air. The first way to ensure that you provide timely individual assistance is to monitor the kinds of assistance students request. Imagine that you just gave instructions for a social studies assignment and eight students surround you, papers rustling, questions poised. Their presence is a sign that you need to reteach: You discover that they do not understand how to read the scale on the map. Stop answering individual questions and reteach the entire group. (See Teaching Tip 8.6.) Or poll the class and pull aside a small group for further explanation of the map's scale. If you have developed a safe environment, students generally will not mind taking you up on your offer to join them in the back for an encore.

After ensuring that students as a group understand concepts and your directions, think about how you can make sure that students get the help they need with as little time away from learning as possible. Following are four strategies teachers find useful:

1. Use praise–prompt–leave (from Figure 6.1). When you address a student's question, give a specific compliment for what he has done right, prompt him quickly on what he needs to do next, and leave. Providing efficient help

RULE OF THUMB FOR RETEACHING

Choose a number, five or fewer, as your limit. Let's say four. If four of your students ask you for the same kind of help, do not answer individual questions; reteach the group: "I did not make this as clear as I had hoped. Many people are asking about __. Let me explain in another way." Stick with your limit.

allows you to interact with more students. Jones (2000) admonishes us to spend no more than 20 seconds as we provide assistance to individuals.

2. If students are seated in groups, teach the students that there can be no *individual* question for the teacher, only a *group* question. That way, students are expected to ask two or three peers before they ask you. You not only save time but also display the expectation that students can and should help each other.

3. Check the work of one person in each row (or group) who is likely to succeed quickly. Put her in charge of answering the questions in her row.

4. Use a signal other than the raised hand. Students can stand a red card on their desks, for example, if they need your assistance. Teach them to work on another section of the task until you arrive.

Making Every Minute Count You want students engaged in learning even when you are not providing formal instruction. Make every minute count by

- having a plan for what students should do if they finish early.
- using "sponges" to soak up spare minutes.

Students work at different rates, and, at least at the elementary level, at some point each will approach you and say "Teacher, I finished. What should I do now?" Develop some instructionally sound responses and teach students—even kindergartners—to select and complete learning activities without your assistance. Write (or draw) acceptable choices on a chart, post the chart, and teach students to follow the chart. Then if they ask, "What should I do now?" you just point to the chart. Add new choices occasionally. Depending on students' age, some widely applicable choices include the following:

- Read a good book.
- Write a letter to a friend in the class. "Send" it through the class post office.
- Study the globe.
- Practice skills (e.g., printing, spelling words, math facts, and vocabulary cards).
- Work at a center (e.g., for science, art, building, puzzles, or technology).
- Play a thinking skills game (e.g., chess, checkers, or a board game).
- Complete independent research. (Allow students to follow their own interests in long-term projects.)

Just as you can count on students finishing at different rates, you can bet there will be downtime, or brief periods when your class is waiting for an assembly, class pictures, or a guest speaker. Soak up those spare minutes with sponges, which are activities that encourage learning but do not require much preparation. For example, when the first assembly runs late and your class is waiting to join the second one, you might ask students of any age, "Have you lived a million seconds?" Students can also estimate their age in minutes, days, weeks, or months. Then you can quickly check their predications by visiting http://www.mathcats.com/explore/age/calculator.html. Calculations are completed so quickly that the site is sure to spark some interesting questions for exploration.

FIGURE 8.6   *Sponges for spare moments.*

1. Read student requests from a book of poetry (anything by Shel Silverstein is a sure bet).
2. Practice logical questioning with a game of 20 Questions.
3. For young students, play Simon Says to hone listening skills. Or, play it in a different language.
4. Count as high as you can as a class by ones, twos, fives, tens, threes, or sevens. A variation is to count by ones and say *buzz* to replace multiples of a given number: "8, 9, buzz, 11," for example, for multiples of five.
5. Individually, in pairs, or as a class, list as many compound words, state capitals, homonyms, mammals, cabinet members, African countries, prime numbers, chemical symbols, or anything else as you can.
6. Sharpen estimation skills by estimating and checking an unknown quantity, amount, or duration of an event. For example, "How many seconds can you stand on one foot? With your eyes closed?" "How many beans fit into my hand?" "What is the total value of the seven coins in my pocket?" "How many insects are on earth?" Use the World Almanac or a book of world records for information.
7. Write brief group stories. One person writes the opening, folds back all but the last line, and passes it to the next author.
8. Practice classification skills with "Who's in My Group?" Call students who meet an unstated criterion of your choosing (such as black hair or earrings or laced shoes) to the front of the room to be members of your group. The rest of the class guesses the rule. Be tricky and use more than one criterion. Or, allow students to make the rule and call up the groups. For older students, draw the dichotomous key to demonstrate your grouping.
9. Pull out a set of simple objects and list scientific observations about them. See how long of a list you can create. Then see if students locate a particular object in the pile purely by reading or listening to peers' observations. Work on improving the quality of their observations over time.
10. Pull down map and play "I'm Thinking of a State (or Region or Island)" by allowing students to ask questions to discover your state. Allow a student to lead the next round. Or, in a less structured activity, find out how many countries are represented in the travels (or ancestries) of your students. Where is the farthest north anyone has traveled? East?
11. Tell students a story. Invite one of them to tell a story or do a trick.
12. Do some genetics research: See how many can curl their tongues, for instance. Who has a hitchhiker's thumb? Attached earlobes?
13. Try some at-your-seat gymnastics. Can students clasp their hands behind their backs if one arm reaches from next to the head and the other comes from below? Can they rub their stomachs and pat their heads at the same time? Drum their fingers starting with the pinkie, then starting with the thumb?
14. Talk about the world. What have students read on the Web today? In the paper? Seen on the news?

The first assembly is *still* not out? Discover what happened on this day in history by checking the headlines: http://dmarie.com/timecap/. Secondary students will be enthralled by http://peteranswers.com. It's magic. Don't ask me. Some additional sample sponges are given in Figure 8.6. Write sponges on index cards, transparencies, or in a small notebook in advance so that you can choose one and get right to work. Students can even be taught to select and lead sponge activities. While you are thinking about time management, you may choose to use Figure 8.10 to make a tentative plan for using classroom time well.

YOUR OWN MANAGEMENT PLAN

You have an empty room, a class list, and sets of texts. Where do you go from here? How will you establish a cohesive community? Figures 8.7 through 8.10 can help you establish an initial classroom management plan that is consistent with the major points of this book and that can set you on your way to establishing a productive and humane learning environment.

FIGURE 8.7 *The big view: Guiding forces in my management plan.*

---

1. The law:

   ☐ Reread Figure 1.2 on teachers' legal responsibilities. Notes:

   ☐ Check with administrator or mentor for expectations and sources for local laws.

   ☐ Things to keep in mind:

2. The setting:

   ☐ Check your work in Figure 1.1 to refresh your thinking about the specific locale and the expectations it provides.

   ☐ Things to keep in mind:

3. My stance toward education:

   ☐ Glance at your work in Chapter 2 to refresh your memory of your big view of teaching.

   ☐ Complete the following stems:
   A good society

   A community

   The purpose of education

   People learn by

   Good teachers

Because some teachers, particularly secondary teachers, "float" from room to room rather than being assigned a single room, Figure 8.11 may be helpful in helping you think about some key management issues within a single period (inspired by Emmer, Evertson, & Worsham, 2002). You will revise your plan in response to your students and your growing expertise, so use this draft to brainstorm. You may wish to first try the exercise in Figure 8.13 at the end of this chapter if you have not yet had many opportunities to observe classrooms. As you complete your management plan, be sure to consider the role that technology plays in it.

FIGURE 8.8 *My plan for creating positive classroom ambience.*

☐ I want my classroom to feel like a _____ .

☐ I will foster a sense of community by:

☐ Physical arrangements to create that tone
 Work space (tables and desks):

 My instruction station:

 Small-group instruction area:

 Special-interest areas:

 Wall and ceiling space:

 My work space and storage areas:

☐ Other furnishings and strategies I will use to create that ambience:

Checkpoints

Does the room provide for

☐ Emotional safety and a sense of belonging?
☐ Intellectual stimulation?
☐ Social interaction?
☐ Pleasant experience?
☐ Student responsibility?

TECHNOLOGY AND CLASSROOM MANAGEMENT

Technology's potential to help us get and stay organized is prodigious, as we know from our personal digital assistants, voice memos, and budget spreadsheets. Technology within the classroom can be used, too, to help teacher and students alike stay organized, create community, and make best use of space, resources, and time.

FIGURE 8.9   *My plan for arranging classroom space.*

The Perfect Classroom: A Map

Checkpoints

☐ Is it safe? Can I monitor?

☐ Does it encourage community?

☐ Is it productive?

☐ Is it efficient?

☐ Does it make full use of available resources?

Creating Community: Managing Classroom Ambience

A large variety of techno tools can support a positive community in your classroom. Many take little time and fit easily into the classroom routine. For example, recordings of music played at strategic moments such as during transitions or at the close of the period or day can go far in enhancing the ambience. This is especially true when students select some of the music or the teacher draws the students' attention to the significance of the piece and adds it to the class's musical library. Some teachers play "Twist and Shout" as their students tidy the classroom. Others ask students to share music of personal significance to start the day. Technologically enhanced sponges can also increase the sense of community. Using the Web during a few spare moments, a teacher might project an engaging, instructionally relevant game onto the screen and challenge the students as a class. Perhaps he uses one like the *New York Time's* Daily News Quiz (http://www.nytimes.com/learning/students/quiz/index.html). As the class laughs and learns together via technology, they are cemented as a group.

Several productivity tools can also help you craft a positive ambience in your classroom. For instance, digitally created banners, signs, and posters can help students feel welcome and can share your important priorities such as your mission statement, motto, or inspirational quotes. Students can also electronically create their own cards, posters, and signs to contribute to a positive, student-centered, content-focused tone in your room.

FIGURE 8.10 *My plan for using classroom time well.*

☐ Check with administrator or mentor for requirements or guidelines on allocated time.

Sample Classroom Schedule

Routines

☐ **Some of my noninstructional routines:**

Taking attendance:

Opening exercises:

Expected behaviors for each area:

Two more routines to use (review Figure 8.4):

☐ **Instructional routines:**

Providing assistance:

Sponges:

Independent work activities:

Involving Families

☐ Routines for involving family and other volunteers:

☐ Routines for communicating regularly with families:

Some teachers take digital photos of students (when appropriate and permitted; check permission slips). They post prints in the room to show the class engaged in important work and to document the class's history. For example, Figure 8.12 shows a small group of preservice teachers on the last day of our foundations class, holding cards with the words and phrases they each selected to represent a core conviction about teaching. This photo became one of many displayed on the class's Web site and during their end-of-program slide show. Teachers of all grade levels often display such images on the password-protected Web pages they create for students and families. They also often

FIGURE 8.11 *Management plan for a single period of the day.*

1. Opening Procedures

   Attendance procedure:

   Location of attendance materials such as tardy and absence slips:

   Procedure for getting work to students returning from absences:

   Instructional activity for students during attendance:

2. Rules and Procedures

   Leaving the room:

   Using classroom resources (e.g., computers):

   Getting assistance:

   Working with peers:

   Submitting work:

   Expectations on format of assignment, allowable resources, late work, extra credit:

   Recording assignments:

   What to do if teacher is occupied by a visitor:

3. Dismissal Routines

   Signal for clean-up time:

   Expectations for the room's condition upon students' leaving:

Teacher Tip 8.7

POST A CLASS WEB SITE

Put up your own site to post upcoming events, assignments, and celebrations. Many sites allow you to post your own Web site at a low cost. Two examples include http://classWebs.net and http://schoolworld.com. Some of the sites you will find when you search "web page builder" allow you to establish your page for free. None of these sites actually allow you to build a page from scratch, but they do allow you to post your content to a site on the Web. Schools also often have a mechanism by which you can establish a site. Protect students' privacy and safety by guarding their names and taking care about the class photos you post. This is of particular importance if the site is not password protected. Check your school's policies on teacher Web sites and postings.

exhibit photos in celebratory slide shows in order establish and maintain a sense of class cohesion and accomplishment.

Managing Physical Space

The increasing presence of classroom computers requires us to carefully plan physical space. The student-to-computer ratio in the United States is approximately 4:1, nearly all schools have Internet access, and about half have wireless connections (U.S. Department of Education, National Center for Education Statistics, 2006a). Take these facts into account as you devise your perfect classroom map (Figure 8.9). You may need, for instance, to include about five classroom computers in your plan. Look around—check local statistics and plan technology accordingly. If your computers are desktops with cords and connections, place them where the cords and cables will not be a safety hazard (often along the perimeter of the room), where you and the students using computers can see each other without peeking over the tops of monitors, and where students can be of assistance to others using the computers without distracting peers who are working in other parts of the room. If your students have laptops (perhaps on a cart?), be sure to include space to store them so that they are safe and accessible as well.

FIGURE 8.12 *Building community through digital media.*

You can also use technology to help you make and record decisions regarding physical space. Check out the interactive classroom map tool at the American Federation of Teacher's Web site listed at the chapter's close. You can select and arrange virtual furniture and view your map from different angles. No more cutting out tiny furniture or shoving around dozens of desks! Finally, rather than creating seating charts by hand and then erasing frequently, create seating charts using a word processing program or other tool. This way you can modify the charts easily and you can print out many copies to use for purposes such as taking attendance, making observational notes, or recording participation rates.

Managing Resources: Managing Technology and Other Stuff

An earlier section of this chapter gave advice for organizing computer use in your classroom. Computer-based technology can also help you manage "the stuff" of teaching. One of your responsibilities will be to establish and manage communications, for example. Keep a contact log for family phone calls and other communications. Word-processed tables and spreadsheets can both be used for this purpose, although spreadsheets make it easier to manipulate your data for different purposes. List the date, time, student, family member, description of the issue, and plans for resolution. Post assignments and major events for students and families via e-mail or through your own Web site. As Chapter 7 discussed, computer-managed student records make efficient use of time, aid in analysis, and foster timely communications with students and families.

Managing Time

Technology as an instructional tool *can* help teachers to maximize academic learning time. However, it must be used wisely to avoid wasting precious instructional minutes. Some teachers use computers only for noninstructional games during reward time, for example. Film and video, too, are sometimes used in ways that do not enhance learning (Hobbs, 2006). Hobbs recommends that, in order to use media well, teachers should:

- Set clear instructional purposes.
- Make use of functions such as pause and review to enhance learning.
- Stay mentally engaged throughout the showing (do not do other things).
- Avoid noninstructional uses such as video as a reward, time filler, or a way to control student behavior.

As with any teaching and learning tool, it is important to maximize learning benefits for time invested via technology by carefully considering your purposes, finding tools that match those purposes, teaching students to use the tools efficiently, monitoring students' engagement and success, and changing tools if time is not well spent.

Technology can also help with time management by capturing the minutes, hours, days, and weeks we spend with students. Year-long, unit, and lesson plans created and stored electronically are easily modified and archived for next time. Class agendas created on the computer similarly allow easy modifications. Some teachers continue to write, longhand, in plan books, which requires them to recopy much information such as times, periods, and regular events (e.g. lunch) on every page. Imagine, instead, creating your plan book as a computer file where recurring events are set as a template or copy/pasted with two or three clicks of a mouse. Your electronic plan book would also save you the inevitable irritation of erasing and moving lessons you "didn't get to" or drawing so many arrows that your book might be mistaken for a football play book rather than a lesson plan book.

Technology can also help teachers track their instructional time minute by minute in the classroom. Many teachers use stopwatches or overhead timers to help build student awareness of time requirements and expenditures. For instance, Jones (2000) recommends that teachers time their students during transitions and other routine events. Seconds not wasted can be spent during preferred activities later. Or, a teacher may set an overhead timer for a specified number of minutes as students begin their small-group work. Recall Teaching Tip 8.3 in this regard.

In sum, technology raises issues that must be addressed as we make decisions—how can all my students have equitable access to classroom computers?—and it presents us with a set of tools that, when used well, can help us build community and use our space, time, and resources to the best advantage.

PARTING WORDS

Your painstaking efforts to maintain a pleasant and productive learning environment will not always result in a happy citizenry living in educational paradise. Sometimes a negative tone can arise if the teacher struggles with discipline, if the students begin to treat each other with disrespect, or if the class fails to establish a sense of group purpose. Chapter 9 provides additional suggestions for keeping the atmosphere positive, for talking through issues to encourage respect, for building community, and for managing students as a group. If you notice that your classroom is beginning to feel unproductive or unpleasant, try running through some of these steps:

1. *Get a sense of perspective.* What are you trying to accomplish with your students? What is interfering with your class's attempts to build a productive environment? A trusted outside observer may be able to offer a fresh view.

2. *Rebuild a sense of community.* Try a classroom meeting during which you set new goals as a class. Choose some high-interest activities and perhaps

some positive consequences that reward students for working as a group. Allow students to make the space their own.

3. *Reestablish your expectations for student behavior.* Open your eyes wide and remind your students that you care so much about them that you cannot allow them to treat each other or their classroom in harmful ways. Clearly outline the kinds of behaviors you need to see and, if necessary, employ logical consequences to help students with their behavior.

4. *Change something.* Add quiet music. Rearrange the desks. Record yourself and listen to your tone. Rework your routines. Flip the schedule. Laugh at the nuisances that would otherwise drive you to distraction. Have lunch with your students.

5. *Never give up.*

WEB SITES

http://www.t-source.org/TeacherResources.aspx
American Federation of Teachers: Teacher Resources. Contains helpful resources such as check sheets and videos. My favorite is the "arranging your classroom" tool, which allows you to build a map of your classroom with a 3D modeling tool.

http://www.educationworld.com/a_curr/archives/class management.shtml
Educator's World: Classroom management. Includes a large variety of tips from different sources. For instance, a tutorial shows how to make an easy-to-update seating chart using Excel. Also check "5-minute fillers" for ideas for using every minute productively.

http://www.middleweb.com
Middleweb: Exploring Middle School Reform. This site addresses management and other issues for teachers of the middle years. For classroom management topics, go to "The First Days of Middle School." The free weekly e-newsletter is very good, and the teacher blogs give a realistic picture of living and learning with middle school students.

http://www.nea.org
National Education Association. Under "Members and Educators," go to "In the Classroom" and view ideas in both "Classroom Management" and "It Works for Me."

http://newmanagement.com
New Management. Rick Morris's Web site. Morris is known for his positive, practical management strategies that emphasize meeting the basic needs of power, love, fun, freedom, and safety. This site gives articles and tips, but it also sells Morris's products.

http://www.proteacher.com/030001.shtml
Pro Teacher: Behavior Management. Includes tips and articles on classic, timely, and practical topics related to discipline and management. I searched the archives for "time management" and received helpful tips from experienced and student teachers.

http://www.theteachersguide.com
The Teachers Guide. Rich resources of a variety of kinds. Go to "class management" under "education" for Internet sites, printouts, and discussion.

OPPORTUNITIES TO PRACTICE

1. Analyze a teacher's management plan using the observation sheet given in Figure 8.13. You have three choices:

   - Analyze the fourth-grade video clip found at the Merrill Teacher Prep Web site Video Classroom, Classroom Management, Module 2, Video 1.

   - Observe an experienced teacher's room environment and classroom management. At the end of the observation jot down a few great ideas that are consistent with your own thinking about management. Incorporate them into your own plan.

   - If you are already teaching, ask a colleague or mentor to observe your own management.

2. Read a professional journal article on classroom management. What is the author's implied stance toward education? Are the strategies consistent with what you know about good teaching?

3. Alfie Kohn (1996) is critical of schools' overreliance on punishment and rewards and the illusion of choice it presents for students. To what extent do you agree with him? What would it take to change the practices that he sees as inhumane?

4. Start a file for promising classroom management ideas. Encourage a share session with peers. Observe more classrooms for ideas on management. Remember that every strategy you consider needs to measure up to the tough standard of your stance toward education and must encourage student learning in humane ways. Plenty of management strategies around today fall short of those criteria.

FIGURE 8.13   *Observing classroom management.*

Management Area	Observation Notes

Ambience
 	
1. This classroom feels like a _____.
2. What things does the teacher actually do and say to create the tone?
3. What are the big ideas about teaching and learning that seem to be conveyed by the classroom ambience?
4. **Community:** How does the environment establish the norms of shared governance and concern?
5. How does the tone establish
   a. Emotional safety?
   b. Intellectual stimulation?
   c. Social interaction and responsibility?
   d. School as a meaningful and pleasant experience?	

Physical Space
 	
6. Observe how the teacher has structured the *physical layout* of the room.
   • Floor space
   • Wall space
   • Instruction station
   • Special-interest areas
   • Other spaces
7. Observe how the teacher has arranged *instructional materials and resources,* including computers.
8. How does the environment promote *physical safety?*
9. **Productivity:** How does the environment allow for
   a. A balance and variety of activities?
   b. All students to see and hear the teacher?
   c. All students to focus on instruction?
10. **Efficiency:** How does the environment allow for ease in
   a. The teacher reaching each student?
   b. Students reaching each other?
   c. The teacher and students reaching materials and other areas of the room?	

Time
 	
11. Find the classroom schedule. How does *allocated time* encourage learning?
12. What evidence is there that students are experiencing *success* during **engaged time**?
13. How does the teacher use *noninstructional routines* effectively? List some routines you observed to be particularly effective.
14. If you observe *instruction,* check
   a. Pacing
   b. Transitions
   c. Provision of assistance
   d. Provisions for students who finish early	

Overall 15. List two or more things you learned about classroom management by observing this teacher and classroom.	

Before You Begin Reading

Take your pick of Exercise A or B; or, if you like, do both.

Warm-Up Exercise A: Encouraging Appropriate Behavior

Think back to a teacher you loved or admired when you were young. Briefly jot down a few notes about that teacher. What specifically did the teacher do to gain your admiration?

What lessons about classroom discipline can you draw from this teacher? (P.S. You can learn lessons from a teacher you disliked as well. Analyze a negative experience too if you like.)

Warm-Up Exercise B: Shopping List of Promising Rules and Tools

Chapter 9 asks you to develop your own discipline program, and it presents much information that can support your efforts. Use this table to keep the big picture in mind as you read Chapter 9, if you like.

Rule: Treat all learners with dignity and respect.
Tools:

Establishing a climate of dignity and respect	Responding to Behavior
❏ Celebrate and suffer	❏ Address the behavior
❏ Active listening	❏ Private correction
❏ Peer listening	❏ Hints
❏ Model and teach	❏ *I*-messages
	❏ Strength refreshers
	❏ Emotional control
	❏ Laughter
	❏ Apologies

Rule: Actively prevent misbehavior.
Tools:
❏ Meaningful curriculum
❏ Motivation and development
❏ Authority
❏ Clear expectations
❏ Anticipation
❏ Positive approach
❏ Nonverbal communication

Rule: View discipline as an opportunity to help students gain independence and responsibility.
Tools:

Establishing a climate that promotes independence	Addressing behaviors in ways that encourage self-control
❏ Choices	❏ Talk it through
❏ Respect for decisions	❏ Self-correction
❏ Clear limits	❏ Avoid power struggles
❏ Consistency	❏ Anger shields
❏ Natural consequences	❏ Conflict resolution

Rule: Address discipline in many ways and on multiple levels.
Tools:
❏ Group size
❏ Overlapping
❏ Intensity of response
❏ Motivation for misbehavior
❏ Redirecting behavior

CHAPTER *Nine*

Encouraging Appropriate Behavior

> *"For the very true beginning of her [wisdom] is the desire of discipline; and the care of discipline is love."*
>
> —The Wisdom of Solomon 6:17

Discipline and *love* in the same sentence? Discipline is not an evil word, although it provokes at least a twinge of anxiety for many teachers. What is it about maintaining classroom discipline that seems inherently troublesome for many teachers, especially novices? The need to discipline students can run counter to new teachers' need to feel loved and accepted. Also, pressing one's own will above that of the students often invokes conflict. Teachers must at times ask students to behave in ways that are at odds with the students' youthful agendas.

You will be most successful as a disciplinarian if you begin with a positive attitude. Teachers who believe they *can* make a difference in students' behavior and handle discipline situations . . . *do* (Rimm-Kaufman & Sawyer, 2004). Teachers who are self-confident about student discipline tend to respond to problematic behavior in ways that are more positive and more consistent with the teachers' overall approach, their stance.

Additionally, your attitude toward student discipline should be positive because encouraging appropriate behavior is not an act of coercion. Rather, it is an act of care and respect by a teacher who values students enough to help them make good decisions about their behavior. Nearly every teacher's philosophy includes the goal of helping students to become considerate citizens who exhibit self-control and take responsibility for their own actions. Because you respect your students, you will be eager to help them grow toward independence—not only academically but behaviorally as well. This chapter offers rules and tools for classroom discipline, and it encourages you to develop your own discipline program.

RULES AND TOOLS FOR CLASSROOM DISCIPLINE

Your classroom management and discipline program, as a reminder from Chapter 8, needs to be coherent, consistent, positive, and proactive (Miller & Hall, 2005). A few basic rules can provide good direction as you create and maintain a warm, respectful, and productive classroom:

1. Treat all learners with dignity and respect.
2. Actively prevent misbehavior.
3. View discipline as an opportunity to help students gain independence and responsibility.
4. Address discipline issues in many ways and on multiple levels.

> **REMEMBER THE LAW**
>
> 1. Teachers are prohibited from
>   - humiliating students.
>   - physically punishing students, except under strict guidelines for corporal punishment (where allowed).
>   - using academic penalties for behavioral offenses.
> 2. Students have rights to due process.
>
> *Refresher from Figure 1.2.*

These four basic rules can be implemented through tools, or specific strategies, such as those addressed in the following sections.

Treat All Learners with Dignity and Respect

> The secret in education lies in respecting the student.
>
> —*Ralph Waldo Emerson*

Every learner—every human—deserves courtesy and kindness. This notion seems basic, yet it is violated daily. Given their lesser size and status, children in our society sometimes receive less thoughtful treatment than do adults: fast-food workers glance over the heads of children waiting at the counter, tired parents are easily irritated, and teachers readily interrupt. Additionally, not all students are treated equally by their teachers. Chapter 3 provided evidence to suggest that students have different classroom experiences based on characteristics such as gender and ethnicity.

The same is true for disability status. In Cook's (2004) study and in several similar ones, general education teachers report feeling less attached to their students with disabilities and reject them at higher rates than they do their nondisabled students. Students who are less attached or are rejected get less positive attention and feedback from their teachers. Therefore, vigilance in accepting all of our students as valuable humans is vital; students must feel that

Caring relationships are based on mutual respect.

Scott Cunningham/Merrill

we respect them as people, are concerned about their needs, and understand their perspectives.

In terms of discipline, as you shape students' behavior, Curwin and Mendler (2001) advise you to protect students' dignity by thinking about your own: How would you respond if a teacher used this strategy with you? By fostering respect and dignity, we offer hope. Make your classroom a refuge where students receive the same consideration as would respected adults, through both the environment you create and the ways you elect to respond to students' behavior.

Following are 12 ways you can treat people with dignity and respect. The first four points establish the climate; the rest of the list show responses to behavior.

1. Celebrate and suffer
2. Active listening
3. Peer listening
4. Model and teach
5. Address the behavior
6. Private correction
7. Hints
8. *I*-messages
9. Strength refreshers
10. Emotional control
11. Laughter
12. Apologies

Establishing a Climate of Dignity and Respect You want students to know that every person in your classroom is important. The sense of community you began to establish through your work in classroom management (Chapter 8) is the starting point for your climate of respect. Use a warm and respectful voice (Kohn, 1999). Show students that you know and value their perspectives (Wormeli, 2001). Learn about the things they care about and remember to see the world from the eyes of someone their age.

Celebrate and suffer

1. *Celebrate and suffer.* One way you can demonstrate respect for your students' thoughts and experiences is by sharing their successes and their slips. When students express emotions, especially sadness or despair, it is tempting for teachers to rush in, quickly analyze the situation, tell students how they should be feeling, fix things, and move on. However, this overly helpful response can serve to take away from another person's experience. You need not feel that you must provide explanations or analyses for every event that causes emotion for your students (Schneider, 1997). A quiet, sad smile, a thumbs-up, or a round of applause may be a terrific way to show students that you understand their positions and respect their experiences. The use of such empathic resonance can help your students feel less alone (Kottler & Kottler, 2007).

Active listening

2. *Active listening.* On a more immediate level, you can show that you value students' words and ideas by practicing active listening (Gordon, 1974). In active listening, the teacher summarizes or reflects the speaker's message. For instance, a teacher may begin his reply to a frustrated student, "You seem to be saying that this homework was hard for you." A question stem such as "Are you saying that . . . ?" can also help to ensure clear communication. Active listening shows students that you value their ideas enough to be certain that you understand them correctly. It allows you to demonstrate that you believe communication involves two parties, each deserving to be heard. Gootman (2001) gives six tips for caring listening:

1. *Show interest.* Show interest and pay attention when students speak. Hold your body still and give your full attention.
2. *Hear them out.* Wait until students are finished speaking before saying anything.

3. *Separate your feelings from their feelings.* Respond to the issue, not the emotion.

4. *Look for nonverbal cues.* Body language can help you find the true meaning of the message.

5. *Put student feelings into words.* Try to interpret the message and emotions by rephrasing what you think you have heard.

6. *Don't argue with students' feelings.* Accept students' rights to feel as they do rather than suggesting that they should feel different emotions.

Gootman's tips can be equally effective for helping students listen to their peers.

Peer listening

3. *Peer listening.* Silent but accepted norms teach students that they need to listen raptly to the teacher but not so carefully to each other. Students need to be encouraged to listen to each other. When we allow children to ignore their peers, we perpetuate their disrespect and interfere with the sense of community we are trying to establish. Following is a typical scenario: The class chatters over Ray as he shares his ideas. The teacher implores, "Stop, Ray, I can't hear you." When the class quiets down, the teacher repeats Ray's words for the class: "Ray was saying . . . " In this scenario, the teacher is the traffic cop who controls the conversation. Let's rewrite the scenario so that it encourages more respectful and caring interactions: The class chatters, but this time the teacher suggests, "Ray, let's wait just a second. Some of your peers can't hear you yet." The class quiets down, and the teacher urges: "Ray, why don't you repeat the last thing you said now that you have all ears on you." Now the teacher sends the message that she expects students to listen to each other. She doesn't repeat Ray's words but directly encourages students to listen to each other.

Model and teach

4. *Model and teach.* This scenario also highlights the importance of directly teaching students to treat others with dignity. Take advantage of the power of modeling to show learners what fairness and dignity look and feel like. When modeling is insufficient, draw students' attention to respectful treatment. If they treat someone disrespectfully, quietly and calmly point out the consequences of what they have done and help them find more dignified alternatives. For example, when students use harsh words to tease, tell them firmly that harsh words can hurt and are not allowed in your classroom. Then give them some acceptable alternatives to teasing. Each of these tools can help you build a supportive climate, but you will also need to address misbehavior in ways that maintain students' dignity.

To watch teachers address misbehavior with low-profile responses, visit the Merrill Teacher Prep Web site Video Classroom, General Methods, Module 4, Video 1. What are the benefits of low-profile responses to misbehavior? What if they fail to change student behavior?

Responding to Behavior How you choose to respond to inappropriate behavior can teach lessons that last a lifetime. You have the power to humiliate or help. Be certain that you redirect inappropriate behavior without embarrassing learners. Remember that, as the sole adult in the classroom, you and your words can carry tremendous power. Students, especially younger ones, depend on adults for messages about who they are and what they are worth. Additionally, your responses to students' misbehavior should cause minimal disruption to the lesson and should signal that you trust in students' ability to solve their own problems.

Address the behavior, not the person

5. *Address the behavior.* A child may carry your words into adulthood, so when you praise or provide correction, address students' actions and not their character. For instance, when your class has listened attentively to a guest speaker, it is more effective to praise specific behaviors ("You all watched and listened with such respect!") than to address students' value as people ("You are so good!"). When you need to correct misbehavior, do not apply words such as lazy, thoughtless, or bad to the students. Instead, provide feedback on what students did that was wrong: "You talked while the guest speaker was talking" instead of "You are so rude!" Say "You left the room a mess" instead of "You are so messy!" When you address behavior and not character, you send the message that students are worthy people, even when they err.

Use private correction

6. *Private correction.* In the instances when most of the class is fine but one student needs redirection, make it a point to speak quietly with her in private. While the others work, approach the student's desk for a calm conversation about her behavior. If you can continue providing adequate supervision, you may elect to hold your conversation in the hall or outside the door. This approach allows the rest of the class to continue without interruption and saves the student from public humiliation. Private communications also lessen the chance that students will respond defensively to your correction to save face.

Start with hints

7. *Hints.* When some or all of the class needs redirection, start with the lowest level of intervention possible: the hint. For example, you may have just assigned a reading task, but you notice that a few students are still working on a fun math activity. You calmly remind students what they should be doing ("Calculators should be put away now. Everyone is finding page 83."). Often no greater intervention is required, and you have shown students that you trust them to follow directions with only a gentle reminder.

Use *I*-messages

8. *I-messages.* Gordon (1974) suggests that students are often unaware of the effects of their actions on others. Teachers can use *I*-statements to state their emotions without anger or blame and without belittling the student. An *I*-statement has three parts:

1. Statement of the problem ("When people sharpen their pencils while I talk . . . ")
2. Specific effect of the problem (" . . . Other students cannot hear me, . . . ")
3. Statement of the teacher's feelings (" . . . and I am frustrated to have to stop and wait.")

Once a teacher uses an *I*-statement, the teacher and students can work on the problem together. *I*-statements express respect by encouraging students to pay attention to their effects on others, allow the teacher to state emotions without humiliating, and convey the teacher's trust that students can address a problem.

Refresh students' memories of their strengths

9. *Strength refreshers.* When students are corrected by their teachers, they may lose perspective that a single mistake is just that: a *single* mistake. You can reaffirm your faith in students' basic goodness by starting your correction with a strength refresher (Schneider, 1997). In a strength refresher, you remind the student of how he typically behaves and point out that this mistake was atypical for him. For instance, when you discover that Roger spit water during a passing period, you pull him aside for a conversation: "Roger, I was surprised to hear that you spit. You usually do a super job of helping us make sure that our school is a safe and clean place." Because you demonstrate your faith in Roger's usual behavior, he will probably feel less guarded about explaining the incident to you and more eager to correct his behavior for tomorrow. Strength refreshers remind students that you see them as good people.

Model emotional control

10. *Emotional control.* Humans are not born with a balance between their emotions or impulses and their conscious knowledge about appropriate behavior. Emotional control or **emotional intelligence** comes through socialization (Good & Brophy, 2000). One way teachers can help children gain emotional control is by modeling it. Derek, one of my middle school students, interrupted me so frequently and so energetically that I wanted to squirt him in the face with a water bottle. Deep within, I knew that squirting a fellow human would serve as an affront to his dignity, but I was sorely tempted.

Sometimes we take personal offense at students' misbehavior, and anger is a natural human emotion. However, you need to have your emotions in check when you address students' behavior. If you are angry, you are not ready

GETTING CALM

If a conversation with a student begins to get tense, imagine the student's parent standing beside the student. This can help you get calm and choose your words carefully.

to respond to your students. And dealing with students who are particularly defiant takes the utmost in emotional maturity (Hall & Hall, 2003). Give yourself a few seconds to collect your emotions, telling students that you will be better able to address the situation when you are calmer. You may, for instance, discover that your class showed no mercy in antagonizing the music teacher. You are furious that they could act that way, and you are embarrassed that their behavior may reflect on you. Instead of yelling, though, you lower your voice and say, "I am shocked and angry to hear about this. In fact, I am so angry that I cannot discuss this with you right now. When my head is clearer, we can discuss this situation."

If you lash out while you are angry, you may need to backtrack later, and you may say something hurtful. Controlling your own anger models your desire that students do the same, and it stops you from attacking a student with your words. Further, when we are angry, other people are in control of us (Jones, 2000). Strength, according to Jones, comes from calm. By calming your body through strategies like relaxed breathing, you calm those around you and you help people get back to work. Rick Morris offers us Teaching Tip 9.1 to help us stay calm.

| Use laughter |

11. *Laughter.* Despite your supportive atmosphere and respectful interactions, there are times when students will manage to push your buttons. It seems to be a quest that marks the progression of childhood: Some students *live* to get a reaction. If you are able to retain your sense of humor, you can use laughter to diffuse tense situations and maintain dignity—the students' and your own (Kottler, 2002).

I know a teacher who entered her room to find an ugly caricature of herself drawn on the board. Instead of standing with her hands on her hips and demanding the name of the offending artist, she said, "Pretty good, but I need my glasses," and added a ridiculous version of her reading glasses to the sketch. What could have been a tense moment passed with smiles throughout the room. Using humor can show that you do not take the world (or yourself) too seriously and that you maintain a positive outlook.

When using humor to address behavior, be certain not to direct your humor at students. Humor is highly individual, and it is cultural. At least until you have a thorough understanding of your students and a cohesive group spirit, use jokes that are directed at yourself or at situations outside the students and be sure that the students see the humor as well. The point is to respond playfully to situations that might otherwise erupt into power struggles or other unproductive interactions.

| Apologize if you make a mistake |

12. *Apologies.* Finally, when despite your best attempts you offend a student's dignity, apologize. You may occasionally speak before you think and hurt feelings. Consider using a calm, apologetic message: "That did not sound at all as I had intended. I apologize if I hurt your feelings. Next time I will choose my words more carefully." You will not lessen your authority by admitting a mistake. You will probably, in fact, gain authority by displaying your willingness to disclose and correct an error: You are fair. You model the humility that you hope students will also display. You demonstrate how humans (teachers!) make a mistake, learn from it, and go on. And you acknowledge that your students deserve respect. In addition to treating students with respect, you can prevent much of the misbehavior that plagues some classrooms.

Actively Prevent Misbehavior

Some misbehavior occurs because it is human nature to press the limits, to test the predictability of our environments. However, misbehavior also occurs when students' educational needs go unmet. Albert (1996) suggests that we can create a sense of belonging that goes a long way in preventing misbehavior by using the three Cs: capable, connect, and contribute. Teachers need to help students see themselves as *capable* by focusing on success and making it acceptable to make mistakes. To help students build personal *connections* with teacher and peers, teachers can accept their students, appreciate their accomplishments, affirm students' positive traits, and show genuine displays of affection. Finally, teachers need to encourage students to *contribute* to their classroom, school, and local community.

Preventing misbehavior through the three Cs requires your thought and advance planning. Seven proactive strategies can help you forestall much of students' misbehavior:

1. Meaningful curriculum
2. Motivation and development
3. Authority
4. Clear expectations
5. Anticipation
6. Positive approach
7. Nonverbal communication

Use meaningful curriculum

1. *Meaningful curriculum.* When students are engaged in relevant and interesting learning experiences, they are often too busy to misbehave. Research reviewed by Miller and Hall (2005) supports the fact that engaged students display fewer misbehaviors. Fortunately, student engagement is in your hands. To engage students, you need to maximize learning time, vary your instructional strategies, and help students find meaning in their work. You may ask yourself a few related questions: Do students see the purpose in what you want them to learn? Are *their* topics *your* topics? How well does school capture issues seen as vital to the students? Three-quarters of the secondary students surveyed agreed either somewhat or strongly with the statement, "Most of my schoolwork is busywork" (Metropolitan Life Insurance Company, 2002).

Check your curriculum to ensure that the content is appropriate and that you are using rich learning strategies that accommodate students' diverse needs. Although some topics may not spark immediate student enthusiasm, if you remember to COME IN (Chapter 5), you increase the chances of engaging students in important learning and thus forestall misbehavior. If you have assessed the curriculum and your plans and have found them sound, a tougher test is to watch a recording of yourself teaching. Is your instruction as engaging as you had hoped? If not, think about when you as a student misbehaved. Teaching Tip 9.2 shows you how to prevent misbehavior by bridging two worlds.

Attend to students' maturation and motivation

2. *Motivation and development.* Study the characteristics of your learners and then align your expectations to their physical and emotional development. For instance, kindergartners should be expected to sit for only about 10 minutes before the activity changes, but older students can succeed with longer periods of sustained activity. Despite the fact that high school students can sit and listen for hour-long periods, as a general rule, it is useful to allow students of all ages to spend about 2 minutes actively processing information for every 10 minutes they spend listening. That means after you provide 10 minutes of information, they need a chance to discuss it. Try some of the "tell each other" strategies (Figure 5.7) to help students process information.

Teaching Tip 9.2

BRIDGING THE STUDENTS' WORLD AND THE SCHOOL'S WORLD

Actively pursue strategies that help *you* incorporate students' worlds into your classroom and help *them* see the importance of what school has to offer.

1. *Listen to the issues students discuss and incorporate them into your instruction.* Some educators suggest that students' issues should be placed firmly at the center of the curriculum. Thematic planning can be used to incorporate issues that are important to students. On a more specific level, a teacher might overhear his students discussing an impending threat of a pandemic flu. He plans a brief series of science lessons that addresses the history, procedures, and sociopolitical and ethical issues pertaining to vaccination.

2. *Use a student survey before you plan a unit to find out what students would like to know about the topic.* A survey may begin, "Students study the American Revolution in many grades, but sometimes they don't find out what they would really like to know. What do you still not know about that war?" An in-class discussion can serve the same purpose: "Let's make a list of the things we wish we knew . . . "

3. *Incorporate students' interests in sports, music, and other aspects of culture into the topics you select and the methods you use to study them.* For example, students may analyze lyrics of rap music for examples of poetic devices. In chemistry, students may make ice cream as an example of a phase change.

4. *Begin every lesson with an opener.* Openers pique students' curiosity and connect their interests and knowledge with the content of the lesson. A mathematics lesson might begin with an interesting problem embedded in a real-life context. A literature lesson on genres might begin with a quick tally of students' favorite books. An art lesson may begin with a guided imagery session using a favorite locale for students.

5. *State the purpose of your lessons.* Tell students how this information or skill will be useful. Or, have them tell you. "You'll need this for the test" or " . . . for next year" tend not to be convincing reasons for many students.

Also match your activities and expectations to factors such as the time of day and year. It is human to be sleepy after lunch and antsy before the last bell rings. Primary teachers are especially good at using games such as Simon Says or Copy My Clap Pattern to refocus students' attention. Secondary teachers can ensure that they provide high-interest activities when students' energy or attention may be likely to wane. They can also ask students to stand, stretch, and listen as they present a few minutes of information. Changing physical location or position gives students a break and allows them to refocus.

In addition to planning for students' developmental capabilities, you can also prevent misbehavior and encourage learning by attending to motivation. Research suggests that many elements that affect student motivation, shown in Figure 9.1, can be directly influenced by the teacher. For example, researchers found that when teachers explicitly focused on student understanding and autonomy in a positive context, students reported positive coping skills and affect (Turner, Meyer, Midgley, & Patrick, 2003). In short, their teachers supported students' motivation. From Figure 9.1, if a student gives up upon viewing a whole sheet of tedious grammar exercises, the teacher may rip the sheet in half to affect the student's *perception of effort and probability of success.* Another teacher works hard to return students' essays shortly after they submit them. He knows *immediate feedback* can increase motivation.

FIGURE 9.1 *Factors of motivation.*

- *Needs and interests.* Motivation increases when physical, psychological, and social needs are met. Examples include feelings of safety from physical and psychological harm and students' perceptions that they are treated fairly.
- *Level of concern.* Motivation is optimized when there is some tension about completing a task but not enough to provoke acute anxiety.
- *Perception of required effort.* Motivation increases when individuals perceive that the amount of effort required to complete a task is reasonable.
- *Probability of success.* Motivation increases when individuals perceive that there is a good chance they will succeed.
- *Knowledge of results.* Motivation increases when individuals have specific, immediate information about the result of their efforts.

When students lack the enthusiasm to stay focused, try tweaking one of the factors of motivation from this figure. For example, Wormeli (2001) advises middle school teachers to support student motivation through strategies such as creating an emotionally safe environment, communicating learning goals clearly, using vivid lessons, building suspense, and providing frequent feedback. By ensuring that your classroom meets students' physical, emotional, cognitive, and social needs, you optimize the probability that they will engage in learning and in appropriate behavior. Although it is true that you cannot *force* students to learn, there are many ways you can tweak *your own* behavior and assignments that can directly affect students' motivation.

3. *Authority.* When students respect their teacher as an authority, they tend to behave well. Teachers establish themselves as authorities using different combinations of power, as described by French and Raven (1959):

> Establish yourself as an authority figure

- *Expert power:* The teacher is perceived by the group as having superior knowledge about the content, about teaching, and about individual needs.
- *Referent power:* The teacher is liked and respected because she is perceived as ethical and concerned about her students.
- *Legitimate power:* The teacher has the right to make certain decisions by the sheer power of her official role as teacher.
- *Reward power:* The teacher has power because she can distribute rewards, including tangible items such as candy and privileges and social awards such as praise and attention.
- *Coercive power:* The teacher has power because she can punish.

Reward power and coercive power predominate in many classrooms, probably because they are often effective for immediate control of student behavior. Examples include "changing the card" systems, table points, and candy as a reward. Unfortunately, teachers who establish no firmer authority base than the use of rewards and punishments run a strong risk of having their power collapse. Additionally, rewards and punishments have limited usefulness if they demean students' dignity, interfere with the development of self-control, or work at cross-purposes with the teachers' larger vision of education.

 A QUESTION FOR SECONDARY TEACHERS

Kohn (2001) cites research indicating that as students move from elementary to middle or junior high school, there is a shift from trying to figure things out to trying to achieve. Does authentic learning remain a motivation for your students?

Instead, Savage (1999) suggests that more lasting and mutually respectful authority is based on the teacher's expert and referent power. Because both of these kinds of power depend on students' perceptions of you—as an expert and as a concerned, trustworthy adult—you can begin to earn students' respect by demonstrating your knowledge and care. Other kinds of power can be used judiciously as supplements, especially in your early years as a teacher.

4. *Clear expectations.* Students make better choices about their behavior when they know what is expected of them. School and classroom rules are an important way to teach students what we expect. One school, for instance, adopted an elegant set of rules that provide direction for behaviors a variety of settings at school such as at the assembly, in the quad, and in the classroom (Lewis, Sugai, & Colvin, 1998). The rules are: be kind, be safe, be cooperative, be respectful, and be peaceful. Note that these are all positively stated. Develop a similar set of classroom rules, either with the students' help or on your own. Keep your list of rules down to about four or five in number and state each rule in positive terms. For instance, "Raise your hand before speaking" is more helpful than "Do not shout out."

If you develop the rules without student input, be certain that students accept the rules as useful and reasonable. If you choose to have the class develop the rules through group discussion, check that their rules are reasonable and address major areas of concern for classroom behavior (when to talk, when to move around, and how to treat each other and belongings). Some teachers operationalize their rules for classroom talk with a color system: "red" for silence, no one out of her seat; "yellow" for whispers in small groups; and "green" for regular conversational level. If you elect to include explicit consequences for following and breaking the rules, be sure that they are logical and humane.

You also need to establish clear expectations for special circumstances. Before a field trip, for instance, teach your students approximately three specific behaviors you expect to see. A primary teacher might hold up three fingers, one for each expectation, and state in positive and clear terms his expectations for student behavior during the trip: "First, you need to stay with your buddy. Second, you need to keep your hands to yourself. Third, you need to stay where you can see an adult at all times." Then the teacher checks for understanding of his rules: "Let's see how many know the first special rule for today. I see 10 hands up. I will wait for another 10. . . . Good. Say it aloud." He reteaches until he is certain that all students know what he expects. Parties, assemblies, and sports activities are other situations when clearly stated expectations are critical.

5. *Anticipation.* You can prevent misbehavior, too, by anticipating and thus avoiding trouble spots. You know that your students are a curious bunch, so if

---

Establish clear expectations

Watch an elementary teacher discuss classroom rules on the first day of class and revisit them later. Go to the Merrill Teacher Prep Web site Video Classroom, Educational Psychology, Module 12, Video 1. How is this teacher's treatment of classroom rules the same or different from how you will treat classroom rules in the early days with your students?

Anticipate behavior

CLASSROOM RULES

Jot down four classroom rules that address major areas for classroom behavior in positive and specific terms:

1.
2.
3.
4.

When you have revised these rules and are happy, include them in your own discipline program. Anticipate and set students up for success.

FIGURE 9.2 *Anticipating and avoiding trouble spots.*

Students are more likely to misbehave when . . .

1. . . . they think you can't see them. So . . .
   - When you stand and talk with an individual, keep your back to the wall and position yourself where you can see the class.
   - Write on an overhead projector rather than the board, especially if you are left-handed.
   - Make eye contact with the students farthest from you as you work with individuals.
2. . . . they are allowed to disengage without clear expectations. So . . .
   - Teach your directions through direct instruction.
   - Plan your transitions between lessons. Think through each aspect of the transition. Make your directions very clear, and minimize the time spent switching activities.
   - Have all your materials ready to go. Lay them out at different stations for quick distribution and collection, as appropriate.
   - Prepare a student to take over if you need to speak with an adult or have another interruption during class. Practice the routine.

---

you leave a bowl of mealworms for your science lesson on the front table while you attempt to teach a social studies lesson, you invite misbehavior. By placing the mealworms out of sight, you help students focus their attention on the lesson at hand. Similarly, if you have passed out pointy compasses for your third-period geometry lesson, collect the compasses as students move into the next phase of the lesson. Removing distractions is a sure bet for preventing misbehavior.

Anticipation is key for preventing individual students from escalating in their misbehaviors as well. If you've spent time in classrooms, you can probably conjure an image of a student who displayed a minor misbehavior that quickly became something larger and more troublesome. Shukla-Mehta and Albin (2003) give 12 helpful strategies to help teachers deescalate potentially explosive behaviors, and several of the strategies focus on stopping the behavior before it starts. Teachers can anticipate difficulties by becoming aware of the triggers for misbehavior, by refusing to engage, and by intervening early. It's a matter of planning. See Figure 9.2 for some other trouble spots that can be avoided with careful planning.

Your ability to anticipate common trouble spots will improve with experience. You can begin by planning instruction and your room environment with an eye toward setting students up for success. Charney (2002) spends the first six weeks of the school year teaching students to monitor their own behavior and use the items in the room safely through her own version of the three *R*s:
- *Reinforcing:* Commenting on the positive behaviors students demonstrate ("I notice that you are solving that problem together.").
- *Reminding:* Asking students to state the expectations for behavior ("Remind me, where do we put the brushes when we are finished?").
- *Redirecting:* Pointing students toward more appropriate behavior ("Rulers are for measuring.").

You will also use your knowledge of your particular students to anticipate possible misbehaviors. Then plan an appropriate response. When you have a few quiet minutes at home, rehearse your calm, productive responses to those behaviors: What will you do and say the next time students chat during a transition time? Having a response ready often helps to forestall problems.

Keep things positive

6. *Positive approach.* Because classrooms are crowded and hurried, it is very easy to focus on those students determined to derail our lessons. However, when we emphasize misbehavior, we contribute to a negative tone and provide attention for the wrong bunch of students. Instead of criticizing the wigglers who

FIGURE 9.3   *Establishing a positive environment from day one.*

1. *Learn students' names immediately (yes, during the first day).* It is an immediate way to show your respect for them as people. Take 10 quick minutes to go up and down the rows or through the tables, repeating students' names as you memorize them. All who learn at least three new names are winners.

2. *Convey your high expectations and enthusiasm for teaching and learning right away.* Examples include enthusiastic messages about being glad for your time together, stories about you as a person to help show that you expect to connect with students as people, and previews of the exciting things students will learn and do in your class.

3. *Teach your classroom rules or have students develop them in a community.* Keep the number brief and state the rules in positive terms.

4. *Provide for learning and for student choice on the first day.* Ask students what they want to learn about certain subjects, either through private journal entries or via a class chart. Teach at least one real lesson on your first day and prime your students to share what they learned when they go home that night.

5. *Immediately establish routines and effective management to prevent misbehavior.* Teach students your procedures and rules regarding pencil sharpening, leaving their seats, using the restroom, submitting finished work, and other routines right away.

are facing the wrong way during your **read-aloud,** glance around the group. You will probably notice that more than half are listening raptly. Concentrate on those students. Smile warmly and say, "More than half of you are eagerly listening! I really appreciate that!" Then wait and praise as the other class members give their attention. Remember, though, that false praise is probably worse than no praise at all; keep your praise genuine. Keep in mind, too, that students' reactions to public praise can vary by age level. Although some teachers use public praise effectively with older students (perhaps with a simple "Thanks, Rogelio. Thanks, Shirley."), older students often view teacher praise about behavior as manipulative. Reactions to public praise also vary among individuals. Some students are embarrassed by public praise and respond better to a private word.

In public and private, praise good behavior specifically and in a way that stresses logical consequences: "Thanks for cleaning up, my friends! When you work so quickly to straighten our room, we have lots more time left for art!" That way you reinforce the notion that students' motivation to behave is not simply to please you, it is to keep the environment productive and enjoyable for all.

A praise statement keeps the atmosphere positive, builds your referent power, and serves as a gentle reminder for what all students should be doing. Emphasize what students do right and you help to prevent misbehavior. Figure 9.3 shares some strategies that can help to establish a positive learning environment—and thus curb misbehavior—from the first day you meet your students. Through effective management, a meaningful curriculum, and genuine concern for your students, you can prevent much behavior that could otherwise distract from learning.

| Use nonverbal communication |

7. *Nonverbal communication.* Many efforts to discipline are communicated not through teachers' words but through their bearing and their actions, or nonverbal communication. Jones (2000) demonstrates vividly the power of body language. Without saying a word, Jones suggests, you can prevent misbehavior by moving purposefully throughout the room, sending the message that you mean business through your direct gaze and relaxed bearing, and by moving your body (turning it, moving it closer to students, and staying long enough to convey your message and ensure compliance, and then moving away). Indeed, effective classroom managers consistently prevent misbehavior by placing themselves where the action is, monitoring carefully, and using eye contact to direct student behavior (Miller & Hall, 2005).

FIGURE 9.4 *The "I mean business" look is captured not just in teachers' stares but in the message sent by their entire bearing. How is this teacher doing?*

You can use nonverbal communication to prevent misbehavior by informing students that you feel confident in your own abilities, that you are aware of their actions, that you care about the students, and that you will help the students make good choices about their actions (see Figure 9.4).

The following four strategies might expand your communications repertoire:

- *Bearing.* Carry yourself in a way that communicates self-confidence. Stand erect and relax. Use eye contact and facial expressions to support your verbal messages. (Remember, though, that your direct gaze may not be returned by students who do not share your cultural norms for conveying respect.)
- *Gestures.* Like a symphony conductor, use your gestures to make requests for behavior. Pointing is rude, but you can lower both hands, palms down, to indicate a need for lower volume. A hand in front of you, palm forward, can support your message to Angela that she stop talking, as can a quiet shake of your head. Nod when she quiets down. Practice in the mirror to develop "the look" that redirects behavior without a word.
- *Physical proximity.* Some teachers are stuck like glue to the front of the room . . . but not you. Move throughout the room so that your physical presence is felt by all. Teach in different parts of the room. When you see two students begin to wander **off task,** move physically closer to them but continue teaching. Often your presence alone will bring them back to attention. If not, try tapping a single finger on their desks. Only when these efforts fail do you need to send a verbal message.
- *Withitness.* An effective teacher knows what is happening in every area of the classroom. Kounin's (1977) term *withitness* describes the childhood conclusion that teachers have eyes on the backs of their heads: Teachers need to be aware of all their students' actions all of the time. Position yourself so that you can see all students and monitor carefully. For instance, using an overhead projector, a projection panel, or a magnetic lap board instead of the whiteboard at the front of the room allows you to face the group as you instruct.

In sum, the powerful conclusion I hope you drew from this section is that much of student behavior is in your hands. You have tremendous power to set students up for success by thinking proactively about discipline and planning purposefully to prevent misbehavior. You can stop many unproductive behaviors before they start when you actively support students' wise decisions. When students misbehave, treat their actions as an opportunity to nudge them toward independence.

View Discipline as an Opportunity to Help Students Gain Independence and Responsibility

> Children today are tyrants. They contradict their parents, gobble their food, and tyrannize their teachers.
>
> —*Socrates (circa 450 BCE)*

Most would agree that humans are not born knowing how to behave in socially responsible ways. Behaviors that allow us to function well as members of a group are *learned* behaviors, and the research in classroom management and discipline is clear: Teachers have a responsibility to *teach* students prosocial behavior. What exactly are these skills? Take a look at your stance and its definition of "the good person" and you will probably find skills and abilities such as self-control and cooperation. Indeed, the K–12 teachers surveyed in one study agreed that the most important skills for success in the classroom are skills for cooperation and self-control (Lane, Pierson, & Givner, 2003).

By examining the literature, Miller and Hall (2005) suggest that teachers first develop a coherent set of skills and behaviors and then equip students with the skills necessary to display those behaviors. This is accomplished through modeling and through direct instruction, which includes opportunities to practice, feedback on performance, and appropriate reteaching. Teachers should consistently check the success of their efforts and adjust as necessary. In addition to the acquisition of skills, the capacity for independent and responsible behavior is also an issue of development.

Human development appears to be driven by two competing forces: (1) the need to be loved and to belong and (2) the need to do for oneself. From the minute they are born, people engage in the quest for self-determination, as evidenced by a child's struggles over time to first feed himself, to tie his own shoes, to set his own curfew, to pierce or tattoo his flesh, and, as an adult, to make his own way. At each stage of this struggle, the child demands a different kind of loving support from the adults in his world. However, the struggle for independence and self-control appears to be a universal one.

Our job as classroom teachers is to provide an atmosphere that ensures emotional security and a sense of belonging that allows students to safely learn to control their impulses and govern their own actions (Gootman, 2001; Savage, 1999). That may sound obvious, but it may not be prevalent practice. For instance, in one study (Lewis, 2001), elementary and secondary students' perceptions were that when faced with student misbehavior, their teachers responded by increasing their use of coercive discipline rather than using techniques that fostered students' development of responsibility.

Teachers' efforts to discipline should channel the fight for self-determination so that it follows productive paths. We need to love our students enough to help them develop, and we can do so by (1) establishing a climate that promotes independence and (2) addressing their behaviors in ways that encourage self-control.

Establishing a Climate that Promotes Independence Your instruction and physical environment should provide safe opportunities for students to think for themselves and to make meaningful choices. Try these five tools for establishing such a climate:

1. Choices
2. Respect for decisions

3. Clear limits
4. Consistency
5. Natural consequences

Offer choices

1. *Choices.* Within safe and acceptable limits, provide repeated and varied opportunities for students to make meaningful decisions. Arrange options so that a range of choices is acceptable. For instance, you can allow students options for the literature group they join, the topics they pursue, the project to represent their learning and the tables they choose at center time. Students can also select places to sprawl during silent reading, the consequences for behavior, classroom jobs, and class fund-raisers. The more mature the student, the broader the range and number of choices he may be able to handle. When students have the opportunity to make meaningful choices, they see that they are capable of making good decisions and that you respect their ability to do so (Coloroso, 1994).

Respect decisions

2. *Respect for decisions.* Once students make choices, respect their decisions. Make it a point to override their choices only if they show themselves unable to follow through or if the consequence of their decisions would be harmful. Students' decisions may not match your own, but unless the consequences are dangerous, students should be allowed to experience them.

Set clear limits

3. *Clear limits.* Not every choice a student makes is acceptable. As children, students still need your help in internalizing standards of conduct that provide for physical safety and respect the rights of others. Gootman (2001, p. 38) calls such limits *waist-high fences.* Waist-high fences are expectations or rules that keep students safe and encourage enjoyable learning for all. Establish clear limits in your classroom so that students know the boundaries of permissible behavior. You can set limits through your class rules, your own modeling, and your interactions. For instance, during sixth period, Steve is a bit too relaxed, leaning back in his chair, fingers laced to cradle his head, feet up on his desk. Privately you tell him, "Steve, this is a place for learning. In this room, your feet belong on the ground and your hands belong near the desk." You finish with a bit of humor and a smile: "If this were my family room couch, you would be welcome to relax."

Here is your chance to support this student in developing self-control. What will you do?

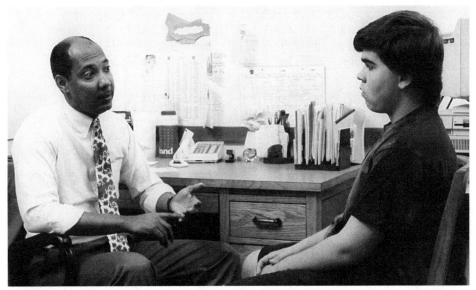

Scott Cunningham/Merrill

Setting limits is sometimes difficult for new teachers, who tend to be concerned that their students like them. However, one of the kindest things you can do for your students is to provide a stable environment with reasonable limits and to forbid travel beyond those limits. Students will push until they find your limits. When they find those boundaries, they can turn their attention to other matters. Do them—and yourself—a favor and make your limits clear at the outset. *Say what you mean . . . and mean what you say.*

4. *Consistency.* Perhaps even more difficult than setting limits is following through to reinforce those limits. Children of all ages find limits to push. One of the most effective ways you can reinforce reasonable limits is by responding consistently to students' requests and behavior. Your consistent responses will help students see that their environment is predictable and that they can rely on stable rules and expectations. When you show them that you mean what you say, you convey to students that you care enough about them to keep your promises. If you are inconsistent, students will learn that they can do as they please and that they cannot trust you to do as you say. "No" must mean "No" every single time (see Figure 9.5). This is a tough one, but your efforts will pay off. Follow through with consequences consistently.

5. *Natural consequences.* People with self-control understand the link between their behaviors and the consequences of their actions. Unfortunately, schools often emphasize rewards and punishments that are not only unrelated to students' behavior but are also delivered by the hands of another, the teacher. Examples include discipline programs that have students copying class rules when they talk out of turn or receiving food for following directions. In programs like these, teachers retain responsibility for delivering the consequences of students' actions, and students may have a harder time establishing authentic

Be consistent: Follow through

Allow for natural consequences or arrange for logical consequences

FIGURE 9.5 Students will push until they find your limits. When you are inconsistent, they may control you rather than controlling themselves.

motivation for appropriate behavior. This is not to say, however, that rewards are inherently ineffective.

Some research indicates that rewards, when used appropriately, can support the development of intrinsic motivation. Witzel and Mercer (2003) reviewed this research and recommend that when deciding whether and how to use rewards, teachers should ask themselves: What is the purpose of using a reward in this situation? Will this reward logically lead to intrinsic motivation? The authors argue that rewards can provide a temporary support until students build internal controls. An example of such an instance may be when a student with a learning disability needs support in facing difficult academic tasks.

To help students build internal controls and take responsibility for their actions, you can also arrange classroom conditions so that they face the natural consequences of their behavior. Natural consequences (Dreikurs, 1968) flow from the behavior and are not arranged by another. For instance, when a student talks while directions are given, he misses the opportunity to gather appropriate materials for his art project. A natural consequence of Ming's running in the lunchroom is that she spills her lunch.

When it would be unsafe or unfeasible for students to experience natural consequences as a deterrent to future misbehavior, provide a consequence that is at least logical. A logical consequence for Sheila's breaking Jaime's pencil out of anger, for instance, is that she supply Jaime with another pencil. Charney (1992) suggests that at least three kinds of logical consequences are available to teachers:

- *Reparations:* When a student or group breaks or loses something, it must be replaced or repaired. The situation must be fixed.
- *Breach of contract and loss of trust:* When a student or group acts in a manner that contradicts the rules of the group, rights are temporarily lost.
- *Time-outs for inappropriate participation:* When a student or group does not participate in a manner consistent with expectations for the situation, the student(s) or group is removed from the situation until better choices are made.

When students live with the consequences of their choices, they come to see that the best discipline is not enforced by an authority but comes from within: They build self-control. In sum, you can foster student self-control by providing a safe environment that allows for choices within reasonable limits and builds the connection between student behavior and its consequences. You can also nurture self-control in the ways you respond to misbehavior.

> No man is free who cannot control himself.
>
> —*Pythagoras*

Addressing Behaviors in Ways that Encourage Self-Control   Your response to misbehavior should be approached as an effort to help students to gain self-discipline. The following five tools can help:

1. Talk it through
2. Self-correction
3. Avoid power struggles
4. Anger shields
5. Conflict resolution

> Talk it through

1. *Talk it through.* Wise teachers do more than put an end to misbehavior: They use misbehavior as an opportunity to teach. For example, when Tyler accidentally swings a baseball bat dangerously close to a friend's face, his teacher responds by moving forward to stop the bat and then intones: "Tyler, look how close that bat came to Dan's face. What could happen if you do not look where you swing?" The teacher guides Tyler to consider the potential harm of his impulsive bat swinging by listening openly to his honest answer and then discussing appropriate alternatives. Before he lopes away, Tyler assures his

teacher: "I will go check out the baseball field because it is less crowded. I will look behind me before I swing." By guiding Tyler to consider hurtful outcomes, his teacher helps him to forge the links between behavior and its consequences.

Talking it through can be difficult when you feel rushed. It takes time to teach students about good behavior. Although you may not have included behavior as a daily objective, no doubt it has a place in your long-range goals, and your time investment will most likely be a good one. Talking it through can also be difficult when you feel irritated because you *just want those monsters to stop it.* There are indeed times when belaboring an incident of misbehavior serves only to prolong it. Talk it through when there is a reasonable chance that students have not considered the potential effects of their actions. Otherwise, address the misbehavior as briefly as possible and move on.

Talking it through is useful because it (1) models the expectation that rational people use words to sort things out, (2) tightens the link between behavior and consequence without actually allowing for dangerous consequences, and (3) works to prevent similar misbehavior in the future. Talking it through can help students see their mistakes not as crimes but as opportunities to do better.

| Allow for self-correction |

2. *Self-correction.* Your goal is that students control themselves, so whenever possible, allow students themselves to find solutions to their problems and to select appropriate behaviors. When faced with the typical barrage of tattling during rug time ("Teacher! She is bothering me!"), a wise teacher I know tells the offended child, "I am sure you can find a quieter place to sit." The student almost invariably moves quietly to another, less provocative spot on the rug, and his talking friends receive a hint about their own behavior. As another example, Doug holds a lively conversation during independent work time. His teacher approaches him for a quiet talk: "Doug, the time to chat has passed. Can you find something more productive to do, or would you like me to help you find an alternative?" Doug shrugs, "I guess I will read my ghost stories." As Doug pulls out his book, the teacher responds with an emphasis on the positive: "Good choice! I was pretty sure you would have a good idea!" The teacher joins another group but follows through by glancing at Doug to ensure that his nose is buried in his book. Allowing students to correct their own behavior provides practice—with a safety net—in controlling their own destiny.

Related to self-correction is peer correction. You need not correct every incidence of misbehavior you notice. First, sometimes drawing unnecessary attention to a fleeting or relatively minor transgression can interrupt instruction and increase the likelihood that the misbehavior will reoccur. Ignoring some misbehaviors can ensure that students are not reinforced for inappropriate behavior. Second, students can serve as a powerful influence on each other's behavior. A cold rebuff from a peer can do more to direct a poking student's behavior than can your admonitions to remember the rules against poking. If students solve problems on their own, pat yourself on the back and resist the urge to intervene.

| Avoid power struggles |

3. *Avoid power struggles.* Independent people have power over their fate in important ways. Children very often have less power than adults—especially in the classroom setting—and growing toward self-determination can mean questing for more power. When a student outwardly defies you and provokes your anger, you are probably engaged in a power struggle. Power struggles rarely end with satisfactory results, mainly because the student is right: You cannot *make* her do anything. Avoid power struggles in three ways:

- *Diffuse the situation.* Use humor, greater physical distance, or a caring voice to allow the anger to dissipate: "I can see that you are angry. It may be better if we talked about this in 5 minutes. I will be back in a few moments to talk." Usually increasing your physical and emotional distance from the student helps to diffuse the student's anger and allows you to approach the situation more calmly.

- *Let the student save face.* Offer an out so that the student can comply with your request without submitting entirely to your authority. If a student's sole choice is to do as you say, she can only lose in her own mind and in the eyes of her peers. As Linda attempts to draw her teacher into a power struggle, for instance, her teacher calmly tells Linda, "You may get out your math book, or, if you have a better idea, I am listening." Still angry, Linda replies, "Yeah! I want to do nothing!" Her teacher's wise response is to accept the student's alternative, even if it is only vaguely appropriate. "All right. Sometimes I want to do nothing, too. That is a fine choice for the next few minutes. I will be happy when you are finished with that and can join us in math. I miss you when you are gone." The teacher has allowed Linda some control, has provided her with an out so that she can join the math group with at least the appearance of her own free will, and she has reinforced the notion that Linda is a likable person with a contribution to make.
- *Give the student the power.* A student in a power struggle may need to make one more comment after your request for quiet, or feed the hamster one more pellet after you ask him to stop. By allowing those "one mores," you convey that students do indeed have some power over *what* they do *when.* Usually a student's behavior will stop with a "one more" (Schneider, 1997). Only if it continues will you need to address the behavior again. You may also elect to abdicate your desire to control the student's behavior entirely: "I certainly cannot force you to use appropriate language, but I must insist on it in my room. You will need to use street language elsewhere." When the student realizes that you are comfortable with your own power—and its limits—he will almost certainly have a lesser need to grab for available power.

Use anger shields

4. *Anger shields.* Expect that, at times, your students will be angry or hurt. Irate parents, similarly, may at times use hostile language with you. Although negative feelings are unavoidable, you and your class deserve to be protected from angry outbursts. Schneider (1997) suggests that you shield yourself and others with comments such as "I know you are hurt, but I care too much about our class to let you say unkind things. You need to find another way to handle these feelings. I can make some suggestions if you get stuck."

In addition, some students will need your help in putting words to powerful feelings. Help them phrase their feelings in ways that do not belittle others. Techniques such as *I*-statements can be useful even for young students.

Anger shields convey the message that every person in your room deserves dignity and respect. Schneider (1997) also suggests that anger shields (1) teach students that although we cannot entirely control our environments, we can control how we will respond, and (2) encourage students to draw on their inner resources to handle their negative emotions.

5. *Conflict resolution.* During the 2003 school year, 3% of K–12 students were the victims of violent crimes at school (U.S Department of Education, National Center for Education Statistics, 2006b). Others were engaged in less severe violence such as bullying (Lincoln, 2002). In 2005, about 28% of sixth through twelfth graders reported having been bullied recently at school (U.S. Department of Education, National Center for Education Statistics, 2006c). In bullying, there is an imbalance of power, and the perpetrator purposefully and repeatedly uses physical aggression (e.g., hitting, pushing, or spitting) or social aggression (e.g., making fun, malicious gossip) against the victim. Bullying tends to peak during the middle school/junior high years. Therefore, teachers in those grades may have a particular responsibility, but students in all grades clearly need adult support in solving conflicts in appropriate ways.

No matter your grade level, your job is to help students build lifelong skills that will assist them in positive interactions throughout their lives. Begin by not

Teaching Tip 9.3

CONFLICT RESOLUTION

1. Set the rules (example: no name calling).
2. Listen. Let each person finish without interrupting.
3. Find common ground. Agree on the facts and the issues important to each.
4. Brainstorm solutions.
5. Negotiate proposed solutions.
6. Agree. Listen as each person states the plan aloud.

Watch a fourth-grade teacher lead a conflict resolution session with two students. Go to the Merrill Teacher Prep Web site Video Classroom, Classroom Management, Module 5, Video 1. How would you lead this session differently for older or younger students?

tolerating hateful acts. Stop your students from using hate speech ("That's so gay!"), and intervene in acts of bullying. Check with your school for policies regarding bullying; schools rightly treat it very seriously. In fact, cyber-bullying policies are now being implemented across the nation.

Fortunately, many programs assist schools and teachers in preventing violence. Many focus on helping students resolve their conflicts in nonviolent ways (see Druck & Kaplwitz, 2005; Johnson & Johnson, 2004; O'Toole & Burton, 2005; Selfridge, 2004). Teaching Tip 9.3 presents a general set of skills you can teach your students in resolving conflict.

The point of each of the mentioned strategies is to address misbehavior in ways that respect students' current power over their own emotions and behaviors and that enhance students' ability to make even better decisions in the future.

Address Discipline Issues in Many Ways and on Multiple Levels

Teaching looks easy . . . from the outside. To maintain a productive learning environment that supports students' bids for independence, though, you will need to draw on a rich repertoire of rules and tools that allows you to respond quickly and on different levels to different numbers of students. Your ability to integrate these different demands for maintaining classroom discipline will increase with experience, especially if you remain vigilant about growth. For now, you can begin to address behavior in multifaceted ways by thinking about (1) group size, (2) overlapping, (3) intensity of response, (4) motivation for misbehavior, and (5) redirecting behavior.

Group Size   Although you will work with individuals daily, much of your time will be spent in working with groups of students. Students behave differently in groups than they do as individuals, and each group tends to develop its own personality. One aspect of encouraging appropriate behavior, then, is to harness the emergent disposition of your class. By working to create a sense of community, you can direct students' energy in productive ways and meet the human social needs for power, affection, and emotional safety. Modeling your concern for students and requiring students to treat each other with respect form the foundation of a solid sense of community. Teachers also use strategies called class builders to create a feeling of fellowship. Community builders were introduced in Chapter 8.

Despite the public's fears of sensational misbehavior in American classrooms, Jones (2000) found that 80% of student misbehavior is simply talking out of turn, and that 15% is general off-task behavior.

For these reasons, you need to develop strategies that will maintain the group's focus. Figure 9.6 suggests some common techniques for managing the behavior of groups. Note that the tips are not punitive. Instead, they focus on

FIGURE 9.6   *Tips for maintaining group focus.*

1. Use a signal to gain students' attention. Don't talk while they talk.
   - Make a clear request: "Attention up here, please. Let's come back together."
   - Follow through: "I'll know you're ready when your eyes are on me and your pencils are down." Or: "Thanks Miguel, I see you're ready. . . . Thanks Pat."
   - "Clap once if you can hear me. Clap twice. Clap once . . ."
   - Just wait.
   - Raise a hand and teach students that when they see your raised hand, they need to stop talking and raise their own hand. Follow through.
   - Flash the classroom lights off then on.
   - Use a noise signal, such as a squeaker toy.
   - Lead a clapping pattern; students who are listening join in until all are with you.
   - Hold up a stopwatch and click to measure how many seconds it takes.
   - Try "Give me five" (Wong, 1998). When you say, "Give me five," students go through five steps: eyes on you, be quiet, be still, empty their hands, and listen.
2. Monitor carefully—especially the back and side edges of the room—and provide feedback on students' behavior.
   - Use hints to maintain on-task behavior: "Your group should be on the second job by now."
   - Allow for self-monitoring: "Check your noise level. Are you using quiet voices?"
   - Play soothing music quietly: "If you can't hear the music, your group needs to quiet down."
   - Use a sound monitoring device that beeps when the noise reaches a certain level.
3. Provide feedback on students' behavior as a group.
   - Use verbal statements: "Groups Two and Three, you're working especially well right now. Thanks." Or: "We are able to accomplish so much when you work this well together. Way to go!"
   - Use table points or class points that add up to time on a desired activity or other reward such as a frozen juice bar or a popcorn party. (Check school policy on food.)
   - Use your stopwatch to award extra seconds for a desired activity when students minimize wasted time.
4. Be fair to individuals when you deal with the larger group. Use strategies that don't penalize all students for the behavior of a few. Conversely, if everyone is talking, do not single out one or two students for consequences. If students perceive you as unfair, your expert and referent power erode.

positive, clear communication of expectations, careful monitoring, and specific feedback. Teachers have individual preferences, and some of these strategies (such as using tangible rewards for behavior) may undermine other elements of your stance toward discipline. Be certain to select tools that are consistent with your own convictions and with what you know about your students.

Thus, one aspect of dealing with behavior on different levels is attending to the needs of students as individuals *and* as members of a larger group. You will also need to handle more than one issue at a time.

Overlapping   To maximize the time your class spends on learning, you need to overlap your tasks. In overlapping, you address discipline issues while you continue to teach. For instance, as you respond to a student's content question, you can also move closer to two others who are embroiled in a pencil fight. While listening to a student read, you can also glance around the rest of the room to ensure that all are on task. You may need to give a "teacher look" and a shake of the head to a student who begins to fold paper airplanes while you work with another group. Through overlapping, you can prevent misbehavior by providing meaningful learning activities, nonverbal communication, and **proximity control** all at once.

Intensity of Response   Your responses to student behavior will vary by level of intensity. Canter (1976) recommends that teachers use assertive requests and that teachers match the response's level of intensity to the seriousness of students' behavior. You may start with a hint: "Everyone should be working now." If students need more support than is provided by your hint, you can use one of these increasingly intense responses:

1. Question about behavior: "What should you be doing right now?" Follow up: "Do you need help in getting started?"
2. Statement of direction using student's name: "Ivy, put away the magazine."
3. Use of eye contact and serious facial expression to match the tone and message: "Ivy, put away the magazine" while you look at her, your eyebrows raised.
4. Use of a gesture in addition to eye contact, serious facial expression, and assertive message: "Ivy, put away the magazine" as you look intently at her and gesture closing the magazine.

When student misbehavior is severely disruptive, more intense responses are appropriate. Many teachers arrange for a "time-out buddy," a fellow respected teacher who can provide a place for students to cool down if they need to be removed from the classroom. If you use time-outs, be certain to send the message that the time-out is a chance to cool down, not to suffer humiliation. Also be certain that you have a system to ensure that students arrive swiftly at the time-out room and that they return promptly. Remember that you have a legal responsibility to provide adequate supervision for every student, so be certain that students are supervised even when removed from the group. Also remember that time away from the group decreases a student's opportunity to learn. There may be a time when students' misbehavior may take the form of physical fighting. Fully one-third of high school students surveyed said they had been in a fight within the past year (Centers for Disease Control and Prevention, 2004). Immediate and considered actions will be necessary; a plan for addressing student fights is suggested in Teacher Tip 9.4 (Fields, 2004).

Finally, you can vary the intensity of your response for positive behavior as well. Consider using unexpected reinforcement to show the intensity of your pleasure at students' good choices. In my sophomore year of high school, for example, my father sent a telegram to my chemistry class, congratulating me for my good grades. At the time, good grades were somewhat of a rarity for me. This surprising and thoughtful display of appreciation still draws a smile from me.

Motivation for Misbehavior   In addition to stopping student misbehavior, teachers need to work on the causes of behavior. When we address the motivations that underlie misbehavior, we can prevent recurrence and foster

Teaching Tip 9.4

ADDRESSING STUDENT FIGHTS

1. Right now—Check policies: What are your legal responsibilities?
2. Next—Create a plan: What will you do? What are your resources?
3. If a fight breaks out:
   - Give a loud, clear verbal command.
   - Make a decision: Is it safe to intervene?
   - If it isn't safe: Get help while still protecting students.
   - If it is safe: Intervene without becoming an aggressor. Try wrapping around from behind.

FIGURE 9.7 *Identifying and responding to mistaken goals.*

Goal	Description	What It Looks Like	How You Might Respond
Attention seeking	In attempting to gain recognition and acceptance, students behave in socially inappropriate ways.	The teacher's first reaction is to yell. The student stops the misbehavior when corrected but starts again soon.	• Persistently ignore misbehavior. • Hold a personal conference to determine how many times the student will be allowed to exhibit the misbehavior. • Monitor and provide feedback based on the conference. • Provide attention for positive actions.
Power seeking	Students revert to unacceptable means—outwardly refusing their teachers' requests—to gain a sense of power.	The teacher's first reaction is to feel challenged. The student's reaction is defiance.	• Refuse to engage in a struggle, perhaps by instead offering a sympathetic response. • Remove the student or the audience from the situation. • Find authentic ways to allow the student to exercise power.
Revenge seeking	Students who feel that they have been wronged seek to get even.	The teacher's first reaction is to feel hurt or defeated. The student is abusive or complains of unfair treatment.	• Change the student's relationship with the teacher and peers. • Foster respect. • Help student gain social skills. • Refuse to retaliate; use matter-of-fact messages about the behavior.
Display of inadequacy	Students who feel incompetent resist help so that they can avoid even trying.	The teacher's first reaction is frustration to the point of giving up. The student does nothing.	• Never give up on the student. • Keep risks low and celebrate small successes.

self-control. Dreikurs, Grunwald, and Pepper (1982) identify four mistaken goals that students pursue. Figure 9.7 describes each of these four goals and suggests reactions that can help you signal the identity of those goals. Dreikurs and colleagues suggest that after you identify the student's goal, you disclose it to the student through questions such as "Could it be that you would like more attention?" Your first impulse to respond to each of these mistaken goals (as suggested in the third column in Figure 9.7) is probably the wrong one. More productive alternatives are given in the fourth column. The key is to respond in a calm and thoughtful manner that helps the student identify his mistaken goal and choose more acceptable avenues for recognition.

Whether you use Dreikurs and colleagues' ideas about mistaken goals or focus on different causes for misbehavior, the point is to realize that a student's

BEHAVIOR ANALYSIS

1. What is the problem behavior?
2. When does it occur?
3. What happens right before and after the behavior?
4. How does the student benefit from this behavior? (Does it help the student avoid something? Gain something else?)
5. What have others tried that has worked to change the behavior?
6. What will you try?
7. (Later) Did your plan work?

persistent misbehavior usually has a cause and that when you and the student can identify the cause, you can work together on more acceptable alternatives.

An appealing alternative to the Golden Rule, the Platinum Rule, can be of use as you help students move beyond their mistaken goals. The Platinum Rule admonishes us to treat others the way they would like to be treated. If, for instance, students need attention, then we can see to it that they receive attention, albeit for positive decisions they make. If students crave power, we can shape our classrooms to ensure that they have some meaningful control over what they do at school.

Understanding students' motivations for misbehavior is important, then, because that understanding provides insights for us as we help students choose more productive paths. Part of your plan to effect improvement is a careful analysis of students' behavior and an empirical approach to modifying it. Try Teaching Tip 9.5 to conduct an analysis of disruptive behavior (based on Danforth & Smith, 2005; Jackson & Panyan, 2002; Ryan, Halsey, & Matthews, 2003). Behavioral analysis is effective with many students, but not necessarily all. Hall and Hall (2003) point out that oppositional children may not be receptive to behaviorist approaches to change their actions. Any tool should be thoughtfully applied with careful attention to the audience.

Short-Term and Long-Term Redirection   To work toward your overarching goal of helping students independently choose appropriate behavior, you will need to enlist strategies that address discipline issues in short- and long-term time spans. Short-term solutions focus on preventing misbehavior or stopping undesirable behavior and replacing it with less harmful alternatives. Short-term solutions are the tools you use immediately and from which you expect quick results. Long-term solutions keep in mind the broader view of your hopes for students. Long-term tools take longer to implement, and results may build incrementally over time. You will no doubt need to use more than one kind of each strategy to fully address discipline issues.

Your fifth-grade student Melanie provides an example. She rarely completes her work during class and has not yet submitted a homework assignment. She shrugs when you lecture her on responsibility and the importance of practice. Frustrated by her apparent indifference, you are determined to help. You begin with a problem-solving conference (e.g., Charney, 1992) to assess Melanie's perspective and interests and to invite her cooperation on working together. You devise a plan, taking the notes shown in Figure 9.8. Notice that your plan includes a multifaceted approach to help Melanie succeed: You will modify your curriculum, check with other specialists, include Melanie's family as part of the education team, and restructure your classroom interactions to encourage Melanie's success. In addition to these long-range approaches, also notice that the plan uses short-term strategies: an extrinsic reinforcer (art time

FIGURE 9.8   *Devising a plan with short- and long-term strategies for redirecting student behavior.*

Short-Term Suggestions	Long-Term Ideas
√ *Conference with Melanie to determine the cause for her not completing work (a la Dreikurs).*	√ *Check curriculum: Differentiate instruction by providing individual projects that tap into her interests. Use read-alouds that inspired her last year (e.g., Baudelaire books).*
√ *Call her father and get his perspective.*	√ *Work on elements of motivation: Break assignments into smaller pieces to increase probability of success and decrease perception of effort required.*
√ *Develop a contract with rewards that she finds appealing (art or science time).*	√ *Reorganize cooperative learning groups and begin to shift reasonable leadership responsibilities to Melanie.*
√ *Find high-interest, low-vocabulary books.*	√ *Use her parents' input about Melanie's out-of-school expertise (e.g., rugby) to build connections in the classroom.*
√ *Start homework sheet where she writes her assignments each day, and her dad signs nightly.*	
√ *Check cumulative record folder to determine if Melanie has any identified learning difficulties.*	
√ *Find a software program that uses reading through science (her interest).*	

as a reward for Melanie's time on task). Although you may be opposed in general to using extrinsic reinforcers, you decide that Melanie needs some immediate success and that the rewards can be dropped later as her successes begin to snowball.

By working on the apathy issue in many ways—with tools you can use tomorrow and tools that will be implemented over the year—you increase the probability of success. You may find that certain aspects of your plan are more effective than others as you work with Melanie, and thus you will drop the least effective tools.

The point is to address discipline issues along several dimensions: prevention and response, curriculum and management, group and individual focus, and cause and immediate redirection. It may sound overwhelming, but you will likely find that a few tools can serve many purposes for different learners.

So there you have it—Four rules to guide teachers' efforts in establishing classroom control and encouraging appropriate behavior are as follows:

1. Treat all learners with dignity and respect.
2. Actively prevent misbehavior.
3. View discipline as an opportunity to help students gain independence.
4. Address discipline issues in many ways and on more than one level.

Each of these rules is supported by a number of tools that bring them to life. No doubt you will find some of these tools more useful than others, and no doubt you will also be more successful at implementing some than others, at least initially. Novice teachers tend to have similar struggles in establishing discipline. Therefore, Figure 9.9 restates a number of the chapter's tools that may be helpful in boosting you over some of the hurdles new teachers typically face as they establish and maintain a positive learning environment. You may wish to review Figure 9.9 during tough days, especially those when your principal or supervisor sits in.

DEVELOPING YOUR OWN DISCIPLINE PROGRAM

This chapter offers a number of tools that may be useful for you in fostering student self-control. Other books and experienced teachers will also propose a number of appealing tips. A few books that you may find helpful, for example, are Rogers (2004), Rudolph (2006), Kottler (2002), Jones (2000), and Wong

FIGURE 9.9 *Discipline boosts for new teachers.*

Direct→Check→Feedback
- Use clear, positive language to *direct* students' behavior.
- *Check* to see whether students comply. Wait and watch.
- Give specific *feedback* on students' efforts to comply.
- Redirect as necessary.

Keep It Positive
- Focus on what students do well.
- Focus on students who deserve attention for making good choices.
- Be genuine and specific in your praise.
- Be fair. Smile. Laugh.

Make Your Presence Felt
- Move around the room to teach and monitor.
- Move closer to students who are beginning to stray.
- Monitor students carefully and subtly let them know that you are aware of their actions.
- Carry yourself with confidence.

Avoid Overreliance on Rewards and Punishments
- Point systems, card systems, token economies, and marble jars can all support a positive classroom environment, but be certain that *you*—not the marble jar, not the principal—are the authority in your classroom.
- Focus on logical consequences and self-control.

(1998). However, no expert—and no book—in the world can tell you the appropriate plan for disciplining *your* students. Charney (1992) urges us to teach authentically. When we teach, according to Charney, we teach from the whole teacher, revealing ourselves every day. We accept our own limitations and mistakes. We act on personal authority: "We stake a claim in the classroom and in the larger context of schools and systems—to what is personally, intimately known and felt. . . . Authenticity involves accepting our personal authority— and the risks that go with it—so that we can be agents of the changes needed in our schools" (p. 259).

To teach authentically, you need to develop your own discipline plan based on your philosophy, personality, and preferences in addition to the research. That plan needs to consider the particular ages, characteristics, and strengths of your students and their families and reflect your genuine appreciation for your students as individuals.

Figure 9.10 provides a planning sheet for your discipline plan. You can begin by once again perusing your stance toward education and asking yourself the following questions:

1. Who do I hope my students will be as adults? What should their character be?
2. How do students learn?
3. What does it mean to teach well?

Then jot down characteristics of your students—the range of their background experiences and their age and developmental levels are examples of characteristics that may be relevant.

Next, consider your own needs, likes, and dislikes (Charles, 1992). Draw from each of these responses to develop your own rules for establishing and maintaining classroom discipline (see Figure 9.11). Remember that "rules" are

FIGURE 9.10 *My personal discipline program.*

This I believe . . . *(List major points from your stance toward education.)*

My students . . . *(List characteristics of your specific students or of students in general.)*

I need . . .

I like . . .

I dislike . . .

My Rules and Some Tools
(Not classroom rules, but principles that guide my approach to discipline.)

My Rule:

Some Tools:

    Establishing an environment

    Preventing misbehavior

    Responding to behavior

My Rule:

Some Tools:

    Establishing an environment

    Preventing misbehavior

    Responding to behavior

My Rule:

Some Tools:

    Establishing an environment

    Preventing misbehavior

    Responding to behavior

My plan for involving families and other team members to help students develop self control

FIGURE 9.11 *Formalize your own set of rules that will govern the decisions you make regarding classroom discipline.*

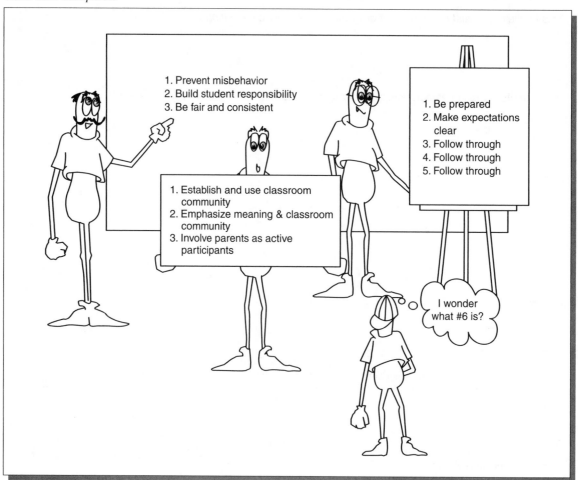

not the rules that govern the students; rather they are the rules that govern *you:* What are the principles by which you will select your actions when it comes to encouraging discipline? Borrow as you see fit from the four rules presented in this chapter or from other sources, or invent your own. Then, flesh out your plan by listing tools—specific strategies—that can help you bring each of your rules to life. Review your list and work from our chapter-opening exercises, your other readings, and your own observations of expert teachers for tools that are consistent with your rules.

Expect your list of tools to grow with your experience. You will receive many discipline suggestions and tools. Before incorporating any tool into your discipline plan, however, be certain that the tool is consistent with the rules that guide your efforts to discipline. If you cannot apply the *tool* to a *rule,* the tip is probably not consistent with your stance on discipline. Stick with the tools that are in concert with what you believe to be good for students. Expect, too, that you will reflect regularly on your plan. Does it overemphasize compliance? Rewards and punishments? Does it preserve human dignity?

Also consider other resources for your discipline program. You are part of a team responsible for educating your students. Your plan needs to respond to the cultural, developmental, linguistic, and personal qualities of your students. Families are experts on their children; no one knows them better. How can you appropriately tap into families' knowledge in order to learn about students and to support their growth? How will you work effectively with parents as team members to support student development? Which specialists can provide assistance? What support can you expect from your site administrators and fellow teachers? Capitalize early on the contributions each of these parties can make to the well-being of your class; do not wait until students misbehave to devise a support system. Finally, try out your discipline program. Revise the aspects that are inhumane, ineffective, or unwieldy. As you plan to assist students in learning to behave appropriately, consider the issues that technology raises.

TECHNOLOGY AND ENCOURAGING APPROPRIATE BEHAVIOR

Technology seems to provide a set of tools to address our *current* issues just as it presents us with a *new* set of issues. Such is the case with technology and student behavior.

Emerging Issues with Technology and Student Behavior

Technological developments have given students new ways to communicate, to express themselves, and, in short, new choices to make regarding their behavior. In a recent case, a group of girls with a history of inappropriate behavior at their high school used technology for many of their reported transgressions. They talked on cell phones during class and rebuffed their teachers' efforts to stop them. They sent racy text messages from their coach's cell phone to others. They posted provocative photos of themselves on their My Space accounts. Thus, technology seems to provide for our students new avenues for making (bad?) choices. Indeed, digital citizenship is now a priority for schools interested in helping students to become responsible inhabitants of the twenty-first century (Ribble, Bailey, & Ross, 2004).

Digital citizenship and related issues force teachers and schools to develop policies and rules related to students and technology. Check your school and district policies related to technology use. Each district has an acceptable use policy that students and parents are required to sign. Locate the policy and discover what it tells you about questions such as:

- When and how are students allowed to use cell phones?
- When and how are students allowed to use digital recording devices (such as cell phone still and video cameras)?
- What policies govern Internet use at school?
- How can we counteract the negative and violent messages that students sometimes encounter in cyberspace?
- What are your responsibilities for preventing students from sending or posting potentially troublesome electronic communications? From violating copyright law?

As an aside, while you verify policies designed to guide students' digital citizenship, also check policies that guide your own. Teachers need to serve as strong models of cyber-citizenship and may be dismissed for immorality if their private behavior affects their duties as educators (Underwood & Webb, 2006). Consequently, as public figures, teachers need to guard that their electronic habits and communications adhere to standards of professionalism.

In addition to school and district policies, you will want to consider additional restrictions or guidelines you place on students' use of technology within your room. Many teachers do not allow students to make or take calls or text message during class, but there may be times when cell communications are appropriate. Determine your own stance on issues such as these, communicate them explicitly to students, and have a plan for consequences if students violate the rules. For example, will you *really* take away their phone if it rings?

Technology as a Tool for Encouraging Appropriate Behavior

Technology does indeed offer promise for helping educators address traditional issues of student behavior. At the most basic level, computers may help prevent misbehavior. When computer-aided instruction is effective, it seems reasonable to expect that it can support student motivation and encourage appropriate behavior. If students are successfully engaged in learning opportunities that are tailored to their needs, they are more likely to behave appropriately. Good computer-based instruction does indeed offer the benefit of adjusting level of difficulty, providing immediate feedback, and providing engaging contexts for learning. However, although some studies explore the link between computer use and factors of student conduct (e.g., Barron, Hogarty, Kromrey, & Lenkway, 1999; Powell, Aeby, & Carpenter-Aeby, 2003), empirical research supporting computer use as a prevention for misbehavior is thus far sparse. Additionally, as students repeatedly use computers at school, the novelty factor often decreases, taking along with it a bit of the power of the computer as a mechanism to prevent misbehavior.

Computer-aided technology also offers promise for helping teachers and schools respond to student behavior. At the schoolwide level, for example, computerized systems for analyzing discipline referrals can help staff members to identify students who may be at risk given their behaviors. Staff can examine patterns in the data such as the type of problem, gender, and grade level (Tobin, Sugai, & Colvin, 2000). Within the classroom, students can create graphs related to problematic behaviors and watch them decrease over time. Also, communication formats such as e-mail—for those who have access—and immediate phone calls home can help teachers and families work together as a team to support appropriate student behavior. For example, many teachers find it powerful indeed to pick up the phone and have a student who has just misbehaved (or behaved laudably) dial a family member on the spot. As you develop your own discipline plan, consider how you can:

- support students in using technology appropriately in your classroom and beyond.
- use computer-based instruction to support student behavior by enhancing motivation and addressing individual needs.
- communicate effectively with families regarding student behavior.

PARTING WORDS

Providing positive classroom discipline is, at the least, strenuous—and it can be downright exhausting. Many, many teachers succeed at establishing fair and productive classrooms, and you can, too. Think about one of these pieces of advice on a day when you feel disheartened about the challenge of helping your students develop self-discipline:

- A bad day is often followed by a good one.
- Classroom discipline is said to be a series of little victories. You and your students build good discipline over time, one interaction at a time. One mistake does not mean you have lost them forever.
- Remember that much of what happens in your classroom is under your control. When students misbehave as a group, ask yourself, "What can *I* do to provide a better environment, help them build skills for self-control, or prevent misbehavior?" Do something.
- If your system does not work, change it.

> If your horse dies, dismount.
> —*U.S. Cavalry Manual from World War I*

WEB SITES

http://www.BehaviorAdvisor.com
Dr. Mac's Amazing Behavior Management Advice Site. This site has many positive, useful ideas for a range of issues.

http://www.gentleteaching.com/
Gentle Teaching International. Gentle teaching is an approach to human interactions that focuses on the values of helping individuals feel safe, valued, and engaged.

http://iris.peabody.vanderbilt.edu/browsebytopic02.html
Behavior: IRIS Center (Ideas and Research for Inclusive Settings). Includes activities, information, and modules for fostering positive behavior for students in inclusive settings. See materials related to other topics (such as Diversity and Management) as well.

http://www.pbis.org
Positive Behavior Interventions and Support. Check the online library for links to resources and implementation examples.

http://www.teachervision.com/lesson-plans/lesson-2943.html
Teacher Vision. "How to Manage Disruptive Behavior in Inclusive Classrooms" provides 10 questions and answers for analyzing behavior in inclusive classrooms.

http://www.disciplinehelp.com/
The "You Can Handle Them All" site. Gives discipline tips, including suggestions for addressing 117 misbehaviors related to the categories of attention, power, revenge, and self-confidence. Recommend the site to families as well.

OPPORTUNITIES TO PRACTICE

1. Watch a teacher in action and analyze his strategies for encouraging appropriate behavior. Visit the Merrill Teacher Prep Web site, Video Classroom, and go to General Methods, Module 8, Video 1. Watch the first few minutes of a middle school teacher's lesson on Bernoulli's principle and analyze his discipline plan. Complete the following chart.

Treating Students with Dignity and Respect		
	How did the teacher convey his respect for the students and treat them with dignity?	What additional teacher actions might you suggest for the teacher to convey dignity and respect?
Preventing Misbehavior		
Physical arrangement	How did the room's physical environment help prevent misbehavior?	What modifications might you suggest?
Curriculum	To what extent does the lesson engage the students?	What lesson additions or modifications might you suggest to further engage students?
Procedures, routines, and past practice	Misbehaviors during the lesson are few. In what ways can you infer that the teacher prevented misbehavior?	What additional ideas do you have for supporting students' good choices throughout the lesson?
Encouraging Independence and Responsibility		
	There are a few low-level misbehaviors from the students. How does he respond to student misbehavior in ways that (a) convey his belief that students can solve their own problems and (b) cause minimal disruption to the lesson?	

2. Start with the students. Try one or both of these strategies to build a discipline plan that is responsive to your learners:

   a. Determine students' preferences for how teachers should discipline, perhaps through a questionnaire or an informal interview with questions such as, "What do good teachers do?" "What advice do you have for new teachers?"

   b. Culture makes a difference too. Spend some time learning about your actual students' experiences and about general patterns for their cultural or ethnic groups. Two sources to get you started are Banks (1997) and Grant (1995). The Internet can also provide information. Use the cultural group's name as a search term.

3. Because authentic authority affects classroom discipline, make a plan to build bridges to your students. Technology is one tool that may help. As I type this chapter in my home office, I can hear my son's history teacher's voice in the next room. What? The teacher is at home playing the game Halo with his son, battling mine online. My son noted that although he has appreciated this teacher for two years at school, it was not until they started interacting occasionally in cyberspace that my son felt connected to him.

   Make a list of some ideas that can help you connect with your students. Share the list with an experienced colleague to double check that your strategies are appropriate and, while friendly, maintain your professional standing. Get your students' opinions too.

4. Observe an experienced teacher in action.

   a. How does the room environment encourage positive behavior?

   b. How does the curriculum prevent misbehavior?

   c. List some strategies the teacher uses to provide feedback to students on their behavior, noting which messages are positive, neutral, or negative.

   d. List some strategies the teacher uses to allow students to monitor and correct their own behavior.

   e. What evidence do you see that the teacher understands and is responsive to students' perspectives?

   f. What else do you notice about the teacher's discipline system?

5. Pick any tool from this chapter. Try it out, either in your classroom or at home when the occasion arises. How did it feel to you as a teacher? To the other party? Remember that there are always effects—usually both intended and unintended. What effects did this tool have in this circumstance?

6. Arrange for a friend to mock interview you for a teaching position, focusing on your approach to discipline. Use your discipline plan (Figure 9.10) as support for the points you make. Your friend could devise difficult scenarios for you to respond to as part of the interview. (Caution: This exercise is harder than it sounds.)

7. Develop a one-page handout of your discipline program that you can share with students, families your master teacher, and other interested parties. You may wish to begin with a credo, or statement of beliefs. (Note: This one-page handout and artifacts such as notes home and photographs of students productively engaged are highly appropriate entries for your professional portfolio.) Invite input, especially from students' families.

8. Choose and respond to one of these critical incidents. Use the rules and tools in this chapter or your own to describe the problem and suggest a plan.

   a. Josh, a ninth grader, walks into fifth period 2 minutes late. His arms are full of books, papers, and notebooks all awaiting a chance to spill to the ground. He gives the teacher a sheepish smile and announces, "Sorry I'm late. My backpack broke at lunch." On the way to his seat, he trips on Brittney's desk. The class bursts out in laughter. Josh's face turns red, and he alone stoops to gather his spilled belongings.

   b. Susana, a first-grade teacher, drags into the lounge at lunch. "What is it, Susana?" asks Brent, a fellow teacher. Susana replies: "I am fed up with my students' constant tattling: 'Teacher, he looked at me.' 'Teacher, she says I copied her.' 'Teacher, she took Dylan's eraser and then put it back when she saw me.' I need this tattling to stop!"

   c. Joseph is a new fifth-grade teacher. He is feeling successful about how his students are treating each other, but their constant talking is wearing him down. When he tells them to quiet down, they do, but within three minutes the noise level is back to being too high. He feels like he is nagging with his constant reminders.

Before You Begin Reading

Chapter Ten

Warm-Up Exercise for Growing in Your Profession

Consider your future. Choose some of the prompts below to jot down some of the possibilities of where you hope to be . . .

- **One Year from Today**
  Professional goals:

  Personal goals:

- **Two Years from Today**
  Professional goals:

  Personal goals:

- **Five Years from Today**
  Professional goals:

  Personal goals:

- **Ten Years from Today**
  Professional goals:

  Personal goals:

CHAPTER Ten

Growing in Your Profession

*A*deunt etiam optima: The best is yet to be.

Obtaining a teaching credential and landing a job are only two very early—and happy!—stages in your professional development. *Good teachers are never finished growing.* Remember Chapter 1's discussion of the National Board for Professional Teaching Standards' core propositions on teaching (2002)? Those propositions state that accomplished teachers reflect on their practice in order to continuously improve. Further, accomplished teachers work effectively with families, communities, and other professionals in order to shape the world of education. They work creatively as members of learning communities. It is your job, starting today and for the rest of your career, to work with others and to grow professionally. In fact, some say that the day teachers stop learning is the day they are finished as classroom teachers. Through its four sections, this chapter encourages you to stretch professionally by

- Engaging in the professional community
- Working with families
- Using professional ethics as your guide
- Providing some advice from the heart

ENGAGING IN THE PROFESSIONAL COMMUNITY

You have chosen a profession that requires you to work with people every day. Your students' success depends in part on your willingness and ability to engage with other professionals in sharing, implementing, and refining professional knowledge. In the future, you will be deeply involved in the life of your school through activities such as committee work and curriculum development. As you consider the type of school in which you would like to work, think about aspects of the school and its functioning that might be deciding factors for you. Is staff collaboration important to you? Is a strong inclusion program important to you?

Three aspects of engagement you may think about right now include becoming an effective staff member, growing from feedback on your teaching, and pursuing more formal opportunities for growth.

Becoming an Effective Staff Member

> The brighter you are, the more you have to learn.
>
> —Don Herold

Success in your job as a teacher extends far beyond your classroom door. Perhaps more than ever teachers are required to work well as team members in support of the goal of rigorous learning—and grade-level proficiency—for all students. From the first day you step on campus, you will want to demonstrate your willingness and ability to listen, learn, and function well as a member of a

New teachers often find that talking with colleagues lessens feelings of isolation or frustration and heightens feelings of professional competence and satisfaction.

Anne Vega/Merrill

Watch a grade-level team meeting. At the Teacher Prep Web site Video Classroom, go to Foundations/Intro to Teaching, Module 5, Video 1. This meeting hints at the many people with whom teachers must successfully interact, including teammates, site administrators, district personnel, family members, guest speakers, and field trip personnel. In what ways is this meeting a reminder of the nature of teaching (Chapter 1)? Two hints: (1) Teaching looks easy from the outside, and (2) teachers are part of a system.

team. Get to know each of the many staff members and volunteers who spend their days at school. Talk with the janitor and office personnel. Find the specialists. Smile and say hello to the family members on site. Learn about your administrators' priorities. Each of these people contributes to school life and learning.

Chances are your colleagues will welcome you with plenty of informal support. Many experienced peers at your site will likely offer assistance to the new teacher on the block. They may advise you as you stand near the photocopy machine or tear off butcher paper for your bulletin boards. Some may even offer more intense help in topics such as arranging your room, working with discipline challenges, getting to know the site, or planning your curriculum.

Some of your less experienced colleagues will also serve as a source of support because of the benefits that can be derived from being new together. Teaching Teaching Tip 10.1 gives some suggestions from new teachers whom I asked for words of wisdom. Their words are encouraging because, despite the fact that they allude to the challenges of teaching (teaching looks easy . . . from the outside!), they also communicate that there are many actions you can take to build your own success.

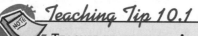 *Teaching Tip 10.1*

TEACHER TO TEACHER: ADVICE FOR THE EARLY DAYS.

- "Be prepared. Plan."
- "Take a break in the middle of the day. Get out of your room. I learned early on, that, for my own sanity, I could not keep kids in during recess."
- "Don't be afraid to ask for help. Connect with another teacher."
- "The first day of teaching is scary. . . . The second day is worse (because you know what you've gotten yourself into!). Take it a day at a time. Don't be overwhelmed by every new thing that comes your way."
- "Be flexible. Leave room in your plan book and in your head for the possibility that this may not be a normal day."
- "Don't take on too many responsibilities in your first year. After-school volunteering, student council meetings, and school board meetings will all be there next year too."

When on-site experienced colleagues give advice or offer to help, your response can be essential to your growth as a professional and for your easy adjustment to the school culture. Experienced teachers emphatically state that the fastest way for a novice to be shunned by a school staff is to act as if she knows it all and has nothing to learn. No one likes a know-it-all. As you respond to well-meaning attempts to help, remember that you bring the enthusiasm of a "new kid," no matter your age. You may be finishing an intense teacher preparation program, so you may not feel that you need every piece of advice that comes your way. Nevertheless, you need to be gracious. You have the gift of enthusiasm; others bring the gift of experience. Find the gem of usefulness—even if it is merely the willingness to help—that each person brings to you. Offer your own advice sparingly. Establish from your first day on site that you are eager to learn and that you respect the wisdom of experienced teachers and staff.

Conversely, you may find yourself in a lonely situation with no offers of help. In this case, be the first to shake a hand, smile, and say hello. Introduce yourself and make it clear that you are thrilled about being part of the team. If you need help, ask. Find another inexperienced friend or a teacher at the same grade level or in the same subject area who is willing to talk shop.

It can be tempting to join in lounge conversations as a way to establish yourself as a member of the group. Sometimes lounge talk, unfortunately, degenerates into negative conversations about students, family members, or school personnel. It will be important for you to avoid such conversations for a number of reasons. Poisonous people can sap your energy and deflect your focus from where it should be. Also, it is unkind and of questionable ethics to speak ill of others. It reflects poorly on you as a professional. Additionally, complaining can serve to make you feel like a victim rather than like the competent professional you are (Kottler, 2002).

Long-term survey data suggest that teachers become less optimistic about student learning and their own ability to make a difference over time (Markow & Martin, 2005). You don't need anyone helping you along that path. When negative conversations come up, you may try changing the subject, or as, Kottler recommends, focusing on one or two *positive* qualities of your students or others. Find the colleague who has been teaching for 25 years and still loves it and learns every day. Keep company with teachers who maintain a positive outlook; they will feed your soul.

In addition to these informal opportunities to integrate into the school staff, you will also engage in a shared journey with your colleagues in support of student learning. Expect to spend many hours examining your students' work and assessment results together. Grade-level and department meetings are examples of teams that may engage in joint reflection and planning. These and other individuals may also form professional learning communities (PLCs), lesson study groups, or other inquiry-based endeavors in support of student learning.

In professional learning communities (introduced in Chapter 7), members of teams create shared values and focus on learning through interaction, analysis of data, and reflection to improve student learning. Teachers, students, and family members can all benefit from the PLC (Roberts & Pruitt, 2003). Lesson study, borrowed from Japan, consists of teachers selecting research questions and then collaboratively planning, teaching, reflecting, and critiquing their lessons (Lewis, Perry, & Hurd, 2004). These and other team approaches have been shown effective in furthering teachers' knowledge growth and practice. In your early days on site, discover what mechanisms exist for you and your teammates to collaborate in pursuit of better teaching and learning.

Growing from Feedback on Your Teaching

In many states, new teachers receive assistance and feedback on their teaching through formally assigned mentors. In fact, 87% of new teachers surveyed across the nation in 2004 were assigned to a mentor or **support provider** (Markow & Martin, 2005). Many are assigned as one component of new teacher **induction programs** that provide comprehensive support systems. Mentors often conduct observations (perhaps formal or informal, but separate from the personnel evaluation process), offer assistance, and help shape professional development activities based on the needs of new teachers.

New teachers report very clearly that the support of a trusted colleague who is officially assigned to help out is a key factor in the new teachers' satisfaction and success. Further, states such as California are finding that teachers stay in the profession at higher rates when induction programs are in place (Reed, Rueben, & Barbour, 2006). Find out what types of mentoring and induction support are offered in your state and district and determine the extent to which you can provide input into the selection of your mentor.

In addition to informal assistance and observations, you will receive structured feedback on your teaching. If you are enrolled in a teacher education program, university personnel and a site supervisor will probably observe you. If you are a paid teacher, you will be probably be observed by your mentor and certainly by your administrator. Sometimes observational support for new teachers is also provided by the district office.

Some feedback on your teaching will be formal, based on an administrator's or other official's evaluation of your teaching. In formal instances, structured observation sessions often begin with a brief preobservation conference at which you may be given the opportunity to direct the observation. The observer may ask what you would like her to focus on. Have an answer ready. If no immediate need comes to mind, consider using one of the principles of instruction: COME IN (you could even provide Figure 5.8 with elements of your choice circled). After the lesson, you will probably have a postobservation conference. The observer may begin by asking for your analysis of the lesson. Be frank and specific in assessing the strengths and weaknesses of your teaching. Then brace yourself for the evidence or advice from the observer.

It can be difficult to accept criticism about something so close to your heart as your teaching. The worst thing to do when you receive suggestions is to take a defensive posture and state immediately why those suggestions do not apply to you or will not work. The observer knows something about teaching or he could not be in the position to offer advice in this format. One of the best things to do when you receive advice (even if you hate it) is to smile, establish eye contact, and say thank you. Then you can add something sincere to show that you understand the point of the suggestions. Honest examples, in order of decreasing enthusiasm, include the following:

- "Thanks. Those are great ideas! No *wonder* they pay you the big bucks!"
- "Thanks. That just might work! I will try it tomorrow."
- "Thanks. You have given me lots of things to think about!"
- "Thanks. I appreciate your ideas. I will need to think about some ways to make them work for my situation."
- "Thanks. Tell me more about how I could make that suggestion work in my room."

Your postobservation conference will probably be helpful and positive. However, if you have limped through a painful postobservation session, you can go home and nurse your wounded pride. Chances are, in a few hours (or days) you will find some kernel of wisdom or helpfulness in the words that stung initially. The point is not to be false in your reaction to criticism but to realize that every teacher has room to grow and that once you can get over a possible initial reaction of hurt, you can appreciate a fresh insight into teaching.

Sometimes advice on your teaching may not be offered, even though you eagerly ask for it. For instance, you may have a formal lesson observation for which the evaluator gives nonspecific feedback: "Wonderful lesson! Great job!" Be ready with some pointed questions that require the sharing of evidence collected by the observer. For instance, you could ask the observer whether your instruction engaged all of the students, or whether the observer noted any evidence that students were mastering the content. (Again, provide Figure 5.7 or your credo of education. Ask the evaluator to gather relevant evidence.)

You may at times need assistance of a more dire nature. For example, you may have a student who is particularly troubled or you may be struggling to meet the needs of a specific group of students. Being a classroom teacher means being part of a team, so be certain that you ask for help. Talk with your principal, mentor, or supervisor about your needs, stating them in a professional, clear way at the appropriate place and time. Do not place blame or suggest that you are not responsible for difficult situations ("I was given the roughest class!"). Your aim is to help your students learn, and you are exactly the person who is responsible for them. Have alternatives ready if you are faced with unfair or difficult practices or procedures. Be assertive and positive, with an effort to serve as part of the solution, not part of the problem. Get your needs met without sacrificing others' rights or dignity. Use *I*-statements (presented in Chapter 9). Convey your sense of self-trust that you have the ability to make a difference and your sense of eagerness to learn. Finally, remember that learning to teach is a developmental affair. The kinds of concerns you have, the sophistication of your thinking and your strategies, and the realm of your influence will almost certainly shift as you grow with experience.

Pursuing Formal Opportunities for Growth

According to Wiggins and McTighe (2006), we teachers grow when we find personal meaning in our work, when we reflect, and when we question ourselves within a supportive environment. Many teachers find that informal and formal opportunities to talk about teaching in its daily context contribute invaluably to their growth. Formal opportunities to pursue professional learning also propel teacher learning.

Seek out resources about teaching, and, as appropriate for the amount of time available to you as a new teacher, make it a point to pursue at least one formal opportunity per year. Formal professional development opportunities range broadly; Figure 10.1 lists some tips for locating and engaging in formal opportunities to learn. Note that to grow in a balanced way you will probably need to select a variety of professional development opportunities over the course of your career. The point is to

- Make better contributions to the lives of students each year.
- Contribute to your profession in broader ways.
- Derive satisfaction from personal and professional growth.

WORKING WITH FAMILIES

Effective teachers realize the incredible potential that strong family–school connections can have for fueling students' success. This section explores the research on family involvement and suggests things you can do right now to build bridges with families.

FIGURE 10.1 *Professional development opportunities.*

Description	Benefits	Drawbacks
1. Attendance at Professional Meetings, Workshops, and Conferences		
Meetings range from general to specific conferences, to focused workshops on working with particular student needs, on specific teaching or assessment strategies, and on subject matter areas. With time, you may be ready to provide workshops that showcase your own expertise!	+ Meetings are readily available (check the teachers' lounge for advertisements). + Meetings can directly address your areas of interest or need. + Meetings can present very practical strategies for immediate implementation.	− Meetings might take you away from the classroom, which adds to your planning load and is often unpopular with students. − Meetings often do not supply the follow-up support needed to implement new techniques.
2. Professional Memberships Many national, state, and local organizations focus on educational concerns.	+ Joining an organization can increase your feelings of belonging to a professional community. + You can select your level of participation, which can vary from minimal to extensive. + Most associations' membership fees include both practical and research journals.	− Dues can be considerable. − If minimal participation is selected, membership may have limited effects on your professional knowledge.
3. Professional Literature Abundant educational resources include practical texts, scholarly texts, research journals, trade magazines, and Internet resources.	+ The variety of education literature is tremendous. + You can select exactly the information you need. + Electronic searches allow you to find large amounts of information specifically related to your needs. + You can read at your own convenience.	− It can be difficult to find the time to gather materials and read. − Some research literature is not written with the classroom teacher in mind. − Reading can be a solitary endeavor unless you can find a discussion partner or study group
4. Professional Travel • Local travel opportunities include visits to nearby classrooms, schools, and field-trip sites. • Educationally related field trips to distant sites to study the culture, language, history, or natural phenomena (e.g., the Galapagos Islands) can provide college course credit.	+ Travel, even to the school down the street, broadens our experiences and views of good practice. + Travel can increase your empathy and subject matter base and the resources you draw from in your classroom teaching.	− Seeing other schools at work usually means leaving your own students during instructional hours. − Travel can be costly and time consuming.

FIGURE 10.1   *Continued.*

Description	Benefits	Drawbacks
5. Advanced Study Advanced study through a university can result in: • a certificate • an advanced credential • a graduate degree	+ Advanced study is often particularly meaningful for teachers because they can draw from the background of their own teaching experience. + Advanced study provides for a greater number of professional options. + Advanced study is the typical mechanism for advancing on the salary scale in public schools.	− Advanced study can be overwhelming as teachers balance the needs of their students and of their educational programs. − New teachers are usually highly focused upon their classrooms and may not be ready to engage in advanced study. − Without financial assistance, advanced study can be expensive.
6. Professional Writing • Informal writings by teachers include private journals and handbooks for local distribution. • Many education journals and magazines, including electronic sources, welcome contributions from practicing teachers. • Findings from action research projects are useful to other professionals when published.	+ When teachers write, they send the message that educators are thoughtful and can build and share knowledge with each other. + You are a great model for your students when you write professionally.	− Writing is among the most time-intensive ways to contribute to the field. − Most teachers find difficulty in splitting their interests among the demands of classroom teaching and of putting ideas on paper.

Tips:

(a) Reread your Warm-Up Exercise for this chapter. Circle some opportunities from those introduced in this figure that will help you reach your goals. Add them to the Warm-Up Exercise.

(b) When expense is involved in professional development, ask your administrator if support is available. Check, too, with your tax advisor to determine and document legitimate professional expenses.

What We Know About Families and Schools

There is overwhelming evidence that parent participation has positive effects on a number of student outcomes (Epstein, 2005; Henderson & Mapp, 2002; Jeynes, 2005; Sheldon & Epstein, 2005). Positive outcomes associated with family involvement include student attendance, social skills and adaptation to school, enrollment in higher-level curricular programs, and achievement (shown in grades, tests scores, course passage, and grade promotion). Family participation is twice as predictive of student success as is family socioeconomic status. Also, parental involvement can counteract factors such as poverty that have a negative effect on students. Clearly it is essential that teachers and schools build connections with families.

Yet many new teachers feel underprepared to work with families. The new K–12 teachers surveyed in the MetLife teacher study named engaging families in support of their students' learning as their biggest challenge (Markow & Martin, 2005). Teachers were twice as likely to worry about family involvement than about preparing students for testing. Some teachers seem to feel that their efforts are unsupported by families. This fact seems reflected in common teachers' lounge talk where frustrated teachers begin their sentences with, "Those parents . . ." or exclaim, "They just don't value education." Teachers have a right to be frustrated by the many pressures and challenges they face in helping students learn. However, these discouraged exclamations are largely unfounded and reflect **deficit thinking,** or the belief that families are faulty in some way and need remediation. Such perceptions can be translated to family members so that families feel unwelcome at school, as was the case for Latino families studied by Quiocho and Daoud (2006). Instead, the research on family involvement indicates that:

- Parents of all races and economic levels do care deeply about their students.
- Parents do value education. What it means to be "well educated" can vary based on culture and other factors, but parents do want their students to succeed.

Based on these positive convictions, effective family involvement programs begin with the assumption that parents are knowledgeable, influential people who have contributions to make to students and their education. According to Nieto (1996), strong parent programs hold parent empowerment as a main goal, commit to serving families with low incomes and draw from the culture, values, language, and experiences of the home.

Many successful examples of schools valuing families and their expertise in order to build partnerships for the benefit of students exist (e.g., Cairney, 2000; Moll, Amanti, Neff, & Gonzalez, 1992). Establishing such successful programs involves a great deal of continued effort on the part of both the family and the teacher. Common threads include:

1. An awareness that each of us is steeped in our own culture and values and a willingness to explore those values and to accept that there are alternatives to them. This awareness allows each partner to be vigilant about remaining sensitive to others' perspectives. The greater the mismatch between a parent's experience and the culture of the school, the greater the likelihood that the parent will feel estranged from the schooling process and the more trust and support in understanding this new culture the teacher may need to establish.

2. Partnerships need to be two-way and balanced. Both parties need to be seen as having valuable knowledge and perspectives.

3. There is mutual accommodation (recall Chapter 3), in that the teacher seeks to learn about the students' communities and cultures and about how to communicate effectively with families. Home visits, translator-mediated conferences, notes home, and research are all examples of teachers learning about their students. Care must be taken not to offend families with requests that they may consider inappropriate (Davidman & Davidman, 1997).

4. There are clear, frequent, and multifaceted attempts to communicate. The communication needs to be respectful, in the language of the home, and it needs to take many forms including both written and oral messages.

5. Partnerships need to expand traditional options for family involvement. Epstein (2002) remind us to broaden our views of family participation, which can exist through six kinds of activities: parenting, communicating, volunteering, learning at home, decision making, and collaborating with the community. Examples include literacy programs where parents join school-based writing clubs and units of study that incorporate the **funds of knowledge** of the community. Funds of knowledge are the rich understandings and networks of support that community members develop and use in daily life. Special effort must be given to draw in parents who speak a language other than English and those who are bicultural (Olivos, 2006).

6. Partnerships need to grow over time, and as trust builds, teachers can provide suggestions for how parents may support their students' school success (Faltis, 2001).

Start Now to Involve Families

From the start, you can work toward effective family participation by encouraging family members to play an active role on the education team. Let parents know that you value their expertise about their children and that you can teach the student together much better than you could alone.

Act on your conviction that the world looks different from their perspective, and that you can benefit by learning about those perspectives. Here's an example. As a 22-year old new middle school teacher, I had little understanding of the stresses that my monthly book reports and 30-minute nightly homework assignments added to families, especially when compounded with students' assignments from other classes and the three or four weekly quizzes students took each Friday. The world looks very different now from my perspective as a parent of two teenagers. And research documents the stress that homework can bring to families (e.g., Solomon, Warrin, & Lewis, 2002). As I teacher, I wish I had challenged my own assumption that the homework I assigned unquestionably supported our learning goals. I wish I had invited families to sit and talk with their students about the content rather than assigning another page from the text. I wish I had asked a few more questions.

Use concrete strategies to welcome family input and to communicate openly. Capitalize on the power that "back-to-school night" and other formal meetings have to establish partnerships, especially since formal meetings are one of the most common avenues for family participation. Teaching Tip 10.2 gives a to do list for back-to-school night; items on the list are meant to help you build bridges with families from the start (Guillaume, Yopp, & Twardos, 2006).

Use a variety of forms of communication as well. For instance, if appropriate, send a letter home during the first week of school asking families about students' experiences and families' hopes and wishes for their children's education. Call or send home a note, written in the home language, during the first month of school to share each student's success. Use a newsletter to keep families

> The test of the morality of a society is what it does for its children.
>
> —*Dietrich Bonhoeffer*

Families and schools should view themselves as serving on the same team in working together to encourage student growth.

Anthony Magnacca/Merrill

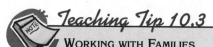

Teaching Tip 10.2

BACK-TO-SCHOOL NIGHT TO-DO LIST

☐ Dress to convey respect.

☐ Use nonverbal communication that is welcoming and conveys your competence. Smile. Stand up. Don't put physical barriers between you and families.

☐ Tell why you are a teacher. Make sure your reasons include students.

☐ Explain the important things students will learn and be able to do as a result of this year.

☐ Show your passion for the subject matter.

☐ Show why your classroom is a good place to be.

☐ Build the family–school team.

☐ Address agenda topics required by your school.

abreast of classroom events. Try e-mail if that is appropriate, or establish telephone trees to spread information to each family. Sometimes standing in front of the school after dismissal allows teachers to talk with parents or other caregivers.

Finally, find different ways for families to be involved in education. For those who can volunteer in your classroom, arrange for activities such as small-group tutoring and materials preparation. Send projects home for parents to complete with their students. Try sending home literacy backpacks (Bright, 2006) or other projects that engage families in working with their students. Include a range of involvement opportunities so that all families can experience success with their students. For example, parents may have the option of (a) listening to their student recount an event from the day or (b) participating in an interview about family experiences related to the day's story. Teaching Tip 10.3 provides additional suggestions for working with families.

Establishing effective partnerships is long, hard work. Despite your best efforts, you may occasionally grumble about an obstinate parent. Sometimes the job may feel more difficult because of actively engaged parents. If you find yourself in this situation, it may help to remember that parents are experts on their children. They have spent years tending these young lives. They know some things about their children that teachers may never understand. They also have a right to make some choices about what they perceive as best for their children. Work to separate your own feelings from a parent's emotional demands. Whether or not you agree with the course of action suggested by the parent, consider the possibility that the parent is motivated by his or her ideas of what is best for the student. Welcome input and retain your stance as an instructional leader.

Another motivation to consider is that parents' egos and protection defenses can be deeply involved. For many parents, nurturing a child is an act without comparison. Many of us discover the depths of love when we become parents. That deep love—and some ego—can color the way parents interact

Teaching Tip 10.3

WORKING WITH FAMILIES

1. Draw on their broad and long history with their children.
2. Remember that parental ego and protection defenses can be deeply involved in parenthood.
3. Make the most helpful assumptions possible.
4. Include families as essential team members. Use inclusive language and plan for solutions together.
5. Provide different ways for families to be involved.

with teachers and other professionals. Please be gentle with parents who defend their children in the face of a perceived threat or criticism or who live through the accomplishments of their children.

Some of the techniques you learned in Chapter 9 for encouraging humane, forthright communication may assist you as you talk with parents. Figure 10.2

FIGURE 10.2 *Suggestions for communicating with parents.*

1. Set a warm and supportive tone for your conversation.

Establish yourself as an authority figure.	Use genuine concern for students and your expert knowledge base to build trust with families. You may be new, but you are a professional.
	Be certain that the care you feel for each of your students is reflected in your words and actions.
Use nonverbal communication.	Communicate your concern for students by choosing a collegial location for conferences (not, for instance, you behind an imposing desk). Share your care and enthusiasm in your handshake, your posture, and your facial expression.
Celebrate and suffer.	Appreciate—don't evaluate—families' successes and struggles with their children. It's hard work to be a parent. Remember, your work with the students stops every day. Families are in for the long haul.
Actively listen.	Use body language to indicate that you are fully attentive.
	Paraphrase your understanding of what parents say. Show that you understand the parents' concerns.
Keep things positive. Use laughter.	Keep the tone of your conference hopeful and assertive: This is an effective team! Express shared commitment and communicate your sense of certainty that together you and the family can help the student. Use humor appropriately to keep a sense of perspective.

2. State your concerns fairly and without evoking defensiveness.

Use a strength refresher.	Begin with a statement of the student's tremendous strengths. Use that as a context for what you can work on next. We can all improve.
Use *I*-messages to communicate your concerns.	You can lessen parents' defensiveness by not placing blame. Not: "*You* aren't checking that homework is done" but "When Joey does not complete homework, *I* worry that he won't master these fundamental concepts."
Address the behavior, not the person.	Talk in specific terms about what you see the student doing and saying. Then talk about the consequences. Steer clear of phrases that label. Provide specific evidence, including work samples and grade-book marks, to illustrate the student's strengths and struggles.

3. Work on addressing issues as a team.

Ask for family insights.	Draw on families' considerable years of experience: "What has been effective in the past?" Talk frankly about what seems effective and ineffective in your own efforts.
Establish clear expectations.	Give parents clear guidelines of things they can do to help. Share professional literature. Give lists of suggestions. Especially if parents are feeling ineffective, you'll need to give concrete suggestions for things to try. Remember, you need a license to be a teacher, but parents typically have no training for their role. We all can use some friendly suggestions, especially when shared by someone we trust and respect.
Offer choices and respect decisions.	Suggest for parents some specific options for strategies to help their students. When parents make a choice, respect it instead of suggesting others.
Follow through.	Do what you say you'll do. Check to see that the parents do the same. If they don't, talk about changing the system to make it more manageable for them.
Talk about addressing issues in many ways and on different levels.	Discuss possible motivations for misbehavior. For example, are things going well for the student at home? In Scouts? In day care? Make a plan to address issues in the short run and in the longer range. Be certain the plan includes both home and school aspects.

continued

FIGURE 10.2   Continued.

---

4. Avoid ugliness.

Model emotional control.

- Even if parents express emotions inappropriately, you need to remain calm and professional.

- If parents have difficulty collecting themselves, use a supportive statement that recognizes their right to feel strongly.

- You may want to suggest that you talk another time.

- Do the same if you are no longer in control: "I care so much about this issue that I'm having trouble remaining calm. I'd like to excuse myself. We can talk again tomorrow evening."

Use anger shields.

- Occasionally parents become so emotional that they can no longer behave with the best interests of their children in mind.

- Don't talk to a parent who angrily interrupts your instruction. Instead suggest that the parent stop by the office and make an appointment to see you after school or during your conference period.

- If a conference takes a hostile turn, stand up and excuse yourself: "I see you care deeply about your student. However, this conversation is no longer professional. I'll be glad to talk to you at another time when the principal is able to join us."

---

recounts some promising strategies from Chapter 9 that may transfer to your informal conversations and your formal conferences.

If you feel frustrated when it appears that parents are falling short of your expectations, it can be helpful to assume the best. Instead of assuming that parents do not care about their child or they would ensure that daily homework is completed, think about what other things might account for the fact that homework is not getting finished: Does the parent perceive that the student needs to take sole responsibility? Does he view it as outside the scope of his authority so that it would be an affront to your professionalism if he were to step in? Is there a tough softball schedule? Is the student caring for younger siblings? When a parent does not come to back-to-school night, remember that school might be an intimidating place for some. Or a parent may work at night. When you assume that families do not care, you close the door on your chances of working with them on behalf of the student. Assume the best. Remember the powerful role you play in forming effective home–school teams and in leading learning. Teachers who think that they *can* make a difference *do*.

USING PROFESSIONAL ETHICS AS YOUR GUIDE

Ethics and **morals** are the often tacit rules that govern how people should treat each other. According to Goodlad (1990), the entire enterprise of education is a moral one; the primary purposes of schools, providing access to knowledge and enculturating the young, are moral callings. Further, teachers are part of a system. When you enter this profession, you accept its code of ethics (Soltis, 1986). You take on the obligation to act in the best interest of your students, including commitments such as protecting them and taking responsibility to help them learn. These are weighty responsibilities. Further, teaching is fraught with tensions and dilemmas that require you to act as a moral agent (Buzzelli & Johnston, 2001; Kidder & Born, 1998–1999).

Finally, you have entered a career in which professionals are typically held to a higher moral standard than the general public. In each of your dealings, be certain that professional ethics inform your choices about how to act and what to say.

Using professional ethics as your guide means that you must advocate for the students and advocate for yourself. Advocating for the students means that you

1. Ensure students' physical and emotional safety. Be certain that you carefully monitor the students and make reasonable efforts to protect them from bodily and psychological harm. Learn to recognize symptoms of stress and distress in students (Kottler & Kottler, 2007).
2. Know students' legal rights and your responsibilities. Protect students' right to privacy. Do not discuss them casually in the lounge.
3. Report suspected abuse. Your role is not to gather evidence to erase doubt. You are legally bound to report *suspected* abuse. Do not rationalize to save yourself—or the family—the pain and trouble.
4. Work to secure appropriate services if you suspect that students' needs are going unmet. Be certain that you watch both male and female students and students of color to assess their potential for gifted programs and check for your own biases when you recommend counseling or other services.
5. Build meaningful partnerships with families and others who are experts. Commit to working as part of a team in the best interests of the students.
6. Begin with the attitude that you *can* serve as a positive influence on students' lives. If you do not know an answer, you can—and will—find one. Teachers with high degrees of **self-efficacy** tend to be more effective than ones who do not believe they can effect change.
7. Think about the long-term consequences of your actions, and consider your choices from a variety of perspectives.
8. Being a professional is more than being an employee. Do everything you need to do to help students learn.
9. Even if it feels like everyone else has, never give up.

Advocating for yourself means that you

1. Know your responsibilities, rights, and benefits. Read your contract. Understand how to obtain legal representation if you need it.
2. Are careful about being alone with students and using physical contact. Check local policies for the conditions under which it is acceptable to touch a student. Find out what to do if a student touches you in a way that makes you uncomfortable.
3. Are a team player. Find the good in each staff member. Steer clear of those who whine or complain, instead associating with these who view the profession with a positive outlook.
4. Volunteer for a committee or two that benefits the school. Do not sign up for every committee in your eagerness, though, because your students (and your personal life) will be shortchanged. Say "yes" to the commitments that you can accomplish well.
5. Strike a balance in your life. Your family—and your students—will benefit from your being well-rounded. See Teaching Tip 10.4 for some ideas for coping with stress.
6. Choose your battles. Not every insult to your sensibilities is worth a fight to the death.
7. Are on time. Stay as late as necessary to do a good job.

COPING WITH STRESS

When you feel stressed . . .

1. Remind yourself aloud that you have the skills to handle this. You've handled plenty of stressful situations.
2. Decide whether this issue is inside your circle of influence. If it isn't, let it go. Confine your worries to the things you can do something about.
3. Choose your reaction. You can't change what people do; you can only choose your own response.
4. Close your eyes and breathe. Three times. Deeply. In through your nose, out through your mouth. Then roll your head forward, left then right.
5. Go for a walk. Or do something else that totally changes your physical and mental location.
6. Think long-term. How much will this matter in a year? In 10 years?
7. Tell yourself what you have learned for next time.
8. Laugh.

8. Eat something healthy once in awhile and get enough sleep.
9. Have confidence in your ability to teach and to improve. Teachers who believe that they can learn, grow, and make a difference . . . do.

Advocating for yourself also includes continuing to press yourself to grow and change as a person and as a professional. Technology will probably figure prominently in your professional growth.

TECHNOLOGY AND GROWING IN YOUR PROFESSION

Technology is likely to play a number of roles in your professional growth. It will nudge you toward updating your technological skills. It will provide opportunities for professional development, and it will provide a variety of ways for you to engage in the professional community.

Technology places requirements upon all of us to become effective twenty-first-century citizens. Because our students are expected to become technologically competent, we as their teachers must build and implement the knowledge and skills that will assist them in doing so. It will, then, behoove you to frequently assess your own knowledge of the technology students are expected to master and to continue to update your skills in the hardware, software, and pedagogy that will allow us to model target competencies, provide instruction, and guide practice to allow students to hit those targets. Additionally, as you encounter students with different needs and as technology changes, it will behoove you to continue to search out and employ assistive and other technologies that will help each of your students succeed. It may help to set a reasonable goal for starting now: Choose one piece of hardware or software that can help you meet a specific need of one of your students. One example is software with text-to-speech capabilities. What do you know about text-to-speech software? Read about it. Watch a skilled teacher model its use. Observe a student interacting with it. Find personnel who can support you in using it. Make a plan to implement it in small steps in service of your students' learning.

In addition to helping you achieve the most important goal of encouraging students' learning, continuing to gain technological competence can also increase your desirability in the job market and allow you to contribute to life and learning at a particular school or district. Many teachers with interest and skill in technology become "technology leads" with plentiful opportunities to play leadership roles in their school communities. In these positions, teachers expand their professional influence by fostering learning for both students and teachers alike.

Technology also expands the avenues available to you for professional development. Informal and formal learning opportunities alike are a click away when you have access to the Internet. Informally, a logical place to begin research on an educational issue is the Internet. Do you wonder about RTI? A quick glance at answers.com (http://www.answers.com) or Wikipedia (http://www.wikipedia) can give you a thumbnail sketch, often composed by experts, of the issue and direct you toward more extensive resources for your research. It can also help you locate resources that could benefit your students. As a side note, it is important to use trustworthy Web sites and to triangulate multiple sources of information to obtain high-quality information from the Internet. In addition to a Web search, you may also maintain user privileges at your university's library and thus obtain scholarly and practical information while you surf at home or school.

More formally, you may decide to pursue professional development online. Are you teaching a unit that includes the Galapagos Islands? Copenhagen? Honolulu? Thanks to the Internet, you might find opportunities to travel and study with other educators, earning course credit to improve your content and pedagogical knowledge. Many organizations such as universities offer single courses, certificate programs, and entire graduate degree opportunities online. If you elect to pursue online instruction, be sure to evaluate the quality of the program as carefully as you would that of a traditional degree program. Review the course catalog or other documents and judge the course's or program's rigor, for example. Determine the program's accreditation status. Check the reputation of the program by speaking with knowledgeable colleagues and potential employers. Just as you would a face-to-face program, select online opportunities that are most likely to enhance your professional knowledge and skills and to open—rather than shut—the door to additional professional opportunities and perhaps further study.

Finally, technology can expand opportunities for you to engage in the community of education. Non-computer-based techno tools such as tape recorders and video recorders can allow you to communicate with families for whom reading English print is a difficult option. Some districts have automated phone systems that allow teachers (and other staff) to record a voice message and send it to a selected group of families, such as those of all students in a class or school. The Internet, too, expands our capacity to communicate with families via Web sites, e-mail, and grade books posted to the Web.

In addition to family members, technology also connects teachers to other members of the community. Chat rooms, electronic bulletin boards, and Web sites all allow us to interface with our colleagues near and far to deliberate practical, pressing, and enduring issues of education. You may have already established regular e-mail communication with your master teacher, mentor, or peers, and online discussions occur at many Web sites. One is the Web site of *Education Week* (http://Edweek.org), which, though fee-based, often hosts online sessions where experts discuss current education topics and respond to questions from the cyber-audience. Other chapters (recall Chapter 1) give Web sites for professional organizations that allow you to join the system of education.

In this, the final chapter, we consider one last time that just as technology presents us with a new issues and demands, it also presents a set of tools for us to use in addressing current issues; we see that technology presents both a set of directives and opportunities for us to grow as members of our profession.

SOME ADVICE FROM THE HEART

> Respect for the fragility of an individual life is still the first mark of the educated man.
>
> —*Norman Cousins*

You are entrusted with one of the greatest privileges I know: shaping young lives in the classroom. My deepest hope for you is that you will approach each day in the classroom with passion and with the burning desire to do one thing better than you did yesterday. My final words of advice for you come from me as a *citizen* who trusts you to bring up the next generation as an informed, compassionate group, as a *teacher* who expects you to lead students to discover the power and beauty of knowledge, and as a *parent* who speaks for others in believing that every day, when we release to your care our cherished children, you will provide a safe and loving atmosphere where their minds and spirits will be uplifted. My final suggestions are these:

1. *Listen to your students.* Teaching is more than telling. When one of my sons was very young, I needled his teacher at back-to-school night to hear some wonderful words about my precious son (remember, parents are ego involved). Her comment? "I am surprised he cannot cut." That teacher, it turns out, said many helpful, positive things about my child over the course of the school year. But at this early moment, I felt like I had been punched in the stomach. My son's teacher did not know that he sat on the couch at age 3 and sang "Nobody knows the troubles I've seen." She did not know that he asked about volcanoes on Mars. She knew he could not cut. She knew him in terms of what he could not yet do, in terms of his deficits. Please think about your students as people. Believe in them as knowers and learners. Listen to their stories. Entertain their questions. Even five-year-olds have lived a lifetime before meeting you.

2. *Be careful with the praise you give.* When you compliment a student, be genuine and specific. Your ultimate goal is not to shore students up with a steady stream of shallow and false praise. You are not the ultimate authority. You probably do not want your students to grow dependent on you—or anyone else—for judgments of their self-worth. Self-esteem should be based instead on students' own assessments of their work and abilities, on their own ability to judge a job done well. Help them recognize good work. Teach them to value themselves for who they are and what they can accomplish.

3. *Do not waste people's time.* You may be new. You may be learning. No doubt you will be better next year. But remember that this year is likely the only chance at 10th (or second or any) grade that your students will ever have. I can promise that some days in the classroom will feel like survival. If you begin to experience entire weeks during which you are searching for activities to keep students occupied, you are wasting people's time. Do not try to justify the educational benefits of a steady diet of word searches. You need to do better. Get some rest and start planning meaningful learning experiences.

4. *Stay only as long as you are effective.* Classroom teaching is not for everyone, and in many cases it is not forever. It is difficult to teach. Even expert teachers have bad days . . . and bad years. If you ever hate your job each morning, you need to change your life. You can change what you do in your classroom. You can change grade levels or school assignments. You can remain in education but leave the classroom. Or you can take your own set of skills and use them in a different field. It is not a disgrace to leave teaching. You will do everyone a service if you leave when it is time to go. There are many ways for each of us to contribute to the world.

> No bubble is so iridescent or floats longer than that blown by the successful teacher.
>
> —*Sir William Osler*

5. *Pull from inner resources.* My personal experience with classroom teaching is that it can bring tremendous emotional highs—watching a student learn can inspire awe—and lows. There may be times when even those who love you the most cannot pick you up after a tough day in the classroom. Instead, you will need to draw on your inner resources to reconsider your motivations and refresh your resolve to have a better day tomorrow. One of the devices I use when I need to encourage myself is a collection of

FIGURE 10.3 *Quotes that have helped me learn about teaching.*

(My apologies to those whose words I've misremembered over time.)

"Now that you have a child, you know how much I love you."

> —LuAnn Munns Berthel, my mother, who taught me in one sentence how deeply one can love.

"They're only children."

> —attributed to Gordon Guillaume, my father-in-law, by Beverly Guillaume, his wife. These words remind me that the job of a child, apparently, is sometimes purely to annoy.

"If you are committed to improving, you probably will."

> —Cheryl Bloom, my master teacher, who taught me to keep working at classroom discipline.

"'Stop worrying so much about *teachers'* questions, and start worrying about *students'* questions."

> —a rough paraphrase of five years with James T. Dillon, who taught me to listen.

"Interesting people do more than teach."

> —Carol Barnes, who taught me that well-educated people have a variety of interests in their lives.

"Assume that people are doing the best they can."

> —Jodi Elmore, my student teacher, who reminds me that I should approach people with the understanding that most of us just keep trying to do the best we can using what we have.

"What you focus on will grow."

> —Ernie Mendes, who reminds me to see people in terms of their strengths rather than in terms of their shortcomings.

Here's a lighter set I've composed to capture my own foibles.

Murphy's Laws for Teachers

1. Things take about two to three times longer than the time you have (or than you expected).
2. The lesson right before (or right after) the one your supervisor (or principal) observes is great.
3. Typos in memos to families are much easier to spot right after you send the papers home.
4. Someone will throw up before winter break.

quotes from people in my life who have helped me learn about teaching. Some of the deposits in my quote bank are shown in Figure 10.3. Try creating your own collection of quotes to provide some advice when you are in need.

6. *Look for the best.* Each person you encounter has something to add to your professional life. The students each offer their own funny idiosyncrasies and their fresh, rough-and-tumble view of the world. Your staff members have been in your place and have learned from it. Finally, *you* have something to contribute to the world through your teaching. Look for the best you have to offer and nurture it. Good wishes to you.

WEB SITES

http://www.ascd.org
Association for Supervision and Curriculum Develop-
ment. Go to "Education Topics" for information on a
number of current issues. A number of professional
development courses are available online.

http://www.bartleby.com/100/
Bartlett's Familiar Quotations, 10th ed. Also try
Creative Quotations (http://www.creativequotations
.com). Sites like these can help you locate
quotations to enhance your lessons and provide a
professional boost.

http://www.csos.jhu.edu/p2000/center.htm
The Center on School, Family, and Community
Partnerships at Johns Hopkins University. This site
includes research, success stories, and ideas for
building connections. Many materials are available
for sale.

http://www.gse.harvard.edu/hfrp/projects/family.html
Family-Schools Partnership Project at Harvard
University. This site includes research and resources
such as teaching cases to help families and schools
work together.

http://www.tc.columbia.edu/lessonstudy/lessonstudy.
html
Lesson Study Research Group. This site at Teachers
College at Columbia University site includes an
overview of the lesson study technique and many
resources for learning about it and becoming
involved in a study.

http://www.nationjob.com/education
Nation Job Network. This is the Education Jobs page.

http://www.pta.org
The National Teacher Parent Association. Includes
information on issues, news, and resources.

http://www.teachervision.com/lesson-plans/lesson-
3730.html
The Teacher Parent Collaboration section of Teacher
Vision Web site offers practical suggestions for
working with parents, including questionnaires and
handouts that can be used for parent education.

http://www.teacherleaders.org/Resources/profcomms.
html
The Teacher Leaders Network. A list of resources for
professional communities.

OPPORTUNITIES TO PRACTICE

1. Watch teachers work with family members by going
    to the Merrill Teacher Prep Web site Video
    Classroom. Choose between a fifth-grade parent
    conference (go to Foundations/Intro to Teaching,
    Module 2, Video 1) and an individual education
    plan (IEP) meeting (go to Special Education,
    Module 2, Video 1). What effective strategies did
    the school personnel employ throughout the
    meetings?

    a. How did the personnel indicate that they value
        the families' expertise?

    b. How did the personnel provide opportunities
        for family members to share their concerns
        and ideas?

    c. How did the personnel demonstrate a positive
        approach to planning for students' success?

    d. What else did you notice?

2. Interview a trusted, respected colleague for some
    advice on professional development. Share your
    work from the chapter-opening exercise and ask for
    insights.

3. Compose a letter to families. Have your principal
    read it over and then send it out.

    a. Introduce yourself.

    b. Let parents know how eager you are to work
        with their students.

    c. Ask families some questions that help you to
        understand their students and their hopes for
        the future.

    d. Include a tear-off portion to enlist family help.

Or, prepare a PowerPoint presentation for back-to-
school night or your own Web page.

4. Make an index card file or a spreadsheet with all of
    your students' names, addresses, and phone
    numbers as available. Develop a plan to contact
    each family throughout the year. Mark each card,
    or record a comment on the spreadsheet, as you
    make each contact.

5. Commit to one formal professional growth
    opportunity right now:

    a. Subscribe to one professional journal.

    b. Conduct research on an issue faced by one or
        more of your students.

    c. Attend a workshop.

    d. Join a professional organization.

    e. Take a field trip to another classroom on your
        site (or beyond).

    f. Write a reflection on your practice. Share it with
        your students.

6. Develop your own quotation collection.

7. How will you know whether you are improving in
    your teaching? Make a list of things you will accept
    as evidence that you are sharpening your
    professional skills. Consider using the self-analysis
    tool found in Figure 1.7 to reanalyze your practice.

GLOSSARY

access to the core curriculum With full access to the core curriculum, each student, including those acquiring English, comprehends instruction related to the academic content seen as central and makes progress in mastering that content.

accommodations Changes to classroom resources, instruction, or conditions that allow students to learn or to show what they know despite specific areas of need such as physical or learning disabilities. Accommodations do not change the learning expectations to which students are held.

accountability The idea that educators and schools should be held responsible for student mastery of the curriculum.

achievement gaps Marked and sustained discrepancies in the academic progress (typically measured by standardized tests) among the scores of certain subgroups of the student population.

active participation Strategies employed by the teacher during a lesson to ensure that every student overtly engages in and responds to the lesson.

analytical trait rubric An assessment tool that allows the reader to rate components of a performance separately, using criteria that are specific to each component.

Asperger syndrome A developmental disorder typified by repetitive behaviors and impaired social interactions.

assistive technology A wide range of built items (noncomputer-based) and computer-based hardware and software that aid people with physical disabilities in functioning, learning, and communicating.

audience response systems A digital technology wherein each audience member (student) has a remote control or other input device and uses it to vote on topics or answer closed-ended questions from the teacher. Each response is tabulated, and results are depicted as a projected image,
often through a graph. Results can be stored and printed.

backwards planning An approach to curricular planning that begins with the end product: the envisioned student performance. With this clear vision of what students should be able to do as a result of instruction, teachers plan instructional events. Specifying performance through rubrics created with students is often a component of backwards planning.

behavior (portion of objective) That portion of the objective that specifies, in observable terms, what the student will be able to do as a result of instruction. The expected student performance.

behavioral intervention plan (BIP) As mandated by IDEA, students with behaviors that impede their learning or the learning of others-as a manifestation of their disability-must receive a functional behavioral analysis and plan to address their behaviors in positive ways.

"big idea" approach An approach to unit planning in which the teacher begins with a focus on the major ideas or generalizations related to the content and then selects activities designed to help students develop those big ideas.

bilingual education programs Programs that teach the native language and target language as subject areas and use both languages as modes of communication. They are based on the conviction that students will learn content more quickly and have additional linguistic skills if they are taught in their native language alongside the target language. Use of the native language typically drops off as use of the target language increases.

caretaker speech Talk that has the purpose of clear communication. It focuses on immediate concerns rather than abstract or distant ideas and is adjusted syntactically to the current linguistic abilities of the listener. Caretaker speech is one way to provide comprehensible input for English learners.

certification The process by which K–12 educators gain official authorizations to teach. States vary in their certification requirements and processes.

classroom meeting A gathering in which all classroom participants have the opportunity to provide input to the agenda and the meeting itself. Classroom meetings can serve a number of purposes such as event planning, open discussion, and problem solving. The teacher facilitates, but students play an active leadership role.

concept map A graphic organizer that is hierarchically organized, presenting a major concept or idea and revealing the connections among the concept and its subconcepts.

conditions (portion of objective) The portion of the objective that specifies relevant aspects of the environment such as the materials, time, or resorces that will be available (or not) to students as they demonstrate mastery of the objective.

content standards Statements of the subject matter teachers are to teach and students are to master. Developed at different levels (national, state, and local), standards describe outcomes that students should demonstrate in given curricular areas throughout the grades.

criteria (portion of objective) The portion of the objective that specifies how well a student is to perform. Criteria provide the standard against which the student performance will be assessed. Criteria are often stated in terms of speed, accuracy, or quality.

criterion-referenced Assessments the compare students' performance to an external standard rather than to the performance of their peers.

critical attributes Those characteristics that define an object, organism, or phenomenon.

curricular integration The combination of two or more traditional content areas in a manner that reveals the connectedness of the subject matter. There are many approaches to curricular integration.

curriculum   That which students are expected to learn at school and that which they actually learn there.

curriculum compacting   An instructional approach undertaken with the aim of teaching only the content students have not previously mastered. The typical sequence is as follows: identification of learning goals, assessment of student progress related to those goals, provision of instruction to meet non mastered learning goals.

deductive strategies   Instructional approaches that move from general rules or principles to specific examples of those principles. Teachers present content directly, and students engage in a
carefully sequenced set of activities to ensure mastery.

deficit thinking   An approach to considering students or families in terms of their failings or in terms of what they do not know rather than in terms of the strengths and experiences they bring to the classroom that can serve as a springboard for further learning.

democratic classrooms   Classrooms where teacher and students share power and responsibility more equally than is the case in traditional classrooms. Shared decision making through democratic processes is an emphasis.

differentiated instruction   An approach to teaching that seeks to maximize student growth by beginning with each student's current knowledge and skills and offering a variety of learning experiences to help each student move forward. Experiences can vary in their difficulty
level, their topic, and their allowances for
students' preferences for learning and
expression.

differentiated instruction   An approach to instruction that provides a range of resources and activities designed to meet students' varying assessed needs and interests. Differentiated tasks should be engaging and challenging and should allow students to work in a variety of instructional formats. Instruction can be differentiated for *content* so that student learn different things, *process* so that they go about learning differently, or *product* so that they select among different ways to show their learning.

digital divide   persistent gaps in access to digital technologies among certain subgroups of the population.

digital natives   Prensky's (2001) term, used to refer to individuals who have grown up with ubiquitous access to digital technologies. Their counterparts are digital immigrants, who learn technologies later in life.

direct instruction   A deductive approach to instruction where the teacher states the major idea or skill early in the lesson and then systematically and explicitly leads students to mastery of the objective.

directed lesson   A lesson in which the teacher maintains careful control of the content, presents it explicitly to the students, and allows them to practice during the lesson as they work toward and demonstrate mastery of the lesson's objective.

dominant culture   In a region, the group of people whose ways of thinking and behaving are predominant. Factors such as historical precedence, population size, and social status influence which culture is dominant in an area at any point in time.

Educational Testing Service (ETS)   According to its Web site (http://www.ets.org), ETS is the world's largest private educational testing and measurement organization. ETS develops tests and other measures to provide information to test takers and other stakeholders. Examples of ETS tests include the Test of English as a Foreign Language (TOEFL), the SAT I and II (formerly the Scholastic Aptitude Test), and the Graduate Record Exam (GRE).

emotional intelligence   A person's ability to understand his own emotions and the emotions of others and to use this understanding in deciding how to act appropriately.

English learners   Students who are in the process of mastering English in addition to one or more other languages, including the home language. Also deemed English language learners.

essential question   A conceptual or overarching question that fans curiosity and frames study throughout an instructional unit. It should be phrased to capture major, enduring ideas related to the content.

ethics   Values related to human conduct in terms of what is right and wrong.

explicit curriculum   The content (knowledge, skills, and attitudes) that schools set out to teach. It is often contained in the adopted texts and other materials as well as in the daily activities selected by teachers and schools.

formative assessment   Assessment of student learning that yields results used to shape future instruction.

free and appropriate public education   A federal right of all U.S. students with disabilities. This right guarantees that each student's education is
paid for by the public (not the student or family) and that the education is suited to the needs of
the student.

funds of knowledge   The bodies of knowledge, social networks, and cultural resources found in students' homes and surrounding communities.

general education   General education classrooms are those in which students with no identified special needs are placed. Smaller numbers of students receiving special services are also typically found within general education classrooms, but general education teachers are not required to hold special certification. Instead, they work as part of a team with special educators to provide appropriate instruction for students with identified needs.

gifted   A student classified as gifted has been identified as possessing demonstrated or potential high ability in specific academic and other performance areas.

Gifted and Talented Education   Programs designed to meet the needs of students identified as academically gifted or otherwise talented. Such programs vary widely across districts and states and offer services through a wide variety of structures such as self-contained classrooms, gifted clusters, and resource programs.

graphic organizers   Visual presentations of information. The displays are organized to reveal important aspects of or patterns in the information. Graphic organizers can be developed by teachers and students at any phase during the instructional cycle.

high-stakes testing   Student or teacher assessments where the consequences are perceived to be very important to one or more groups of stakeholders. For students, grade retention or graduation are examples of high-stakes decisions that can result from their test scores.

highly qualified teachers   As stipulated by the No Child Left Behind act, highly qualified teachers (a) have demonstrated competence in each core subject area they teach, (b) hold at least a bachelor's degree, and (c) are fully licensed by the state.

holistic rubric   An assessment tool that allows the reader to give an overall rating to a performance. Performances are rated as being consistent with particular levels of overall quality.

Home schooling   The practice of educating students outside the school context, most notably within the home. Home schooling became legal in all U.S. states in 1993 and is a growing trend.

implicit curriculum   The lessons students learn without their teachers having consciously selected or taught them. Students learn the implicit curriculum by drawing inferences about correct ways to think and behave based on their experiences in schools.

Inclusion   A practice of educating students with disabilities-to the maximum extent possible-with their non disabled peers.

Individual education program (IEP)   A legally binding document that details the educational plan for a student who is identified as having one or more disabilities. The plan states the student's disability and provides present levels of performance, instructional objectives, assessment plans, and a statement of the least restrictive environment for the student. It is reviewed annually.

Individuals with Disabilities Education Act (IDEA) Formerly P.L. 94–142, this law requires all states that receive federal education funds to provide individuals with disabilities between the ages of 3 and 21 with a free and appropriate public education designed to meet the student's specific needs and prepare them for independence and employment.

induction programs   Programs designed to assist new teachers through the induction, or early, years of teaching.

inductive strategies   Instructional approaches that begin with specific data and help students find a rule or pattern. Discovery learning is an inductive strategy.

inquiry lesson   An inductive lesson wherein students pursue a question or problem by using scientific processes such as observation, inference, and hypothesis testing to arrive at one or more answers.

instructional strategies   Ways of arranging parts of a lesson according to particular patterns of student and teacher behaviors to accomplish certain goals. Some examples include inquiry, cooperative learning, and direct instruction.

interactional   Phenomena wherein parties affect each other through reciprocal action.

Interactive whiteboard   An electronic writing surface typically driven by a computer. It can capture and store the information recorded upon it, and it can be used to control (through touch) computer-generated images displayed on the screen.

learning styles   A combination of factors that together indicate how a person perceives information, interacts with it, and responds to the learning environment. Several schemes can be used to describe students' preferred learning styles.

learning centers   Stations designed for small groups of students to focus on particular content or activities. Students may all rotate through a series of centers, or students may work at centers that meet their interests or targeted needs.

least restrictive environment   Holds that students with disabilities should be educated with their non disabled peers to the maximum extent possible and should have access to the curriculum, activities, and programs available to non-disabled students. The severity of a student's disability determines the appropriate degree of restrictiveness in the educational environment. Restrictive environments are those that contain only students with disabilities.

linguistic   Of or pertaining to language.

literature circles   Essentially book clubs for students. Typically, students select from a variety of works (often fiction but increasingly nonfiction as well) and meet in small groups with assigned roles to study and appreciate their selected texts.

local assessments   Measures used with the intent of gathering information about student performance at the classroom, school, or district level. The purpose is not to compare student performance with that of students in other places, but to gather specific information related to local curricular and instructional efforts and student learning within the immediate context.

metacognition   Thinking about thinking. Understanding of one's own thinking.

mentors   Individuals who support the growth and development of less experienced peers, often in a partner relationship. Mentors can be formally assigned and complete a prescribed set of tasks, or they can work informally with their protegees and offer less structured support.

modifications   Changes to classroom resources, instruction, or conditions to allow students to learn or show what they know despite areas of need such as physical or learning disabilities. Modifications substantially alter the learning expectations to which students are held.

monitor   To actively observe students for specified purposes, often to ensure that they are safe and engaged in learning activities.

morals   Principles of right and wrong in relation to human conduct.

multimedia projects   Computer-based projects that combine different media such as sound, text, animation, and images to create an integrated product.

multiple embodiments   Varied examples of a single concept. Embodiments should be selected to portray the critical attributes of the concept.

multiple measures   A variety of assessment strategies used as part of a system to obtain a valid portrait of student performance and growth.

mutual accommodation   The notion that both the teacher and the students must actively work to learn about the members of the classroom community and the content. Through mutual accommodation, learning is not the sole responsibility of the student; the teacher must take an active role in learning about students and increasing her professional knowledge and skills to foster learning effectively.

National Assessment of Educational Progress (NAEP)
Conducted for more than 40 years, the NAEP is a test that provides information about how U.S. students achieve in various subject areas. Representative samples of students in private and public schools from all 50 U.S. states are assessed in grades 4, 8, and 12. Long-term trend data and data by state, subject area, and student subgroups are available. Data are not reported for individual students or schools.

National Board certification An advanced level of certification available to teachers across the nation. This optional certification process compares a teacher's practices to a set of standards through performance-based assessments such as portfolios, videotaped lessons, and student work samples. It also includes a written examination. Many states offer financial compensation for the application process and some sort of incentive for certified teachers.

National Board for Professional Teaching Standards (NBPTS) An independent, nonprofit, and nonpartisan organization comprised of teachers and other educational leaders. The NBPTS's core conviction is that the key to improving student learning is to strengthen teaching. The NBPTS developed performance-based assessments of teacher performance in relation to sets of professional teaching standards. See also *National Board certification.*

No Child Left Behind Act of 2001 Federal legislation that revises the Elementary and Secondary Education Act, first enacted in 1965 and modified at several other points in history. The act is designed to fuel gains in student achievement and hold states and schools more accountable for student progress. Students in low-performing schools are a special focus. The legislation increases the role of the federal government in education.

norm-referenced Assessments that compare one student's performance with that of others.

null curriculum The content that is not explicitly taught in schools. One example from many places in the United States, some may argue, is physical fitness in terms of whole-body wellness and skills. General patterns for the null curriculum exist based on factors such as geographical region, local values, and historical context. The null curriculum is also a product of an individual's idiosyncratic experiences in school.

off task A description of the behaviors students exhibit when they are engaged in activities other than those specified by the lesson objective or the task at hand.

on task A description of the behaviors students exhibit when they are actively engaged in activities related to the task at hand or the lesson objective.

opportunity gap Persistent discrepancies in the educational experiences afforded certain subgroups in the U.S. student population.

pacing guide A document that specifies the content to be addressed in a certain sequence for a given period of time, such as for the day, week, month, or term.

Praxis A series of Educational Testing Service tests for beginning teachers designed to measure academic skills (Praxis I, taken to enter a teacher education program), subject-matter knowledge (Praxis II, taken to demonstrate competence in the subject matter related to the prospective credential area), and classroom performance (Praxis III, completed for licensure).

preassessment See *preinstructional assessments.*

preinstructional assessments Measures used before instruction begins to determine students' current knowledge, attitudes, or skills. Preinstructional assessment results help teachers plan learning experiences that most closely address students' needs.

primacy effect The tendency for humans to remember the first stimuli or information to which they are exposed in a given situation.

proximity control Based on the fact that students who are physically farthest from the teacher tend to misbehave, proximity control has teachers moving closer to students to prevent and redirect misbehavior.

read-aloud The portion of the day in which teachers read text to the class, often for the primary purposes of fostering appreciation for the work and enjoyment in the act of reading. Can also refer to the selected text itself.

realia Real-life materials that can support students' understanding of the content. Examples include actual objects such as coins, tools, and articles of clothing.

recency effect The tendency for humans to remember the last stimuli or information to which they are exposed in a given situation.

reliable An instrument is reliable if it delivers consistent results. Reliable instruments yield similar results with different scorers and when given under varied conditions.

response to intervention (RTI) An educational approach that focuses on collecting data on student progress, providing a systematic instructional intervention, and then frequently assessing changes in student progress. Currently RTI can be used in place of or in addition to traditional means for determining specific learning disabilities.

reteach Efforts taken by a teacher to present content to students who did not master it as a result of an earlier presentation.

rubrics Sets of guidelines that specify the relevant criteria for a student product and indicate levels of performance.

school accountability The notion that schools should be held responsible for student achievement, usually determined by student test scores. Accountability typically is defined through rewards or punishments at varying levels, including, for example, financial incentives for high student performance or the takeover of schools that fail to demonstrate growth in student achievement.

School Report Card Mandated by No Child Left Behind, the report card is a document that must be made publicly available each year. It must specify, in understandable language, student performance at three levels (basic, proficient, and advanced), and must show achievement data by student sub group. The report card must also must disclose if the school has been identified as needing improvement or other action.

scope and sequence A section in teacher's editions of classroom texts that specifies the content that is addressed in the text (scope) and suggests plans for laying out the content over time (sequence). It is typically presented in the form of a chart that displays not only the grade level addressed in the text, but also its connection to the content of the text of other grade levels as well.

self-efficacy   One's own judgements of one's abilities to produce desired results, to succeed, or to control one's circumstances.

semantic   Of or pertaining to meaning.

service learning   Projects through which students continue their own learning of some content or topic by providing assistance related to the topic to individuals, groups, or organizations.

sheltered instruction   Instruction that "shelters" the linguistic demands of a lesson while simultaneously seeking to ensure that English learners master the content of the lesson. Sheltered instruction includes both discrete strategies such as teaching key vocabulary terms as well as general approaches such as building classroom environments where students feel safe to communicate.

simulation   An instructional strategy wherein students undergo a series of activities designed to replicate a real-life situation, the conditions faced within that situation, and the decision-making processes required to succeed in that situation.

social action   Planned efforts by individuals or groups to address social issues they hold as important.

social justice   An ideal that holds that all individuals and groups within a society should receive fair treatment and a just share of benefits of society.

Social Reconstructionism   A branch of educational thought that views schools as active agents to improve society. Schools, in this view, serve as transformers rather than as transmitters of the status quo. Notable proponents include George S. Counts and Harold Rugg.

sociocultural   An adjective that describes factors pertaining to both the social and cultural aspects of a phenomenon. Sociocultural elements describe those ways of behaving and living that are developed by people in groups and transmitted to future generations.

socioeconomic status   Some measure of a person's or group's income level and social class.

specific learning disabilities   Disabilities possessed by individuals who have adequate cognitive functioning in general and the ability to learn some things easily. Specific learning disabilities can relate to basic psychological processes involved in learning and using mathematics or in understanding and using spoken or written language.

speech or language disorders   Disorders related to the transfer of knowledge or information such as ideas and feelings. Speech disorders are specifically related to the verbal components of the communication process.

standards-based instruction   Teaching to a set of outcomes prescribed through local, state, or national content standards. Standards-based instruction may offer benefits such as uniformly high expectations for all students and close alignment among materials, instruction, and assessment. Potential drawbacks include a narrowing of the curriculum to what is prescribed in the standards and curriculum and lessons that are less responsive to local students and community needs.

student achievement   Student knowledge and skills, often as measured by test scores. Some people are concerned that achievement is currently construed too narrowly and should be more broadly conceived of through a variety of goals pertaining to student growth and how it is measured.

student-led conferences   In contrast to traditional teacher-led conferences with families, student-led conferences ask students to take the leadership role in sharing and evaluating their work and articulating their growth. Student-led conferences seek to engage students, parents, and teachers in dialogue about student learning by shifting the power away from the teacher, who acts as a facilitator at the conference, and more equally into the hands of the student and family members.

student performance standards   Explicit statements of the educational outcomes students are to attain. Typically student performance standards specify the content, behavior, and level at which students are expected to perform.

support provider   An experienced colleague who is formally assigned to assist a new teacher throughout the induction (or early) years in the teaching profession.

task analyze   To break a complex skill or idea into its subcomponents and order those subcomponents in a logical way. Teachers task analyze academic content in order to decide how to teach the complex task effectively.

teachable moment   An often unexpected opportunity for the teacher and students to explore an event or idea that arises from daily life or classroom events.

teacher testing   Efforts to assess teachers' professional knowledge and skills. Though teacher testing has a long history in America, interest in it has heightened with current concerns over accountability.

teacher's editions   The teachers' versions of classroom texts. Teachers editions typically include many kinds of assistance for teachers, including the answers to exercises, suggested lesson sequences, prompts for using the materials with students, and suggestions for reteaching or extending the material presented in the text.

textbook adoptions   The processes by which schools commit to using particular text series. Typically, state boards of education approve works from among competing publishers, and districts select from among the approved texts those they feel are most appropriate for their local setting. The adoption cycle allows schools to obtain current materials for a variety of subject areas after a set number of years.

thematic instruction   An approach that organizes curriculum around themes that cut across traditional subject areas rather than using the subjects themselves as the organizing principle.

think aloud   A strategy in which one describes one's thought processes while carrying out a target activity. The point is to help students sense the critical attributes of the target activity and the important decisions requried by it.

tracking   A practice of arranging students into stable, relatively homogeneous groups based on perceived ability or demonstrated achievement. Research on tracking suggest that it frequently does not improve achievement for students in the lower tracks, as these students often receive lower-quality instruction. Conversely, many teachers feel that tracking helps them meet students' needs better by reducing the range of performance in their classes.

trade books   Commercial books, often sold in bookstores.

unit   A collection of lessons that address a common goal or topic.

unschooling   An approach to education wherein learning is based on students' interests and goals rather than upon a set curriculum. Unschooling is often considered one form of home schooling, with adults providing resources and guiding students to access them as their needs and interests dictate.

valid   A measure is valid to the extent to which it measures what it is intended to measure.

REFERENCES

Adams, G. L., & Engelmann, S. (1996). *Research on direct instruction: 25 years beyond DISTAR*. Seattle, WA: Educational Achievement Systems.

Adams, J. (1780, May 12). Letter to his wife Abigail Adams. Retrieved May 6, 2007, from http://www.creativequotations.com.

Albert, L. (1996). *Cooperative discipline*. Circle Pines, MN: American Guidance Service.

Alexander, K., & Alexander, M. D.(2005). *American public school law* (6th ed.). Belmont, CA: Wadsworth.

Allchin, D. (2005). "Hands-off" dissection? *American Biology Teacher, 67*, 369–373.

Allen, J. B., Ed. (1999). *Class actions: Teaching for social justice in elementary and middle school*. New York: Teachers College Press.

Allen, R. (2003). The democratic aims of service learning. *Educational Leadership, 60*(6), 51–54.

Amrein, A. L., & Berliner, D. C. (2002). High-stakes testing and student learning. *Policy Analysis Archives, 10*(18) Retrieved May 6, 2007 from http://epaa.asu.edu.lib-proxy.fullertonedu/epaa/vlon/8/.

Amrein, A. L., & Berliner, D. C. (2003). The effects of high-stakes testing on student motivation and learning. *Educational Leadership, 60*(5), 32–38.

Anderson, L. W. (2005). Objectives, evaluation, and the improvement of education. *Studies in Educational Evaluation, 31*(2–3), 102–113.

Anderson, L. W. (Ed.), Krathwohl, D. R. (Ed.), Airasian, P. W., Cruikshank, K. A., Mayer, R. E., Pintrich, P. R., Raths, J., & Wittrock, M. C. (2001). *A taxonomy for learning, teaching, and assessing: A revision of Bloom's Taxonomy of Educational Objectives*. Boston: Allyn & Bacon.

Annenberg Institute for School Reform. (2004). Professional learning communities: Professional development strategies that improve instruction. Retrieved May 6, 2007, from http://www.annenberginstitute.org/images/ProfLearning.pdf.

Arter, J. A., & McTighe, J. (2001). *Scoring rubrics in the classroom: Using performance criteria for assessing and improving student performance*. Thousand Oaks, CA: Corwin Press.

Ashlock, R. B. (2005). *Error patterns in computation. Using error patterns to improve instruction* (9th ed.). Upper Saddle River, NJ: Merrill/Prentice Hall.

Atkin, J. M., Coffey, J. E., Moorthy, S., Sato, M., & Thibeault, M. (2005). *Designing everyday assessment in the science classroom*. New York: Teachers College Press.

Audet, R. H., & Jordan, L. K. (Eds.). (2005). *Integrating inquiry across the curriculum*. Thousand Oaks, CA: Corwin.

Bailey, J. M., & Guskey, T. R. (2001). *Implementing student-led conferences*. Thousand Oaks, CA: Corwin Press.

Baker, S., Gersten, R., & Lee, D. S. (2002). A synthesis of empirical research on teaching mathematics to low-achieving students. *The Elementary School Journal, 103*(1), 51–73.

Ball, B. (2003). Teaching and learning mathematics with an interactive whiteboard. *Micromath, 19*(1), 4–7.

Banks, J. (1997). *Teaching strategies for ethnic studies* (6th ed.). Needham Heights, MA: Allyn & Bacon.

Banks, J. A. (2005). Multicultural education: Characteristics and goals. In J. A. Banks and C. A. M. Banks (Eds.), *Multicultural education: Issues and perspectives* (5th ed, pp. 3–30). Hoboken, NJ: Wiley.

Barron, A. E., Hogarty, K. Y., Kromrey, J. D., & Lenkway, P. (1999). An examination of the relationships between student conduct and the number of computers per student in Florida schools. *Journal of Research on Computing in Education, 32*(1), 98–107.

Bartolome, L. I. (1994). Beyond the methods fetish: Toward a humanizing pedagogy. *Harvard Educational Review, 64*(2), 173–194.

Bateson, D. (1994). Psychometric and philosophic problems in "authentic" assessment: Performance tasks and portfolios. *Alberta Journal of Educational Research, 40*, 233–245.

Becker, R. R. (2000). The critical role of students' questions in literacy development. *Educational Forum, 64*, 261–271.

Bennett, C. I. (1995). *Comprehensive multicultural education: Theory and practice* (3rd ed.). Boston: Allyn & Bacon.

Benson, B., & Barnett, S. (2005). *Student-led conferencing using showcase portfolios*. (2nd ed.). Thousand Oaks, CA: Corwin Press.

Benzel, K. N. (Ed.). (1997). *Western landscaping book*. Menlo Park, CA: Sunset Books.

Berliner, D. (2006). Our impoverished view of educational research. *Teachers College Record, 108*, 949–995.

Berliner, D. C. (2004). Describing the behavior and documenting the accomplishments of expert teachers. *Bulletin of Science Technology and Society, 24*(3), 200–212.

Bilingual Education Act of 1994, Public Law No. 103–382. Section 7102.

Black, S. (2001). Ask me a question. How teachers use inquiry in the classroom. *American School Board Journal, 188*(5), 43–45.

Bloom, B., Englehart, M., Hill, W., Furst, E., & Krathwohl, D. (1956). *Taxonomy of educational objectives: The classification of education goals. Handbook I: Cognitive domain*. New York: Longman Green.

Blosser, P. E. (1990). Using questions in science classrooms. Research matters—to the science teacher. No. 9001. National Association of Research in Science Teaching. Retrieved May 6, 2007, from http://www.narst.org/publications/research/question.htm.

Bohn, C. M., Roehrig, A. D., & Pressley, M. (2004). The first days of school in the classrooms of two more effective and four less effective primary-grade teachers. *The Elementary School Journal, 104*, 269–287.

Bomer, R., & Bomer, K. (2001). *For a better world: Reading and writing for social action*. Portsmouth, NH: Heinemann.

Booher-Jennings, J. (2006). Rationing education in an era of accountability. *Phi Delta Kappan, 87*, 756–761.

Bowen, C. W. (2000). A quantitative literature review of cooperative learning effects on high school and college chemistry achievement. *Journal of Chemical Education, 77*(1), 116–119.

Brand, S., Dunn, R., & Greb, F. (2002). Learning styles of students with attention deficit hyperactivity disorder: Who are they and how can we teach them? *Clearing House, 75*(5), 268–273.

Bransford, J. (2000). *How people learn: Brain, mind, experience, and school.* Washington, DC: National Academy Press.

Bright, R. M. (2006). Literacy backpacks in teacher education: Launching support for home and school literacy. *Journal of Reading Education, 31*(2), 24–34.

Bromley, K., Irwin-De Vitis, L., & Modlo, M. (1995). *Graphic Organizers: Visual Strategies for active learning.* New York: Scholastic.

Brophy, J. (1997). Effective instruction. In H. J. Walberg & G. D. Haertel (Eds.), *Psychology and educational practice* (pp. 212–232). Berkeley: McCutchan.

Bruer, J. T. (1997). Education and the brain: A bridge too far. *Educational Researcher, 26*(8), 4–26.

Bruner, J. (1960). *The process of education.* Boston: Harvard University Press.

Bruner, J. (1986). *Actual minds, possible worlds.* Cambridge, MA: Harvard University Press.

Bruner, J. B., Goodnow, J. J., & Austin, G. A. (1960). *A study of thinking.* New York: John Wiley & Sons.

Burniske, R. W. (2000). Civil literacy and the cyber-pilot's license. *National Teaching & Learning Forum, 9*(5) (no page number). Retrieved May 6, 2007, from http://oira.syr.edu/cstl2/Home/ Teaching%20Support/Resources/Subscriptions/NTLF/V9n5/viewpoint.htm.

Buzzelli, C., & Johnston, B. (2001). Authority, power, and morality in classroom discourse. *Teaching and Teacher Education, 17,* 873–884.

Caine, G., & Caine, R. N. (2001). *The brain, education, and the competitive edge.* Lantham, MD: Scarecrow Press.

Caine, R. M., & Caine, G. (1994). *Making connections: Teaching and the human brain.* Menlo Park, CA: Addison-Wesley.

Caine, R. N., Caine, G., McClintic, C. L., & Klimek, K. J. (2005). *12 brain/mind learning principles in action.* Thousand Oaks, CA: Corwin.

Cairney, T. H. (2000). Beyond the classroom walls: The rediscovery of the family and community as partners in education. *Educational Review, 52*(2), 163–174.

Caldwell, J. S., & Ford, M. P. (2002). *Where have all the bluebirds gone? How to soar flexible grouping.* Portsmouth, NH: Heinemann.

California Department of Education. (2005). *Physical education model content standards for California public schools kindergarten through grade twelve.* Sacramento: California Department of Education.

California Department of Education. (2006). William's case. Retrieved May 6, 2007, from http://www.cde.ca.gov/eo/ce/wc/index.asp.

California Department of Education & California Association for the Gifted. (1994). *Differentiating the core curriculum and instruction to provide advanced learning opportunities.* Sacramento: California Department of Education. Retrieved May 6, 2007, from http://eric.ed.gov/ERICDocs/data/ericdocs2/content_storage_01/0000000b/80/23/2c/b9.pdf.

Canter, L. (1976). *Assertive discipline: A take-charge approach for today's educator.* Seal Beach, CA: Canter & Associates.

Cavanaugh, S. (2006, November 16). Technology helps teachers home in on student needs. *Education Week, 26*(12), 10–11. Retrieved May 6, 2007, from http://www.edweek.org/ew/articles/2006/11/15/12calculators.h26.html.

Cavanaugh, S. (2006 October 25). To tailor schedules, students log in to online classes. *Education Week, 26*(9), 1, 24. Retrieved May 6, 2007 from http://www.edweek.org/ew/articles/2006/10/25/09online.h26.html?qs=to_tailor_schedules.

Cazden, C. (1986). Classroom discourse. In M. Wittrock (Ed.), *Handbook of research on teaching* (3rd ed., pp. 432–462). New York: Macmillan.

Center for Applied Special Technology (CAST). (2006). What is Universal Design for Learning? Retrieved May 6, 2007, from http://www.cast.org/research/udl/index.html.

Center for Research on Education, Diversity & Excellence. (2002). The five standards for effective pedagogy. Retrieved May 6, 2007, from http://crede.berkeley.edu/standards/standards.html.

Center for the Study of Mathematics Curriculum. (2006). The intended mathematics curriculum as represented in state-level curriculum standards: Consensus or confusion? Executive summary. Retrieved May 6, 2007, from http://www.mathcurriculumcenter.org/st_std_exec_sum.pdf.

Center on Education Policy. (2006). From the capital to the classroom: Year 4 of the No Child Left Behind Act. Retrieved May 6, 2007, from http://www.cep-dc.org/nclb/Year4/CEP-NCLB-Report-4.pdf.

Centers for Disease Control and Prevention. (2004) Youth risk behavior surveillance—United States, 2003. MMWR Surveillance Summaries [Introduction] 2004; 53(SS02), pp 1–96. Retrieved May 6, 2007, from www.cdc.gov/mmwr/preview/ mmwrhtml/ss5302a1.htm.

Central Intelligence Agency. (2006). *The world factbook.* Retrieved May 6, 2007, from https://www.cia.gov/cia/publications/factbook/index.html.

Charles, C. M. (1992). *Building classroom discipline* (4th ed.). White Plains, NY: Longman.

Charney, R. S. (1997). *Habits of goodness.* Greenfield, MA: Northeast Foundation for Children.

Charney, R. S. (2002). *Teaching children to care: Classroom management for ethical and academic growth, K–8.* Greenfield, MA: Northeast Foundation for Children.

Chin, C., & Brown, D. E. (2000). Learning in science: A comparison of deep and surface approaches. *Journal of Research in Science Teaching, 37*(2), 109–38.

Chorzempa, B. F., & Graham, S. (2006). Primary-grade teachers' use of within–class ability grouping in reading. *Journal of Educational Psychology, 98,* 529–541.

Cochran-Smith, M. (2003). The unforgiving complexity of teaching: Avoiding simplicity in the age of accountability. *Journal of Teacher Education, 54*(1), 3–5.

Coffield, F., Moseley, D., Hall, E., & Ecclestone, K. (2004). *Learning styles and pedagogy in post-16 learning. A systematic and critical review.* London: Learning and Skills Research Centre. Retrieved May 6, 2007, from http://www.lsda.org.uk/files/PDF/1543.pdf.

Cole, R. W. (Ed.). (1995). *Educating everybody's children: Diverse teaching strategies for diverse learners. What research and practice say about improving achievement.* Alexandria, VA: Association for Supervision and Curriculum Development.

Coles, G. (July 2000). "Direct, explicit, and systematic"— bad reading science. *Language Arts, 77* 543–545.

Coloroso, B. (1994). *Kids are worth it! Giving your child the gift of inner discipline.* New York: William Morrow.

Cook, B. G. (2004). Inclusive teachers' attitudes toward their students with disabilities: A replication and extension. *The Elementary School Journal, 104*(4), 307–320.

Cortes, C. E. (2000). *The children are watching: How the media teach about diversity.* New York: Teachers College Press.

Costa, A., & Kallick, B. (Eds.). (2000). *Assessing and reporting on habits of mind.* Alexandria, VA: Association for Supervision and Curriculum Development.

Costa, J., Caldeira, H., Gallastegui, J. R., & Otero, J. (2000). An analysis of question asking on scientific texts explaining natural phenomena. *Journal of Research in Science Teaching, 37*, 602–614.

Cotton, K. (2001). Close-up #5: Classroom questioning School Improvement Research Series (SIRS): Research You Can Use. Northwest Regional Educational Laboratory Retrieved May 2, 2007 from http://www.nwrel.org/scpd/sirs/3/cu5.htm.

Cozzul, M. C., Freeze, R., Lutfiyya, Z. M., & Van Walleghem, J. (2004). The roles of nondisabled peers in promoting the social competence of students with intellectual disabilities in inclusive classrooms. *Exceptionality Education Canada, 14*(1) 23–41.

Csikszentmihalyi, M., & Csikszentmihalyi, I. S. (Eds.). (2006). *A life worth living: Contributions to positive psychology.* Oxford: Oxford University Press.

Cuban, L. (2006). The laptop revolution has no clothes. *Education Week, 26*(8), 29.

Cummins, J. (1981). The role of primary language development in promoting educational success for language minority students. In California State Department of Education (Ed.), *Schooling and language minority students: A theoretical framework* (pp. 3–49). Los Angeles: National Dissemination and Assessment Center. (ERIC Document Reproduction Service No. 249 773)

Cunningham, C. A., & Billingsley, M. (2003). *Curriculum webs: A practical guide to weaving the web into teaching and learning.* Boston: Allyn & Bacon.

Curwin, R., & Mendler, A. N. (2001). *Discipline with dignity.* Upper Saddle River, NJ: Merrill/Prentice Hall.

Danforth, S., & Smith, T. J. (2005). *Engaging troubling students: A constructivist approach.* Thousand Oaks, CA: Corwin.

Daniels, H. (2002). *Literature circles: Voice and choice in book clubs and reading groups* (2nd ed.). Portland, ME: Stenhouse.

Danielson, C. (1996). *Enhancing professional practice: A framework for teaching.* Alexandria, VA: Association for Supervision and Curriculum Development.

Darling-Hammond, L. (2000). Teacher quality and student achievement: A review of state policy evidence. *Educational Policy Analysis Archives, 8*(1). Retrieved May 6, 2007, from http://epaa.asu.edu/epaa/v8n1/.

Darling-Hammond, L., French, J., & Garcia-Lopez, S. (Eds.). (2002). *Learning to teach for social justice.* New York: Teachers College Press.

Davidman, L., & Davidman, P. T. (1997). *Teaching with a multicultural perspective: A practical guide.* New York: Longman.

DeBell, M., & Chapman, C. (2006). *Computer and Internet use by students in 2003 (NCES 2006-065).* U.S. Department of Education. Washington, DC: National Center for Education Statistics.

Delpit, L. (1995). *Other people's children: Cultural conflict in the classroom.* New York: New Press.

Dillon, J. T. (1987). Unpublished course syllabus for Education 139: Curriculum and Instruction, University of California at Riverside.

Dillon, J. T. (1988a). The remedial status of student questioning. *Journal of Curriculum Studies, 20*, 197–210.

Dillon, J. T. (1988b). *Questioning and teaching: A manual of practice.* New York: Teachers College Press.

Dillon, J. T. (1990). *The practice of questioning.* London: Routledge.

Din, F. S. (2000). Use direct instruction to improve reading skills quickly. *Rural Educator, 21*(3), 1–4.

Dorrell, L. D., & Busch, A. (2000). Censorship in schools: The impact of conservative Christian pressure. *Quest, 28*(3), 24–26.

Downing, J. E., & Eichinger, J. (2003). Creating learning opportunities for students with severe disabilities in inclusive classrooms. *Teaching Exceptional Children, 36*(1), 26–31.

Doyle, W. (1986). Classroom organization and management. In M. Wittrock (Ed.), *Handbook of research on teaching* (3rd ed., pp. 392–431). New York: Macmillan.

Dreikurs, R. (1968). *Psychology in the classroom* (2nd ed.). New York: Harper & Row.

Dreikurs, R., Grunwald, B., & Pepper, F. (1982). *Maintaining sanity in the classroom: Classroom management techniques* (3rd ed.). New York: Harper & Row.

Driscoll, M. P. (2002). *How people learn (and what technology might have to do with it).* ERIC Digest. (ERIC Document Reproduction Service No. ED470032 2002-10-00)

Driver, R. (1981). Pupils' alternative frameworks in science. *European Journal of Science Education, 3*, 93–101.

Driver, R. (1989a). Changing conceptions. In P. Adey (Ed.), *Adolescent development and school science.* London: Falmer.

Driver, R. (1989b). Students' conceptions and the learning of science. *International Journal of Science Education, 11*, 481–490.

Druck, K., & Kaplowitz, M. (2005). Preventing classroom violence. *Education Digest: Essential Readings Condensed for Quick Review, 71*(2), 40–43.

Duckworth, E. R. (1996). *The having of wonderful ideas and other essays on teaching and learning* (2nd ed.). New York: Teachers College Press.

Duffy, D. G. (1998, June). Teaching and the balancing of round stones. *Phi Delta Kappan, 79*, 777–780.

Dunn, M. A. (2000). Closing the book on social studies: Four classroom teachers go beyond the text. *Social Studies, 91*(3), 132–136.

Eastin, D. (2002). Students who serve. *American School Board Journal, 189*(4), 42–44.

Echevarria, J., & Graves, A. (1998). *Sheltered content instruction: Teaching English-language learners with diverse abilities.* Boston: Allyn & Bacon.

Echevarria, J., Vogt, M. E., & Short, D. (2004). *Making content comprehensible for English language learners: The SIOP model* (2nd ed.). Boston: Allyn & Bacon.

Education Commission of the States. (2000). *Every student a citizen: Creating the democratic self (executive summary).* Denver, CO: Education Commission of the States. Retrieved January 31, 2007, from http://www.ecs.org/clearinghouse/ 16/77/1677.pdf.

Education Week. (2006, May 4). The information edge: Using data to accelerate achievement. *Education Week, 25*(35), 8–9. Retrieved May 6, 2007, from http://www.edweek.org/ ew/ articles/2006/05/04/35intro.h25.html.

Educational Testing Service. (2002). Pathwise/Praxis III domains. Retrieved January 31, 2007, from http://www.ets.org.

Edwards, J., & Fraser, K. (1983). Concept maps as reflectors of conceptual understanding. *Research in Science Education, 13*, 19–26.

Edwards, J., Hartnell, M., & Martin, R. (2002). Interactive whiteboards: Some lessons from the classroom. *Micromath, 18*(2), 30–33.

Effrat, A., & Schimmel, D. (2003). Walking the democratic talk: Introduction to the special issue on collaborative rule making as preparation for democratic citizenship. *American Secondary Education, 31*(3), 3–15.

Eisner, E. (1979). *The educational imagination: On the design and evaluation of school programs* (3rd ed., pp. 87–107). Upper Saddle River, NJ: Merrill/Prentice Hall.

Eisner, E. (2006). The satisfactions of teaching. *Educational Leadership, 63*(6), 44–46.

Elias, M. J., & Arnold, H. (Eds.). (2006). *The educator's guide to emotional intelligence and academic achievement: Social-emotional learning in the classroom.* Thousand Oaks, CA: Corwin.

Ellis, A. K. (1998). *Teaching and learning elementary social studies* (6th ed.). Boston: Allyn & Bacon.

Elmore, R. F. (1979–1980). Backward mapping: Implementation research and policy decisions. *Political Science Quarterly, 94*, 601–616.

Emmer, E. T., Evertson, C., & Worsham, M. E. (2002). *Classroom management for secondary teachers* (6th ed.). Boston: Allyn & Bacon.

Emmer, E., Evertson, C., & Anderson, L. (1980). Effective classroom management at the beginning of the school year. *Elementary School Journal, 80*, 219–231.

Epstein, J. L. (2005). Developing and sustaining research-based programs of school, family, and community partnerships: Summary of five years of NNPS research. National Network of Partnership Schools. Retrieved May 6, 2007, from http://www.csos.jhu.edu/p2000/pdf/Research%20Summary.pdf.

Epstein, J. (2002). *School, family, and community partnerships: Your handbook for action* (2nd ed.). Thousand Oaks, CA: Corwin Press.

Erikson, E. (1968). *Identity: Youth and crisis.* New York: W. W. Norton.

Evertson, C., & Emmer, E. (1982). Effective classroom management at the beginning of the school year in junior high classes. *Journal of Educational Psychology, 74*, 485–498.

Fairlie, R. W., London, R. A., Rosner, M., & Pastor, M. (2006). *Crossing the divide: Immigrant youth and digital disparity in California.* University of California, Santa Cruz: Center for Justice, Tolerance, and Community. Retrieved May 6, 2007, from http://cjtc.ucsc.edu/docs/digital.pdf.

Faltis, C. (2001). *Joinfostering: Teaching and learning in multilingual classrooms* (3rd ed.). Upper Saddle River, NJ: Merrill/Prentice Hall.

Federation of American Scientists. (2006). Harnessing the power of video games for learning: Summit on educational games. Retrieved May 6, 2007, from http://fas.org/gamesummit/Resources/Summit%20-on%20Educational%20Games.pdf.

Fields, L. (2004). Handling student fights. *The Clearinghouse, 77*(3), 108–110.

Fillmore, L. W. (1982) Instructional language as linguistic input: Second language learning in classrooms. In L. C. Wilkinson (Ed.), *Communicating in the classroom* (pp. 283–296). New York: Academic Press.

Finkel, D. L. (2000). *Teaching with your mouth shut.* Portsmouth, NH: Boynton/Cook.

Fischer, L., Schimmel, D., & Kelly, C. (1999). *Teachers and the law* (5th ed.). New York: Longman.

Flowers, C. P., Hancock, D. R., & Joyner, R. E. (2000). Effects of instructional strategies and conceptual levels on students' motivation and achievement in a technology course. *Journal of Research and Development in Education, 33*(3), 187–194.

Fordham Foundation. (2006). How well are states educating our neediest children? The Thomas F. Fordham Foundation. Retrieved May 6, 2007 from http://www.fordhamfoundation.org/doc/TFR06FUL-LREPORT.pdf.

Frank, C. (1999). *Ethnographic eyes: A teacher's guide to classroom observation.* Portsmouth, NH: Heineman.

Frederickson, N., Warren, L., & Turner, J. (2005). "Circle of friends"—an exploration of impact over time. *Educational Psychology in Practice, 21*(3), 197–217.

French, J. R. P., & Raven, B. (1959). Bases of social power. In D. Cartwright (Ed.), *Studies in social power.* Ann Arbor, MI: University of Michigan.

Frey, N., Fisher, D., & Moore, K. (2005). *Designing responsive curriculum: Planning lessons that work.* Lanham, MD: Rowman & Littlefield Education.

Fuchs, D., & Fuchs, L. S. (2005). Responsiveness-to-interventions: A blueprint for practitioners, policymakers, and parents. *Teaching Exceptional Children, 38*(1), 57–61.

Fuchs, L. S., Fuchs, D., Hamlett, C. L., Phillips, N. B., & Bentz, J. (1994). Class-wide curriculum-based measurement: Helping general educators meet the challenge of student diversity. *Exceptional Children, 60*, 518–537.

Fuhrman, S., & Lazerson, M. (Eds.). (2005). *The public schools.* Oxford, NY: Oxford University Press.

Fulghum, R. (1988). *All I really need to know I learned in kindergarten: Uncommon thoughts on common things.* New York: Villard Books.

Gagne, R. (1985). *The conditions of learning* (4th ed.). New York: Holt, Rinehart & Winston.

Gagnon, G. W., Jr., & Collay, M. (2001). *Designing for learning: Six elements in constructivist classrooms.* Thousand Oaks, CA: Corwin Press.

Gardner, H. (1983). *Frames of mind: The theory of multiple intelligences.* New York: Basic Books.

Gardner, H. (1993). *Multiple intelligences: The theory in practice.* New York: Basic books.

Gardner, H. (1999). *Intelligence reframed: Multiple intelligences for the 21st century.* New York: Basic Books.

Gardner, H. (2006). *Multiple intelligences: New horizons.* New York: Basic Books.

Gardner, J. E., Wissick, C. A., Schweder, W., Canter, L. S. (2003). Enhancing interdisciplinary instruction in general and special education. *Remedial & Special Education, 24*(3), 161–172.

Garrett, J. L. (2006). Educating the whole child. *Kappa Delta Pi Record, 42*(4), 154–155.

Gatto, J. T. (1992). *Dumbing us down: The hidden curriculum of compulsory schooling.* Philadelphia: New Society *Publishers.*

Gatto, J. T. (2001). The underground history of American education: A schoolteacher's intimate investigation into the problem of modern schooling. New York: Oxford Village Press.

Gega, P. C., & Peters, J. M. (2002). *Science in elementary education* (9th ed.). Upper Saddle River, NJ: Merrill/Prentice Hall.

Glasser, W. (1986). *Control Theory in the Classroom*. New York: Harper & Row.

Glasgow, N. A. (1997). *New curriculum for new times: A guide to student–centered, problem-based learning*. Thousand Oaks, CA: Corwin Press.

Goleman, D. (1995). *Emotional intelligence*. New York: Bantam Books.

Goleman, D. (1998). *Working with emotional intelligence*. New York: Bantam Books.

Gonzalez, N., Andrade, R., Civil, M., & Moll, L. (2001). Bridging funds of distributed knowledge: Creating zones of practices in mathematics. *Journal of Education for Students Placed at Risk (JESPAR)*, 6(1–2), 115–132.

Good, T. L., & Brophy, J. E. (1987). *Looking in classrooms* (4th ed.). New York: Harper & Row.

Good, T. L., & Brophy, J. E. (2000). *Looking in classrooms* (8th ed.). New York: Longman.

Goodlad, J. (1984). *A place called school*. New York: McGraw-Hill.

Goodlad, J. I. (1990). The occupation of teaching in schools. In J. I. Goodlad, R. Soder, & K. A. Sirotnik (Eds.), *The moral dimensions of teaching*. San Francisco: Jossey-Bass.

Goodlad, J. I. (1997). *In praise of education*. New York: Teachers College Press.

Gootman, M. E. (2001). *The caring teacher's guide to discipline: Helping young students learn self-control, responsibility, and respect* (2nd ed.). Thousand Oaks, CA: Corwin Press.

Gordon, T. (1974). *Teacher effectiveness training*. New York: David McKay.

Grant, C. A., & Sleeter, C. E. (1998). *Turning on learning: Five approaches for multicultural teaching plans for race, class, gender, and disability* (2nd ed.). Upper Saddle River, NJ: Merrill/Prentice Hall.

Grant, C. A., (Ed.). (1995). *Educating for diversity: An anthology of multicultural voices*. Boston: Allyn & Bacon.

Green, T. D., & Brown, A. (2002). *Multimedia projects in the classroom: A guide to development and evaluation*. Thousand Oaks, CA: Corwin.

Gregory, G. H., & Kuzmich, L. (2004). *Data driven differentiation in the standard-based classroom*. Thousand Oaks, CA: Corwin.

Grisham-Brown, J., Hallam, R., & Brookshire, R. (2006). Using authentic assessment to evidence children's progress toward early learning standards. *Early Childhood Education Journal, 34*(1), 45–51.

Gronlund, N. E. (2004). *Writing instructional objectives for teaching and assessment* (7th ed.). Upper Saddle River, NJ: Merrill/Prentice Hall.

Guillaume, A. M., & Kirtman, L. (2005). Learning lessons about lessons: Preservice elementary teachers' memories of mathematics instruction. *Teaching Children Mathematics, 11*, 302–309.

Guillaume, A. M., & Spencer, B. (2006, April). Developing science vocabulary through the learning cycle. Session presented at the annual meeting of the National Science Teachers Association, Anaheim, CA.

Guillaume, A. M., Yopp, R., & Twardos, K. (2006). Helping new teachers: Forging family links. Presentation at the State BTSA and Intern Directors' Meeting, Sacramento, CA.

Guillaume, A. M., Yopp, R. H., & Yopp, H. K. (1996). Accessible science. *Journal of Educational Issues for Language Minority Students, 17*, 67–85.

Guillaume, A. M., Yopp, R. H., & Yopp, H. K. (2007). *50 strategies for active teaching: Engaging K –12 learners in the classroom*. Upper Saddle River, NJ: Merrill/Prentice Hall.

Guskey, T. (2002). Computerized gradebooks and the myth of objectivity. *Phi Delta Kappan, 83*, 775–780.

Haar, J., Hall, G., Schoepp, P. & Smith, D. H. (2002). How teachers teach to students with different learning styles. *Clearing House, 75*(3), 142–145.

Hall, P. S., & Hall, N. D. (2003). *Educating oppositional and defiant children*. Alexandria, VA: Association for Supervision and Curriculum Development.

Hall, T., & Stegila, A. (2003). *Peer mediated instruction and intervention*. Wakefield, MA: National Center on Accessing the General Curriculum. Retrieved May 6, 2007, from http:// www.cast.org/publications/ncac/ ncac_peermii.html.

Hamm, M., & Adams, D. (2002). Collaborative inquiry: Working toward shared goals. *Kappa Delta Pi Record, 38*(3), 115–118.

Hargreaves, M., Shorrocks-Taylor, D., Swinnerton, B., Tait, K., & Threlfall, J. (2004). Computer or paper? That is the question: Does the medium in which assessment questions are presented affect children's performance in mathematics? *Educational Research, 46*(1), 29–42.

Harrison, G., Andrews, J., & Saklofske, D. (2003). Current perspectives on cognitive and learning styles. *Education Canada, 43*(2), 44–47.

Harrow, A. (1969). *A taxonomy of the psychomotor domain: A guide for developing behavioral objectives*. New York: David Mckay.

Hawkins, J. (2002). The pit boss: A new Native American stereotype? *Multicultural Education, 9*(4), 15–17.

Hebert, E. A. (2001). *The power of portfolios: What children can teach us about learning and assessment*. San Francisco: Jossey-Bass.

Henderson, M. T., & Mapp, K. L. (2002). *A new wave of evidence: The impact of school, family, and community connections on student achievement*. Austin, TX: National Center for Family & Community Connections with Schools and Southwest Educational Development Laboratory. Retrieved May 6, 2007, from http://www.sedl.org/ connections/resources/evidence.pdf.

Herman, J. L., Aschbacher, P. R., & Winters, L. (1992). *A practical guide to alternative assessment*. Alexandria, VA: Association for Supervision and Curriculum Development.

Herman, J. L., Osmundson, E., Ayala, C., Schneider, S. & Timms, S. M. (2006). *The nature and impact of teachers' formative assessment practices. CSE Report 703*. Los Angeles: CRESST/University of California.

Hill, J. D., & Flynn, K. M. (2006). *Classroom instruction that works with English language learners*. Alexandria, VA: Association for Supervision and Curriculum Development.

Hobbs, R. (2006). Non-optimal uses of video in the classroom. *Learning, Media & Technology, 31*(1), 35–50.

Hoffman, M. (1979). Development of moral thought, feeling, and behavior. *American Psychologist, 34*, 958–968.

Holt, J. C. (2004). *Instead of education: Ways to help people do things better*. Boulder, CO: Sentient Publications.

Hoover, R. L., & Kindsvatter, R. (1997). *Democratic discipline: Foundation and practice*. Upper Saddle River, NJ: Merrill/Prentice Hall.

Horgan, D. D. (1995). *Achieving gender equity: Strategies for the classroom*. Boston: Allyn & Bacon.

Horton, P.B., McConney, A. A., Gallo, M., Woods, A.L., Senn, G.J., & Hamelin, D. (1993). An investigation of the effectiveness of concept mapping as an instructional tool. *Science Education 77*(1) 95–111.

Howell, K. W., Bigelow, S., Moore, E., & Evoy, A. (1993). Bias in authentic assessment. *Diagnositique, 19*, 387–400.

Hunter, M. (1982). *Mastery teaching.* El Segundo, CA: Instructional Dynamics.

Hurt, J. (2003). *Taming the standards: A commonsense approach to higher student achievement, K–12.* Portsmouth, NH: Heinemann.

International Society for Technology Education. (1998). Technology standards for students. Retrieved May 6 2007, from http://cnets.iste.org/docs/ NETSUM.pdf.

Jackson, L. & Panyan, M. V. (2002). *Positive behavioral support in the classroom.* Baltimore: Paul H. Brookes.

Jackson, P. (1986). *The practice of teaching.* New York: Teachers College Press.

Jacob, E. (1999). *Cooperative learning in context: An educational innovation in everyday classrooms.* Alban; State University of New York Press.

Jehlen, A. (2000). Science texts flunk the test. *NEA Today, 18*(7), 29.

Jensen, E. (2000). Brain-based learning: A reality check. *Educational Leadership, 57*(7), 76–80.

Jensen, E. (2005). *Teaching with the brain in mind.* Alexandria, VA: Association for Supervision and Curriculum Development.

Jeynes, W. H. (2005). A meta-analysis of the relation of parental involvement to urban elementary school student academic achievement. *Urban Education, 40,* 237–269.

Johnson, D. W., & Johnson, R. T. (1999). *Learning together and alone: Cooperative, competitive, and individualistic learning* (5th ed.). Boston: Allyn & Bacon.

Johnson, D. W., & Johnson, R. T. (2004). Implementing the "Teaching Students to Be Peacemakers Program." *Theory into Practice, 43*(1), 68–79.

Jones, F. (1987). *Positive classroom discipline.* New York: McGraw-Hill.

Jones, F. (2000). *Tools for teaching: Discipline, instruction, motivation.* Santa Cruz, CA: Frederic H. Jones & Associates.

Jones, R. (2000). Textbook troubles. *American School Board Journal, 187*(12), 18–21.

Kagan, S. (1994). *Cooperative learning.* San Juan Capistrano, CA: Kagan Cooperative Learning.

Kagan, S. (2000). *Silly sports and goofy games.* San Clemente, CA: Kagan Publishing.

Kajder, S. (2006). *Bringing the outside in: Visual ways to engage reluctant readers.* Portland, ME: Stenhouse.

Kaplan, S. (2003). Advocacy as teaching: The teacher as advocate. *Gifted Child Today, 26*(3).

Keller, J. B., & Bichelmeyer, B. A. (2004). What happens when accountability meets technology integration. *TechTrends: Linking Research & Practice to Improve Learning, 48*(3), 17–24.

Kidder, R. M., & Born, P. L. (1998–1999, December– January). Resolving ethical dilemmas in the classroom. *Educational Leadership, 56*(4), 38–41.

King, M. L., Jr. (1947). *The purpose of education.* Excerpted in the Papers of Martin Luther King., The Martin Luther King, Jr. Papers Project, Stanford University. Retrieved May 6, 2007, from http://www. stanford.edu/group/King/Publications/ papers/vol1/ 470100-The_Purpose_of_Education.htm

Kingston, P. W., Hubbard, R., Lapp, B., Schroeder P., & Wilson, J. (2003). Why education matters. *Sociology of Education, 76*(1), 53–70.

Kleiner, A., & Lewis, L. (2004). Internet access in U.S. public schools and classrooms: 1994–2002. *Education Statistics Quarterly, 5*(4). Retrieved May 6, 2007, from http://nces.ed.gov/programs/ quarterly/vol_5/5_4/2_2.asp.

Kliebard, H. M. (2002). *Changing course: American curriculum reform in the 20th century.* New York: Teachers College Press.

Kohlberg, L. (1963). *Essays on moral development.* San Francisco, CA: Harper & Row.

Kohn, A. (1996). *Beyond discipline: From compliance to community.* Alexandria, VA: American Society of Curriculum and Development.

Kohn, A. (1998). Beyond bribes and threats: How not to get control of the classroom. *NAMTA Journal, 23*(1), 6–61.

Kohn, A. (1999). *The schools our children deserve: Moving beyond traditional classrooms and "tougher standards."* Boston: Houghton Mifflin.

Kohn, A. (1999, September). Constant frustration and occasional violence. *American School Board Journal, 186*(9), 20–24.

Kohn, A. (2001). Fighting the tests. *Phi Delta Kappan, 82*(5), 348–347.

Kottler, J. A. (1997). *What's really said in the teacher's lounge: Provocative ideas about cultures and classrooms.* Thousand Oaks, CA: Corwin Press.

Kottler, J. A. (2002). *Students who drive you crazy.* Thousand Oaks, CA: Corwin.

Kottler, J. A., & Kottler, E. (2007). *Counseling skills for teachers.* Thousand Oaks, CA: Corwin.

Kounin, J. (1977). *Discipline and group management in classrooms.* New York: Holt, Rinehart & Winston.

Kounin, J. (1983, November). Classrooms: Individuals or behavioral settings? *Monographs in Teaching and Learning.* Bloomington, IN: Indiana University.

Kovalik, S. (1993). *ITI: The model. Integrated Thematic Instruction* (2nd ed.). Village of Oak Creek, AZ: Books for Educators.

Kovalik, S. J., & Olsen, K. D. (2001). *Exceeding expectations: A user's guide to implementing brain research in the classroom.* (3rd ed.). Federal Way, WA: Books for Educators.

Kozol, J. (1991). *Savage inequalities: Children in America's schools.* New York: Crown.

Kozol, J. (2000). An unequal education. *School Library Journal, 46*(5), 46–49.

Kozol, J. (2005). *The shame of the nation: The restoration of apartheid schooling in America.* New York: Crown.

Krashen, S. (1997). Why bilingual education? ERIC Digest. Retrieved May 6, 2007, from http://ericae.net/ericdb/ED403101.htm.

Krashen, S. D. (1981). *Second language acquisition and second language learning.* Pergamon Press. Retrieved May 6, 2007, from http://www. sdkrashen.com/ SL_Acquisition_and_Learning/index.html.

Krathwohl, D., Bloom, B., & Masia, B. (1964). *Taxonomy of educational objectives: The classification of educational goals. Handbook II: Affective domain.* New York: David McKay.

Kulik, C., & Kulik, J. A. (1982). Effects of ability grouping on secondary schools and students: A meta-analysis of evaluation findings. *American Educational Research Journal, 19,* 415–428.

Kulik, C. C., & Kulik, J. A. (1991). Effectiveness of computer-based instruction: An updated analysis. *Computers in Human Behavior, 7*(1–2), 75–94.

Kulik, J. A. (1993, Spring). An analysis of the research on ability grouping. *The National Research Center on the Gifted and Talented Newsletter,* 8–9.

Kulik, J. A., & Kulik, C. L. (1989). Effects of ability grouping on Student achievement. *Equity and Excellence, 23*(1–2), 22–30.

LaCelle-Peterson, M., & Rivera, C. (1994). Is it real for all kids? A framework for equitable assessment policies for English language learners. *Harvard Educational Review, 64*(1), 55–75.

Lachat, M. A. (2004). *Standards-based instruction and assessment for English language learners.* Thousand Oaks, CA: Corwin.

Laczko-Kerr, I., & Berliner, D. C. (2002). The effectiveness of "Teach for America" and other under-certified teachers on student academic achievement: A case of harmful public policy. *Education Policy Analysis Archives, 10*(37). Retrieved May 6, 2007 from http://epaa.asu.edu/epaa/v10n37.

Laczko-Kerr, I., & Berliner, D. C. (2003). In harm's way: How undercertified teachers hurt their students. *Educational Leadership, 60*(8), 34–39.

Ladson-Billings, G. (2003, March). I used to love science...and then I went to school: The challenge of school science in urban schools. Plenary Session at the Annual Meeting of the National Association for Research in Science Teaching, Philadelphia, PA.

Ladson-Billings, G. (2006). From the achievement gap to the education debt: Understanding achievement in U.S. schools. *Educational Researcher, 35*(7), 3–12.

Laitsch, D. (2006). Assessment, high stakes, and alternative visions: Appropriate use of the right tools to leverage improvement. Education Policy Research Unit, EPSL-0611-222-EPRU. Retrieved May 6, 2007, from http://epsl.asu.edu/epru/ documents/EPSL-0611-222-EPRU.pdf.

Lambros, A. (2002). *Problem-based learning in K–8 classrooms.* Thousand Oaks, CA: Corwin.

Lane, K. L., Pierson, M. R., & Givner, C. C. (2003). Teacher expectations of student behavior: Which skills do elementary and secondary teachers deem necessary for success in the classroom? *Education and Treatment of Children, 26*, 413–430.

Lau v. Nichols, 1974, Public Law 414, U.S. 563.

Layton, C. A., & Lock, R. H. (2007). 20 ways to . . . Use authentic assessment techniques to fulfill the promise of No Child Left Behind. *Intervention in School and Clinic, 42*(3), 169–173.

Lazarus, W., & Mora, F. (2000). *Online content for low-income and underserved Americans: The digital divide's new frontier. A strategic audit of activities and opportunities.* Santa Monica, CA: Children's Partnership. (ERIC Document Reproduction Service No. ED 440 190)

Lee, J. (2006). *Tracking achievement gaps and assessing the impact of NCLB on the gaps: An indepth look into national and state reading and math outcome trends.* Cambridge, MA: The Civil Rights Project at Harvard University.

Lenski, S. D. (2001). Intertextual connections during discussions about literature. *Reading Psychology, 22*(4), 313–335.

Levy, T. (2000). Lookout point: The character of their content. *Social Education, 64*(5), 2.

Lewis, R. (2001). Classroom discipline and student responbibility: The students' view. *Teaching and Teacher Education, 17*, 307–319.

Lewis, C., Perry, R., & Hurd, J. (2004). A deeper look at lesson study. *Educational Leadership, 61*(5), 6–11.

Lewis, T., Sugai, G. & Colvin, G. (1998). Reducing problem behavior through a school-wide system of effective behavioral support: Investigation of a school-wide social skills training program and contextual interventions. *School Psychology Review, 27*(3), 446–459.

Lieberman, L. J., James, A. R., & Ludwa, N. (2004). The impact of inclusion in general physical education for all students. *Journal of Physical Education Recreation and Dance, 75*(5), 37–42.

Lincoln, M. (2002). *Conflict resolution communication.* Laham, MD: Scarecrow Education.

Loewen, J. W. (1996). *Lies my teacher told me: Everything your American history textbook got wrong.* New York: Simon & Schuster.

Lou, Y., Abrami, P., Spence, J. C., Poulsen, C., Chambers, B., & d'Apolliana, S. (1996). Within-class grouping: A meta-analysis. *Review of Educational Research, 66*, 423–458.

MacIver, M. A., & Kemper, E. (2002). The impact of direct instruction on elementary students' reading achievement in an urban school district. *Journal of Education for Students Placed at Risk, 7*(2), 197–220.

Mager, R. F. (1997). *Preparing instructional objectives. A critical tool in the development of effective instruction* (3rd ed.). Atlanta: Center for Effective Performance.

Maheady, L., Michielli-Pendl, J., Mallette, B., & Harper, G. F. (2002). A collaborative research project to improve the academic performance of a diverse sixth grade science class. *Teacher Education and Special Education, 25*(1), 55–70.

Maloney, R. S. (2002). Virtual fetal pig dissection as an agent of knowledge acquisition and attitudinal change in female high school biology students. Unpublished doctoral dissertation for New Orleans University. Retrieved May 6, 2007, from http://louisdl.louislibraries.org/cgi-bin/showfile.exe?CISOROOT=/NOD&CISOPTR=29&filename=30.pdf.

Manning, S. (2006). Recognizing gifted students: A practical guide for teachers. *Kappa Delta Pi Record, 42*(2), 64–68.

Markow, D., & Martin, S. (2005). The MetLife survey of the American teacher, 2004–2005: Transitions and the role of supportive relationships. Retrieved May 6, 2007, from http://www.metlife.com/ WPSAssets/34996838801118758796V1FATS_2004.pdf.

Markow, D., & Scheer, M. (2002). The MetLife survey of the American teacher, 2002: Student life—school. Retrieved May 6, 2007, from http://www. metlife.com/WPSAssets/11738669411033654558V1FBook%20v.3.pdf.

Marlowe, B. A., & Page, M. L. (1998). *Creating and sustaining the constructivist classroom.* Thousand Oaks, CA: Corwin Press.

Marx A., Fuhrer U., & Hartig T. (1999). Effects of classroom seating arrangements on children's question-asking. *Learning Environments Research, 2*, 249–263.

Marzano, R. J. (2004). *Building background knowledge for academic achievement.* Alexandria, VA: Association of Supervision and Curriculum Development.

Marzano, R. J., & Kendall, J. S. (1998). *Implementing standards-based education.* Washington, DC: National Education Association.

Marzano, R. J., Pickering, D. J., & Pollock, J. E. (2001). *Classroom instruction that works: Research-based strategies for increasing student achievement.* Alexandria, VA: Association for Supervision and Curriculum Development.

Matsumura, L. C., & Pascal, J. (2003). *Teachers' assignments and student work: Opening a window on classroom practice.* CSE Report 602. Los Angeles: CRESST/University of California.

McCarthy, M. M., Cambron-McCabe, N. H., & Thomas, S. B. (1998). *Public school law: Teachers' and students' rights* (4th ed.). Boston: Allyn & Bacon.

McDaniel, T. R. (1979). The teacher's ten commandments: School law in the classroom. *Phi Delta Kappan, 60,* 703–708.

McIntosh, R., Vaughn, S., Schumm, J., Haager D., & Lee, O. (1993). Observations of students with learning disabilities in general education classrooms. *Exceptional Children, 60,* 249–261.

Medina-Jerez, W., Clark, D. B., & Medina, A. (2007). Science for ELLs: Rethinking our approach. *The Science Teacher, 74*(3), 52–56.

Metiri Group. (2006). Technology in schools: What the research says. Cisco Systems. Retrieved May 6, 2007, from http://www.cisco.com/web/strategy/docs/education/TechnologyinSchoolsReport.pdf.

Metropolitan Life Insurance Company. (2002). *The Metlife survey of the American teacher. Student life: School, home and community.* New York: Author. Retrieved May 6, 2007, from http://www.metlife. com/Applications/Corporate/WPS/CDA/PageGenerator/0,1674,P2817,00.html.

Meyer, L. M. (2000). Barriers to meaningful instruction for English learners. *Theory into Practice, 39*(4), 228–236.

Middlecamp, C. H., & Nickel, A. L. (2000). Doing science and asking questions: An interactive exercise. *Journal of Chemical Education, 77*(1), 50–52.

Miller, G., & Hall, T. (2005). *Classroom management.* Wakefield, MA: National Center on Accessing the General Curriculum. Retrieved May 6, 2007, from http://www.cast.org/publications/ncac/ncac_classroom.html.

Miller, G. A. (1956). The magical number seven, plus or minus two: Some limits on our capacity for processing information. *Psychological Review, 63,* 81–97.

Miller, G. A., Galanter, E., & Pribram, K. H. (1960). *Plans and the structure of behavior.* New York: Holt, Rinehart & Winston.

Modern Language Association. (2006). *The Modern Language Association language map.* Retrieved May 6, 2007, from http://www.mla.org/map_main.

Moll, L. C., Amanti, C., Neff, D., & Gonzalez, N. (1992). Funds of knowledge for teaching: Using a qualitative approach to connect homes and classrooms. *Theory into Practice, 31*(1), 132–141.

Morris, R. (2000). *New management handbook: A step-by-step guide for creating a happier, more productive classroom.* San Diego: New Management.

Mosher, R. S. (2001). Silence, listening, teaching, and the space of what is not. *Language Arts, 78,* 366–370.

Murphy, S. (1994). Writing portfolios in K–12 schools: Implications for linguistically diverse students. In L. Black, D. A. Daiker, J. Sommers, & G. Stygall (Eds.), *New directions in portfolio assessment* (pp. 141–156). Portsmouth, NH: Boynton/Cook.

Myles, B. S., & Simpson, R. (2001). Understanding the hidden curriculum: An essential social skill for children and youth with Asperger syndrome. *Intervention in School and Clinic, 36,* 279–286.

National Association of School Psychologists. (2002). Social skills: promoting positive behavior, academic success, and school safety. Retrieved January 31, 2007, from http://www.naspcenter. org/factsheets/socialskills_fs.html.

National Board for Professional Teaching Standards. (2002). The five propositions of accomplished teaching. Retrieved May 6, 2007, from http://www.nasponline.org/resources/factsheets/socialskills_fs.aspx.

National Center for Education Statistics. (2003). Highlights from the TIMMS 1999 video study of eighth-grade mathematics teaching. Retrieved May 6, 2007, from http://nces.ed.gov/ pubs2003/timssvideo/.

National Center for Education Statistics. (2005a). Digest of education statistics: Percentage of elementary and secondary school children whose parents were involved in school activities, by selected child, parent, and school characteristics: 1999 and 2003. Retrieved May 6, 2007, from http://www.nces.ed.gov/programs/digest/d05/tables/dt05_023.asp.

National Center for Education Statistics. (2005b). Digest of education statistics: Children 3 through 21 years old served in federally supported programs for the disabled, by type of disability: Selected years, 1976–77 through 2003–04. Retrieved May 6, 2007, from http://nces.ed.gov/programs/digestd05/tables/dt05_050.asp.

National Center for Education Statistics. (2005c). Digest of education statistics: Number and percentage of gifted and talented students in public elementary and secondary schools, by sex and state: 2000. Retrieved May 6, 2007, from http://nces.ed.gov/programs/digest/d05/tables/dt05_053.asp.

National Center for Education Statistics. (2006a). Condition of Education. (See Participation in Education, Elementary/Secondary Education). *Retrieved May 6, 2007, from http://nces.ed.gov/ programs/coe/list/index.asp.*

National Center for Education Statistics. (2006b). Public elementary and secondary students, staff, schools, and school districts: School year 2003–04. Retrieved May 6, 2007, from http://nces.ed. gov/pubs2006/2006307.pdf.

National Commission on Excellence in Education. (1983). A nation at risk. Retrieved May 6, 2007, from http://www.ed.gov/pubs/ NatAtRisk/index.html.

National Research Council. (1996). *National science education standards.* Washington, DC: National Academy Press.

National Research Council. (2000). *How people learn: Brain, mind, experience, and school.* J. Bransford, A. L. Brown, & R. R. Cocking (Eds.). Washington, DC: National Academies Press.

Newmann, V. (1994). *Math journals: Tools for authentic assessment.* San Leandro, CA: Teaching Resource Center.

Nieto, S. (1996). *Affirming diversity: The sociopolitical context of multicultural education* (2nd ed.). White Plains, NY: Longman.

Nieto, S. (2004). *Affirming diversity: The sociopolitical context of multicultural education* (4th ed.). Boston: Allyn & Bacon.

Noble, T. (2004). Integrating the revised Bloom's taxonomy with multiple intelligences: A planning tool for curriculum differentiation. *Teachers College Record, 106,* 193–211.

Noddings, N. (1995). *Philosophy of education.* Boulder, CO: Westview Press.

Novak, J. D. (1990). Concept maps and Venn diagrams: Two metacognitive tools for science and mathematics education. *Instructional Science, 19,* 29–52.

Novak, J. D. (1991). Clarify with concept maps: A tool for students and teachers alike. *The Science Teacher, 58*(7), 45–49.

Novak, J. D. (1998). *Learning, creating, and using knowledge: Concept maps as facilitative tools in schools and corporations.* Mahwah, NJ: Lawrence Erlbaum.

Novak, J. D., & Gowin, D. B. (1984). *Learning how to learn.* New York: Cambridge University Press.

Oakes, J. (2005). *Keeping track: How schools structure inequality* (2nd ed.). New Haven, CT: Yale University Press.

Obenchain, K. M., & Abernathy, T. V. (2003). 20 ways to build community and empower students. *School Intervention in School and Clinic, 39*(1), 55–60.

Ohio Department of Education. (2001). Mathematics academic content standards. Retrieved May 6, 2007, from http://www.ode.state.oh.us.

Olivos, E. M. (2006). *Power parents: A critical perspective of bicultural parent involvement in public schools.* New York: Peter Lang.

Orsborn, E., Patrick, H., Dixon, R. S., & Moore, D. W. (1995). The effects of reducing teacher questions and increasing pauses on child talk during morning news. *Journal of Behavioral Education, 5,* 347–357.

O'Shea, M. R. (2005). *From standards to success.* Alexandria, VA: Association for Supervision and Curriculum Development.

O'Toole, J., Burton, B. (2005). Acting against conflict and bullying. The Brisbane Dracon Project 1996–2004—emergent findings and outcomes. *Research in Drama Education, 10,* 269–283.

Owen, M. (2004). The myth of the digital native. *Futurelab: Viewpoint—article.* Retrieved May 6, 2007, from http://www.futurelab.org.uk/ viewpoint/art26.htm.

Pai, Y., Adler, S. A., & Shadiow, L. (2006). *Cultural foundations of education* (4th ed). Upper Saddle River, NJ: Merrill/Prentice Hall.

Pappas, C. C., Kiefer, B. Z., & Levstik, L. S. (2006). *An integrated language perspective in the elementary schools: An action approach* (4th ed.). Boston: Allyn and Bacon.

Parish, T. B. et al. (2006). *Effects of the implementation of Proposition 227 on the education of English learners, K–12: Findings from a five-year evaluation* (Final report for AB56 and AB 1116, submitted to the California Department of Education). Palo Alto, CA: American Institutes for Research. Summary retrieved May 6, 2007, from http://www.wested.org/online_pubs/CC-06-06.pdf.

Partnership for 21st Century Skills. (2004). Learning for the 21st century: A report and mile guide for 21st century skills. Retrieved May 6, 2007, from http:// www.21stcenturyskills.org/downloads/P21_Report.pdf.

Patrick, N. (2004). *National education technology plan.* Washington, DC: U.S. Department of Education, Office of Educational Technology.

Piaget, J. (1952). *Origins of intelligence in children.* New York: W. W. Norton.

Pisha, B., & Coyne, P. (2001). Smart from the start: The promise of Universal Design for Learning. *Remedial and Special Education, 22,* 197–203.

Popham, W. J., & Baker, E. (1970). *Establishing instructional goals.* Upper Saddle River, NJ: Prentice Hall.

Powell, J. V., Aeby, V. G., Jr., & Carpenter-Aeby, T. (2003). A comparison of student outcomes with and without teacher facilitated computer-based instruction. *Computers & Education, 40*(2), 183–191.

Powers, J. M. (2004). High-stakes accountability and equity: Using evidence from California's Public Schools Accountability Act to address the issues in *Williams v. State of California. American Educational Research Journal, 41,* 763–795.

Prakash, M. S., & Waks, L. J. (1985). Four conceptions of excellence. *Teachers College Record, 87*(1), 79–101.

Predavec, M. (2001). Evaluation of E-Rat, a computer-based rat dissection, in terms of student learning outcomes. *Journal of Biological Education, 35*(2) 75–80.

Prensky, M. (2001). Digital natives, digital immigrants. *On the Horizon, 9*(5). Retrieved May 6, 2007, from http://www.marcprensky.com/writing/Prensky%20-%20Digital%20Natives,%20Digital%20Immigrants%20-%20Part1.pdf.

Prensky, M. (2005/2006). Listen to the natives. *Educational Leadership, 63*(4), 8–13.

Project WILD. (2001). *Project WILD: K–12 curriculum & activity guide.* Houston, TX: Council for Environmental Education.

Prouty, A. (2006). Score one for alternative assessment. *Science Scope, 30*(1), 34–37.

Quiocho, A. M. L., & Daoud, A. M. (2006). Dispelling myths about Latino parent participation in schools. *The Educational Forum, 70,* 255–267.

Rabinowitz, S., & Brandt, T. (2001). Computer-based assessment: Can it deliver on its promise? WestED Knowledge Brief. Retrieved May 6, 2007, from http://www.wested.org/online_pubs/kn-01-05.pdf.

Ravitch, D. (2003a). Thin gruel: How the language police drain the life and content from our texts. *American Educator, 27*(2), 6–19.

Ravitch, D. (2003b). Leaving reality out: How textbooks (don't) teach about tyranny. *American Educator, 27*(3), 32–38.

Reed, D., Rueben, K., & Barbour, E. (2006). Retention of new teachers in California. Public Policy Institute of California. Retrieved May 6, 2007, from http://www.ppic.org/ content/pubs/rb/RB_206DRRB.pdf.

Reineke, R. A. (1998). *Challenging the mind, touching the heart: Best assessment practices.* Thousand Oaks, CA: Corwin Press.

Reis, S. M., & Renzulli, J. S. (1995). Curriculum compacting: A systematic procedure for modifying the curriculum for above average ability students. *Gifted Education Communicator, 26*(2). Retrieved May 6, 2007, from http://www.sp.uconn.edu/ ~nrcgt/sem/semart08.html.

Rettig, M. D., McCullough, L. L., Santos, K. E., & Watson, C. R. (2004). *From rigorous standards to student achievement: A practical process.* Larchmont, NY: Eye on Education.

Reynolds, A. (1992). What is competent beginning teaching? A review of the literature. *Review of Educational Research, 62*(1), 1–35.

Ribble, M. S., Bailey, G. D., & Ross, T. W. (2004). Digital citizenship: Addressing appropriate technology behavior. *Learning and Leading with Technology, 32*(1), 6–9, 11.

Rimm-Kaufman, S. E., & Sawyer, B. E. (2004). Primary-grade teachers' self-efficacy beliefs, attitudes toward teaching, and discipline and teaching practice priorities in relation to the "responsive classroom" approach. *The Elementary School Journal, 104,* 321–341.

Roberts, P. L., & Kellough, R. D. (2008). *A guide for developing interdisciplinary thematic units* (4th ed). Upper Saddle River, NJ: Merrill/Prentile Hall.

Roberts, S. M., & Pruitt, E. Z. (2003). *Schools as professional learning communities.* Thousand Oaks, CA: Corwin.

Rogers, B. (Ed.). (2004). *How to manage children's challenging behaviour.* London: Paul Chapman.

Rogers, S., Ludington, J., & Graham, S. (1998). *Motivation and learning.* Evergreen, CO: Peak Learning Systems.

Rose, L. C. (2004). No Child Left Behind: The mathematics of guaranteed failure. *Educational Horizons, 82*(2), 121–130.

Rowe, M. (1986). Wait-time: Slowing down may be a way of speeding up. *Journal of Teacher Education, 37*(1), 43–50.

Rudolph, A. M. (2006). *Techniques in classroom management: A resource for secondary teachers.* Lanham, MD: Rowman & Littlefield Education.

Rush, S. E. (2006). *Huck Finn's "hidden" lessons: Teaching and learning across the color line.* Lanham, MD: Rowman & Littlefield.

Russell, H. R. (1990). *Ten-minute field trips* (2nd ed.). Washington, DC: National Science Teachers Association.

Ryan, A. L., Halsey, H. N., & Matthews, W. J. (2003). Using functional assessment to promote desirable student behavior in schools. *Teaching Exceptional Children, 35*(4), 8–15.

Ryan, T. G. (2006). Performance assessment: Critics, criticism, and controversy. *International Journal of Testing 6*(1) 97–104.

Sadler, J. E. (1966). *J. A. Comenius and the concept of universal education.* New York: Barnes & Noble.

Savage, T. V. (1999). *Teaching self-control through management and discipline* (2nd ed.) Boston: Allyn & Bacon.

Savage, T. V., & Armstrong, D. (2000). *Effective teaching in elementary social studies* (4th ed.). Upper Saddle River, NJ: Merrill/Prentice Hall.

Schifini, A. (1994). Language, literacy, and content instruction: Strategies for teachers. In K. Spangenberg-Urbschat & R. Pritchard (Eds.), *Kids come in all languages: Reading instruction for ESL students* (pp. 158–179). Newark, DE: International Reading Association.

Schipper, B., & Rossi, J. (1997). *Portfolios in the classroom: Tools for learning and instruction.* York, ME: Stenhouse.

Schmidt, W. H., Wang, H. C., & McKnight, C. C. (2005). Curriculum coherence: An examination of U.S. mathematics and science content standards from an international perspective. *Journal of Curriculum Studies, 37,* 525–559.

Schneider, M. F. (1997). *25 of the best parenting techniques ever.* New York: St. Martin's Press.

Schofield, J. W. (2005). The colorblind perspective in school: Causes and consequence. In J. A. Banks & C. A. M. Banks (Eds.), *Multicultural education: Issues and perspectives* (5th ed, pp. 265–288). Hoboken, NJ: Wiley Jossey-Bass.

Schultz, K. (2003). *Listening: A framework for teaching across differences.* New York: Teachers College Press.

Schultz-Zander, R., Buchter, A., & Dalmer, R. (2002). The role of ICT as a promoter of students' cooperation. *Journal of Computer Assisted Learning, 18,* 438–448.

Selfridge, J. (2004). The Resolving Conflict Creatively Program: How we know it works. *Theory into Practice, 43*(1), 59–67.

Shaywitz, S. E., Holahan, J. M., Freudenheim, D. A., Fletcher, J. M., Makuch, R. W., & Shaywitz, B. A. (2001). Heterogeneity within the gifted: Higher IQ boys exhibit behaviors resembling boys with learning disabilities. *Gifted Child Quarterly, 45,* 16–23.

Sheldon, S. B., & Epstein, J. L. (2005) Involvement counts: Family and community partnerships and mathematics achievement. *Journal of Educational Research, 98*(4), 196–206.

Shukla-Mehta, S. M., & Albin, R. W. (2003). Twelve practical strategies to prevent behavioral escalation in classroom settings. *Preventing School Failure, 47*(4), 156–161.

Silberman, M. (1996). *Active learning: 101 strategies to teach any subject.* Boston: Allyn & Bacon.

Skinner, B. F. (1971). *Beyond freedom and dignity.* New York: Knopf.

Slavin, R. E. (1995). *Cooperative learning* (2nd ed.). Boston: Allyn & Bacon.

Slavin, R. E. (1997). *Educational psychology: Theory and practice* (5th ed.). Boston: Allyn & Bacon.

Slavin, R. E. (2003). A reader's guide to scientifically based research. *Educational Leadership, 60*(5), 12–16.

Slavin-Baden, M., & Major, C. H. (2004). *Foundations of problem-based learning.* New York: Society for Research into Higher Education & Open University Press.

Smith, F., Hardman, F., Wall, K., & Mroz, M. (2004). Interactive whole class teaching in the National Literacy and Numercy Strategies. *British Educational Research Journal, 30,* 395–411.

Smutny, J. F. (2003). *Gifted education: Promising practices.* Bloomington, IN: Phi Delta Kappa Educational Foundation.

Solomon, Y., Warrin, J., & Lewis, C. (2002). Helping with homework? Homework as a site of tension for parents and teenagers. *British Education Research Journal, 28,* 603–622.

Soltis, J. F. (1986). Teaching professional ethics. *Journal of Teacher Education, 37*(3), 2–4.

Spencer, B., & Guillaume, A. M. (2006). Integrating curriculum through the learning cycle: Content-based reading and vocabulary instruction. *The Reading Teacher, 60,* 206–219.

St. John, E. P., Manset, G., Chung, C. G., & Worthington, K. (2001). *Assessing the rationales for educational reforms: A test of the professional development, comprehensive reform, and direct instruction hypotheses.* Policy Research Report. Bloomington: Indiana University. Education Policy Center. (ERIC Document Reproduction Service No. ED458 641)

Steelman, J. D. (2005). Multimedia makes its mark. *Learning & Leading with Technology, 33*(1), 16–19.

Stefanakis, E. H. (2002). *Multiple intelligences and portfolios: A window into the learner's mind.* Portsmouth, NH: Heinemann.

Sternberg, R. J. (1994). Answering questions and questioning answers: Guiding children to intellectual excellence. *Phi Delta Kappan, 76*(2), 136–138.

Stephens, L. S. (1995). *The complete guide to learning through community service: Grades K–9.* Needham Heights, MA: Allyn & Bacon.

Sternberg, R. J. (1997a). Successful intelligence: A broader view of who's smart in school and in life. *International Schools Journal, 17*(1), 19–31.

Sternberg, R. J. (1997b). What does it mean to be smart? *Educational Leadership, 54*(6), 20–24.

Stevens, D. D., & Levi, A. J. (2005). *Introduction to rubrics.* Sterling, VA: Sylus.

Stiggins, R. J. (2001). *Student-involved classroom assessment* (3rd ed.). Upper Saddle River, NJ: Merrill/Prentice Hall.

Stronge, J. H. (2002). *Qualities of effective teachers.* Alexandria, VA: ASCD.

Suchman, J. R. (1962). *The elementary school training program in scientific inquiry.* Report to the U.S. Office of Education, Project Title VII, Project 216. Urbana, IL: University of Illinois.

Swain, M. (1985). Communicative competence: Some roles of comprehensible input and comprehensible output in its development. In S. Gass & C. Madden (Eds.), *Input in second language acquisition.* Rowley, MA: Newbury House (pp. 235–253).

Swanson, H. L. (2001). Searching for the best model for instructing students with learning disabilities. *Focus on Exceptional Children, 34*(2), 1–15.

Swanson, H. L., & Sachse-Lee, C. (2000, March/April). A meta-analysis of single-subject-design intervention research for students with LD. *Journal of Learning Disabilities, 33*(2), 114–136.

Taba, H. (1967). *Teacher's handbook for elementary social studies.* Reading, MA: Addison-Wesley.

Tannenbaum, R., & Rosenfeld, M. (1997). *Evaluation criteria of teaching practices: A study of job-relatedness and training needs assessment.* Princeton, NJ: Educational Testing Service. Retrieved May 6, 2007, from http://www.ets.org/ Media/Research/pdf/RR-97-23.pdf.

Thomas, W. P., & Collier, V. P. (2001). A national study of school effectiveness for language minority students' long-term academic achievement. Center for Research on Education, Diversity and Excellence. Retrieved May 6, 2007, from http://crede.berkeley.edu/research/llaa/ 1.1_final.html.

Thorson, S. A. (2003). *Listening to students: Reflections on secondary school classroom management.* Boston: Allyn & Bacon.

Tiedt, P. L., & Tiedt, I. M. (2005). *Multicultural teaching: A handbook of activities, information, and resources* (7th ed.). Boston: Allyn & Bacon.

Tobin, T., Sugai, G., & Colvin, G. (2000). Using discipline referrals to make decisions. *NASSP Bulletin, 84*(616), 106–117.

Tomlinson, C. A. (2001). *How to differentiate instruction in mixed-ability classrooms* (2nd ed.). Alexandria, VA: Association for Supervision and Curriculum Development.

Tomlinson, C. A., Kaplan, S. N., Renzulli, J. S., Purcell, J., Leppien, J., & Burns, D. (2002). *The parallel curriculum: A design to develop high potential and challenge high-ability learners.* Thousand Oaks, CA: Corwin.

Totten, S. (2001). Addressing the "null curriculum": Teaching about genocides other than the Holocaust. *Social Education, 65,* 309–313.

Turner, J. C., Meyer, D. K., Midgley, C., & Patrick, H. (2003). Teacher discourse and sixth-graders' reported affect and achievement behaviors in two high-mastery/high-performance mathematics classrooms. *The Elementary School Journal, 103,* 357–382.

Tyack, D. (2003). *Seeking common ground: Public schools in a diverse society.* Cambridge: Harvard University.

Tyack, D., & Cuban, L. (1995). *Tinkering toward utopia: A century of public school reform.* Cambridge: Harvard University.

Tyson, K. (2003). Notes from the back of the room: Problems and paradoxes in the schooling of young black students. *Sociology of Education, 76,* 326–343.

Underwood, J. (2004). Legal protections gay students must receive. *Education Digest: Essential Readings Condensed for Quick Review, 70*(4), 16–26.

Underwood, J., & Webb, L. D. (2006). *School law for teachers.* Upper Saddle River, NJ: Merrill/Prentice Hall

U.S. Department of Education. (2003). Meeting the highly qualified teachers challenge: The secretary's second annual report of teacher quality. Retrieved May 6, 2007, from http://www.ed.gov/about/reports/annual/ teachprep/2003title-ii-report.pdf.

U.S. Department of Education. (2006). No Child Left Behind is working. Retrieved May 6, 2007, from http:// www.ed.gov/nclb/overview/importance/nclbworking.pdf.

U.S. Department of Education, National Center for Education Statistics. (2006a). Internet access in U.S. public schools and classrooms: 1994–2005 (NCES 2007-020). Retrieved May 6, 2007, http://www.nces.ed.gov/fastfacts/display. asp?id=46.

U.S. Department of Education, National Center for Education Statistics. (2006b). *The condition of education: 2006. Ratings of school violence and crime,* NCES 2006-071. Washington, DC: U.S. Government Printing Office.

Retrieved May 6, 2007, from http://nces.ed.gov/ programs/coe/2006/pdf/39_2006.pdf.

U.S.Department of Education National Center for Education Statistics. Indicators of School Crime and Safety (2006c) Indicator 11: Bullying at School. Retrieved May 5, 2007 from http://nces.ed.gov/programs/ crimeindicators/ind_11.asp.

Vacca, J. J. (2007). Incorporating interests and structure to improve participation of a child with autism in a standardized assessment: A case study analysis. *Focus on Autism and Other Developmental Disabilities, 22*(1), 51–59.

Valencia, R., & Block, M. S. (2002). "Mexican Americans don't value education!": The basics of the myth, mythmaking, and debunking. *Journal of Latinos and Education, 1*(2) 81–103.

van Zee, E. H., Iwasyk, M., Kurose, A., Simpson, D., & Wild, J. (2001). Student and teacher questioning during conversations about science. *Journal of Research in Science Teaching, 38*(2), 59–90.

Vaughn, S., Hughes, M. T., Moody, S. W., & Elbaum, B. (2001). Instructional grouping for reading for students with LD: Implications for practice. *Intervention in School and Clinic, 36*(3), 131–137.

Vygotsky, L. S. (1978). *Mind in society: The development of higher psychological processes.* M. Cole, V. John-Steiner, S. Scribner, & E. Souberman, Eds. Cambridge, MA: Harvard University Press.

Wahl, L., & Duffield, J. (2005). Using flexible technology to meet the needs of diverse learners. WestEd Knowledge Brief. Retrieved May 6, 2007, from http:// www.wested.org/online_pubs/kn-05-01.pdf.

Wakefield, J. F. (2006, April). Textbook usage in the United States: The case of U.S. history. Paper presented at the International Seminar on Textbooks, Santiago, Chile. Retrieved May 6, 2007, from http://www.eric.ed.gov/ ERICDocs/data/ericdocs2/content_storage_01/0000000b /80/32/ba/3f.pdf.

Walsch, J. A., & Sattes, B. D. (2005). *Quality questioning: Research-based practices to engage every learner.* Thousand Oaks, CA: Corwin.

Walvoord, B. E., & Anderson, V. J. (1998). *Effective grading: A tool for learning and assessment.* San Francisco, CA: Jossey-Bass.

Webb, P. T. (2002). Teacher power: The exercise of professional autonomy in an era of strict accountability. *Teacher Development, 6*(1), 47–62.

Wellesley College Center for Research on Women. (1992). *The AAUW report: How schools shortchange girls.* Washington, DC: American Association of University Women Educational Foundation.

Wenglinsky, H. (2000). *How teaching matters: Bringing the classroom back into discussions of teacher quality.* Princeton, NJ: Milken Family Foundation and Educational Testing Service.

Whitehurst, T., & Howells, A. (2006). "When something is different people fear it": Children's perceptions of an arts-based inclusion project. *Support for Learning, 21*(1), 40–44.

Wiggins, G., & McTighe, J. (2005). *Understanding by design,* (2nd ed). Alexandria, VA: Association for Curriculum and Supervision.

Wiggins, G., & McTighe, J. (2006). Examining the teaching life. *Educational Leadership, 63*(3), 26–29.

Wilkins, M. M., Wilkins, J. L. M., & Oliver, T. (2006). Differentiating the curriculum for elementary gifted mathematics students. *Teaching Children Mathematics, 13*(1), 6–13.

Wimer, J. W., Ridenour, C. S., Thomas, K., & Place, A. W. (2001). Higher order teacher questioning of boys and girls in elementary mathematics classrooms. *Journal of Educational Research, 95*(2), 84–92.

Wisconsin Model Academic Standards. (1998). Retrieved May 6, 2007, from http://dpi.wi.gov/standards/elaa12.html.

Witzel, B. S., & Mercer, C. D. (2003). Using rewards to teach students with disabilities: Implications for motivation. *Remedial and Special Education, 24*(2), 88–96.

Wong, H. (1998). *The first days of school.* Mountain View, CA: Harry K. Wong Publications.

Wormeli, R. (2001). *Meet me in the middle: Becoming an accomplished middle-level teacher.* Portland, ME: Stenhouse.

Wormeli, R. (2006). *Fair isn't always equal: Assessing and grading in the differentiated classroom.* Portland, ME: Stenhouse.

Wren, D. (1999). School culture: Exploring the hidden curriculum. *Adolescence, 34,* 593–596.

Younger, M. R., & Warrington, M. (2006). Would Harry and Hermione have done better in single-sex classes? A review of single-sex teaching in coeducational secondary schools in the United Kingdom. *American Educational Research Journal, 43,* 579–620.

Yu, L., & Rachor, R. (2000). *The two-year evaluation of the three-year direct instruction program in an urban public school system.* (ERIC Document Reproduction Service No. ED 441 831)

INDEX